Gilles Deleuze's Transcendental Empiricism

Plateaus – New Directions in Deleuze Studies

'It's not a matter of bringing all sorts of things together under a single concept but rather of relating each concept to variables that explain its mutations.'
Gilles Deleuze, *Negotiations*

Series Editors

Ian Buchanan, University of Wollongong
Claire Colebrook, Penn State University

Editorial Advisory Board

Keith Ansell Pearson
Ronald Bogue
Constantin V. Boundas
Rosi Braidotti
Eugene Holland
Gregg Lambert
Dorothea Olkowski
Paul Patton
Daniel Smith
James Williams

Titles available in the series

Christian Kerslake, *Immanence and the Vertigo of Philosophy: From Kant to Deleuze*
Jean-Clet Martin, *Variations: The Philosophy of Gilles Deleuze*, translated by Constantin V. Boundas and Susan Dyrkton
Simone Bignall, *Postcolonial Agency: Critique and Constructivism*
Miguel de Beistegui, *Immanence – Deleuze and Philosophy*
Jean-Jacques Lecercle, *Badiou and Deleuze Read Literature*
Ronald Bogue, *Deleuzian Fabulation and the Scars of History*
Sean Bowden, *The Priority of Events: Deleuze's Logic of Sense*
Craig Lundy, *History and Becoming: Deleuze's Philosophy of Creativity*
Aidan Tynan, *Deleuze's Literary Clinic: Criticism and the Politics of Symptoms*
Thomas Nail, *Returning to Revolution: Deleuze, Guattari and Zapatismo*
François Zourabichvili, *Deleuze: A Philosophy of the Event* with *The Vocabulary of Deleuze* edited by Gregg Lambert and Daniel W. Smith, translated by Kieran Aarons
Frida Beckman, *Between Desire and Pleasure: A Deleuzian Theory of Sexuality*
Nadine Boljkovac, *Untimely Affects: Gilles Deleuze and an Ethics of Cinema*
Daniela Voss, *Conditions of Thought: Deleuze and Transcendental Ideas*
Daniel Barber, *Deleuze and the Naming of God: Post-Secularism and the Future of Immanence*
F. LeRon Shults, *Iconoclastic Theology: Gilles Deleuze and the Secretion of Atheism*
Janae Sholtz, *The Invention of a People: Heidegger and Deleuze on Art and the Political*
Marco Altamirano, *Time, Technology and Environment: An Essay on the Philosophy of Nature*
Sean McQueen, *Deleuze and Baudrillard: From Cyberpunk to Biopunk*
Ridvan Askin, *Narrative and Becoming*
Marc Rölli, *Gilles Deleuze's Transcendental Empiricism: From Tradition to Difference* translated by Peter Hertz-Ohmes
Guillaume Collett, *The Psychoanalysis of Sense: Deleuze and the Lacanian School*
Ryan Johnson, *The Deleuze-Lucretius Encounter*

Forthcoming volumes

Cheri Carr, *Deleuze's Kantian Ethos: Critique as a Way of Life*
Alex Tissandier, *Affirming Divergence: Deleuze's Reading of Leibniz*

Visit the Plateaus website at edinburghuniversitypress.com/series/plat

GILLES DELEUZE'S TRANSCENDENTAL EMPIRICISM
From Tradition to Difference

Marc Rölli

Translated and edited by Peter Hertz-Ohmes

EDINBURGH
University Press

Edinburgh University Press is one of the leading university presses in the UK. We publish academic books and journals in our selected subject areas across the humanities and social sciences, combining cutting-edge scholarship with high editorial and production values to produce academic works of lasting importance. For more information visit our website: edinburghuniversitypress.com

Gilles Deleuze: Philosophie des transzendentalen Empirismus by Marc Rölli
© Verlag Turia + Kant, 2003, 2012
English translation © Peter Hertz-Ohmes, 2016

Edinburgh University Press Ltd
The Tun – Holyrood Road
12(2f) Jackson's Entry
Edinburgh EH8 8PJ

Typeset in Sabon by
Servis Filmsetting Ltd, Stockport, Cheshire

A CIP record for this book is available from the British Library

ISBN 978 1 4744 1488 3 (hardback)
ISBN 978 1 4744 1489 0 (webready PDF)
ISBN 978 1 4744 1490 6 (epub)

The right of Marc Rölli to be identified as the author of this work has been asserted in accordance with the Copyright, Designs and Patents Act 1988, and the Copyright and Related Rights Regulations 2003 (SI No. 2498).

Contents

Translator's Note	vi
Author's Foreword	ix
Introduction: Can Empiricism Have a Transcendental Aspect?	1

PART I: EMPIRICISM / TRANSCENDENTALISM

1	Hume's Logic of External Relations	23
2	The Ambiguity of Kantian Thought	34
3	Kant's Transcendental Critique of Classical Empiricism	51

PART II: FROM PHENOMENON TO EVENT

4	Husserl's Concept of Passive Synthesis	95
5	Heidegger's Metaphysics of Finitude	128

PART III: DELEUZE'S TRANSCENDENTAL EMPIRICISM

6	The Paradoxical Nature of Difference	157
7	Virtuality of Concepts	165
8	Subjectivity and Immanence	224

Conclusion: Where Do We Go from Here? Lines of Flight	281
Bibliography	287
Index	302

Translator's Note

Thanks to a paper I wrote on Deleuze and humour (Hertz 1988), I received an invitation from Ian Buchanan to Perth, Australia, for the first 'Deleuze Studies' conference. Then by chance in 2003 I found Marc Rölli's book in an Erfurt bookstore a few kilometres from my current residence in Mühlhausen, Thüringen. I was immediately impressed and contacted Marc through his publisher. I expected an older fellow like myself. Marc was considerably younger. Nevertheless, I proposed a trial translation as something to do in early retirement. That's how this project started.

In German the book has recently received a second edition (2012). Most of the last chapter of my translation appeared in Buchanan's *Deleuze Studies*, v. 3.1. (2009). I want to thank Ian for his support in getting this English version published. I am also indebted to all the translators of Deleuze's works and other cited philosophers from Kant on up. My own effort has certainly been an education for me, as important at this point in my life as John Herman Randall's lectures on the *Career of Philosophy* were to me at Columbia University half a century ago. (See in particular 'Building the German Tradition' in Randall 1965: vol. 2, bk 5, 3–412.)

Rölli's book might be considered the first in-depth treatment of Deleuze as if he were an integral part of so-called continental philosophy. But that is an illusion. Gilles Deleuze's 'empiricism' is the product of intense reassessment. If anything, Deleuze 'dis-integrates' continental philosophy. He is spurred by problems that are vague at first but stubborn, problems that lead to the scrapping of pre-existing notions and concepts. As Nietzsche puts it, 'Sometimes someone has to find the strength to shatter an established wisdom and sweep up the pieces in order to live. This is done by holding court, scrupulously questioning the evidence, and finally making judgement' (Nietzsche 1883, in KSA 1988: v.1, 269) (*Untimely Meditations*, v. 2. sec. 3).

In this sense Deleuze is even more radical than Heidegger. I say this because I translated Heidegger when he was still hot (Heidegger 1967, 1971). What interested me then was the challenge of Heidegger's

Translator's Note

deliberate untranslatability. Had we lost our way to language itself, or better, to its onto-theological source? It occurred to me even then, as a student, that the absolute status of the WORD, behind all the multitude of words which we utilise, was philosophically a dead end. But it took a long time until Deleuze, thanks to Rölli, showed me a better use of transcendental power.

For Deleuze, the 'transcendental' plane is a plane of pure potentiality, not of restricted possibility, a plane where thought takes place without the interference of a not yet constituted Cartesian or Heideggerian authority. There is room, then, although under constant and conscious attack, for unmitigated difference, for the actualisation of unsuspected virtual constructions, for creative intuition – in short, for translatability. I undertook the translation of Rölli's book to convince myself of this working hypothesis.

What, then, has been my role here as translator and editor? First I moved the text from German to English, languages which, philosophically at least, do not overlap, as not only the Heidegger chapter makes all too obvious. Then behind the German there was French, and French philosophy as such. Another lack of overlap. Citations from English rather than German translations of Deleuze and others obviously met this problem half way. But I had to translate some sources myself, and marked them as such in the text.

Second, although the book is long, I have not abridged its substance. Nevertheless, I have drastically edited its scholarly apparatus. The Germanic tradition of footnoting even the footnotes with extended comments distracts mightily from the flow of the main argument. This English version dispenses with all 1,667 footnotes in the German first edition, although many have been tacitly absorbed into the text. Also retained in the text are copious bibliographical references not only to the works of Deleuze and to his primary sources, but also to the standard secondary literature.

Third, it is sometimes necessary in philosophy, especially in German, to slog through interminable sentences of dubious clarity with all the verbs at the end, in order to begin to discern just why the gist can't be made any clearer. Both Rölli and I have avoided such sentences, but whole paragraphs can also develop a certain weight before they sublimate into enlightenment. The reader skips such paragraphs at his or her peril. I know. I also skipped pages, only to go back to rescue the force of the argument from drifting away.

Finally, as Oscar Wilde might have said in his play on *Importance*, I have by dint of this translation become a confirmed Deleuzian.

These days I can actually understand, perhaps even anticipate, what Deleuze himself says in his own books. I now rank him philosophically above Foucault, whom I once met at Stanford, or Heidegger, whom I once translated. Although, as I have already said, I am a couple of generations older than Marc Rölli, I am now proud to be his friend. So I don't mind recommending his book as a first-class philosophic eye-opener.

Author's Foreword

The name 'Deleuze' presents a philosophical challenge on all possible and impossible levels. Concepts like difference, immanence, event, virtuality, de- and reterritorialising, or rhizome send signals. His works are extensively employed in cultural studies, in art and media theory, in political inquiry and in the humanities. This employment wavers between true topicality and trendiness, conceptual investigation and jargon. Thus in recent years authors like Michael Hardt and Antonio Negri, Manuel Delanda, Alain Badiou and Slavoj Žižek, in publishing on Deleuze, have effectively drawn attention not only to him but also to themselves. These efforts are not always philosophically relevant, but they underscore how adaptable to cultural studies Deleuze's concepts can be.

Academic philosophy, on the other hand, has resisted involvement and kept its respectful distance. One doesn't want to get one's hands dirty. It is better not to engage in a philosophical adventure if it isn't yet clear whether it is worth the work. The philosopher Deleuze's language and style come across as strange, complex and confusing. At the same time, his alliance with Félix Guattari on the theme of 'Capitalism and Schizophrenia' counts as a less philosophical and more experimentally directed project that perhaps conveys excitement and inspiration, but doesn't boast really serious intent.

The present book on transcendental empiricism first appeared in 2003. It grew out of a dissertation in the field of philosophy, written mainly between 1999 and 2001, which was overseen by Bernhard Waldenfels in Bochum. In those days the academic situation was as tricky as now. A wide reception of Deleuze developed in North America, concentrated primarily in non-philosophical fields. In German-speaking regions, all of his books were translated but reception was limited to a few areas like film theory or the critique of psychoanalysis. Deleuze and Deleuze-Guattari shared the ambiguous 'fame' of so-called 'poststructuralist' or 'postmodern' authors, and counted in philosophy as outsiders and radicals who terminated all modernisation projects and thus also the emancipation efforts of the Enlightenment.

These reproaches, as raised by Jürgen Habermas or Manfred Frank, have in the meantime considerably cooled down. The whole modern-postmodern discussion looks today like a relic of the last century. In recent years cultural studies departments have grown so strong and have been able to establish themselves in international terms to such a degree that their intensive investigations of Deleuze, and of Guattari as well, now speak for themselves. Around the globe rather comprehensive conferences have taken place and continue to do so, while many journals and book series are dedicated to examining their works. Every year ten new monographs and just as many new editions appear, which also to some extent consider purely philosophical aspects of Deleuzian works. Here I want to mention in particular the *Deleuze Studies* journal produced since 2007 by Edinburgh University Press.

All of this cultural studies expansion of Deleuzian reception cannot help but profit philosophy departments, which still (in their own departments) relegate this reception to borderline status but nevertheless bask in the enormous reputation they themselves derive from non-philosophical sources.

Given this background, it may seem curious that a second edition in German of the present book was recently undertaken. After all, in the meantime many more texts have been published which give knowledgeable and detailed insights into Deleuze's philosophy and his cooperation with Guattari. However, the steady requests I received, together with their wish that the work could be condensed, motivated me to do a revision. [Translator's note: The new edition appeared in 2012 in Vienna with the same title, again from Turia + Kant Publishers.] At the same time the thought of an English translation, thanks to Peter Hertz-Ohmes, convinced me of the ongoing relevance of a Deleuze study that specifically spelled out its philosophical consequences.

After all these years, the question raises itself: how one would write such a book today? What changes and corrections would be necessary? What has become obsolete, and what new research would need to be incorporated? I have decided not to bring the contents up to date. It is, in my view, not a revisable textbook which simply reflects current research. The main thrust of the book speaks against such a goal, apart from the practical impossibility of realising it. The book develops a particular interpretational perspective. The focus is on 'transcendental empiricism' and this gives it a multifaceted and well-established point of view.[1]

Author's Foreword

No doubt years of constant academic occupation do not go by without leaving traces on a book. For the new edition of the German and for the present translation I got rid of a certain amount of accumulated scholastic 'ballast'. Footnotes were jettisoned, passages shortened, chapters restructured for clarity, and some major points reformulated. In this way one notices that the book is primarily interested in confronting Deleuze with philosophical tradition and vice versa. The idea is to show what significance (and what plausibility) can be gained from his difference theoretical approach, together with the critiques he derives from this approach and applies to classical empiricism, transcendental philosophy, dialectic thought and phenomenology.[2] In addition, it is about the conception of philosophy as not only taking up systematically an 'oppositional' stance toward tradition, but also as furthering new, unprejudiced readings of 'congenial' classic texts like those of Leibniz or Spinoza, Bergson or Nietzsche.

I have refrained from fiddling with the book's contents, although here and there this might have proved helpful. Here are only a couple of instances. Example one: new studies have shown that the pragmatist critique of empiricism (by William James and John Dewey) carries more weight with respect to Deleuze's elaboration of 'higher empiricism' than was previously suspected.[3] When Dewey rebukes the *Quest for Certainty*, he is aiming for an overturning of metaphysical fundamentals that will culminate in a concept of experience that is constituted of associations and concatenations arising in heterogeneous contexts of problematic situations and habits. In the name of a generalised pragmatic, Deleuze and Guattari, in *A Thousand Plateaus*, criticise (linguistic) structuralism and find a way to think collective configurations (assemblages, agencements) as 'tiny' or minoritary, as unstable or incomplete, that is, as precarious and situational pragmatic structures.[4] This idea also finds confirmation in the way Peirce's semiotic is applied in the Cinema books.

The second example involves the introduction of the power problematic in connection with Foucault's *will to knowledge*. Apparently the virtual occurs twice, once on the plane of immanence and once on the plane of power relations. Accordingly, power relations lie in virtual microstructures and make it impossible to construct a simple opposition between the virtual and the actual. As modal power theoretician, Deleuze is interested in calling attention to microstructural rules of actions that emphasise the productive and relational character of power, that is, virtual (unactualised) aspects that result in a world of representation. However, immanence conditions should be distinguished from power conditions because they display a nomadological form of organisation and block themselves against homogenising and hierarchical effects (of normalisation and control).[5]

I would never have been able to finish this kind of revision if I hadn't received a generous research grant from the International Research Institute for Cultural Techniques and Media Philosophy (IKKM) at the Bauhaus University in Weimar for the winter semester, 2011–12. For the wonderful work atmosphere they provided, I would like to thank the directors of the Institute, Lorenz Engell and Bernhard Siegert, as well as Oliver Tege and all the colleagues and fellows with whom I came in contact. Thanks go as well to Fatih University in Istanbul, and especially to my colleagues in the philosophy department who gave me leave to accept the grant.

Peter Hertz-Ohmes managed with his translation project to enable me to get first-hand knowledge of Deleuze research in North America. His work allowed me to see that Deleuze could be 'popularised', taken in the sense of, say, Heinrich Heine. Not equivocation or simplification, nor mere conveyance of profundity, but popularisation as a clarification or expression that rejects the profound when that means (from a political or social perspective) esoteric triviality or scholastic autism.[6]

Cooperation with Ralf Krause, Friedrich Balke and Zafer Aracagök as well as with the editorial staff of the online journal *Deleuze International*, Rainer Becker, Kai Denker and Christian Diel, have helped me find ever new perspectives, rough spots and discursive points of contact in the work of Deleuze, and to keep an eye on new publications that appear yearly.

Finally let me mention my gratitude toward Ingo Vavra of Turia + Kant Publishers and Carol Macdonald of Edinburgh University Press for making it possible for the present translation to appear in print.

Notes

1. This may be the place to mention other recent books with related aims. See for example Anne Sauvagnargues, *Deleuze: L'empirisme transcendental* (Paris: Presses Universitaires de France, 2010); Daniel W. Smith, *Essays on Deleuze* (Edinburgh: Edinburgh University Press, 2012); James Williams, *The Transversal Thought of Gilles Deleuze: Encounters & Influences* (Manchester: Clinamen Press, 2005) and James Williams, *Gilles Deleuze's Philosophy of Time* (Edinburgh: Edinburgh University

Press, 2011). I should also mention Levi R. Bryant, *Difference and Givenness: Deleuze's Transcendental Empiricism and the Ontology of Immanence* (Evanston, IL: Northwestern University Press, 2008), although in his book the traditions of post-Kantianism and phenomenology are only occasionally considered.

2. In recent years many exciting works have appeared in English on these themes. See for example Jeffrey Bell, *Deleuze's Hume: Philosophy, Culture and the Scottish Enlightenment* (Edinburgh: Edinburgh University Press, 2009). Bell makes clear the relevance of Hume's philosophy for Deleuze, but pays less attention to the differences and points of criticism that push Deleuze to a (transcendentally directed) radicalisation of empiricism. Daniela Voss, on the other hand, in her convincing study *Conditions of Thought: Deleuze and Transcendental Ideas* (Edinburgh: Edinburgh University Press, 2013), refers to classical transcendental positions (Leibniz, Kant, Maimon). Yet for her Kant's transcendental dialectic hardly has the importance that it has for Deleuze (and his concept of the problematic idea), where it presents, by way of Bergson and Nietzsche, a structuralist reworking of the classic type of transcendental philosophy. With respect to Leibniz, see in particular Sean Bowden, *The Priority of Events* (Edinburgh: Edinburgh University Press, 2011), § 56–87, and Niamh McDonnell and Sjoerd van Tuinen (eds), *Deleuze and The Fold: A Critical Reader* (London: Palgrave Macmillan, 2010). For a reflection on the difficult relations to Hegel, see Karen Houle and Jim Vernon (eds), *Hegel and Deleuze: Together Again for the First Time* (Evanston, IL: Northwestern University Press, 2013). The phenomenological background to Deleuze's concept of genesis is treated by Joe Hughes, *Deleuze and the Genesis of Representation* (London and New York: Continuum International Publishing Group, 2008), § 3–19, p. 105 ff. Finally, Miguel de Beistegui, *Immanence – Deleuze and Philosophy* (Edinburgh: Edinburgh University Press, 2010), § 8–18, p. 24 ff., examines the genetic thought process as an independent ontological draft of a plane of immanence.

3. See Sean Bowden, Simone Bignall and Paul Patton (eds), *Deleuze and Pragmatism* (New York and London: Routledge, 2015); David Lapoujade, *William James: Empirisme et Pragmatisme* (Paris: Empêcheurs de Penser en Rond, 2007); Lapoujade, *Deleuze, Les Mouvements Aberrants* (Paris: Les Editions de Minuit, 2014).

4. Marc Rölli, 'Gilles Deleuze's pragmatic move beyond Structuralism', *Deleuze International*, Issue 1 (2007), http://deleuze.tausendplateaus.de/?p=37 (last accessed 8 April 2016). See also my lecture at IKKM in Weimar 2012, '"We Need Reasons to Believe in This World": Outline of a Pragmatic Theory of Situated Knowledge', https://vimeo.com/33290237 (last accessed 8 April 2016).

5. Marc Rölli, 'Sensibilität – Virtualität – Macht: Widerstandslinien in der

Kontrollgesellschaft', in Hans. J. Lenger, Michaela Ott, Sarah Speck and Harald Strauss (eds), *Virtualität und Kontrolle* (Hamburg, 2010), § 90–9.
6. See Rölli and Trzaskalik, *Heinrich Heine und die Philosophie: Vier Beiträge zur Popularität des Denkens.*

Introduction: Can Empiricism Have a Transcendental Aspect?

> We always rediscover the necessity of reversing the supposed relations or divisions between the empirical and the transcendental. (Deleuze 1994: 167)

The central focus of Gilles Deleuze's thinking is on a necessary reversal of the relationship between the transcendental and the empirical. That is why he calls his philosophy 'transcendental empiricism' (see Deleuze 1994: 56–7, 143–4). This label should be taken literally since it underscores the possibility of conceptualising empiricism *as* transcendental philosophy. Within this possibility is concealed the entire 'paradox' of Deleuzian thought.

Let's face it, almost everyone, both historically and philosophically, is convinced that the systematic positions taken respectively by empiricists and transcendental philosophers are incommensurable. The intention of the present work is to *relativise* that conviction by accounting for the advent of transcendental empiricism as a coherent form of philosophical thought. One cannot simply assert that the concept of transcendental empiricism incorporates an oxymoron: it is precisely the paradoxical structure of this concept that will necessarily be a major theme of this study. We want to get at a fundamental issue inherent in the stated incommensurability of the two classic positions. Deleuze is neither interested in uncovering the transcendental roots of classical empiricism nor the empirical sources of Kant's critical philosophy. His philosophy implies instead a complex intertwining of these two directions of thought. We can therefore assert that within transcendental empiricism an empiricist critique is applied to transcendental philosophy which commits it in a strong sense to experience, while at the same time a transcendental critique is applied to empiricism which brings to light its philosophical assumptions regarding consciousness.

At the heart of this reciprocal critique is the crucial concept of difference. The philosophy of difference, which culminates in the work of Deleuze, deserves to be better situated among current humanistic and philosophic movements. It must not be discussed in isolation, relegated perhaps to matters of aesthetics, but should be tested, along with its consequences, in the philosophical mainstream. Characteristically, Deleuze starts his philosophical studies with a book on David Hume, who is for him the primary exponent of classical empiricism. It is important to go all the way back to this Hume interpretation to work out his concept of empiricism. No doubt one can say – as does, for example, Michael Hardt – that Bergson, Nietzsche and Spinoza should be considered Deleuze's closest 'intellectual kin' (Hardt 1993: XIV). Yet the philosophical reach of his difference-oriented theoretical conceptions can only be recognised if one tracks the critical insights which he develops regarding certain firmly established systematic trends within the history of philosophy.

Even if it were possible to develop transcendental empiricism directly by starting from Nietzsche's late philosophy – and thus to be true in this sense to the great admiration that Deleuze has for him – it is prudent to study the necessary lines of thought running from Hume and Kant directly through Husserl and Heidegger. In this way we can measure the distance that lies between classical empiricism à la Hume and a higher empiricism à la Nietzsche. Nietzsche himself clearly does not relate in a systematic, compact way to the kind of classical empiricism we want to discuss here, so that an interpretation of Nietzsche's thinking concerning empiricism and transcendental philosophy would have to make use of precisely those presuppositions which are made explicit by Husserl and Heidegger regarding Kant and Hume. Furthermore, Deleuze's discussions of Nietzsche also reposition Nietzsche's philosophy on a 'post-phenomenological' and difference-oriented (post-Heideggerian) level. The important aspects which carry Nietzsche beyond Husserl and Heidegger in the conception of transcendental empiricism match in many cases Deleuze's own motivations for his distancing himself from, say, Heidegger or for his broadening of phenomenological investigation. Thus we start with Hume and include a treatment of the Nietzschean (and Bergsonian and Spinozian) influences when we get to Deleuze's own thoughts in a later chapter.

Further elaboration in the direction of transcendental empiricism after Hume recurs here implicitly – and occasionally also explicitly – in specific empirico-critical examinations of Kantianism and phenomenology. It makes sense for several reasons to carry out a presentation of Deleuzian philosophy in this later context as well. First, it can show how French difference-thinking stands up against

Introduction

traditional German schools of thought. In addition, it can show how Deleuze, in spite of his critical transformation of empiricist thought, nevertheless holds on to an empiricist position which steadfastly opposes its supposedly necessary deposition. If there is lasting potential in Deleuzian philosophy, it is because it resolutely follows the traditional path of a critical continuation of a 'metaphysics of finitude' while refusing to let go of its empiricist or immanent foundations – along and beyond the line of Kant, Husserl and Heidegger. In this way we gain access to a source of inspiration and connection in recent French philosophy which hasn't been adequately treated. Whatever its form or label, empiricism's critical stance toward metaphysics has always proclaimed a radicalism imperceptible only by wearing dogmatic blinders.

Consequently this book is divided into three primary parts. In Part I Deleuze's philosophy will first be reconstructed as an empiricist theory by starting from its roots in Hume and his predecessors. Then we come to Kant. It turns out that empiricism and transcendental philosophy need not confront each other irreconcilably as opposites, but rather it is possible to demonstrate with Deleuze that the deficiencies in the classical theories of Hume and Kant can be removed if they are critically related to one another in a certain way. Part II brings us to Husserl and Heidegger. We find that the project of a critical conjoining of empiricist and transcendental thinking places Deleuze's philosophy to a certain extent in the phenomenological tradition. The meaning of its difference-thinking reveals itself in the way the philosophical thoughts of Husserl and Heidegger are critically extrapolated. Finally, in Part III, transcendental empiricism as such will be systematically developed out of Deleuze's *Difference and Repetition* (published in French in 1968).

To give initial contours to transcendental empiricism, let me state four fundamental themes right at the beginning. Starting from his critique of Kant, Husserl and Heidegger, Deleuze demonstrates that a) sense-data have to be reorganised as intensities; b) the doctrine of association must be given a time-theoretical foundation within the context of a theory of passive syntheses; c) empiricism needs to be equipped with a conceptual theory that enables it to have a difference-oriented idea of experience; and d) the traditional empiricist drive of scepticism and critique of metaphysics can only attain its end if the representational image of experience is subverted with the help of an ontology inspired by Nietzsche and Heidegger.

With these points in mind let's see how Deleuze understands

empiricism and transcendental philosophy and then discuss in a preliminary way certain key terms indispensable to the Deleuzian project: difference, virtuality, representation and immanence.

Empiricism

'Transcendental empiricism' is not the arbitrary nameplate of a philosophy of difference meant simply to muddle thoroughly the orders and categories already in place in the history of philosophy. On the contrary, Deleuze develops a novel, 'optimal', concept of empiricism which can work critically on the classic tradition. The historical, epochal concept 'empiricism' has been in use since Kant to designate a certain direction in the philosophy of the seventeenth and eighteenth centuries – from Francis Bacon by way of John Locke to David Hume (and beyond). It is not at all a 'value-neutral' term. Kant introduces it in his questionable project of a systematic distinction between empiricism and rationalism. Accordingly the two movements are declared to be one-sided, antagonistic positions which can only be reconciled and surmounted through a third movement: namely, critical philosophy. Already in his work on Hume, Deleuze rejects the Kantian definition of empiricism.

> The classical definition of empiricism proposed by the Kantian tradition is this: empiricism is the theory according to which knowledge not only begins with experience but is derived from it. [. . .] This definition, to be sure, has at least the advantage of avoiding a piece of nonsense: were empiricism to be presented simply as a theory according to which knowledge begins only with experience, there would not have been any philosophy or philosophers [. . .] who would not be empiricists. (Deleuze 1991: 107; see Kant 1998: B 1f)

Deleuze gives several interdependent explanations why the definition given by Kant – 'in a reverse relationship to rationalism' – is not satisfactory (Deleuze 2001: 35). First and primary, Kant attaches to experience a 'constitutive character' that it doesn't have, as Deleuze shows through Hume's work. That means that, for Hume, the relations relevant to cognition cannot be derived from experience taken as 'the stock of distinct perceptions', since they are effects of principles of human nature given non-empirically (Deleuze 1991: 107–8). Thus empiricism makes use of principles (like those of association) which express themselves in experience insofar as they constitute a subject which is able to go beyond the immediate stock of experi-

Introduction

ence – for example, in the belief in the regularities deposited within habit. The epistemological orientation of the Kantian definition of empiricism, which is governed by the question of whether there are concepts which do not stem from experience, makes the empiricist position on 'origination' problematic in a one-sided way by asserting that 'the intelligible "comes" from the sensible' (Deleuze and Parnet 1987: 54). Deleuze, on the contrary, wants to say that Hume's philosophy at least demands a concept of empiricism that essentially draws on the logic of its external relations. This is the sense of his requirement that we push back the difference between ideas and impressions in favour of the difference between impressions of sense and impressions of reflexion, or in favour of the difference between associations and their terms.

> In effect if relations are external and irreducible to their terms, then the difference cannot be between the sensible and the intelligible, between experience and thought, [...] but only between two [...] sorts of experiences: that of terms and that of relations. (Deleuze and Parnet 1987: 55–6)

The difference between simple perceptions and relations like associations takes on a special value because the latter remain exterior to the former. Relations are neither empirically derivable nor empirically reducible: immediate experience cannot serve as their epistemological foundation. Deleuze takes as his starting point what to other authors – for example, Kant or Reid – must appear as the end of empiricism: its (apparently disastrous) culmination in Humean scepticism. The only thing they have in common is the assessment that Hume, in his style of unbridled Enlightenment, draws the ultimate philosophical consequences out of the basic assumptions of empiricism. Yet whether these consequences prove the empiricist position to be untenable depends on the chosen perspective. Deleuze interprets Hume's 'modern scepticism' through a pragmatic theory of truth as it was developed by such different authors as Bergson, Nietzsche or William James toward the end of the nineteenth century. Here I will address only two aspects of this interpretation. First, Hume drops the natural belief in truth by 'substituting for the traditional concept of error a concept of [...] illusion' (Deleuze 2001: 42). With this substitution the philosophical image of thought undergoes a lasting change, since 'the memory, senses, and understanding are all of them founded on the imagination' (Hume 2001: 173). Hume's scepticism is clearly directed against the 'presumptuousness' of human understanding, which literally overlooks its weaknesses without investigating the corresponding practical motives for doing so. Second, Deleuze points out that the actual secret of empiricism is to be found in the 'anti-Platonic experiment' of pluralism, which sets multiplicity as the normative value. 'The multiple is no longer an adjective which is still subordinate to the One which divides it or the Being which encompasses it. It has become a noun, a multiplicity which constantly inhabits each thing' (Deleuze and Parnet 1987: 57).

The culmination of empiricism in scepticism only then means its dissolution and its ruin if for certain epistemological validity claims one sticks (for example) with a philosophy of common sense. It is just the legitimacy of such claims that Hume doubts. As will become more apparent, it is correct to define empiricism using its primary notion of experience, and the sceptical consequences are in any case directly connected with the empiricist conception of pure experience. However, this connection exhibits the collapse of the empiricist project only if it is assumed that experience has to serve as the scientific basis for objective verification of theoretical laws. In so-called *neo-pragmatism* since Quine, it has been shown that this assumption is *dogmatic*, so that for a viable empiricist philosophy one rightly demands that it takes seriously the critique of representationalism and gives up its fundamentalism in the philosophy of science (see Quine 1953: 20–46 and Rorty 1990).

In this context it is noteworthy that Deleuze orients his early reading of Hume on the pragmatically radicalised version of empiricism promulgated by William James. Taking his cue from Hume's critical views of metaphysics, Deleuze turns against the theoretical assumptions of traditional versions of knowledge. In this he is supported by a concept of experience that allows reconstruction of the process by which habits and beliefs are generated in practical circumstances. In the eyes of the early Deleuze, the concept of experience must be seen as dual: on the one hand it is *atomistic*, in the sense of a radical experience made up of different perceptions 'which succeed each other with an inconceivable rapidity, and are in a perpetual flux and movement' (Hume 2001: 165), and on the other hand it is *associative*, so that the differences communicate with one another directly, without mediation by way of prefigured rational controls. In later years Deleuze will turn aside this strict dualism. Here we merely want to state that Deleuze develops his concept of experience from the beginning in direct relation to the empiricist tradition, in such a way that the pure 'sense-datum-experience' by right is not

Introduction

contaminated by substantialist presuppositions, but organises itself by association. Deleuze understands the doctrine of association as a theory of *passive synthesis*, which makes it possible to think differences and transitions simultaneously without sublating them into one homogeneous totality. 'Sense-data-experience', which Deleuze at first does not strictly separate from atomistic and naturalistic handicaps, determines generally and essentially the empiricist concept of experience. Deleuze interprets it in proximity to William James's 'pure experience' and provides, especially in *Difference and Repetition* and with Nietzsche, a theory of intensity which tries to conceptualise in a new way the 'sense data' experience, that is to say, the experience of 'affects' and 'percepts'. In fact, Deleuze himself never talks of 'sense data' to avoid physicalistic, and later also elementaristic connotations. I am putting this idea into play (provisionally) for the simple reason that the definition of empiricism has to keep going back to its concept of experience, which in recent times is usually explicated as 'sense data' (see Hirst 1959 and 1965). The modern expression 'sense datum' often replaces the classic expression 'perception' and in the debate between Austin and Ayer, as well as for Hume himself, the two technical terms occur primarily in phenomenological usage. In *Sense and Sensibilia* Austin characterises the fundamental thesis of his empiricist opponents as follows:

> The general doctrine, generally stated, goes like this: we never see or otherwise perceive [...], or anyhow we never directly perceive or sense, material objects [...], but only sense-data (or our own ideas, impressions, sensa, sense-perceptions, percepts, etc.) (Austin 1962: 2, 21)

Deleuze interprets the method of empiricist reduction as a structural reduction of experience to its phenomenological immanence. The question which emerges for a transcendental empiricist is this: how must unmediated experience be thought if it is to be freed from unacceptable ontological and epistemological dogmas? As long as there are still presuppositions of one kind or another reigning in classical and logical empiricism, presuppositions that implicitly ameliorate the metaphysically critical and anti-representational primacy of experience, the empiricist onset of thought must be radicalised in a difference-oriented way.

No doubt the immanent scepticism of classical empiricism and its critical examination of the traditional prejudices of substance metaphysics before the tribunal of experience have been sufficiently tempered by naturalistic and 'everyday thinking' tendencies, so that the everyday experience of existing things can easily be interpreted empirically. In other words, the so-called factually apparent phenomenological connections can somehow be reconstructed from sense-data (see Strawson 1983: 12–13 and Laird 1967: 185). To put it in simple terms, ordinary objects more or less correspond to a heaping up of perceptions which, thanks to the association laws inherent in human nature, get hooked together in a certain way. But here Deleuze calls a halt. This is the point where Deleuze, in view of Kant's critical investigations of empiricism, demands that we grasp the difference between objects and perceptions even more radically. The danger of empiricism does not lie in side-stepping the habits of common sense, but in trying to explain only commonly acknowledged givens of experience, a misuse of the means provided by its radicalised thought initiatives. Berkeley's assurance that his philosophy was completely beholden to *common sense* already made his contemporaries somewhat dizzy. Ever since the theoretician of common sense, Thomas Reid, carried out a thorough critique of the fundamentals of empiricism, very few still believe in the *good will* of empiricist thought. The retreat back to experience seems to be a 'step back' from characteristic language usage, as *ordinary language philosophy* has repeatedly shown (see Ryle 2000 and Austin 1962). Clearly sense-data theory flagrantly contradicts the natural realism of human-being-in-the-world. Therefore one cannot ignore the feeling that the more specific ideas of empiricism are falling by the wayside if empiricism recurs explicitly only as a cloudy subarea of positivism, theory of science and logic. Putnam emphasises how touchy the problem is by formulating it smugly as follows:

> But why should a theory which only a few philosophers have ever believed, the theory that the only objects whose existence is not of a highly derived kind are sense-qualia – that sense-qualia are the furniture of the universe – be more credible than the worldview of science and common sense? (Putnam 1985: 26)

This question is justified to the degree that the empirically pure experience of data cannot be translated into the terminology of a pure language of observation, which is then able to legitimise the validity claims of scientific theories. Deleuze quite agrees and will show that it is precisely the loss of objective reference which makes sense-data dysfunctional in a correspondence-theoretical way. Therefore the reductionist thesis bound up with empiricism cannot be used foundationally, to set up and retain higher, complex and derived knowledge on its basis. The mediation of concepts and sense impressions can only succeed with an even more basic idea. In Deleuze's difference philosophy this will turn out to be the empiricist idea of pre-objective, virtual sense-data or virtual perceptions.

Transcendental Philosophy

The concept 'transcendental' has various meanings in the Kantian philosophy. When Deleuze uses the concept, he relates primarily to its methodological sense, which is to say, to demonstrate the constitutive structures in the formation of knowledge as well as the conditions of the possibility of experience or the mode of cognition of objects *a priori* (see Kant 1998: B 25). He sees empiricist connections especially in those places where Kant situates the structures of experience within the 'transcendental consciousness'. The method of so-called *transcendental psychology* consists in regarding the pure syntheses of the power of imagination as requirements *vis-à-vis* the possibility of experience. However, this methodological point of departure cannot be pursued very far within the Kantian philosophy, because on the one hand it stands in conflict with the foundational claims of transcendental cognition but on the other hand it is bound to these claims in a highly problematical fashion. That is why Deleuze orients himself not only on Kantian terminology but also relies on Salomon Maimon's *Essay on Transcendental Philosophy*. Above all, however, he follows Husserl's lead, in which the concept 'transcendental' receives a new, phenomenological definition.

Before I sketch in a few sentences how Deleuze assesses the possibility of a post-Kantian transcendental philosophy, let me point to two important aspects of Kant's presentation of a *transcendental criticism* of empiricism, for this prepares us for the necessary 'deepening' of empiricist foundations. First Kant requires a non-empirical, objective principle to be able to ground the factual regularities of association. This is the *epistemological* aspect of his critique and the related inquiry into the objective validity of the laws of nature. Second, Kant makes it clear that empiricists give up the *phenomenological* objectivity of experience whenever they rely rigorously on their theory of perception. Perceptions that cannot be synthesised according to standards of categorial ideas of unification remain completely uncoordinated, cannot group themselves around an objective pole, and slip away from the ego's overview. The loss of the intentionality of consciousness ends accordingly in the 'milling around' of pre-subjective perceptions (see Kant 1998: A 111). In this sense the transcendental critique forces empiricism either to reject its theoretical axioms or instead to affirm their sceptical consequences without tempering them naturalistically. Thus we are again forced to face the problem of immediate sense-data, data that do not appear in consciousness as discrete phenomenal data or as quasi-objects.

Kant's discovery of the *transcendental synthesis* can, however, help to modify the empiricist theory of successive states of consciousness. For the fundamental fact of empiricist intuition implies that the manifold of impressions are always already apprehended and unified in a temporal order and are thus not given to consciousness as atomistic perceptions. By introducing time as a form of internal sense which *interiorises* the manifold, Kant can meaningfully distance himself from certain Cartesian premises of philosophising still at work in classical empiricism. Of course, when starting from judgements of experience, these inquiries remain methodologically regressive as long as merely the objective reality of concepts, and not objective reality itself, is supposed to be schematically reconstructed. Husserl – and after him, Heidegger – exposed this ambiguity in the Kantian enterprise. Accordingly, there has to be a distinction made between the 'incomprehensibly mythical' vocabulary of the *Critique*, with its rationalist foundations, and the development of a truly transcendental method, one that systematically uncovers the implicit intentionality of the constitutive understanding (see Husserl 1970a: 114f). Husserl talks about Kant's 'overwhelming genius', which becomes obvious in the analysis of the three syntheses within the framework of the *transcendental deduction* in the first edition of the *Critique of Pure Reason*, but he has reservations about the result.

> Kant makes an approach to a direct grounding, one which descends to the original sources, only to break off again almost at once without arriving at the genuine problems of foundation which are to be opened up from this supposedly psychological side. (Husserl 1970a: 104)

Even though Kant starts with the 'representative' fact of experience, that is, with the scientific or ordinary cognition of objects, and orients his transcendental insights in a direction that legitimises the demands formulated in the judgements of experience, remaining general rather than specific, his analyses nevertheless move in the twilight zone that detours around the *genetic conditions* of experience. According to Husserl, it is the task of phenomenology to describe the procedures of the transcendental syntheses well enough to keep them from being taken for granted, and to make them 'intuitively evident'. This clarified idea of the transcendental, as that which immanently defines experience, is the heart and soul of the empiricism which Deleuze has in mind.

Another person whom Deleuze finds useful in orienting his post-Kantianism is the somewhat less well-known Salomon Maimon, who already in 1790, in his Leibniz-inspired *Essay on Transcendental Philosophy*, undermines Kant's duality between concept and intuition by interpreting perceptions with the help of the limit concept of the *differential*. Deleuze in his work often points out that one can extract a genetic method regarding the immanent determination of experience out of Maimon's psychology of perception, a method with which one can home in on the transcendental aspects of Maimon's 'higher empiricism' (see Deleuze 1994: 170, 173–4, and Deleuze 1993: 89). It is with Maimon that Deleuze conceptualises for example *intensity*, his fundamental empiricist concept, by way of Hermann Cohen, who uses differential quantity to interpret the second Kantian axiom regarding the *anticipation of perception*, which is to say, to define the intensity of all *quanta continua*. With the help of these transcendental ideas, Deleuze attempts a critical transformation of the classical theory of perception. 'Sense-data' are henceforth not isolated perceptions, but instead are concerned with differential, imperceptible moments of experience that organise themselves in transcendental syntheses. In this way multiplicities are formed which, as they step over the threshold of consciousness, are perceived as unified or integrated.

Even when Maimon cites Hume to question the presuppositions of Kant's deduction of pure concepts, he simultaneously adapts Kant's idea of a transcendental synthesis when he goes on to inquire about the 'conditions of perception' (Maimon 2010: 137). He defines as *differentials* the pure, unconscious givens of receptivity (Maimon 2010: 19–20). 'These differentials of objects are the so-called *noumena*, but the objects themselves arising from them are the *phenomena*' (Maimon 2010: 21). The *noumena* cannot be consciously recognised, but have to be thought by a finite understanding as idea, for, as Deleuze says, 'an object outside experience can be represented only in problematic form' (Deleuze 1994: 169). The differential sense-data, comprehended as *petites perceptions*, define the manifold of sensible intuition which must be conceptualised not as discrete multiplicity, as classical empiricism suggests, but as *continuous* multiplicity. This is how Maimon puts it:

> [T]he great Leibniz came upon the discovery of the differential calculus through his system of the Monadology. [...] However, in mathematics as much as in philosophy they [the differentials] are mere ideas that do not represent objects but only the way objects arise, i.e. they are mere limit concepts [*Gränzbegriffe*], which we can approach nearer and nearer to, but never reach. They arise through a continuous regress or through the diminution to infinity of the consciousness of an intuition. (Maimon 2010: 19)

Dx is the symbol for the ideal characterisation of consciousness and its objects insofar as their appearance is derived genetically from the determinable relationship of their sub-representable elements. As Maimon shows, one can elicit from calculus a purely philosophical, that is to say, a transcendental method. He uses the differentials to imagine the 'mode of origin of objects', not in any way the objects themselves. 'With respect to intuition = 0, the differential of any such object in itself is $dx = 0$, $dy = 0$ etc.; however, their relations are not = 0, but rather be given determinately [*bestimmt angegeben*] in the intuitions arising from them' (Maimon 2010: 21). The differential elements unfold their ideal characteristic genetic potential whenever they enter into appropriate relationships of reciprocal syntheses. It is the *transcendental power of imagination* that makes these syntheses possible. In his book on Leibniz, Deleuze describes Maimon's central thoughts as follows:

> Inconspicuous perceptions are thus not parts of conscious perception, but requisites or genetic elements, 'differentials of consciousness'. Even more than Fichte, Salomon Maimon – the first post-Kantian who returns to Leibniz – draws all the consequences from this kind of psychic automatism of perception. Far from having perception presuppose an object capable of affecting us, and conditions in which we would be apt to be affected, the reciprocal determination of the differentials dy/dx brings about the complete determination of the object as a perception, and the determinability of space-time as a condition. Beyond the Kantian method of conditioning, Maimon restores an internal subjective method of genesis. [...] The physical object and mathematical space both refer to a transcendental (differential and genetic) psychology of perception. (Deleuze 1993: 89)

This transcendental psychology operates with differential *intensities* which are never to be confused with mere experiential *material* that would have to be conceptually mediated. Deleuze conceives of inconspicuous sensations (following Maimon's example) in such a way that they don't need this mediation. The flux of sensations possesses

Introduction

as such an ideally definable *virtual reality*. In this way a systematic circle is described that characterises the new empiricist image of thought. For the sensible can *only* be thought if it is conceptualised ideally as that which can only be sensed (Deleuze 1994: 144–5). Within this idea of the transcendental, the genetic dimensions of experience can be recuperated and the inability of thought to ground itself and to illuminate itself can be conceptualised. In thinking, there is a repetition of maximum difference when thought thinks about its immanent definition, and realises that it can *only* be thought.

Transcendental Empiricism

In a discussion with Deleuze in *Negotiations* (1995), Raymond Bellour and François Ewald distinguish three periods in Deleuze's work: first a 'history of philosophy' phase beginning with *Empiricism and Subjectivity* (first published in French in 1953 and in English in 1991) and reaching in 1969 to the *Logic of Sense* (1990b), then a period of cooperation with Félix Guattari from *Anti-Oedipus* (1972) to *A Thousand Plateaus* (1980) and finally his occupation with painting and cinema in the 1980s. His last works on Foucault (1988b), on Leibniz (1993) and – let's not forget – on *What Is Philosophy?* (1994) would 'again connect with a more classical approach to philosophy' and round out the picture. Deleuze did not deny this periodisation, but he was against the impression that it meant three work phases, separated from one another by radical changes. On the contrary, as Deleuze continues a bit later in the same interview, only a single crisis – simultaneously biographical as well as philosophical – affected his thought: a crisis situated in time between the books on Hume (1953) and on Nietzsche (1962), and which began with writer's block. We will have an opportunity later to inquire more specifically into the philosophical implications of this break. Here we shall merely point out that Deleuze's empiricism doesn't take form as *transcendental* empiricism until the 1960s. The transition to transcendental empiricism can be more exactly pinpointed with the advent of the concept of *virtuality*. Missing from Humean empiricism and its atomistic foundation – even in Deleuze's interpretation – is a transcendental or virtual dimension which would give him the possibility of taking on his dialectical critics in a consequential way. It is precisely the difference principle in empiricism, which says that all separable objects can be distinguished from one another and all distinguished objects can be separated, that proves to be inconsistent. The point-like sense-data would have to be pure 'thisness', not resulting from genetic processes and therefore also not organised and concretised with the help of such processes.

Deleuze's planned shift of 'transcendental' and 'empirical' affects the concept of experience in classical empiricism as well as in transcendental philosophy. Sense-data are no longer to be taken as the fundamental givens of empiricism, but as *transcendental singularities* which structurally define and actualise themselves (Deleuze 1990b: 103). Thus the transcendental structures cannot be grasped merely as possible conditions for a presupposed experience. Rather, they determine the *actual* experience, which, as empirical result, differs essentially from the transcendental syntheses preliminary to it. In line with Foucault, Deleuze turns against the mere *lifting off* or *calqueing* something transcendental from empirical facts, whereby, starting from the experience of banal acts of recognition, one tries to reconstruct those general regularities which claim by right to have objective and necessary validity for knowledge. Deleuze contrasts this *méthode du décalque* with transcendental empiricism, which 'is the only way to avoid tracing the transcendental from the outlines of the empirical' (Deleuze 1994: 144). In a variation of a remark by Husserl, one could say that Deleuze brackets the image of thought relating to representation to 'lay open an infinite realm of being [...] as the sphere of a new kind of experience: *transcendental experience*' (Husserl 1999: 27). Deleuze demands a radicalisation of transcendental reduction which questions the postulates of representational logic held by a naturalistic belief system, with the result that one can no longer cling to some form of consciousness within the transcendental (see Deleuze 1990b: 105).

> We rediscover in all the postulates of the dogmatic image the same confusion: elevating a simple empirical figure to the status of a transcendental, at the risk of allowing the real structures of the transcendental to fall into the empirical. (Deleuze 1994: 154)

Foucault in *The Order of Things* takes his cue from Heidegger's critique of representational thinking and shows that the preliminary structures of Being (e.g. language) do not coincide with empirical facts within a framework of foundational logic (see Foucault 1970: 303–43). Deleuze ties in with these reflections when he gives priority to the (virtual) being of the sensible, as the irretrievable starting point of thought, over the objective givens of consciousness. With the concept of the *virtual* he succeeds in conceptualising a transcendental

Introduction

region which does not emerge out of a doubling of the empirical and therefore does not determine experience's *a priori* forms with abstracted realms of possibility. The essential difference is thereby localised where the transcendental and the empirical, the virtual and the actual are distinguished from one another. But this difference does not prevent the virtual structures from actualising themselves, nor the transcendental conditions from determining experience as its genetic conditions. Of course the empirical results of these preliminary constitutional processes are not at all the same as the processes themselves. Whenever the actualities are cut off from their virtual backgrounds, there is a growing danger that one tries 'regressively' to peel off their foundational structures. According to Deleuze, the standard image of experience, which is to say, the ordinary or everyday cognition of objects, is problematic because it rests on arbitrary presuppositions which need to be investigated. Objects of recognition must be distinguished from signs and events on the plane of immanence, whose self-structuration makes it possible that we can have objectively oriented experiences at all. It is a widely circulated phenomenological misconception to assert that concrete experience is always the one that holds on to a noematic object-pole that concentrates upon itself all the achievements of the different faculties. The well-defined perceptions of things imply manifold processes of becoming. Underneath the things visible in natural light glimmer in semidarkness the minute perceptions: only *counter-effectuation*, perhaps a rising feeling of panic in the face of pure immanence, transfers us into the paradoxical play of faculties which do not all focus on a single common reference point. 'I have, it's true, spent a lot of time writing about this notion of event: you see, I don't believe in things' (Deleuze 1995: 160).

The empiricist orientation toward the 'event' in no way ties Deleuze to a general dismissal of philosophical concepts as if they were derived from the actual truths of life and, as abstract 'guardian convictions', would screen these truths or make them bearable under a cloak of forgetfulness. Deleuze's concern, in contrast to diverse romantic attempts at reviving empiricist ideas in the contexts of various philosophies of life, is to make full use of the constructive potential of conceptual thinking in the strict sense of an enlightened empiricism. In his theory of concepts he leaves behind the representational *copy-principle* which asserts that simple 'ideas' immediately reflect corresponding sense impressions. For him ideas and concepts have their very own 'sources', and although these sources of reason are neither pure nor original, at least they cannot be traced back to the continuous experience of immediate *sensory*-given life. It was a mistake for the 'radical' empiricism of Mach and James, and in many respects for Bergson and Nietzsche as well, to explain the 'nature' of philosophical concepts through the abstraction theory of classical empiricism. Thus, for example, in a lecture on 'Bergson and his Critique of Intellectualism', James writes:

> All these abstract concepts are but as flowers gathered, they are only moments dipped out from the stream of time, snap-shots taken, as by a kinetoscopic camera, of a life that in its original coming is continuous. (James 1987: 735–6)

Although a certain progress can be attributed to insights into the instrumental character of concepts, it is not enough to be satisfied with their peculiar propensity to be cut apart and then made to fit (see Adorno 1981). Rather, the point is to construct concepts in such a way that, from a difference perspective, they are *not* subjugated to a thinking that seems inevitably intent on making identifications. In this spirit I will close the introduction by giving a short presentation of some key concepts of Deleuze's philosophy.

Difference (différence)

Deleuze's concept of difference will be analysed in detail in the section 'Metaphysics and Difference Philosophy' (within Chapter 7). Here I will advance only a few brief remarks. Deleuze speaks of 'difference in itself' (*différence en elle-même*), which is distinct from a merely notional, mediated or superficial difference. What then is really at stake here? In answering the question it is helpful to recall Heidegger's concept of *ontological difference*, which strongly influenced Deleuze. In his essay *Identity and Difference* Heidegger declares that difference has not been adequately considered in the metaphysical tradition because it has only been viewed in terms of a pre-introduced identity: either Aristotelian, as distinction between things of the same sort or of sorts of the same genus and so on, or Hegelian, as distinction within a concept, identical with itself, which sets itself apart from itself. This 'forgetfulness of difference' in the metaphysical tradition is countered by Heidegger with the challenge to think Being as difference, which means thinking the time-determined event-structures which result on their own insofar as they take place before their foundation in representational logic

Introduction

can be worked out. Deleuze takes up Heidegger's train of thought by calling attention to the self-constitutive achievements of experience by letting something that distinguishes *itself* – by leaping out of the undifferentiated background – become noticeable or conspicuous.

> Lightning, for example, distinguishes itself from the black sky but must also trail it behind, as though it were distinguishing itself from that which does not distinguish itself from it. It is as if the ground rose to the surface, without ceasing to be ground. (Deleuze 1994: 28)

Deleuze understands difference not dialectically as difference between something indefinite and something definite, but as the *unilateral* and *asymmetrical* distinctiveness of THE determination in general. Thus self-distinction does not define itself through negative logic as that from which it distinguishes itself. Lightning remains bound in darkness and cannot cancel it out with its light. The 'indifference' of sub-actual genetic processes cannot be defined by actual differentiated results, but rather, these latter are defined in reverse by the former. Difference cannot be located either speculatively in the interior of the concept, because in this way its non-conceptual relations disappear from view, nor can it be conceptualised as *empirical* difference between diverse things. Difference is not given, but is that *through which* the given is given. Difference has to be thought *in itself*, so that it does not become subverted by the four mediational forms of representation: identity, analogy, opposition and similarity. That is how one prevents difference from being spread over the 'surface of the identical'.

Virtuality *(virtualité)*

A further key concept of Deleuzian philosophy is virtuality. Deleuze borrows it from Bergson, 'who develops the notion of the *virtual* to its highest degree and bases a whole philosophy of memory and life on it' (Deleuze 1988a: 43). Virtuality or the virtual (*le virtuel*) denotes in *Matter and Memory* the ontological form of pure past or unconscious memory. In *Sur les données immédiates de la conscience* (*Time and Free Will*) this concept denotes the subjective-qualitative manifold character of time consciousness (*durée*). Deleuze combines the two aspects of manifold and pure past, thereby making the present actuality of consciousness dependent on the unconscious actualisation processes of a 'structure' considered as a virtual manifold. Accordingly, the differential elements and relations of the structure are not conscious, but they nevertheless have reality as genetic factors within experience. Deleuze first distinguishes between the reality of the virtual and the reality of the actual in line with Bergson's contrasted multiplicities of time and space, subject and object. Objectivity is after all a *numerical* multiplicity without hidden or held back potencies; this multiplicity doesn't undergo fundamental change when divided up. In the field of the objectively actual, possibility displays in its (not realised) variety all the determinations of reality that can be anticipated. On the other hand, subjectivity defines itself as a *continuous* multiplicity which radically changes if it divides up or differentiates. For example, 'minute perceptions' or confused feelings which are implicit within the virtual background of actual states of consciousness lose their virtual status as actual and explicit moments of reality. Whereas a possibility displays itself as a variety of the actual only after the fact and in the process *doubles* in consciousness the defining features of the actual, the virtual possesses a reality that can self-actualise. In contrast to the mere *possibility* of a concept, a possibility which lays down rules regarding appearance within homogeneous forms of intuition, the *virtuality* of structure self-actualises as a time and a space which are immanent to that structure.

If, therefore, the proper line of demarcation runs between the actual or empirical objects of representation on the one hand and the virtual signs or transcendental singularities on the other hand, then it does so to prevent the identification of the virtual with an abstract form of possibility.

Representation (représentation)

According to Deleuze, representation doesn't just stand as one of many postulates in the *dogmatic* image of thought that is responsible for the displacement of difference and its repetition processes, but defines this image of thought as such. In this regard Deleuze leans on Foucault, who in his archaeological studies in *The Order of Things* finds in representation the principle of order governing universally the classic *episteme* (Foucault 1970: 63ff; see Deleuze 1994: 262, 137f). Of course, Deleuze is just as dissatisfied as Foucault to claim a paradigm change, beginning with Kant's critical philosophy, between the historical formations of knowledge of the 'classic' philosophers and those of the nineteenth century. In contrast to the classical theory of sign as representation of idea, which in turn represents the perceived object (and the significance incorporated therein), Kant rejects a copy-derived ontology. He admittedly defines representation epistemically in such a way that objects orient themselves as appearances according to our cognitive faculties (Kant 1998: B xxi–xxiv). Yet he retains certain assumptions of consciousness which continue to shape his concept of experience as representational (compare Kant 1998: A 320/B 376). Deleuze treats these relationships thematically by showing that the classical image of thought, primarily Cartesian, which Kant tries critically to undermine, is in some respects given new support and consolidation. Not to be overlooked, therefore, is that Deleuze defines his concept of representation in the context of the Kantian theory of knowledge, with particular emphasis on Kant's distinction between presentation (*Darstellung*) and representation (*Vorstellung*) as it was bandied about in wide circles of nineteenth-century philosophy.

> The important thing in representation is the prefix: *re*-presentation implies an active taking up of that which is presented; hence an activity and a unity distinct from the passivity and diversity which characterise sensibility as such. From this standpoint we no longer need to define knowledge as a synthesis of representations. It is the representation itself which is defined as knowledge, that is to say as *the synthesis of that which is presented*. (Deleuze 1984: 8)

Immediately present phenomena (presentations) can only be re-presented if they are reproduced based on a conceptual form of identity and thereby mediated. Thus we have this shorthand for representation: making something present as something. No wonder, then, that Deleuze finds the transcendental image of representation in *recognition* as it occurs in Kant's theory of synthesis (see Deleuze 1994: 133). Recognition defines itself by means of the cooperation of faculties in the unity of a thinking subject, faculties that converge about an identical object. Therefore the prefix RE, which also adheres in the concept of repetition, favours the categorial generalities of representation. These generalities are, however, burdened by their inability to think difference in itself or to discover 'the lived reality of a sub-representative region' (Deleuze 1994: 69).

Immanence (immanence)

Toward the end of his life Deleuze wrote a short text in which he asserted that pure immanence, that is the immanence of immanence, is A LIFE and nothing else (Deleuze 2001: 27). Doesn't this thesis proclaim an empiricist vitalism, a 'pious discourse on life and creation', as Alain Badiou thinks? In opposition to a tradition of thought that favours an *original self-transcending leap* by the subject in the direction of an outside world which is set over against it, Deleuze insists on the point of view of immanence, which *abjures* any kind of transcendence of subject or object.

Immanence is defined by Deleuze as the transcendental field of an ego-less and non-intentional stream of consciousness, whereby consciousness only then becomes factum 'when a subject is produced at the same time as its object, both being outside of the field and appearing as "transcendents"' (Deleuze 2001: 26). All transcendents are revealed by Deleuze to be products of immanence that construct themselves in the a-subjective realm of experience. Instead of speculating about a pre-given subject that is forced because of its abstract selfhood to transcend *itself*, Deleuze begins in the reverse direction by thinking about the self-actualisation of experience without recourse to previous instances thereof. Thus Deleuze's transcendental empiricism does not culminate in the continuous immediacy and indifference of a philosophy of life, since this kind of actualisation-practice always runs within the framework of temporal processes of subjectivisation.

> The indefinite aspects in a life lose all indetermination to the degree that they fill out a plane of immanence or, what amounts to the same thing, to the degree that they constitute the elements of a transcendental field (individual life, on the other hand, remains inseparable from empirical determinations). The indefinite as such is the mark not of an empirical indetermination but of a determination by immanence or a transcendental determinability. The indefinite article is the indetermination of the person only because it is determination of the singular. The One is not the transcendent that might contain immanence but the immanent contained within a transcendental field. One is always the index of a multiplicity: an event, a singularity, a life . . . (Deleuze 2001: 30)

A life consists entirely of virtuals that actualise themselves – in a consciousness to which they attribute themselves. Nevertheless nothing that can be considered 'as non-actualised (indefinite)' is lost to the virtual event. The virtual is of course inseparable from its actualisation but it doesn't melt together with the facts in which it actualises itself. For 'there is a big difference between the virtuals that define the immanence of the transcendental field and the possible forms that actualise them and transform them into something transcendent' (Deleuze 2001: 32).

PART I
Empiricism/Transcendentalism

1
Hume's Logic of External Relations

Hume's philosophy is a sharp critique of representation. (Deleuze 1991: 30)

Deleuze was twenty-eight when he wrote his study on Hume. This early exercise, published in Paris in 1953 under the title *Empirisme et subjectivité. Essai sur la nature humaine selon Hume*, stands somewhat isolated from his later achievements. Its peripheral existence has led some interpreters to reserve interest in the book, implying that it is not yet on the level of subsequent works. Nor can we presume to find in it a fundamental first draft of the philosophy of difference which Deleuze developed primarily in the 1960s. At the very least, however, the Hume book needs to be considered as a self-evident starting point for any attempt to present Deleuze as a possible empiricist. Indeed, it goes much further, for it introduces a radicalisation of classical empiricism by taking seriously Hume's logic of external relations.

The young Deleuze intentionally plays the doctrine of association off against sense-atomism to ground a theory of practical subjectivity. This brings to the fore his criticist distance regarding basic scientific assumptions in the empiricist theory of perception. In his implicit distancing, Deleuze not only puts forth certain theorems which prefigure a compelling radical empiricism, he also finds in Hume's philosophy itself the necessary prerequisites for its critical reactualisation. To get there he certainly allowed himself to be inspired by pluralist and pragmatist ideas stemming from William James, which were probably known to him through courses or books by Jean Wahl. Not for nothing does he designate Jean Wahl, apart from Sartre, as the 'most important French philosopher' (Deleuze and Guattari 1987: 57–8), exploring the 'possibilities within empiricism [...] on the non-Hegelian relations' (Deleuze 1994: 311). In *Les philosophies pluralistes d'Angleterre et d'Amerique* Wahl states succinctly that the so-called 'radical empiricism' of William James is based on a logic of external relations which not only rejects classic atomism within sense-data theory, but also and in addition is accompanied by a critique of monistic-speculative philosophy and its theory of inner relations (Wahl 1920: 122f.).

Even if it is true that evident agreements exist between Deleuze and James regarding the critical progression of the empiricist tradition, it is to our advantage to avoid two possible over-interpretations. *First*, Deleuze's presentation of Hume distinguishes itself from others by deciphering the status of external relations *within* Humean philosophy. The critique of the concept of inner relations which derives from this approach is not related by Deleuze to Francis H. Bradley, Josiah Royce and the Anglo-Saxon neo-Hegelians, but to Kant and transcendental philosophy. The latter characterises for him at this point the rationalist image of thought which counters the empiricist position. *Second*, it would be presumptuous to equate radical empiricism in the Jamesian sense with Deleuze's transcendental empiricism. This equation or approximation of the two theories gets encouragement from Deleuze insofar as he often speaks in the 1970s of external relations like the conjunctive enchainings introduced in *Anti-Oedipus* (see Deleuze and Parnet 1987: 54–9, and Deleuze 2001: 37f.). In this way he seems to produce a direct relationship between the difference-based concept of transcendental synthesis and his early, Jamesian-inspired book on Hume (see Hayden 1998: 89). The situation becomes somewhat more complicated, for in transcendental empiricism the positions championed by Deleuze in the Hume book have developed considerably further. Nevertheless, *Empiricism and Subjectivity* represents an important preliminary step in the formation of transcendental empiricism. This early work makes clear how Deleuze unfolds his empiricism against the background of Hume's thinking and allows us to understand later developments in the context of his readings of Hume. Finally, it pinpoints the problematic places where Deleuze will be forced to revise his own earlier position. If in this way we can make the history of its origins comprehensible, it will simplify the understanding of transcendental empiricism and its critical relevance for systematic empiricist questioning.

Referring constantly to the three books that make up the *Treatise of Human Nature* (Hume 1739–40), Deleuze begins his explications of Humean empiricism by stating the thesis – clearly in need of interpretation – that Hume is not interested in a 'psychology of mind' (*psychologie de l'esprit*), but rather in a 'psychology of the mind's affections' (*psychologie des affections de l'esprit*) (Deleuze 1991: 21). This thesis proposes that the doctrine of human nature put forth by Hume is less a problem of *origins* and rather more a problem regarding the *subjectivation* of mind or spirit. As Jean Wahl puts it, 'We won't ask questions of origins, we will only try to determine relations' (Wahl 1920: 122–3). Deleuze would naturally agree that Humean empiricism is founded on *atomism*. However, he thinks that the problems of cognition and morality can only be explained *associatively*. Although the individual and indivisible *ideas* or mental givens do represent corresponding impressions, they cannot as such be made the object of a psychology of human nature.

> The point of view of the origin, according to which every idea derives from a preexisting impression and represents it, does not have the importance that people attribute to it: it merely gives the mind a simple origin and frees the ideas from the obligation of having to represent *things*. (Deleuze 1991: 31)

The consistent application of the fundamental principle of empiricism that simple ideas represent simple impressions makes it impossible for ideas to represent things. Getting ahead of the game, we might say that the operation of reducing complex ideas to simple facts of experience cannot take on 'central importance' because it is, according to Deleuze, not practicable. In the region of factual cognition, for example, the necessary transcendence of what is given rests on a natural act of belief, which includes *in every case* a use of the imagination which cannot be legitimised empirically. No doubt the genetic problem which Hume develops is justified when it questions how we come to believe in independently separable things. But precisely this transcendence of what is given, which takes place in belief, points not to the problem of origin but rather to that of subjectivation. Only simple perceptions that come and go without ceasing are the *given*: 'It is the totality of that which appears, being which equals appearance' (Deleuze 1991: 87).

Deleuze takes from empiricist atomism the idea of a radically immanent experience which rests on the *principle of difference* as established by Hume. This *empirical* principle asserts that there cannot be inseparable impressions or representations. Perceptions that are different are distinguishable and thus separable, and vice versa.

> Therefore, experience is succession, or the movement of separable ideas, insofar as they are different, and different, insofar as they are separable. We must begin with *this* experience because it is *the* experience. It does not presuppose anything else and nothing else precedes it. It is not the

affection of an implicated subject, nor the modification or mode of a substance. (Deleuze 1991: 87–8)

The perceptions have no need of anything to support their existence; they are the only substances there are. They do not exhibit any subjective or objective features. They do not represent any object-related qualities, but must be considered from the point of view of quantity. Deleuze looks to the second section of the first book of the *Treatise* to determine more closely the status of the given in the *smallest perceptions*. It is a question of impressions or representations that cannot be reduced any further without endangering their very existence. As indivisible unitary points – perceptible, not mathematical, points – they constitute the ontological foundation of assembled perceptions (see below, Chapter 8). As Hume says, the representations of time and space are not special representations but consist only of the *succession* of individual perceptions. Yet it is precisely this succession that transcends the status of the elementary givens. 'The given is [. . .] taken up by a movement, and in a movement that transcends it. The mind becomes human nature. The subject [. . .] *is a synthesis of the mind*' (Deleuze 1991: 92). The decisive issue that Hume's philosophy raises, according to Deleuze, has to do with the becoming-subject of the mind. Hume poses the genuine empiricist question regarding the constitution of the subject within the given, but in no way does he ask about the constitution of the given in the subject.

Before we get to the problem of the subject and – connected to that – to the theory of relations and associations, let's quickly clarify how Deleuze later judges critically his reading of sense-atomism. On the one hand he will continually refer to Hume and his intuition of a radical experience. Accordingly, the pure ego-less and objectless perceptions will define the structure of experience *by right*. However, this structure is not determined in the most fundamental sense: the individually disparate and unstable experiences stand in conflict with the possibility of consolidating complex representations on their basis. Thus, on the other hand, Deleuze will demand a *transcendental experience* which is better able to articulate the aforementioned empirical intuition. Whereas in the Hume book the atomistic assumptions are only corrected to the degree that it is already necessary, within the framework of subjectivation, to transcend the empirical givens associatively, Deleuze will later develop a concept of transcendental connection which makes problematical the very construction of the given. This process of construction will for its part take place on the naturally deeper level of passive syntheses relating to subjectivation.

The critique of atomistic leftovers in the early work, once the argument has gone to 'greater depth', can be made plausible regarding Hume's principle of difference. Here we have an *empirical* principle that declares that the smallest perceptions are sense perceptible or perceivable atoms. In contrast, Deleuze develops in later years a *transcendental* principle of difference that isn't about the *diversity* of the diverse, but about the *givenness* of the given. It isn't about the empirical difference between different given perceptions, but about the transcendental difference that distinguishes the given from that through which it is given. The theory of intensity which Deleuze presents in *Difference and Repetition* (1994) formulates an answer to the question of how it is possible to think non-atomistically the fundamental experience of empiricism. The talk about *smallest* perceptions will have to transmute into talk about *small* or minute perceptions. In this way the conception of the former's elementary minimal size, which sets the fundamental measure of extensive quantities, can be replaced by a conception of the latter's continuous and intensive quantity.

First Deleuze attempts to uncover the subjectivist implications of Hume's philosophy to illuminate its fundamental pragmatism. When one looks for the *empirical foundation* from which to derive knowledge, the empiricist orientation toward immanence is less of an issue than the place where contingent processes of connection or ordering take place within experience, processes not steered from the outside (dependent on a transcendent point of reference). Insofar as the principles of association affect the mind, individual representations are regularly bound together not *through* imagination (*par l'imagination*) but *in* it (*dans l'imagination*) (Deleuze 1991: 23). This self-affectation describes the passive synthesis of habit, which defines the subjective necessity according to which a given representation relates *by itself* to another, not-given representation.

> The coherent paradox of Hume's philosophy is that it offers a subjectivity which transcends itself, without being any less passive. Subjectivity is determined as an effect; it is in fact an *impression of reflection*. The mind, having been affected by the principles, turns now into a subject. (Deleuze 1991: 26)

Deleuze lays great value on the separation, undertaken by Hume, between *impressions of sensation* and *impressions of reflection*.

Whereas the former signify only original sense-data, the latter signify 'the effects of principles in the mind' (Deleuze 1991: 31). Deleuze is mainly interested in that inner impression on which, according to Hume, the *idea of necessary connection* is based. This impression is only called forth by habit, namely when it forces us to expect, in a given situation, what at other times – under similar circumstances – has always happened. Under the influence of the principles of human nature, this is how causal relations show up in the imagination, relations based in beliefs that result from habit. Hume constantly asserts that precisely in the case of causal relations the *relata* do not show any special characteristics which label them as effects or as causes. The repetition of similar objects changes nothing about the objects themselves: only in the mind that observes them does the repetition call forth something new. 'These instances [of repetition] are in themselves totally distinct from each other, and have no union but in the mind, which observes them [. . .]' (Hume 2001: 111). Only through this observation is there a resulting *necessity* or the reflective impression of a *compulsion* 'to carry our thoughts from one object to another' (Hume 2001: 111). Deleuze interprets this prevalent interiorising of repetition as the temporal synthesis of habit, which derives the rule for the future from the ongoing power of the past within the present. But as *belief* and anticipation develop, the subject forms itself within the mind.

> It is not necessary to force the [Humean] texts in order to find in the habit-anticipation most of the characteristics of the Bergsonian *durée* or memory. Habit is the constitutive root of the subject, and the subject, at root, is the synthesis of time – the synthesis of the present and the past in light of the future. (Deleuze 1991: 92–3)

It is significant for Deleuze's further advance that he understands the process of subjectivation as temporal synthesis. In *Difference and Repetition* habit is introduced as the model for the *passive synthesis* of the present, in direct connection with his earlier, Hume-oriented thinking. On the other hand, that again strengthens the objection that Deleuze could not offer, in his Hume study, a plausible solution for the *dualistic* constitution of empiricism. With Bergson in mind one could say that the synthesis of habit was not yet presented there with duration understood as virtual manifold (*mémoire souvenir*), but only in the sense of compressed or associational memory (*mémoire habitude*). That's enough, however, to characterise association as passive synthesis, a synthesis which – as affected by the principles of human nature – links perceptions within imagination, linkages that precede the active syntheses of memory and understanding.

From the perspective of the motives of transcendental empiricism, which Deleuze will later place in the centre of his thought, it is altogether natural to take a closer look at precisely the *antirepresentationalist* aspects of the Humean philosophy that Deleuze detected early on. They come into view if we take as our theme the already mentioned logic of relations. This theme is all the more pressing because until now the highlighted problem of subjectivation has remained somewhat indeterminate. As we have noted, Deleuze follows James when he claims that not only the given is given but that 'the transcendence itself is also given, in an altogether different sense and manner – it is given as practice, as an affection of the mind, and as an impression of reflection' (Deleuze 1991: 28). Deleuze therefore distinguishes two meanings for Hume's concept of experience: on the one hand the collection of distinct perceptions, on the other hand the diversely defined system of relations within which the perceptions are linked by habit. It is important to notice that relations do not derive from experience. The *principles of human nature* – for the moment, the principles of association: causality, contiguity, similarity – are the ones that put together within experience a subject and its corresponding structures. Human nature, says Hume, can only be studied through its observable effects, which is to say, in the assembled representations (relations, modes, substances) that it produces.

> We can now see the special ground of empiricism: nothing in the mind transcends human nature, because it is human nature that, in its principles, transcends the mind; nothing is ever transcendental. (Deleuze 1991: 24)

The principles of human nature have only a *quasi-transcendental* status, says Deleuze. They determine the passive procedure of subjectivation and are not to be understood as *a priori* functions of judgement belonging to an already constituted transcendental subject that makes active connections between appearances. Deleuze refuses to accept the Kantian definition of empiricism, which, since even for Hume all knowledge of facts has as its prerequisite a *transcendence* of experience, specifically insists on the *derivative* nature of all knowledge from experience. Not so, he says. Empiricism, in Deleuze's eyes, must not be confused with an empirical or 'genetic' psychology of mind. The 'relations are not the product of a genesis, but rather the effect of principles' (Deleuze 1991: 108). The principles of association, although not sufficient conditions of relations, are certainly necessary. They make it possible for relations to be produced between a present impression on the one hand and absent ones on the other, similar to those which are normally connected to 'that' impression (or again, more precisely, to a similar, earlier impression). In addition, the principles empower the imagination to move from the experience of coherence and consistency among similar perceptions to the idea (ultimately deceptive but in practice believable) of the persistent and isolated existence of the object of perception. In both cases, to be precise, it is the principles which bring about a (second) nature by calling forth in imagination *beliefs* or rather fictions that transcend the given: they are not capable of being generated out of experience, nor are they 'schematically' mediated through experience.

The foundation of the mechanism of association in human nature explains the *exteriority* of relations. 'That an idea naturally introduces another is not a quality of the idea, but rather a quality of human nature' (Deleuze 1991: 101). As Hume himself says, the exterior relations are not based in the nature of the ideas that are related to one another. Relations 'may be chang'd [. . .] without any change on the objects themselves or on their ideas' (Hume 2001: 50). In any case, self-resembling yet different ideas (representations) can only be associated with each other if they pass through a synthesis exterior to them. In particular, commonly conceived causation cannot, for Hume, establish objectively grounded connections between ideas. His theory of causality makes clear that all empirical knowledge is based in imagination, which is not capable of legitimising its own constructs but rather gets involved in an endless conflict with understanding. The latter – ignoring everyday pragmatic considerations – keeps trying to undermine those constructions with scepticism.

Deleuze sees in the Humean logic of relations a fundamental critique of metaphysics which fights any rationalist mediation between sense perceptions and conceptual relations. Deleuze contrasts this empiricist logic directly with transcendental logic à la Kant. Counter to an *empiricist* critique, which takes a 'purely immanent position' and makes the process of subjectivation problematic, the *transcendental* critique works with requirements that make possible the experience as given to a subject.

> Thus, for Kant, relations depend on the nature of things in the sense that, as phenomena, things presuppose a synthesis whose source is the same as

the source of relations. This is why critical philosophy is not an empiricism. (Deleuze 1991: 111)

For Kant the appearance of empirical givens is directed from the outset toward the subject and its *a priori* structures of comprehension. Thus the object of experience mirrors, as it were, the corresponding subjective forms of objectification, whereas for Hume the principles of experience are not principles for the objects of experience. In anticipation of a terminology developed decades later, Deleuze says enigmatically of the Kantian procedure, 'The transcendental is what makes transcendence [the pure empirical fact; auth.] immanent to something = X' (Deleuze 1991: 111). For although Kant correctly discusses Hume's epistemological concerns on the level of imagination (*Einbildungskraft*), Deleuze nevertheless senses within its heart the dominating force of the understanding, which manipulates experience *on the inside* instead of transcending it *on the outside*. 'The *a priori* synthesis of the imagination sends us over to the synthetic unity of apperception which encompasses it' (Deleuze 1991: 111).

One may ask what Deleuze gains when he speculates on human nature to avoid the conceptions of psychologism and transcendentalism. He wants to come up with his own concept of a practical subjectivity that constitutes itself in the process of transcending the given. In this way the given should be able to hold off conceptual organisation pressures while allowing organisational structures based on habit, rather than on established rules, to exhibit a moment of ungrounded positivity. To put it another way, the relations that can be derived from human nature shouldn't, thanks to their exteriority, restrict the immanence of experience, but instead ought to produce a principle regarding differentiation of difference. In that way reason, in the process of articulating itself among the already linked ideas, still remains on the outside of a preexisting world which it doesn't define but merely transcends. In this exterior relationship Deleuze seeks 'the motive of [Humean] philosophy' (Deleuze 1991: 33) because it requires that reason itself be put into question. The assumption of a structure of experience ordered in advance of reason combines with the other assumption that all conclusions from experience are based on belief because they cannot be objectively grounded. Deleuze will pursue these two essential themes of empiricism all his life. Experience, which is not coextensive with reason, denotes reason's utterly intractable problematic core and forever changes the rationalist image of thought. Deleuze will always cling to the concept of *necessity* as developed by Hume, which obliges reason to confront *self*-generated problems.

Human nature is defined by a collection of principles which articulate the *transitional forms* from one idea to another. Yet we must always remember that the principles of association do not exhaust the principles of human nature. They merely explain the *formalism* of consciousness, whereas the principles of affect, which have to do with the given circumstances, deliver the *sufficient ground* of concrete relations. 'Everything takes place as if the principles of association provided the subject with its necessary form, whereas the principles of the passions provided it with its singular content. The latter function as the principle for the individuation of the subject' (Deleuze 1991: 104). The association of ideas is not only managed by the affective circumstances, but the relations gain an irreversible sense 'in the service of passion' (Deleuze 1991: 120), insofar as subjective inclinations, in tune with passion's principles, originate out of the reflection of affects in imagination. When Deleuze tells us that affectivity makes a 'differential psychology' possible, he is anticipating his later thoughts regarding the 'transcendental status' of the pleasure principle, which is rooted beneath the 'possible structure' of the subject, as mediated by association, in the 'real structure' of its affects and passions. (Deleuze 1991: 120) The concept of human nature allows Deleuze to consider quasi-transcendental principles which are neither empirically derivable nor inscribed in a pre-existing subject. Instead, these principles determine processes of subjectivation which accompany the associative self-organisation of experience. They refer to a structural realm that is non-empirical, a realm that in his Hume book still appears largely undefined, but nevertheless grounds the exterior status of relations.

Human nature is not a transcendental authority in the narrow sense, since it allows the conception of a genuine empiricist logic of external relations. It thus becomes clear that Hume's critical attitude applies only to those relations conceived through a logic of representation, because they alone claim an intrinsic connection between the subjective functions of understanding and their objects. Representation is not capable of presenting relations of association because it assumes general ideas which 'cannot be constituted within experience' (Deleuze 1991: 30) in its primary sense.

In spite of all critique of representationalism, the components of external relations still remain no more than atomistic-composed perceptions which hardly relinquish their actual empirical character. One might say that the quick dispatching of transcendentalism, which Deleuze in *Empiricism and Subjectivity* combines with the doctrine of external relations, serves as an indication that the relations and syntheses are not anchored deeply enough in experience. The virtual structures of (trans-)'human nature' do not yet come into view. Instead we see only the actual structures of their relationally arranged effects. Missing are the *transcendental* time-syntheses, which have still to be thought through regarding the self-constitution-processes of subjectivation.

2

The Ambiguity of Kantian Thought

Of all philosophers, Kant is the one who discovers the prodigious domain of the transcendental. He is the analogue of a great explorer – not of another world, but of the upper or lower reaches of this one. But what exactly does he do? (Deleuze 1994: 135)

Recent French philosophy of difference seldom refers to Kantian philosophy. Diverse references regarding the dependence of French postwar philosophy on Hegel, Husserl and Heidegger as well as on Marx, Freud and Nietzsche are so extensive that hardly any room remains for consideration of their relationships to Kant. With the exception of Lyotard's *Lessons on the Analytic of the Sublime*, such neglect seems justified, because already familiar dialectical, phenomenological or ontological interpretations of Kant are the rule, at least in the area of the aforementioned 'poststructuralist' philosophy. This assessment of the situation is unfortunately superficial. Deleuze's position regarding critical philosophy can indeed characterise his project of transcendental empiricism in its entirety. It is significant that Deleuze takes as his starting point the *ambiguity* of Kantian thought. On the one hand it grounds the 'reign of representation' while on the other hand it has the critical resources at its disposal which, if properly applied, can undermine precisely this reign. Thus to a large extent Kant's thought defines for Deleuze the framework of philosophical practice, because it points out the problem areas of epistemology, ethics and aesthetics and at least partially anticipates their proper treatment.

This chapter tracks the essential points of Deleuze's planned empiricist radicalisation of transcendental philosophy. The first section of the chapter reviews Deleuze's explicitly formulated critical attitude toward Kantian philosophy, while the second part examines certain systematic problems having to do with the transcendental critique of empiricism. This should clarify how transcendental empiricism manages rigorously to transpose the two classic positions and then go beyond them.

The Ambiguity of Kantian Thought

Kant and Nietzsche: Initial Discrediting of Truth, Reason and Harmony

In the works of Deleuze there are two popular comments that relate to Kant. Curiously enough, they describe seemingly contradictory positions. The chronologically prior comment is found in the context of a methodological reflection on the writing of a history of philosophy. Here Deleuze recommends that one keep on *penetrating* philosophical authors and their writings until one has revealed the ulterior motives of their thought. Deleuze explains expressly that in his 'book about an enemy' he wanted to unlock the conceptual structure of the three *Critiques* in this way. Thus clarification regarding the conceptual assumptions of critical philosophy consists in *sniffing out* the fundamental problems and *exposing* their representational resolution. The author that undergoes such treatment should be made to say in his own words what he stands accused of from a distance, namely that he is acting 'hypocritically' if he persists in holding on to the postulates of common sense.

The second comment is far more famous – and circulates in many debates on the poststructuralist infiltration of the metaphysics of subject. It has to do with one of those 'four pieces of poetry that could summarise Kantian philosophy' and stems from Rimbaud: 'I is an other' (Deleuze 1997: 29–31). Original here is how Deleuze verifies this maxim repeatedly within Kant's theoretical philosophy. It opens the way to an interpretation of subjectivity that breaks rigorously with the reflexive model of self-consciousness. I will get back to this point later. For now we simply note that for Deleuze there exist *prima facie* incompatible positions regarding Kant. On the one hand Kant has to be pushed until he confesses his collaboration with the values and powers of representation. On the other hand his 'dissolution' of the Cartesian *cogito* allows the opportune discovery of a specific sort of difference that is up to mischief in the sub-representational region.

In *Difference and Repetition* Deleuze reformulates such incompatibility of positions as the *ambiguity* of Kant's philosophy. A too hasty interpretation of this state of affairs might lead one to suspect that Deleuze rejects from the beginning the 'essentially' Kantian train of thought, and that his point of departure is based on a fundamental misunderstanding. However, things are not that simple. Deleuze's early clear rejection of transcendentalism in his Hume book gets visibly more complex in later years. *Difference and Repetition* presents, as it were, the result of a further examination of Kant's philosophy, which Deleuze has steadily undertaken since his books on Nietzsche (1962) and Kant (1963).

No one doubts that Deleuze (at the latest since the beginning of the 1960s) picks up the Kantian project of an immanent critique of human rationality and claims to radicalise it (Smith 1997: 2). In his book *Nietzsche and Philosophy*, Deleuze welcomes Kant's revolutionary impetus: the replacement of metaphysical thought regarding the agreement between thinking and Being with the transcendental principle of a necessary subordination of nature to legislative understanding. This impetus has a liberating effect in so far as the new imperative character of thinking motivates us increasingly to let go of the previous posture of obedience to a previously established natural order. That doesn't mean, of course, that in Deleuze's eyes Kant adequately reflects on the instrumental character of rationality.

In this regard Deleuze turns to the *will to power*, which operates in the depth of human intellect and from the very beginning can lay the groundwork for the critical project. For Deleuze, the *Critique of Pure Reason* remains stuck in the fog of theological prejudices because it nowhere makes a problem out of truth as such with respect to ethics, knowledge or religion. Kant tries to distinguish the legitimate from the illegitimate use of reason, so that the boundaries as well as the possibilities of experience can be defined. Nietzsche counters this optimistic project, which postulates the competence of reason to mark its own boundaries, with his pessimistic view of reason, according to which there is no way to get around the internal mindset of a reason never wholly transparent to itself. The conditions of thought, conditions we can never completely catch up with, require a genealogical angle of vision for which they can be followed thematically. Genealogical investigations of thought come to the conclusion that truths are context-dependent or bound to a will that cannot escape an inherent perspectivism. Therefore Deleuze, along with Nietzsche, insists on a critical thinking that doesn't just inventory reigning values but rather – reasonably – rebels against 'reason' itself.

> Kant lacked a method which permitted reason to be judged from the inside without giving it the task of being its own judge. And, in fact, Kant does not realise his project of immanent critique. Transcendental philosophy discovers conditions which still remain external to the conditioned. Transcendental principles are principles of conditioning and not of internal genesis. We require a genesis of reason itself, as well as a genesis of

The Ambiguity of Kantian Thought

the understanding and its categories: what are the forces of reason and of the understanding? What is the will which hides and expresses itself in reason? What stands behind reason, in reason itself? In the will to power and the method which derives from it Nietzsche had at his disposal a principle of internal genesis. (Deleuze 1983: 91)

Nietzsche endeavours to intensify the critique of reason to get rid of the moral-theological vestiges in terms of an enlightened empiricism. Kant's *Critiques* managed to achieve a 'theologian's success', consisting mainly in passing on their newly conceived art of dialectical argumentation. So in the Nietzsche book Deleuze insists on separating the one side of Kantian thought, the side which Nietzsche picked up and developed further, from the other side, which culminates in Hegel's idealistic *Encyclopaedia*. Nowhere does Deleuze take on Hegel so vehemently as in his Nietzsche study, which amounts to a general repudiation of any *one-sided* reading of the *Critiques*.

Put another way, Kant's own understanding of his philosophy as leaving behind both rationalism *and* empiricism had to make Deleuze suspicious. To be sure, he greets the critical turn that thwarted the purely transcendental use of concepts and ideas. Yet he rejected the anti-empiricist inquiry into matters of pure reason. That is why he recommends a *Nietzschean empiricism* through which the last theological concessions are meant to be banished. By resolutely carrying out his agenda within the framework of a detailed Nietzsche study, he established his reputation in France. The 'generalised anti-Hegelianism' which Deleuze proclaims in the preface to *Difference and Repetition* springs from his systematic interpretation of Nietzsche's philosophy. His book on Kant is an extension of this line of interpretation. By showing the conceptual union of the three *Critiques*, Deleuze intends to make plain Kant's adhesion to representational thought while at the same time retaining whatever heterogeneous and truly critical potential is to be found in his philosophy. At first glance Deleuze seems to give no more than a didactic introduction to Kant, but behind the façade of straightforward instruction something more subtle is concealed, concerning the deconstruction of a syndrome.

Deleuze tackles Kant – with careful hints, strategic resolve and many citations – to elicit from him the true critique, somewhat in the manner of a staged self-accusation. Central to the systematic construction of his presentation of Kant's critical philosophy is the problem of harmony. Deleuze wants to show that this problem infuses all forms of common sense, and this produces a necessary connection between the three *Critiques*. 'As a consequence, Kant's notion of common sense can now be seen to be variously defined by particular relations of harmony between appropriate faculties' (Meerbote 1986: 351).

Clearly revolutionary in the *Critique of Pure Reason* is the interiorising of the Cartesian problem of ego-world-relationship, in that it is transferred to the plane of subjective faculties. Kant introduces an essential difference between the two 'main sources of soul' (*Gemüt*) and uses that difference in conceptualising the critical image of thought. 'One of the most original points of Kantianism' – as Deleuze asserts repeatedly – 'is the idea of a *difference in nature between our faculties*' (Deleuze 1984: 22). Yet Kant is most interested in the conciliatory cooperation of these faculties, as the analysis of his model of recognition shows, an analysis which Deleuze undertakes regarding the concept of *representation*. Representation is defined as the synthesis of that which presents itself and takes place in two steps: first as the synthesis of the imagination, then as active unifying recognition in understanding. Borrowing from the terminology of the deduction chapter in the first edition of the *Critique of Pure Reason*, Deleuze speaks of the syntheses of *apprehension* and *reproduction* as belonging to imagination (Kant 1998: A78/B103). The synthesis of imagination is carried out at the sub-representational level; as such, it doesn't make any cognition possible unless understanding comes to its aid and guarantees its *categorial unity*.

> In fact knowledge implies two things which go beyond synthesis itself: it implies consciousness, or more precisely the belonging of representations to a single consciousness within which they must be linked. Now the synthesis of the imagination, taken in itself, is not at all self-conscious. On the other hand, knowledge implies a necessary relation to an object. That which constitutes knowledge is not simply the act by which the manifold is synthesised, but the act by which the represented manifold is related to an object. This is a table, this is an apple . . . (Deleuze 1984: 15)

Deleuze says the synthesis of imagination should not simply coincide with its preparatory cognitive function, which is passed to it out of the 'retrospective' of an experience already completely defined through understanding. The transcendental model of recognition, we find, is built on the foundation of active forces of understanding which regulate the process of synthesis so harmoniously that objective experience must be the result.

The Ambiguity of Kantian Thought

Deleuze then analyses the experience of representation from another angle, in view of Kant's distinction between intellectual and figurative synthesis. First, the distinction is based on a purely intellectual understanding of the objective unity of transcendental apperception, because objectivity as such is only an expression of formal objectification of the *cogito*. It then turns out that the real *figurative* determination of purely sensual presentations in the schematism is subordinated to the cognitive aim of understanding. The harmony which this approach to space-time and conceptual relationships manages to elicit is neither mysterious nor enigmatic because it somehow posits hidden sources. No, the secret lies only in a problem which is skilfully skipped over in representational thinking.

Deleuze criticises this state of affairs through the example of logical common sense. He begins by reiterating that Kant sharply distinguishes between the receptive faculties of the senses and the spontaneity of understanding.

> Kant invokes the synthesis and the schematism of the imagination which is applicable *a priori* to the forms of sensibility in conformity with concepts. But in this way the problem is merely shifted: for the imagination and the understanding themselves differ in nature, and the accord between these two active faculties is no less 'mysterious'. (Deleuze 1984: 22)

Deleuze admits that Kant has shifted the harmony problem in an original way, which is to say by internalising it. He disputes that this shift – seen critically – is either sufficient or satisfactory. The renewed 'mysteriousness' of the *concordia facultatum* points ironically to the failed attempt to solve the harmony problem through common sense. The problem itself is somewhat distorted in the transcendental glare of representation. Deleuze considers it 'fatal' that common sense appears as an unanalysable, *a priori* fact and points out that Kant – much like his predecessors – 'invokes a supreme finalist and theological principle' to further harmonisation (Deleuze 1984: 23).

Simultaneously with the 'passive' synthesis and the difference among faculties, which Kant tracks down during the investigation of metaphysical fundamentals, he also discovers transcendental illusions and ideas, which originate in the interior of reason and call for self-criticism. Again Deleuze holds apart what for Kant belongs together. For the general assumptions of representative thinking are shaken if reason relinquishes the ability to legitimise its use as unambiguous and illusion-free. Kant sticks to the subjective principle of common sense, that is to say the 'idea of a good nature of the faculties, of a healthy and upright nature which allows them [...] to form harmonious proportions' (Deleuze 1984: 21). Thus the question, can Kant somehow reconcile opposing assumptions regarding two such natures of reason? Their compatibility, as required by common sense, makes Kant undertake complicated and exhausting speculations. Nevertheless, logical common sense goes way beyond itself insofar as phenomena need to be in accord not only formally with the understanding but also in material terms with the ideas of reason.

At this point we arrive at the transition to the *Critique of Judgement*. 'Any determinate accord of the faculties under a determining and legislative faculty presupposes the existence and the possibility of a free, indeterminate accord' (Deleuze 1984: 60). Deleuze is in this context primarily interested in the *free play* of faculties which do not subordinate themselves to one another, reproduce only themselves, and still manage to stimulate: we have here a case of related, communicating differences. The pleasurable sensation regarding beautiful objects consists for Kant in the formal accord of imagination with indeterminate understanding. Deleuze adds that this aesthetic common sense must itself be the object of a transcendental genesis. How then is the free accord of faculties to be produced? By so asking, Deleuze wishes to show that even in the case of an aesthetic common sense, harmony presents an extremely questionable theoretical construct, conceptualised in beauty on teleological grounds and in the sublime on moral ones. The multiplication of common sense corresponds perhaps to the quicksand underlying representation, which has to reach ever further afield to find solid footing. Thus the art of reading as practiced by Deleuze with his characteristic sense of humour seeks to turn the whole problem of representation upside down.

Preliminary Shifts in the Meaning of Transcendental and Empirical

We have seen that Deleuze allows Kant's critical philosophy to function under the rule of common sense, while at the same time undertaking several – rather indeterminate – movements to set himself apart from the monopoly of thought's good nature: lines of flight that overlie critical perspectives. This ambiguous disposition regarding Kant's consummate consolidation of metaphysics manifests itself very clearly in *Difference and Repetition*. Deleuze constructs here a conceptually differentiated, ideal type of representational thought

The Ambiguity of Kantian Thought

going back to essential foundations of transcendental logic. This *image of thought* is set over against 'higher' empiricism, an empiricism that is also inspired in important aspects by Kant and his 'discoveries'. Thus a continuity in Deleuze's thought becomes visible: the theorems presented in the Kant book that are made dependent on the ideal of common sense get a second look once the existing *image of thought* has been broken down, and the critique applied to this dogmatic image stems above all from Nietzsche and his broadened genealogical method.

As Deleuze develops in *Difference and Repetition*, thought as such has an inherent genealogical dimension which is crowded out by the *image* of thought.

> Conceptual philosophical thought has as its implicit presupposition a pre-philosophical and natural image of thought, borrowed from the pure element of common sense. According to this image, thought has an affinity with the true; it formally possesses the true and materially wants the true. It is in terms of this image that everybody knows and is presumed to know what it means to think. Therefore it matters little whether philosophy begins with the object or the subject, with Being or with beings, as long as thought remains subject to this image which already prejudges everything: the distribution of the object and the subject as well as that of Being and beings. (Deleuze 1994: 131)

This 'image' (in the singular) designates a certain combination of opinions, principles and presuppositions which define thought's *illusionary transcendence*. Image in this sense combines a shopping list of different images (plural): for every philosophy is built up on a very specific (pre-philosophical) niveau which slips its implicit assumptions into the current image. Every philosophy has a particular image of itself, which simply depends on the choice of what belongs to thought *de jure* rather than *de facto*. This choice takes effect as the pre-thematic draft of implicit requirements of thought, coexisting always with the acts of thought; they allow themselves to be conceptually reflected and 'recuperated'. In Kant's case the partition of transcendental and empirical realms corresponds to the circumscription of reason's legitimate sphere of operation. It is Deleuze's intent to analyse Kant's partition, to make clear that it belongs to the quintessence of representation.

Kant's concept of *recognition* gives expression to this partition and thereby influences greatly the image of thought. In the next chapter I will explicate more closely Deleuze's analysis of the concept by way of the Kantian text. Here it suffices to indicate that Deleuze first defines recognition very generally by way of the harmonious use of the faculties with an object that is assumed to be the same for all faculties. This objective form of identity corresponds, according to Deleuze, to a unified self-consciousness that is able to put together representations. Only in such activities of correlation or of judgement does a subject establish an identity with itself. Objective *reproduction* within a concept is to be understood as the correlate of subjective *reflection*, which cloaks itself in the certainty of appearance but in achieving certainty comes to terms with itself. The transcendental model of recognition assumes a well-organised experience which merely requires this assurance of its possibility. So it isn't important on what grounds Kant starts with experience: whether the transcendental method systematically assumes it in the sense of 'worldly possessions' and then reconstructs it in detail – or whether accumulated mathematical-physical knowledge is to be given philosophical legitimation. In each case Deleuze calls it self-evident that Kant simply reduplicates the empirical – through abstraction from general features – in the transcendental. He says that the transcendental is 'traced' from the empirical but with such an 'all too obvious tracing method' one can only miss the truly transcendental.

> Of all philosophers, Kant is the one who discovers the prodigious domain of the transcendental. [. . .] However, what does he do? In the first edition of the *Critique of Pure Reason* he describes in detail three syntheses which measure the respective contributions of the thinking faculties, all culminating in the third, that of recognition, which is expressed in the form of the unspecified object as correlate of the 'I think' to which all the faculties are related. It is clear that, in this manner, Kant traces the so-called transcendental structures from the empirical acts of a psychological consciousness: the transcendental synthesis of apprehension is directly induced from an empirical apprehension, and so on. In order to hide this all too obvious procedure, Kant suppressed this text in the second edition. Although it is better hidden, the tracing method, with all its 'psychologism', nevertheless subsists. (Deleuze 1994: 135)

This text excerpt is directed with rare clarity against Heidegger's Kant interpretation. I will have an opportunity to talk about this later. The second reference, obvious and affirmative, is to Michel Foucault and his concept of the *empirico-transcendental doublet* (Foucault 1970: 318, 336). In *The Order of Things* Foucault shows that the problem of modern philosophy, beginning with Kant's critiques, exists in the self-reflection of that finitude which tries to

The Ambiguity of Kantian Thought

ground the possibility of knowledge (*Wissen*) using the limits of cognition (*Erkenntnis*) (Foucault 1970: 316). However, this grounding cannot succeed, according to Foucault, because the human being is founded in structures which precede him: work, life, language. That is why Kant's so-called 'transcendental', put together by privileging selected characteristics of the empirically given, has to be 'lifted' (*aufgehoben*) in favour of a new and different kind of transcendental, one not resulting from a reduplication of an experience set in advance. The *cogito* revolves non-stop around itself, without being able to track down within itself a solid base of certainty, for it depends on something unthought (a transcendental field) from which it cannot separate itself. This is the sense in which Deleuze characterises these problems and structures as 'transcendental' – one could talk with Husserl about a *contingent a priori* – insofar as they set down in advance the effective requirements of thought, requirements that are essential and yet cannot otherwise be grasped as a whole.

The problematic of a transcendental critique can also be seen in the *paradox of transcendental cognition*, as presented by Jaakko Hintikka (Hintikka 1989: 243–57). According to him, restricting the legitimate domain of theoretical reason to the world of appearances won't work the instant one has to postulate, along with these limits, an unknowable being-in-itself that corresponds to the general opacity of human cognitive processes. The epistemologically non-recuperable being-in-itself marks the blind spot of cognition. The blind spot spans both the purely empirical manifold of sense-data and the transcendental synthesis of the imagination as long as the latter, provisionally, has not yet terminated in recognition. Deleuze picks up on these two aspects of Kant's transcendental psychology and uses them to map out a very definite new course for post-Kantianism – as will be clearly demonstrated later.

The inability of thought to penetrate itself should, therefore, not be marginalised: this irrevocable negative side of thought topples its 'moral' self-image. That is why Deleuze discovers in the Kantian concept of transcendental appearance (*Schein*) a truly critical moment that seriously endangers the priority of common sense:

> [W]hen Kant shows that thought is threatened less by error than by inevitable illusions that come from within reason, as if from an internal arctic zone where the needle of every compass goes bad, a reorientation of the whole of thought becomes necessary at the same time as it is in principle penetrated by a certain delirium. (Deleuze and Guattari 1994: 52)

Deleuze never tires of reminding us that the idea of common sense gives every citizen the right to participate in rational thought. Every human being possesses *de jure* the possibility of thinking and finds himself only on empirical grounds, that is provisionally, in untruth. This untruth is therefore defined as error and can in principle be corrected by conceptual labour. But the relationship to truth is problematic because thought must always be stimulated or forced from outside: thought is occasioned by a problem. 'Most thought-provoking is that we are still not thinking' (Heidegger 1968: 4). Deleuze loves to quote this maxim from Heidegger and points to signs, situations and questions that stir up thinking in its natural lethargy. Thought isn't hampered by mere incorrectness, but rather gets its start from what is at first immanently unthinkable, so that it is the powerlessness of thought that determines its rightful image and exposes the self-satisfaction of pure reason as a theological substrate. 'Error is a fact which is then arbitrarily extrapolated and arbitrarily projected into the transcendental, and the true transcendental structures of thought [. . .] must be sought elsewhere' (Deleuze 1994: 150). It follows that the most thought-provoking aspect of thought is its natural inability to think its own foundation.

Let us remember that Deleuze strictly dissociates signs and affects which move thought from objects of recognition. Signs mean problems and become noticeable wherever transcendental illusions darken the image of representational thought. These signs cannot be grasped by common sense since they are defined as what first can *only* be felt. Objects of recognition, on the other hand, affect not only the senses but also allow themselves to be remembered, imagined and above all, judged. In this way Deleuze counters the empirical employment of abilities with a 'transcendental' employment, characterised by its implicit aversion to common sense. This transcendental use of abilities is oriented around the conflict between imagination and understanding, as Kant analyses it in the feeling of the *sublime*. To be sure, that disjunction is now spread over all the higher and lower abilities, for Deleuze is not satisfied with localising differences under the competence of common sense. Instead he is thinking about 'sublime' communication among all the separated abilities: each carries over to the other exactly that power that drives it to its own limit, because every limit refers to a transition which the abilities require of each other. The sign, which is neither a recognisable object nor the specific quality of such an object, sets the limit of sense and refers to its own immanent idea, which runs through all the abili-

The Ambiguity of Kantian Thought

ties without becoming an empirical object of any particular one of them. Deleuze's desire to radicalise critical philosophy leads him to aesthetic dissonances which effectively underlie the harmonies. This reversal of preferences concurrently affects the relationship between transcendental and empirical – it turns it upside down:

> The transcendental exercise must not be traced from the empirical exercise precisely because it apprehends that which cannot be grasped from the point of view of common sense, that which measures the empirical operation of all the faculties according to that which pertains to each, given the form of their collaboration. That is why the transcendental is answerable to a superior empiricism which alone is capable of exploring its domain and its regions. Contrary to Kant's belief, it cannot be induced from the ordinary empirical forms in the manner in which these appear under the determination of common sense. [...] Transcendental empiricism is the only way to avoid tracing the transcendental from the outlines of the empirical. (Deleuze 1994: 144)

As we have seen, one of the central motives of Deleuze's philosophy has to do with the *disquiet* of thought resulting from confusion: thought is only then capable of thinking if something (a sign) strikes or encounters it and provokes it. From the point of view of the empirical employment of the abilities, which is to say, for recognition, the sign is that which cannot be felt since it is neither the material part of some experience complex nor the qualitative aspect of an object. Deleuze insists instead that the sign, as the veritable being of the sensible, is not a given but rather that through which the given is given (see Deleuze 1994: 57, 140). We will show in due time that herewith he names the transcendental principle of difference. At this point we want to emphasise that all the abilities can only be set in motion by the sensible and its sign. The sensible signifies itself by the fact that 'in an encounter, what forces sensation and that which can only be sensed are one and the same thing, whereas in other cases the two instances are distinct' (Deleuze 1994:144–5). The non-intentional consciousness feels at first to be an egoless field of individuation: a bundle of intensities that signals to itself its present state. The *tautogoric* essence of the feeling expresses a first self-affection of thought, that feels itself insofar as it implicitly informs itself about its situation: the pressure of explication manifests itself then in sufficiently clear perceptions, memories, concepts. It is exactly for this reason that Deleuze considers the building of concepts to be genuinely empiricist: the philosophical thought process gets moving when sensible experience is left to its own devices. Concepts evolve on the *transcendental field of immanence* which defines the empiricist image of thought.

Deleuze endorses an empiricism that doesn't see philosophical concepts *per se* as products of abstraction, an empiricism that results from the transcendental critique of the metaphysical foundations of Cartesianism. Decisive in this regard is Kant's questioning of the immediate connection of thought (*cogito*) and existence (*sum*). It allows us to have at our disposal a new form which regulates the determination of 'I am' by means of 'I think', namely *time*. That means that the indeterminate existence of 'I am', which is implied by the *cogito*, can only be fixed as the existence of a passive I. Where Kant speaks of the *paradox of inner sense*, Deleuze believes he can see an empiricist model of passive synthesis that introduces the form of time into thought: 'the greatest initiative of transcendental philosophy' (Deleuze 1994: 87). The introduction of time fractures the integrity of the subject to the point that it is always fixed as merely a receptive empirical I, whereas the activity of determination is awarded to a spontaneously thinking entity. According to Deleuze it is impossible to bring these two halves into line, because they continuously displace one another. The pure forms of understanding are loaded onto the passive I 'from the outside', for it possesses no spontaneous intellectual abilities. Time as pure form of inner sense thus marks the self-inadequacy of thought: thought must be anchored in time so that it can open itself to something unthought (see Deleuze 1994: 86).

Again the ambiguity of Kant's thought becomes noticeable and Deleuze takes advantage of it to pick apart counter-running strands of interpretation. For the critique of speculative reason commits the pure concepts of understanding to the pure forms of sensibility only with the help of an *a priori self-affection* of inner sense. Heidegger is the first to have worked out the foundational meaning of the doctrine of self-affection in the transcendental analytic of the first *Critique*. Deleuze follows carefully in his footsteps. Without a doubt the temporising of productive imagination, which undermines the primacy of understanding, is what inspires him to construct his theory of the passive syntheses. It would be oversimplifying to say that Deleuze sees pure self-affection at work in the time-forming syntheses of apprehension and reproduction but not in the schematism. Deleuze's primary interest is to internalise time, that is to comprehend it as the transcendental form of the inner sense. From his perspective Kant managed in revolutionary fashion to change the classical definition of time as succession by exposing how time actually operates in the process of the (transcendental) synthesis of differential elements.

'I is an other.' Time – as the form of self-affection – continuously separates what is determined from undetermined existence and thereby continuously sets up a new field of individuation that can be described in a positive manner. The emphatic rejection of the 'subject' is thus relegated to the critical sidelines, insofar as the transcendental form of time is reapplied to the figurative synthesis within the framework of Kant's theory of recognition. However, the unity of *a priori* self-affection as effected within pure sensibility by the understanding is no longer an issue. Self-affection now means that the (exterior) form of determinability evolves into a (genetic) principle of reciprocal determination, thus characterising in a positive way the *ideal synthesis of difference* in contrast to the repetitional structure of representation.

Kant nevertheless reconstitutes the unity of the subject by conceiving of an active synthesis of understanding and using it to appeal for a new form of identity in self-consciousness. But the unreserved acknowledgement of the understanding as the only faculty that can achieve the connection of the manifold corresponds on the other hand to a receptivity without any synthesising power. The so-called Kantian *duality* affirms a merely external difference between intuition and understanding. A number of pure concepts establishes the possibility of experience, which is to say, they determine upon which foundation the intuited givens can be represented. Yet these general concepts are merely abstract conditions which remain exterior to what is conditioned, whereas the sensible manifold of intuition is already given within the wholly undetermined milieu of space and time. This reduction of the transcendental instantiation of a conditioning without genetic claims, says Deleuze, delivers to post-Kantianism its true motive for getting beyond Kant. Deleuze refers to Salomon Maimon in this regard, citing his 'fundamental reformulation of the *Critique* and an overcoming of the Kantian duality of concept and intuition' (Deleuze 1994: 173).

The external relationship between what is spatially given and conceptually thought must, according to Maimon, be internalised in the problematic Idea and may certainly not be mediated by means of hidden harmonies. In the words of Deleuze, this means that 'determinability must itself be conceived as pointing towards a principle of reciprocal determination. [...] The reciprocal synthesis of differential relations [is] the source of the production of real objects' (Deleuze 1994: 173). Maimon's attempt to come up with a genetic transcendental philosophy understands distinct experience to be the result of a differentiating process regarding the Idea, immanent to spatial-temporal dynamics which determine its actualisation. Here we meet an argument from the realm of a Leibnizian transcendental psychology: conscious perception emerges out of the shadow of vague impressions insofar as a differential relationship chooses a few (at least two) among unconscious singularities and relates them to one another.

The philosophical idea of experience as Deleuze conceives it rests on the principle of the *interiority of the manifold*. This principle is directed on the one hand against the dogmatic intent to incorporate the manifold within the concept, and on the other hand against the empirical doctrine of only externally separated perceptions. For example, although Hegel's infinite representation sublimates the 'conflict of consciousness', it remains dogmatic because it puts difference squarely within the interior of the concept. Classical empiricism, on the contrary, believes positivistically in the pure givenness of externally separated 'macro-perceptions'. According to Deleuze, the mutual determination of the differentials refers to little perceptions – 'a lapping of waves, a rumour, a fog, or a mass of dancing particles of dust' (Deleuze 1993: 86) – therefore not to an infinite understanding but rather to an unconsciousness of finite thinking. Thus a noticeable aspect of the world actualises itself through a process of filtration, which resolves a clear form out of a dark ground.

There is probably something a bit romantic in Deleuze's empiricism, but the poetic idea of an infinity which ironically makes the antithesis of a logic of reflection impossible to sublimate is also full of aesthetic mystery which until now has not been 'demystified' by difference philosophy. In the *Logic of Sense* Deleuze states repeatedly that even the alternative between the determinations of representation and the undifferentiated abyss is incorrectly stipulated (see for example Deleuze 1990b: 103). True post-Kantianism undermines both of these mutually exclusive possibilities, since the passive ego, as Daniel Smith underscores, 'is itself constituted by a prodigious domain of unconscious and passive syntheses that precede and condition the activity of the "I think"' (Smith 1996: 37). Therefore Deleuze conceives of the Idea as a system of differential relations between reciprocally determinable genetic elements which are brought to expression by the differential unconscious of pure

The Ambiguity of Kantian Thought

thought (see Deleuze 1994: 173–4). Thinking is forced to think the seat of its origin, an *empty field*, without which it would have to remain impossible and unmotivated. In this way the interiorising of difference is completed and so is the final rejection of Kantian duality.

The theory of passive synthesis, as Deleuze develops it in the second chapter of *Difference and Repetition*, runs through the famous three syntheses which Kant presents in the first edition of the *Critique of Pure Reason* to carry out with their help the transcendental deduction of the pure concepts of understanding as well as to unfold analytically the concept of experience. Taking his cue from Heidegger, Deleuze understands the transcendental synthesis as the sub-representative form of self-affection in the genesis of normal acts of recognition, which in their temporal way of operating ground a new kind of 'experience of being'. Yet Deleuze distances himself in other respects from Heidegger's views, as has already been mentioned. Deleuze thinks that Heidegger still orients himself on Kant's common sense, as the doubling of the empirical in the transcendental suggests. This criticism can be made more concrete by looking at four aspects of agreement between Heidegger and Kant. First, both distinguish an empirical element and a related pure or transcendental synthesis as condition of possibility in the syntheses of apprehension, reproduction and recognition. Second, both emphasise the unity of the three syntheses, insofar as they only constitute analytical moments of a totality. Third, for each one the doctrine of synthesis is conceptually ruled by the third synthesis of recognition, in which the other two 'culminate'. Fourth, the task of mediation is handed to the power of imagination, which for unexplainable reasons seems to be able to regulate the necessary concordance of abilities. That is why one should mistrust Heidegger's view that Kant crossed out the text in the second edition to retreat from the (altogether unbearable) abyss of origin that would have endangered the reign of understanding. The great importance that Heidegger attached to the schematism results accordingly from the 'profound' mediation which it manages to cause in the modality of the transcendental synthesis of recognition. But for Deleuze the riddle of ontological synthesis can very well be resolved:

> If the spatial order of extrinsic differences and the conceptual order of intrinsic differences are finally in harmony, as the schema shows they are, this is ultimately due to this intensive differential element, this synthesis of continuity at a given moment which, in form of a *continua repetitio*,

first gives rise internally to the space corresponding to Ideas. (Deleuze 1994: 26)

The clear rejection of schematism in this quote stretches to include rejection of the primacy of recognition in the doctrine of the synthesis. For Heidegger future time, which can be drawn out of the third synthesis, corresponds to the conceptual horizon of 'what is held up' in general, before which beings can reproduce and identify themselves. But transcendental possibility, inscribing a tablet of concepts, blocks the virtual Idea, which integrates for itself the forms of sensibility. The ontological foundation of philosophy therefore requires, above all, a clarification about the kind of recognition which fixes thinking dogmatically.

> The criticism that must be addressed to this image of thought is precisely that it has based its supposed principle upon extrapolation from [...] particularly insignificant facts such as Recognition, everyday banality in person; as though thought should not seek its models among stranger and more compromising adventures. (Deleuze 1994: 135)

According to Deleuze, philosophy characterises itself through the experimental use of concepts whose status is non-categorial and extra-propositional. Even in the case of Deleuze's theory of concepts, direct relations to Kant's transcendental logic exist only incidentally, and then presupposing ambivalence. For while there is no doubt that Deleuze rejects the desire to deduce concepts in a completely empirical way just as he rejects the scholastic acceptance of a handful of categories which function as equivocal interpretations of Being, yet Deleuze never explicitly undertakes a conceptually based theoretical critique of the classic position of empiricism, not even with regard to the Kantian objections. It is after all of fundamental importance for the development of a critical empiricism to ground the concepts non-empirically in the region of transcendental virtuality. In what follows, especially in the section on schematism, we will also, considering the Deleuzian project, be on the lookout in the Kantian analytic for a possibility to undermine critically the empiricist theory of abstraction.

3

Kant's Transcendental Critique of Classical Empiricism

It is common anecdotal knowledge that Kant awoke from his dogmatic slumber thanks to Hume's scepticism. Inversely, a seldom articulated hope lies hidden in the name 'transcendental empiricism': could empiricism possibly profit from the same transcendental method that is meant to override it? Deleuze does in fact attempt to modify empiricist theory with a philosophically transcendental approach. Our engagement with Kant stands under this directive. It entails neither a retreat from Kant nor the simple adoption of his critique of empiricism. Rather, armed with relevant Deleuzian deliberations, the transcendental critique will – as far as possible – be assimilated empirically, whereby the 'leftovers' that cannot be integrated will undergo a further empiricist critique. In short, putting Kant's position on the scales should lead to two results: to adopt philosophically transcendental components for the empiricist theory and in the process convincingly prevent turning the empiricist project as such into an impossibility.

The transcendental critique of empiricist philosophy will be presented in what follows in such a way that its positive incentives for promoting further advances in empiricism are distinguishable from its obstructive and dogmatic aspects. As textual reference, the chapter on the transcendental deduction in the *Critique of Pure Reason* commends itself, since it bears upon the theoretical principles of empiricism. In that chapter Kant contrasts his concept of experience with the empiricist doctrine of association. The deductive argument for the objective reality of categories tries in a typically transcendental way to override empiricism and its sceptical consequences. Not for nothing do the debates over the possibility of transcendental philosophy revolve around this segment of theory. Since the reconstruction of the transcendental deduction which I am presenting here primarily rests on the distinction between two stages of the proof in the B-edition, namely the distinction between intellectual and figural synthesis, Kant's counter-empiricist arguments will be introduced and criticised in two successive steps. This will uncover the fundamental structure of the transcendental argument as it tries to refute Humean epistemological scepticism. I want to make clear that although Kant fails in the end to carry out his proof, he manages along the way not only to expose inconsistencies in English empiricism but also to develop theoretical starting points for resolving them beneficially. In particular, the necessary transition from the intellectual to the figural synthesis shows conclusively the significance of so-called transcendental psychology. This theory – especially its doctrine of synthesis – was rediscovered in Husserl's phenomenology. Here is where the transcendental field of a critical empiricism comes into view, so that the interpretation of the 'psychological' moments within the transcendental analytic makes transparent how positivist interpretations of empiricism run astray. Note that time proves to be a pure form of inner sense and that concepts cannot be derived directly from experience. Simple objective perception conceals a transcendental problem.

Intellectual Synthesis

> I [. . .] cannot approve of that expeditious way, which some take with the skeptics, to reject at once all their arguments without enquiry or examination. If the skeptical reasonings be strong, say they, 'tis a proof, that reason may have some force and authority: If weak, they can never be sufficient to invalidate all the conclusions of our understanding. This argument is not just. (Hume 2001: 124–5)

The pressing task of the following discussion of Kant's critique of empiricism is to illuminate its unwarranted claim to be rigorous. I will show that the primary aim of transcendental deduction, namely the consolidation of experience solely on conceptually necessary combinations of 'representations', breaks down. If not, empiricism would be finished off for all time. As I pointed out in the first chapter, Deleuze already saw the failure of Kant's representationalism in his book on Hume. Only in his later writings did he formulate that the model of recognition, which Kant introduced, came to characterise an 'image of thought' that was critically in need of help. Nevertheless, Deleuze's observations hardly touch directly upon the Kantian text, so that only a few directives leading to a concrete interpretation of the foundations of critical thinking can be gleaned from his rather arbitrary comments on transcendentalism. Here I want to pick up on Deleuze's 'intuition' and work it out in the context of certain well-posed questions, so that one can catch sight of the conceptual consistency of his thought and the correspondingly relevant historic relations. Accompanying Heidegger's interpretation of the transcendental function of imagination – and viewing critically the ideal of a harmony of faculties as well as their 'threefold unity', to which the deduction chapter is strategically indebted – Deleuze turns against the epistemological stabilisation of Kantian thought.

Kant's transcendental approach sets up an epistemological problem that can only be construed and resolved by using newly coined concepts, and this fundamentally takes place within the framework of the transcendental deduction. It is well known that Kant develops his philosophy within a double constraint, on the one hand against rationalism and on the other hand against empiricism: 'thoughts without content are empty and intuitions without concepts are blind'. Kant begins where Locke and Leibniz both failed, insofar as they postulated a merely gradual difference between intuition and understanding. That is to say, Kant divided his philosophy into aesthetics and logic. Logic, in the *Critique of Pure Reason*, is called transcendental because it explains how concepts *a priori* can be related to objects. Transcendental logic draws content from transcendental aesthetics, for 'concepts cannot arise analytically with respect to content' (Kant 1998: A 77/B 103). To put it simply, intuition conveys the material for empirical knowledge. That is why any hasty mixture of the two fundamental sources of human cognitive faculties has to be carefully avoided. Transcendental philosophy emerges precisely at the spot where, in a new way, the two moments combine, which have been separated. The question concerning the relationship of intuition and understanding marks the problem to which Kant seeks an answer through the transcendental deduction of pure concepts of understanding. This answer is generally considered to be 'cryptic'. Most interpreters have trouble with it, so at best a so-called transcendental argument is all they can make of it. Patricia Kitcher is persuasive when she traces the reasons for the widespread rejection of the deduction chapter by other interpreters to too much transcendental psychology on Kant's part (see Kitcher 1990: 63).

The division of the argument's structure into two halves, as mentioned above, reflects this interpretational stance. It makes sense to discuss the purely intellectual-analytical connection first, separated from the transcendental synthesis of imagination. According to Strawson, the doctrine of the synthesis is supposed to be surpassed by the establishment of a direct analytic connection between the unity of consciousness and the unified objectivity of the world of our experience (see Strawson 1966: 97). The analytic interpretation of experience, which requires a self-conscious being to control a collection of privileged concepts to be at all able to identify, spatially and temporally, individuals different from itself, can readily follow from Kant's initial remarks on synthesis. After all, the construction of the intellectual synthesis gives, in a formal sense, an account of the intentional structure of apperception. We shall see that the attempt to catch the sceptical empiricist position in a pragmatic self-contradiction won't work in the last instance (see Strawson 1959: 35).

According to Kant, the objective validity of the pure concepts of understanding can be deduced if it can be shown that only through them – that is, through the intellectual synthesis – will objects of a possible experience be thinkable. Later, in the second step of the B-deduction argument, Kant treats the question of how the objective synthetic unity of the manifold can be obtained in intuition with the help of those concepts – that is, through the figural synthesis – and he does so by referring to the 'subjective machinery' of the faculties, without which it would remain completely impossible to explain how empirical knowledge comes about. Kant starts from the everyday experience that an object is comprehensible as identical within a prolonged flow of perceptions. However, since empirical consciousness itself lacks a stable identity – 'for the empirical consciousness which accompanies different representations is in itself fragmentary and disunited, and without relation to the identity of the subject' (Kant 1998: B 133) – the possibility of the specification of an identical object presupposes a transcendentally grounded unitary self-consciousness. In other words, if a series of representations is to be related to the same object, then there must be a guarantee that all these representations are 'each mine', for, without that guarantee, the 'identical' empirical likeness, that is, the objective unification pole of diverse representations, simply could not be sustained. This 'each mine' is for Kant a necessary condition of recognition. But a transcendental subject matter (*Gegenstand*) of a possible experience in general is needed as well, which corresponds to the formal unity of consciousness in the categorial synthesis of the manifold that is given in intuition. That is because the original consciousness of self-identity consists only in the consciousness of the necessary unity of the synthesis of all appearances (*Erscheinungen*) in accord with concepts or in the possibility of self-attribution of object-related representations. Subject and object come into being equi-originally in the process of objective cognition. Kant postulates the transcendental unity of subject and object as a purely intellectual relationship, insofar as cognition is only possible when an object is re-identifiable as object, which in turn is only possible if there is an identifying subject that for its part can only gain necessary self-assurance through acts of recognition. Thus the categories must simultaneously be representations of the unity of consciousness and, as such, predicates of some object. In this sense the unity of the cogito is pure understanding itself. Self-consciousness, which cannot become conscious of itself as such (*an sich*), preserves itself solely by 'losing' itself in the general logical functions of synthesis, without which its continuous, unbroken identity cannot be thought.

To this point we have been concerned with the purely intellectual synthesis that Kant discusses in the first step in the proof of the B-deduction, and which makes itself at home in the circular argument of representational thinking. For only under the assumption of a pure self-consciousness Q (or a 'privileged class Q' of propositions which express necessary conditions for meaning in language to occur at all) is objective knowledge E (experience) possible, which for its part is the condition of possibility of a self-consciousness, since the latter can only realise itself in categorial acts (see Stroud 1968: 252ff.). If the point of the transcendental argument of the deduction is to explicate the *a priori* necessary structures of immanent rationality or categorial determination of correspondingly presupposed experience, then this explication cannot make plausible its implicitly presumed assumptions: neither in recourse to the subject nor in recourse to the object, which both first consolidate themselves in that experience. It is not surprising that, in the process, the inferential structure of the transcendental argument proves to be tautological. The first premise, 'E', and the second premise, 'If E, then Q', leads, according to the deductive pattern, to the conclusion, 'therefore Q' (see Stevenson 1982: 5ff.). In this case we have an elenctic form of argumentation, a form which neither allows nor needs further elaboration. Instead we merely wish to keep in mind that the intended refutation of the sceptic (who, for example, doubts that causal laws can be objectively grounded in judgements concerning matters of fact) is left to rely on the sceptic's own good nature. If the sceptic contests the second premise, which establishes the concept of experience transcendentally, he becomes irrefutable. The question remains if he can 'afford' to contest that second premise, which might have unforeseen consequences.

This transcendental connection defines experience in terms of its self-referentiality insofar as it must assume, or at least imply, conditions for its possibility, conditions which determine (explicitly or not) experience. Transcendental (self-)reflection, which accompanies every empirical cognition within a homogeneous consciousness, characterises, according to Deleuze, 'representative thought' (see Deleuze 1994: 80). The faulty proof power of anti-sceptical analytic-deductive arguments is reflected in a general comment which Deleuze makes in the context of the transcendental problem of foundation and its onto-theological reasoning:

> Is this not the most general characteristic of the ground namely, that the circle which it organises is also the vicious circle of philosophical 'proof', in which representation must prove what proves it, just as for Kant the possibility of experience serves as the proof of its own proof? (Deleuze 1994: 274)

With this rhetorical question Deleuze points to the problem involved in the first argumentational step of the transcendental deduction. Up to here, Kant showed only that objective knowledge, when it is possible, is possible solely with the help of categories, whose unifying origin lies in pure apperception which in turn gets its (self-reflexive) determination only with (object-related) categories. Although Kant rightly feels obliged to undertake a second step for the clarification of the legitimacy of objective claims to knowledge, we can also see here, thanks to circularity, the weakness of the 'transcendental argument', which wants to assert that the epistemological sceptic refutes himself, because, to explicate his assumptions, he seems to need a conceptual framework whose validity he concurrently denies. If the sceptic accepts experience in the Kantian sense, he is made aware of the transcendental conditions which the corresponding experience presupposes. Naturally, however, the theorist of association – the sceptic par excellence – will deny having an experience defined in such a manner. One need not look long to find a suitable example: David Hume and the foundation of all empirical knowledge in habit and belief.

With the transcendental synthesis, Kant develops a model that is counter to empiricist association. When Kant introduces an objective ground for the validity of the laws of association, so as to be able to guarantee the associability of representations, he finds that ground in the unity of apperception, to which all perceptions are subordinate. 'The objective unity of all (empirical) consciousness in one consciousness (of original apperception) is thus the necessary condition even of every possible perception [. . .]' (Kant 1998: A 123). This intentionality of pure understanding, which is conceived on the basis of the intellectual synthesis, is used to justify – together with the range of proofs we discussed above – the assumption of a transcendental critique of association.

In the present discussion, my objection to the Kantian type of transcendental argumentation does not restrict itself to exposing the conditions of possibility for such argumentation as merely necessary but never sufficient to exclude in principle any alternative. The insinuated necessity of analytically derivable sense conditions, which are introduced as refutation of sense-data experience, refers to assumptions which are circularly bound with one another, assumptions that are not necessarily made by any reasonable person. Two of these assumptions, which both refer to the necessity to undertake, with Kant, that second argumentational step leading into the domain of the figural synthesis, will now be held up for examination. First issue: the unity of apperception cannot be the inevitable starting point of a post-Cartesian philosophy which sees itself facing the Humean challenge. Second issue: the intentionality thesis implies no more than a dogmatic fixation on what is empirically the normal case.

Figural Synthesis

(First issue.) Deleuze again and again pointed out that the comprehensive critique of the Cartesian cogito in Kant's paralogism chapter (Kant 1998: A 341–B 432) was not merely concerned with the immortality of the soul, but rather, and above all, with the stable unity of personal identity: it is precisely the incapability of achieving immediate self-intuition, which Kant analyses as the paradox of inner sense, that leads to the divergence between *a posteriori* and *a priori* self-affection (see Deleuze 1994: 86). For Kant, the unity of the thinking self exists only while carrying out the pure, conceptually determined, object-oriented synthesis of the manifold of representations (Kant 1998: B 135–6). At any rate, the self-attribution theorem used in Kant's analytical interpretation to explicate the transcendental ego does not problematise the highest instance of apperception (nor does it appear to guarantee the objective meaning of representations, which can only 'belong to me'). Instead, the transcendental cogito makes possible the categorial relation to the object, and it first constitutes itself as selfness in the synthesising act of 'subsuming' the manifold. The transcendental deduction turns against Hume's concept of experience precisely by trying in a (critically inspired) new way to guarantee the unity of self-consciousness. Accordingly, we can only have representations if the synthetic unity of apperception is presumed, so that *a priori* every experience is bound up in a cross-reference with other experiences (see Kitcher 1990: 91ff.). The representationality of representations depends on the concordance of perception, remembrance and understanding, as Kant summarises in the synthesis of recognition. This necessary synthetic unity of diverse cognitive states leads to the productive power of imagination, which prepares conceptually the intuition of things – and only raises suspicion because it illuminates certain genetic aspects of experience which somehow ought simply to be given. We remind ourselves that the transcendental synthesis undertaken by the power of imagination is called figural.

(Second issue.) The problem of intentionality in Kant's work, on the other hand, has to do with his critique of association, which is primarily worked out with the means prepared in the second step of the argument. We begin by noting that the analytic philosophers' rejection of the doctrine of synthesis fails to convince, because it cannot explain the genetic processes involved in the constitution of the intentional relationship to the object. However, this explanation is required if non-arbitrary alternatives are to be found to set over against the empirical model of object-oriented experience. Hoppe has made it clear in this context that for Kant the bare association of representations serves as prime example for deviations from the norm (see Hoppe 1983: 19). If association is not just accepted in a factually subjective way as a pre-scientific realm of mere perceptual opinions, but is treated instead as categorially accidental, it exemplifies an objectless experience, which, according to Kant, simply cannot be the case (see Kant 1998: A 111). One could say that Kant pathologises empirical experience, as the many text examples support that deal with the 'swarm of appearances'. This image, says Kant, exposes the 'chaos' of a pure empiricism and indicates from the start the lack of a real alternative by which the critical programme can revitalise metaphysics as science. What is important is that Kant, in his 'falling out' regarding Hume's latent irrationalism, paints the picture of a radicalised empiricism, of a non-intentional and 'ego-less' consciousness, that wanders around, distraught, in the non-coordinated (abstract) stream of feelings and ideas. The critique, which Kant exaggerates here metaphorically, does hit upon a fundamental problem of empiricism: individual and simple representations, as isolated incidents in consciousness, cannot have intentional relations to objects. Insofar as representations do relate to objects, they also thereby take part in categorial reference connections.

So it almost seems one could agree with Jaakko Hintikka that the debate about the transcendental argument has little to do with Kant, since nowhere are the requirements for the possibility of experience identified from the point of view of the transcendental functions of cognitive powers (see Hintikka 1972: 274f.). The intellectual synthesis exposes an undigestible aspect of the classic assumptions of empiricism, namely that simple representations are separated from one another and yet are also lined up objectively. It is the figural synthesis that first shows how the manifold-like multitude given to intuition becomes conceptually unified. Thereby it opens a way out of the empirical dilemma, which got little more than a negative characterisation from Kant in the first step of the proof. The transcendental synthesis must bring about a connection between the individual empirically given representations, a connection which is founded upon the categorial determination of a formal horizon of objectivity-in-general, so that, ultimately, it is indeed – contrary to a 'connection of association' – inscribed within the completely determined experience.

The problem of the transcendental founding of association, the fact that the categorially necessary associability of all the contents of consciousness guarantees, from the beginning, the regularity of experience, is reflected in Kant's introductory remarks on the transcendental deduction of the concepts of understanding in the answer to the question of why this deduction is indispensable. Obviously the critique of association is a central aspect of the deduction chapter. Kant explains that the categories, in counterdistinction to the pure forms of intuition, have to be deduced – the justification for their use has to be set out – because the categories are not requirements for which objects are given to intuition. It is within the framework of the deduction chapter that one can first clarify whether there can be appearances that do not necessarily relate to functions of the understanding. Up to this point it would be possible that appearances are of such a nature that they might not fit in with the requirements of their unification through understanding. That would mean to sink down into the 'blind play of representations' or into unregulated heaps of association, 'less [real] than a dream' (Kant 1998: A 112). A famous letter to Markus Herz, dated 1789, distinguishes succinctly between the (unconscious) experience of sense-data – which nonetheless has at its disposal associative connections of its elements – and well-organised human experience, which makes possible objective cognition through the categorially necessary synthesis of appearances.

> I would not even be able to *know that I have sense data; consequently for me, as a knowing being* [*als erkennendes Wesen*], they would be absolutely nothing. They could still (I imagine myself to be an animal) carry on their play in an orderly fashion, as representations connected according to empirical laws of association, and thus even have an influence on my feeling and desire [*auf Gefühl und Begehrungsvermögen*], without my being aware of them (assuming that I am even conscious of each individual representation, but not of their relation to the unity of representations of their object, by means of the synthetic unity of their apperception). This might be so without my knowing the slightest thing thereby, not even what my own condition [*Zustand*] is. (Kant 1789: 313–14)

If one ascertains that Kant, in the transcendental deduction, primarily aims at the critique of empiricism, it becomes clear that the process of legitimising pure concepts demands the genetic-constitutive model of synthesis. How else could the objective reality of the categories be proven if not by showing how they take possession of experience? That would show that there simply cannot be any representation that doesn't acquire demonstrable reality within the synthetic functioning of understanding.

The transcendental unity of apperception founds the formal framework of intentionality for all representations relevant to cognition, and it divides itself up into the logical judgement functions which unify the intuitions into a concept of the object. As Deleuze shows in his book on *Kant's Critical Philosophy*, this theory of cognition is carried by the doctrine of synthesis. No doubt, the productive power of imagination is in sole possession of the ability to synthesise the manifold of sense intuitions, that is, *a priori* to determine 'sensibility internally with regard to the manifold that may be given to it in accordance with the form of its intuition' (Kant 1998: B153). It is the sensualism in Kant's transcendental philosophy that makes synthesis necessary in the place where it belongs. The sensualist initial position of the Critique demands a constructive founding of objective reference, which Kant must achieve in the synthesis theory. From the Kantian perspective, one has to accuse classical empiricism of not having completed this achievement, that is, with associationism to have gotten stuck in the mire of an experience that ultimately is without objects.

The aim of Kant's proof in the transcendental deduction, 'that only by means of the categories an object can be thought', demands therefore that 'we must first assess [. . .] the transcendental constitution of the subjective sources that comprise the *a priori* foundations for the possibility of experience' (Kant 1998: A 97). Not only must the possibility of the relation of understanding to objects-in-general be explained, but also the working together of all faculties which are involved in the whole of cognition. Therefore it is of decisive importance that, in the second step of the proof of the cognitive value of the categories, one restricts oneself to objects of possible experience. That calls for figural synthesis which treats the *a priori* self-affection of the inner sense in terms of understanding qua the power of imagination. This theorem does not merely explain that something like a manifold given in intuition is then properly thought, by means of the intellectual synthesis of reason, to belong to the unity of apperception, but also how 'this manifold is given to an empirical intuition', which unifies itself thanks to the categories. As Kant writes, 'The aim of the deduction will first be fully attained by the explanation of the *a priori* validity of [the categories] in regard to all objects of our senses' (Kant 1998: B145). The figural synthesis is nothing but transcendental synthesis through the power of imagination – that is, the productive ability to determine sensibility *a priori*, so that reason can be applied in principle to objects of possible intuition (Kant 1998: B 151). Thus the categories bring about objective reality, because they possess a schematic rule that allows them to relate to intuitive manifold diversity.

If pure reason can be related to the pure manifold of time in the inner sense, then its relation to empirical reality is also established (see Kant 1998: B 160–1). It follows that every empirically given manifold has to be able to be thought by me at once, and in that way it is thought as possible object of experience. One can say that this objectively representational point of reference – we are not talking here of the object, but of objective representationality – is first produced by categorial thinking in its application to sensibility.

Kant reaches the projected goal of his proof of the deduction by means of the presupposition that all experience agrees with the laws of reason, that is, that the synthesis of apprehension is in concordance with that of apperception. The syntheses are inseparable within the totality of experience and the first two moments of apprehension and reproduction belong as 'preliminary steps' to the synthesis of recognition, the 'last and highest' synthesis, containing concepts which ground the formal unity of experience (see Kant 1998: A 125).

> However, the possibility, indeed even the necessity of these categories rests on the relation that the entire sensibility, and with it also all possible

> appearances, have to the original apperception, in which everything is necessarily in agreement with the conditions of the thoroughgoing unity of self-consciousness, i.e., must stand under universal functions of synthesis, namely of the synthesis in accordance with concepts, as that in which alone apperception can demonstrate *a priori* its thoroughgoing and necessary identity. (Kant 1998: A 111–12)

Every perception must be accompanied by an original consciousness, or it would be nothing for us. A perception only represents something if it belongs with others to a single consciousness within which they can be bound together. The transcendental synthesis, which underlies all empirical ones, is carried out by productive imagination. It connects the various impressions, which 'are encountered dispersed and separate in the mind' in the synthesis of apprehension (Kant 1998: A 120). The synthetic function of imagination is intellectualised provided it is added to the 'standing and lasting' unity of apperception, bringing about a conceptual relationship to sensible intuition. The pure synthesis undertaken by imagination is subordinate to this apperceptive unity. Strictly speaking, experience in the Kantian sense is only empirical cognition. Whatever is not suited to cognition can also not be experienced, so that the understanding 'is always busy poring through the appearances with the aim of finding some sort of rule in them' (Kant 1998: A 126). But objective rules are primarily the pure concepts of understanding, which is why the understanding looks deeply at the appearances until they completely give back what has been 'put into' them. Although deepened, this is what constitutes, in spite of everything, the tautological argument of the deduction: Kant proceeds from a concept of experience that is modelled in such a way that it must verify the objective validity of the categories. Everything that doesn't fit would be nothing. The sensual chaos of non-referential feelings lies below the horizon of successful human experience, no more than a 'meaningless' fiction, as Kant says to defame his philosophical opponents.

> Unity of synthesis in accordance with empirical concepts would be entirely contingent, and, were it not grounded on a transcendental ground of unity, it would be possible for a swarm of appearances to fill up our soul without experience ever being able to arise from it. But in that case all relation of cognition to objects would also disappear, since the appearances would lack connection in accordance with universal and necessary laws, and would thus be intuition without thought, but never cognition, and would therefore be as good as nothing for us. (Kant 1998: A111)

Kant probably thinks he has refuted the possible occurrence of an experience that rests exclusively on association. But it is highly questionable whether every consciousness is necessarily bound up in the objective unity of apperception (see Paton 1936: I 331). As Hoppe suggests, in the clinical field pathological isolation of representations, as well as derailments and slips indicating a loss of objectively coherent sense and reference, are all too present (Hoppe 1983: 129ff.). The sensuality of localised, intensive feelings, which rumbles around in the background of Kantian thought, continues to populate the scorned 'forefront' of Kantian experience. 'Experience for Kant always involves objects. Merely having sensations is not experience,' as Rolf George stresses (George 1981: 249). Yet this 'forefront' persists not only in stark contrast to Kant's tautological concept of experience, but it also makes it possible to go one step further and describe the transcendental synthesis undertaken by imagination from a new perspective: from below. The famous three syntheses, which substitute for the thinking of self-affection in the first version of the deduction, will be summoned at the end of this chapter to show how Kantian sensuality already evokes the idea of passive syntheses in the *Critique of Pure Reason*. First, to be sure, certain aspects of Kant's critical reflections on empiricism will have to be discussed, aspects which compel essential progress in this field. We begin with the conceptual doctrine regarding schematism and then pass on to Kant's principle regarding the intensive magnitude of sensual qualities.

Schematism and Pure Concepts

The transcendental schematism is a pain in the neck for many Kant scholars. If it is possible to uncover its roots in the deduction chapter, then it will be possible to bring some clarity into the matter. In the last section we discovered that schematism founds pure concepts of understanding through the figural synthesis, 'which is an effect of the understanding on sensibility and its first application (and at the same time the ground of all others) to objects of the intuition that is possible for us' (Kant 1998: B152). Categories are schemata, if indeed they are rules for the synthesis of manifolds given inner sense. The problem of how to apply pure concepts, proposed in the schematism chapter, corresponds to the problem, in the deduction chapter, of how categories can *de jure* claim for themselves objective reality. Transcendental schematism's 'subsumption procedure' obeys the metaphysical structures to be a mediating instance between intuition and understanding. This mediating function has often been given as standard criterion when evaluating the meaning of the schematism chapter. Deleuze, however, holds the fundamental position that the schemata, if indeed Kant unduly 'subsumed' them to the categories, are 'reduced to the status of simple mediations in the world of representation', something to be generally rejected (Deleuze 1994: 285). It isn't the failure of mediation that Deleuze objects to, but the theoretical strategy itself and its corresponding conceptual realisation. This clearly negative opinion is nevertheless relativised by Deleuze insofar as there may be an anticipation of an a-categorial type of concept in schematism: conceptual schemata taken as nomadic 'complexes of space and time, no doubt transportable but on condition that they impose their own scenery, that they set up camp there where they rest momentarily . . .' (Deleuze 1994: 285).

First let's examine more carefully the thesis that schematism is scarcely more than an appendage to the deduction chapter. As we said, the theorem of the figural synthesis is the primary subject of the chapter on schematism. Accordingly, the reality problem of the deduction first appears definitively in the transition to the second step of the proof, where it merges with the problem of applying schematism. As Kant shows in these pages, pure concepts of understanding which are strictly confined to their empirical usage gain objective significance for the very reason that they are rules of synthesis of the pure forms of intuition, in which all empirical reality is given (Kant 1998: B150; see also Chipman 1972: 36–50). As Heidegger pointed out, this restriction belongs to the innermost constitution of the categories: they must distinguish themselves by their definitive (schematic) relationship to intuition, in order to be able to produce the necessary connection of individual representations, given here and now, into judgements, as is required if all representations are to belong to a single unified self-consciousness (Heidegger 1990: 62ff.). Precisely this relationship of categories to the pure form of inner sense is what schematism realises, just as the figural synthesis makes it possible in general in the *a priori* self-affection. The categories are significant when they contain 'formal conditions of inner sense', namely schemata as temporal determinations *a priori* according to rules (Kant 1998: A 139–40/ B 179).

> From this it is clear that the schematism of the understanding through the transcendental synthesis of imagination comes down to nothing other

> than the unity of all the manifold of intuition in inner sense, and thus indirectly to the unity of apperception, as the function that corresponds to inner sense (to a receptivity). Thus the schemata of the concepts of pure understanding are the true and sole conditions for providing them with a relation to objects, and so with significance [...] (Kant 1998: A145–6/B 185)

The understanding, which instructs imagination in the figural synthesis to determine inner sense, thereby brings about schematically for each individual category the proper unity of the manifold of intuition. Here we see that a particular role is left over for schematism, in spite of its embeddedness in the deduction problematic, namely to produce the categorial time-determinations in each individual case. However, contrary to appearances, what has just been said leads our research into an unfortunate dilemma. The back and forth between deduction and schematism, which gave us a convincing interpretation of the latter, also has an inadvertant drawback. Based on our present discussion of the application problem, we note that, as Detel formulates, 'we cannot avoid the conclusion [...] that, according to Kant's interpretation, schematization grants [...] objective reality to the categories and that therefore the schemata of the pure concepts of understanding are nothing but the schematised categories' (Detel 1978: 40). Schematism, understood as schematised categories, represents in a particular way the transcendental mediation problem. We should keep in mind that the category in no way 'degrades' to a product of imagination, because synthesis and schematism – as mentioned above – are to be distinguished in an important sense. Following Deleuze we can say that the transcendental synthesis of the manifold (as well as its schematising) is for Kant the business of imagination, whereas the formal unity of the synthesis (as well as its schematic rule) is already categorially at hand, that is, it does not originate in imagination. But insofar as concepts and schemata have the same rules of synthesis, 'external to the concept, it is not clear how [the schema] can ensure the harmony of the understanding and sensibility, since it does not even have the means to ensure its own harmony with the understanding [...]' (Deleuze 1994: 275). For Deleuze the schema transforms the formal possibility, as thought 'within' the concept, into transcendental possibility. In so doing, Kant lays the schema open to attack as a 'second' category, so that the imagination reflects only conceptual determinations on the plane of pure forms of intuition but never reconciles the two sides in a mutual sublimation. Curtius anticipated the interpretational results we have been discussing. First, he demonstrated that Kant introduces the theorem of the figural synthesis productively as the foundation for schematism. This means, second, that by specifying, in the schematism chapter, the forms according to which the figural synthesis takes place, the deduction is complemented (more exactly: is elaborated in the direction of the foundational problem). Third, however, Curtius didn't let himself be bowled over by the nimbleness of Kant's arguments, but rather exposed the one-sided orientation of the schema toward the category, which simply doesn't allow for the necessary similarity of schema and sensibility required for mediation. Kant seems to have 'solved' the problem of mediation by simply 'commanding' it. 'However heterogeneous intuition and concepts may be, as Kant first announces, he connects them in the schema with the decree: fit yourselves together!' (Zschocke 1907: 169, as cited in Curtius 1914: 362).

So the unavoidable question remains regarding the starting point for schematism, namely the application of pure concepts of understanding. Kant differentiates, as we know, the empirical use of concepts from the non-empirical. Accordingly, propositions which are formed using non-referential conceptual rules possess no empirical relevance, which is why Kant poses the application problem for categories in the first place (see Körner 1955: 55–60). To legitimise his epistemological claims, Kant needs pure concepts which can be properly applied to the world of appearances. Deleuze thinks that here the problem, how concepts determine experience, is posed incorrectly. In his opinion the significance of pure concepts which cannot be derived empirically does not lie in the determination of the form of possible experience. So it would be a digression to try to sniff out by way of schematism a revisionist possibility, through the use of quasi-empirical 'correspondence rules', that might legitimise theoretical terminology that cannot be explicated empirically. The absolute necessity of non-empirical, that is to say philosophical concepts must be honoured as such, so that it can be made crystal clear what constitutes the real productive power of schematism: its immanent critique of empiricism.

Kant uses schematism to get rid of the empiricist copy theory of the concept. The schemata of pure concepts are not like images which themselves copy empirical reality. The transcendental schema is the 'representation of a general procedure [...] for providing a concept with its image [...] The schema is to be distinguished from an image' (Kant 1998: A 140/B 179). It is a rule for the extra-propositional presentation of the categories in the figural synthesis. The pure schema-likeness determines the pure form of inner sense, so that it implies an unspecified but specifiable object as pure possibility. The categorial set of rules, originally presented in the pure schema, works, in the empirical situation, through the material of experience to attain reality. The schematic concepts contain the rules of their intuitive fulfilment – that is, they possess intuitive content. Therefore Kant's theory of concepts does not exhaust itself by thrusting given objects under concepts (subordination doctrine), but systematically grafts appearances onto concepts, that is to say, to produce them as something. These empirico-ideal 'schemategories' possess a constructive potential to the degree that their inner conceptual relations determine their actualisation, so that they function as genetic conditions of experience. Transcendental schemas pre-form whatever experience is made in the environment and how it is to be assimilated.

Concepts as rules for synthetic unity of disparate representations do not in principle have their source in experience, but rather bring experience into being. Kant's rationalist insight into the significance of pure concepts as constitutive of experience undermines the dogmatic abstraction theory of empiricism. The latter explains the construction of concepts as brought about by the naturally habitual, purely subjective connectivity of simple representations, a process which can never be objectively legitimised. Concepts are therefore complex collections of individual representations which are taken from their original settings and reassembled in accordance with subjective necessity. It is a question of abstractions that are derived empirically and that have always occurred in language, without reflecting in any particular way their origin or their remoteness with respect to the direct truths of sense. This opens up room for discussion and allows the empiricist to exercise his methodology regarding the criticism of metaphysics. However, this critique tends to orient itself too quickly on the logical abstraction relation which universal concepts and laws maintain toward immediate givens and complains about the distortion of the latter by the former, instead of paying attention to the productive valence of the intellectual fictions which truly overstep their 'basis in experience'. In spite of everything, a certain potential to criticise concepts is gaining force in empiricism and its nominalist tendencies, a potential that is doing the necessary spadework for ongoing philosophical attempts to conceive of concepts that resist the reproach of 'instrumental thinking'.

Explaining concept-building via abstraction is mirrored in the corresponding confirmation or testing theory of empiricism. Hume never tires of asking the same question: 'From what impression is this representation derived?' (Hume 1956: 20–1), so as not to submit to the 'gibberish' of metaphysics. The keen critique of dogmatic empiricism since Quine concentrates particularly on the reductionist idea of a 'concept-neutral' empirical foundation, which stands behind the aforementioned 'logico-positivist' interrogation. Accordingly, classic and modern empiricism both suggest, falsely, that theoretical propositions can be verified, sentence for sentence, before the tribunal of experience. But as has been shown, especially in studies in the history of science, there is no observation tower from which the synthetic achievement of various conceptual schemata could be compared, because the 'empirical content' transported by them is not theory-neutral. To put it another way, it cannot be alleged that various concepts organise the same undetermined experiential material, because the realities from which they are supposed to recur cannot be found out without concepts. In accordance with these results we conclude that empirical confirmation is itself, for the most part, a theoretical procedure. 'Any statement can be held true come what may, if we make drastic enough adjustments elsewhere in the system' (Quine 1953: 43). The metaphorical rhetoric regarding 'agreement', 'connection', 'reproducibility' and so on will all have to be revised pragmatically. Concepts which do not prove to be purely empirical cannot be purely empirically derived: they permeate only that experience that they are capable of determining. Knowledge is not a construction 'placed directly upon raw sense data by the mind' (Kuhn 1970: 96). Rather, every scientific procedure presupposes a particular theoretical paradigm (see Kuhn 1970: 129–30).

At this point it becomes obvious that Kant, in the interest of speculation, plays down the difference inscribed in his dualist system. Although he specifically distinguishes the thinking of problematic ideas from rational recognising of empirical facts, yet on the whole his epistemological claim predominates and dictates the necessary harmony of the faculties participating in the cognitive process. Therefore Kant disregards the strict parallel of concept and sense, which nowhere allows a crossover *de jure* (see Walsh 1957: 100). Hume's sceptical position leads Kant to insight into the questionability of objective meaning of pure concepts, which is why he pushes forward into the transcendental 'twilight zone' of synthesis. But this is where the compass of understanding goes wrong. Concepts neither order nor permeate any material of experience, which remains radically separated from them. Instead, they stand in a more or less complex net of relationships with other, carefully coordinated, concepts. Experience is nothing but the limiting condition of such a conceptuality (see Quine 1953: 45). If, therefore, as Deleuze suggests, a non-referential use is supposed to take place in the philosophy of concepts and ideas, then this usage is only answerable to pragmatic criteria of application, which must still be evaluated. With that we reach the level at which the real, complex intermingling of the visible and the articulable can be analysed into paradigmatic formations of knowledge (Deleuze 1988b: 70ff.). Some results: a) Extra-conceptual facts are, to be sure, not intrinsically determined by concepts, yet the facts are *de facto* anticipated by them. b) The non-conceptual field of experience does not allow itself to be transferred 'without a break' into the experience of the concept unless, in fact, the concept is already privileged as pure immediacy. c) The non-conceptual experience can stimulate thinking toward concepts, even if these do not harmonise with the experience but rather unfold their efficacy in an informal milieu of forces in its vicinity. Surely, then, it is one of the special achievements of Deleuze's transcendental empiricism that he can reconcile empiricist theory with a doctrine of concepts, a doctrine that can be transcribed back into the traditions of Kantianism and Hegelianism. (See also the section 'Structuralism of Ideas and Concepts', in Chapter 7 of this book.)

Sense Perception and Intensities

> Among all the means at the disposal of consciousness, sensation is the most indescribable, most ambiguous, and simultaneously the most indispensable and the most definitive with respect to addressing and expressing objectivity. Therefore it is the foundation of sensualism and the stumbling block of idealism. (Cohen 1987: 753–4)

The pathos of immediate experience overshadows the philosophical reflection of empiricism. Sense-data theory is what formulates empiricism's fundamental propositions. Simple, unconnected and passively given impressions, from which the classical theory of perception takes its start, can be grasped, at first glance, as sense-data. It is conventional to use the term 'sense-data' to designate a one-time, directly perceived, non-physical 'object'. The well-known argument from illusion that Alfred Ayer develops in detail points to the phenomenological singularity of every sense-data experience, which lies at the foundation of all complex representations of higher cognition faculties (see Ayer 1940: 1–57). 'Sensible things are only such that are immediately perceived by the senses' (Berkeley 1988: 14–15), as George Berkeley is stressing. On this basis the empiricists construct a second type of experience which leans toward the views of common sense. With the help of association theory, Hume explains how ordinary experience as well as the belief in persistent and separate physical objects is put together, namely through habitual overstepping, according to certain rules of human nature, of merely receptively encountered impressions.

As we have seen, Kant's critique of association wants to show – to put it simply – that the empiricist relationship between immediate experience of data and higher indirect representations is inconsistent and has to be replaced with his doctrine of synthesis. Kant argues first that the actual regularity of appearances cannot be explained as long as no transcendental foundation exists for the association of simple representations. Second, he asserts that, with the loss of this categorial foundation, unified experience is no longer confirmable, so that a sensibility might be possible that doesn't conform to the general requirements of cognition. With that, the epistemological method essentially reverses itself. The empiricists search for the pure fundamentals of experience, in order to determine on a firm foundation the limits and possibilities of knowledge, whereas Kant tosses aside these empiricist maxims because the idea of an immediate, present stream of sensations does not conform with any concrete experience regarding the objective recognition of things, and therefore cannot be justified epistemologically. Accordingly, Kant paints the picture of a literally impossible non-conceptual experience, the consequence of empiricist assumptions which in a curiously threatening way denies all scientific claims.

One has to pay attention to the reasons which lead Kant to his metaphoric turn away from empiricism. Kant works through the 'reasonable' aspects of empiricist realism in systematic fashion. There remains, however, a meaningless residue on which traces of the critique remain stuck, meaningless in the sense of a pure sense-data experience which apparently exhibits no objectively binding inclusions. From this we conclude that Kant not only pushes empiricism to the point of caricature, but immanently radicalises it by eliminating certain weaknesses in its theoretical structure or forcing the resolution of inner contradictions. With the intention of demonstrating the groundlessness of empiricism, he overstates his image of an impossible experience and thereby – as shown above – signals the breakdown of the deduction if the epistemological claims formulated there become enclosed within the tautological framework of the possible. At the same time the fixed boundary between the possible and the impossible is shot full of holes in making the transition to the figural synthesis from the inside out, namely in a transcendental-psychological manner. Kant does more than exhibit the positivist adherence of classical empiricism to a common sense understanding of physical objects. He clearly opens up completely new genetically constitutive perspectives. It is this transcendental background which provides empiricism with the necessary critical depth. We don't have to give up the sense-data theory, but it needs serious modification. Sense-data can neither be identified phenomenologically with exterior objects nor applied to them representationally. Above all they shirk from idealist sublimation within understanding. As Hume made clear, if we begin with sensible data, then only the genetic question, rather than the epistemological one, can be asked regarding why we believe in a world of exterior objects, independent of us and continuously existing. This belief is a product of imagination; it can be attributed neither to the senses nor to reason and is also incapable of justification. Kant's discussion of transcendental functions relative to imagination forces, first, empiricist theory to reconsider objectivity as such. This gives rise to a problem that, second, expands to the concept of simple perceptions and undermines the empiricist theory of abstraction. Third, the Kantian concept of sensation clarifies the equivocal usage of simple and complex perceptions. Intensity, as Kant speaks about in the second principle of pure understanding, can be employed to modify the sense-datum aiming at resolving the empiricist antinomy of consciousness. It all depends on moving from the sense-datum, as it has traditionally been understood in empiricism, toward a sensualist-virtual complex, that is to the (Deleuzian) idea of the sensible. This transition, which, after all, was initiated by Kant, finally bestows upon empiricism its transcendental character.

We shall now go into detail regarding the three points just made.

1. We start with the problem of the object (*Gegenstand*) with respect to our annotations to Kant's doctrine of synthesis. It is well known that empiricists deny that spatially extended material things can be immediately perceived. However, they do not dispute that simple and individual representations can be intentionally imposed on objects. To put it differently, and historically more accurately, empiricists constantly talk about things whenever they talk about their immediate observations. But as Kant has shown, the empiricist

conception of the original manifold of experience is incompatible with the objective validity or even the objective orientation of its elementary perceptions.

> Counter to Hume's empiricist starting point, that there can be, to be sure, scattered objective cognition but no consequent objective experience of connections among things, Kant asserts that also the perception or experience of isolated events always already assumes an original and necessary connection of the whole manifold given to us in terms of pure concepts of understanding. (Hoppe 1983: 61)

Hoppe correctly insists that classical empiricism breaks down on the problem of intentionality, whereas Kant takes this breakdown to heart and – based on his dispute with Hume – reacts to it with his critical project. Thus the transcendental synthesis mediates the positions, at first glance incompatible, taken by sensible manifolds of data on the one hand and the issue of objective reference on the other. Kant makes it clear that Hume's scepticism has to be radicalised even more: the talk of scattered objective cognition cannot be empirically grounded. The object-oriented experience, which implies a categorially necessary connection of empirically unconnected appearances within a concept of an object, stands over against an objectless experience of merely subjective occurrences of consciousness. Classical empiricism contradicts itself in the implicit assumption that individual representations exhibit intentional relations to objects. Kant's critique of empiricism asserts that, in the case of objective cognition, the sensible givens are connected according to conceptual rules of reproduction and are related in a unified manner to an object-form that is not given but is attributed to them. With the aid of categorial connectivity functions, the original apperception sets up synthetic referential bonds between individual perceptions, which are thereby tied together within the identity form of the transcendental object (*transzendentaler Gegenstand*). Kant's model of recognition is behind the common-sense understanding of direct realism, insofar as we make the necessary assumption about several faculties working beforehand in a regulated way to assure the stable perception of things. It takes the coordination of disparate perceptions through the understanding to enable an object to attain meaning independent of its actual mode of givenness. A thing gains independence when it doesn't rely on willy-nilly approaches, or – as Piaget would have it – on individual action-schemes, but rather conforms to the conceptual formation of the noematic core of perception, which is never given to intuition as such. Isolated representations, which follow one another randomly, never coalesce into object-related constellations of sense, which suggests that radical empiricism is in need of some pathological guidelines. Whoever loses the objective unity of apperception, loses simultaneously his hold on things.

In wholly general terms Kant analyses the fact of inner-worldly experience as it persists, unnoticed, relative to the object, with the intention of consolidating its subliminally practised, objective achievement in terms of synthetic *a priori* judgements. Empiricists, on the other hand, are deceived by objectivity and unwittingly keep falling for its all too natural efficacy as an implicit assumption of classical thought. For isolated occurrences of consciousness that are qualified through sense are tacitly extracted from requirements for the perception of objects. In what follows we will have to insist, therefore, on returning to transcendental synthesis with a well-protected empirical attitude. Sense-data that are established based on their non-perceivable status – as Kant showed, impressions apprehended in perception are never unbound, isolated impressions – require connective structures which organise themselves, never spontaneously within understanding, but passively according to habitual rules. 'Bundles', 'heaps' or 'packages' of sensible impressions result from the transcendental association of 'simple perceptions' in the imagination. If it is possible to construct a critical philosophy of empiricism or to decipher one in the works of Deleuze, then it must also be possible to think a passive synthesis of sensory data and then – following Hume – to deliver an (improved) genetic explanation of intentional acts of recognition.

2. If the necessary radicalisation of empiricism, which Kant calls for, is to take place, we'll have to give up trying to refer simple perceptions to objects and turn instead to more complex perceptions. These can neither be thought of as built up of otherwise unchanged bits and pieces, nor are they, in the Kantian sense, an objectively necessary assemblage achieved through pure reason. In the next chapter we will take a look at Husserl's phenomenology to clarify just how the passive syntheses lie in anticipation of the active cognition of objects. Right now we must still convince ourselves that the principles of association cannot be ascertained with the help of empirical regularities. For these regularities are abstract representations which are supposed to explain how simple representations appear together, although the latter are also products of abstraction stemming from observed regularities involving successive sense impressions. The empiricists presume a fully described situation while pretending to

take the situation by the hand and giving it for the very first time the means to describe it. The principles of association assume facts – that is, representations bound together out of subjective necessity, which they have already implicitly determined.

If that which is empirically the case involves transcendental genetic processes, then the problem of association changes in an essential way. One has often argued against cognitive atomism that it makes no sense to start with a concept of simple perception, because perceptions always refer to structured wholes, i.e., only realise themselves as bound together. Complex perceptions therefore become primary facts of consciousness and require us to revise the classic relationship between simple and complex perceptions. The problem of intentionality stretches to cover the relationship of unity and multiplicity. Object-directed perception refers immediately to the phenomenal Gestalt of a thing, which stands out against an unthematic background and becomes bound into meaningful referential contexts. Gestalt theory counters sense-atomism only insofar as the empirical theoreticians of cognition regard sense-data as facts of consciousness. Quine recommends that empiricists no longer talk of sense-data but move to the purely receptive plane of sense stimuli.

> Sensory receptors operate at the level of reception, and Gestalt operates at the level of perception. The old antagonism was due to the epistemologist's straining toward reception while still requiring awareness, which belongs to perception. (Quine 1974: 4)

Classical empiricists thought they perceived sense-data: simple perceptions that phenomenologically quickly lose their simplicity and reveal themselves to be constructions. The very doubling of expressions – perceiving perceptions, for example – already gives the game away and for good reason provokes criticism from the Oxford ordinary language programme.

As long as simple sense impressions form the foundation of cognition and determine the tabula rasa of blank consciousness, the understanding is obliged to overstep actively the passively received data and work the given material into complex ideas which then claim quasi-fictional validity for themselves. Conversely, the theory of abstraction starts with completely undetermined complex ideas and begins to select general patterns having characteristics which can then be employed as simple representations. So we see both particular and complex perceptions, as well as individual and simple ones, function as fundamental building blocks of experience, whereas on the other hand first complex, then simple perceptions result from the reflection of reason.

> To summarise this discussion, clearly simple ideas are not given immediately, but rather that one is confronted, based on experience, with infinitely complex 'particular ideas', which only later are decomposed into irreducible units. The materials of cognition, the atomic facts as Locke first called them, become right away the products of cognition. At the decisive point, Locke's structure turns out to be inconsistent. (Kambartel 1968: 26)

This ruinous conflict within the classical theory has its roots in the belief in simple perceptions which won't let themselves be organised into complex assemblages below the threshold of consciousness.

Let us consider just what would happen if indeed sense-data were not construed as simple facts of consciousness but were instead thought to be virtual moments of complex affections! Deleuze devotes himself to working out this transcendentally inspired alternative to simple empiricism, while at the same time countering any idealist revocation of physicality. Individual perceptions persist *ab ovo* in synthetic relations with other perceptions: they can only be understood as atomistic elements within the framework of a structural model that allows existing facts to be analysed subsequently into their components. Usually, however, such models serve idealist interpretations and, in the case of a concretely structured experience, the abstract material – the basic substratum of that experience – is completely sublimated. In contrast, the empiricist position has to gain possession of a structural model that begins with differential elements which are neither given to consciousness directly in punctilious simplicity nor, as abstract particles, merely serve to assist reconstruction of an already determined experience. It follows that sense-data must have a virtual status as the differential moments of an ideal manifold. That version of the sensible is what Deleuze has in mind. We will go on to show that the idea of a virtual structure of small perceptions and affects allows comprehension of the genesis of conscious acts without letting these be totally assimilated into the resulting actual cognitions. On the contrary, the virtual extracts itself from the actual: it insinuates itself as counter-actuality (as event) into the actualities of representation (experience in the narrower sense).

3. Surprisingly, it is again Kant who, in his reflections, anticipates the intensive magnitude of all sensations and thereby provides empiricism with the critical means to renew itself. For it is its sensual

borrowing which makes the Kantian concept of sensation capable of problematising the intensity of sensual affection. Sensation characterises the boundary of his metaphysics of finitude anyway, insofar as that metaphysic is forced to speculate on material ground to impart to intuition a real complement for exterior facts. 'Intuition and thought can indeed be suspected to be pure fantasies, whereas in sensation we again establish a rapport with the outside world' (Cohen 1987: 541). Kant contrasts sensations and cognitions and defines the former as without object, unextended and sense-specific. The sensation as such does not refer to an object, which would have to be differentiated from the act of sensing. Sensing is different from all other faculties in that it only elicits a subjective, self-affecting modification of one's disposition. 'The consciousness of the homogeneous manifold in intuition [makes] the representation of the object first possible', whereas 'sensation in itself is not an objective representation' (Kant 1998: B 203, A 166/B 208). Unlike the homogeneous parts, which are apprehended in successive synthesis into the extensive magnitude of the pure form of intuition, sensations are instantaneously bound together in an absolute unit. It follows that there is a temporal mode of apprehension, belonging to imagination, which brings sensations into a unit of magnitude which is not composed of similar and simple parts.

> Apprehension, merely by means of sensation, fills only an instant [. . .] As something in the appearance, the apprehension of which is not a successive synthesis, proceeding from the parts to the whole representation, it therefore has no extensive magnitude. (Kant 1998: A 167/B 209)

Kant is here pointing to what is fundamentally the only possible *a priori* cognition with respect to sensations, namely that, regardless of its empirical quality, it must have at its disposal a specific grade of intensity. The intensive magnitude of affection therefore stands over against the extensive magnitude of intuition. Brightness, weight, colour, etc., can vary quantitatively while extension remains constant. In contrast to the extensive magnitude, the intensive magnitude is apprehended as a unit 'in which multiplicity can only be represented through approximation to negation = 0' (Kant 1998: A 168/B 210). This limit marks the point at which the empirical consciousness disappears, insofar as it is no longer affected from outside and thus relinquishes all reality, so that a purely formal consciousness *a priori* of time and space is all that remains. On this negative film of pure intuition, the reality of the intensive stands out, positively and in any magnitude. In this way perception gets the material substrate of sensation vis-à-vis the extensive form of intuition.

Every intensive magnitude can always be gradually diminished, so that we must assume a continuum of infinitely many intermediate sensations from real to zero. The intensive magnitude is not the result of adding simple bits of sensation; on the contrary, it is an indivisible whole that consists of infinitely many partial moments, no one of which is most minute. For every intensive moment which might be apprehended as a unit has to distinguish itself by right from negation, so that a continuous differential to the zero point is taken into account. 'This was the necessity', as Hermann Cohen put it, 'which drove toward the infinitely small: to set something which becomes unity not with respect to one but to zero' (Cohen 1987: 547). Accordingly, intensity is to be conceived in the Leibnizian manner as a differential magnitude. The unit of this limit-value reality can be quantified if one directs one's attention to the manifold states which led to its creation in time. The intensive magnitude defines itself out of the gradual change of state of the non-extensive, non-referential complex of sensations. 'By means of this procedure the real should not be conceived as a sum of given reals but precisely as the sum of reality differences, of state differences' (Böhme 1986: 88). Thus inner differences of sensation can be shown to exist – which Kant considered highly questionable. But it is this concept of differential intensities that forms the empiricist foundation of Deleuze's philosophy: 'Intensity is the form of difference in so far as this is the reason of the sensible' (Deleuze 1994: 222). The whole, as he writes in his film book on the *Movement-Image*,

> has no parts except in a very special sense, since it cannot be divided without changing qualitatively at each stage of the division. The real whole might well be [...] an indivisible continuity. [...] The whole creates itself, and constantly creates itself in another dimension without parts, like that which carries along the set of one qualitative state to another, like the pure ceaseless becoming which passes through these states. (Deleuze 1986: 10)

Deleuze apprehends the 'whole' – speaking with Kant – as a 'reality' that is meant as the product of a 'continuous generation [...] in time' (Kant 1998: A 143/B 183). Of course, according to Kant it is the schematised category of reality that attributes intensive magnitude to all appearances that affect our senses. We will deal later with the problem of schematism involved in the case of the anticipation of perception. But first we cannot avoid a remark on the differing definition of time as succession or as instant.

Kant makes it clear that time generates itself as pure form of intuition in the successive synthesis, as 'the way in which the mind is affected by its own activity' (Kant 1998: B 68). On the other hand, the synthesis of sense in an instant means that immediate sensations, which are not given as simple and separate, are apprehended as integrated. This apprehension of a magnitude in its immediacy (that is without thinking how large it is) is presented by Kant in an exemplary way, in the *Critique of Judgement*, as comprehensio aesthetica. In the aesthetic estimation of magnitude the 'partial representations of the intuited sensations' which follow one another are apprehended as an intuitive unit which as such precedes in principle its parts. The temporal sequence is 'set aside' in imagination whenever it allows a living presence within the aesthetic simultaneity of 'partial representations', 'by which it [imagination] does violence to the internal sense; this must be the more noticeable, the greater the quantum is which the Imagination comprehends in one intuition' (Kant 1914: 122). The imagination synthesises 'regressively' in an instant impressions given 'progressively', all in keeping with its capacity to apprehend such impressions. Böhme, who defines the aesthetically estimated fundamental measure as intensive magnitude, states in this context that the empirical instant embraces a non-arbitrary temporal magnitude, the result of the corresponding synthesis of the imagination. The intensive magnitude enjoys an 'ontological precedence' over the extensive one, which can easily be read off from the variable duration of an aesthetic time synthesis of the present. Thus intensity functions as the transcendental principle of all empirical qualities. It designates in Deleuze's transcendental empiricism the 'reason of sense'. Sensual intensities vary accordingly in time duration and define themselves mutually with respect to their differential position. Therefore they are only sensed while stimulating thought to explicate its state. The intensity differential must, according to Deleuze, 'first be sensed as that which gives diversity to be sensed. Moreover, it must be thought as that which creates diversity' (Deleuze 1994: 226). The sensations 'without qualities', the ones not oriented objectively, form within a temporally defined synthesis an indivisible magnitude which can only be 'parted' if it undergoes change. Deleuze refers here to Bergsonian duration, which stands opposite the extensive multitudes as a virtually manifold whole. Thus time cannot be defined *strictu sensu* as the pure form of intuition, which would lead to the conclusion that the intensive magnitude can only be anticipated by empirical intuition in such a way that it solely qualifies appearances (as extensive magnitudes).

The treatment of the intensive magnitude by Kant served until now to hedge his texts. Kant speaks of the intensive magnitude of sense *and* of the reality to which the sense corresponds. He also speaks of the synthesis that functions here as apprehension of sensation *and* schematising the reality category. We must remember that the active schematising of the reality category affects only the pure form of the inner sense and doesn't coincide with the passive apprehension of sense in an empirical consciousness. Kant suggests the congruence of both syntheses to the degree that the schematic definition of inner sense concerns the form of time, so that it can function at all as the transcendental form of the synthesis of sensual qualities in an empirical consciousness. With that Kant reaches the goal of his proofs, which is to get objective validity for the concept of intensive magnitude, or rather, to be exact, only for the reality that corresponds to the concept of an object of sense and not for the sense itself. The problems of mediation which again come to the fore in the *Critique* solve themselves if one takes the form of time necessary to define the intensity directly out of the synthesis of the sensual manifold, a synthesis which, according to Deleuze, is determined ideally. Deleuze places himself firmly in the tradition from Maimon to Cohen, which idealises the forms of intuition and thereby opens the possibility of conceiving space and time as intensive magnitudes. For Deleuze, the idea of the sensual embraces differential moments of sense which are mutually related when they are temporalised and apprehended. Time must be grasped as a form of inner sense, as resulting from the passive syntheses. In no way can the intuition be schematised *a priori*, letting the intensities be referred only to extension. Deleuze is aiming systematically at a pure intensive sensuality which is implicated in thought as the non-explicable and which roils thought from within. Thus thought is forced to interpret the non-conceptual signs and to actualise them, even though the virtual intensities evade their explication in the forms of representation. They coexist as confused and unnoticed little genetic affections along with the clear and distinct facts of consciousness. For Deleuze it would be false to say that we perceive sense-data: sense-data are not immediate facts of consciousness but little genetic moments of experience which evade their own actualisation.

Three Syntheses

In the first edition of the *Critique of Pure Reason* Kant finds it necessary to precede the third section of the deduction of the pure concepts of understanding – in which the explication of the 'relationship of understanding to objects in general' is for the first time supposed to be 'systematically' brought to 'complete illumination' – with a 'preliminary reminder', a kind of guideline, for the purpose of leading the reader through the 'obscurity that is initially unavoidable in a path that is thus far entirely unexplored' (Kant 1998: A 98). Now it appears that most interpreters think that Kant has not really dispelled the obscurity relating to his presentation of the three syntheses. His procedure seems to be 'psychologistically' prejudiced insofar as he reflects on real developing constituent outputs instead of investigating the rules of evaluation for experience as determined in advance by science or ordinary language. Heidegger's famous lectures on Kant and the Problem of Metaphysics, which 'lay out' the 'threefold essential unity' of the original synthesis, set out to produce the 'proof of the inner temporal character of the transcendental power of imagination' and thus confirm this underlying prejudice when they attempt to intensify the obscurity within the 'abyss of finiteness' to the point of uncanniness (Heidegger 1990: 120f). The lectures confirm the underlying prejudice because they want to see the problem which Kant poses in the doctrine of the synthesis regarding the mediation of intuition and understanding treated in its appropriate – and necessarily obscure – context, which is that of 'actual time'.

Nevertheless, in the end Heidegger rejects the suspicion of psychologism regarding the Kantian synthesis doctrine. He can base his rejection on Husserl, who in his *Analysis of the Passive Synthesis* attests to phenomenological qualities in the 'system of transcendental syntheses' which Kant drafted 'with almost overwhelming geniality in the transcendental deduction of the first edition of the *Critique*' (Husserl 2001: 171, trans. mod.). According to Husserl, Kant at the very least succeeded in anticipating phenomenologically demonstrable constitutive structures for the 'genesis of a subjectivity', which is to say, structures which are accessible within experience – in the sense of what Husserl calls 'transcendental experience'. In *Difference and Repetition*, Deleuze for his part develops a model for three syntheses as passive syntheses (Deleuze 1994: 70ff.). He uses as his point of departure both Husserl's phenomenological interpretation of the 'psychological' aspects of the Kantian doctrine of powers and Heidegger's interpretation of the syntheses as temporal syntheses. However, he avoids the temptation to determine the meaning of the syntheses in terms of their mediational function. The abyss-like aspect of which Heidegger speaks still stems from the indefinite nature of a badly stated problem: the power of imagination as ability to synthesise is transfigured ontologically instead of being dissected phenomenologically. When Deleuze, together with Guattari, emphasises in *Anti-Oedipus* that the roots of his theory of the syntheses lie in Kantian thought, it immediately implies reference to its immanent character and removes itself at a critical distance from Heidegger's concept of transcendence.

> For a simple reason, we again make use of Kantian terminology. In what he termed the critical revolution, Kant intended to discover criteria immanent to understanding so as to distinguish the legitimate and the illegitimate use of the syntheses of consciousness. In the name of transcendental philosophy (immanence of criteria), he therefore denounced the transcendent use of syntheses such as appeared in metaphysics. (Deleuze and Guattari 1983: 74–5)

We will later go into detail on how Deleuze unfolds his concept of the passive synthesis in *Difference and Repetition*, and we will do it in a way that shows how he conflates the sense of 'transcendental' with the sense of 'immanent' (compare Chapter 8). Here we want to emphasise the criticism of empiricism which makes Kant's doctrine of synthesis attractive for Deleuze. In what follows we will therefore discuss the applicable text excerpts from the A-deduction by taking that latter perspective, but we will not completely neglect Deleuze's ultimate interpretation, especially where there are noticeable divergences from Heidegger's understanding of Kant.

Kant leads us into the problem of the synthesis, within the framework of the project relating to the deduction of the pure concepts of understanding, with the thesis that the objective reality of the categories rests on the fact that they 'must always contain the pure necessities *a priori* of a possible experience' (Kant 1998: A 96). Concepts, however, which cannot be related in advance to intuitions or to the 'field [. . .] of possible experience', are merely 'empty' logical forms through which nothing can be thought. The success of the deduction stands and falls with the answer to the question: how shall understanding relate to objects? The explication of the possibility of this relation requires, says Kant, that 'we must first assess [. . .] the transcendental constitution of the subjective sources that comprise the *a priori* foundations for the possibility of experience' (Kant 1998: A 97). The justification of the categories by proving 'that by means of them alone an object can be thought' only holds water if we can clarify as well why intuitions must also agree in advance with the logical use of understanding. At this point Kant begins to carry out the deduction in the first edition (Kant 1998: A 95ff.), somewhat on the level of the figural synthesis insofar as the 'synthesis of the manifold of sensible intuition *a priori*' by the power of imagination is taken as the object of investigation (see Kant 1998: B 151).

In the first section on the synthesis of apprehension in the intuition Kant begins by asserting that our representations in general belong to the inner sense as 'modifications of the mind' and that they are subordinate to time as the form of inner sense. So only if we begin with the assumption of a temporal differentiation among consecutive impressions is it possible that an empirical intuition which contains a manifold is given or apprehended as 'absolute unity' in a single moment. Thus, based on its temporal determination, apprehension involves synthetic processes which have always already organised the empirical data entering receptivity. In other words, apprehension is synthetically composed within itself. Kant characterises synthesis in the mode of apprehension as a dual activity: the running through and taking together of the manifold sensible impressions. As he writes later in summary form, the power of imagination must take up the manifold impressions and bring them together into an 'image', so that the appearances can be perceived consciously.

> The first thing that is given to us is appearance, which, if it is combined with consciousness, is called perception (without the relation to an at least possible consciousness appearance could never become an object of cognition for us, and would therefore be nothing for us [...]). But since every appearance contains a manifold, thus different perceptions by themselves are encountered dispersed and separate in the mind, a combination of them, which they cannot have in sense itself, is therefore necessary. There is thus an active faculty of the synthesis of this manifold in us, which we call imagination, and whose action exercised immediately upon perceptions I call apprehension. For the imagination is to bring the manifold of intuition into an image; it must therefore antecedently take up the impressions into its activity, i.e., apprehend them. (Kant 1998: A 120)

In an important footnote to this paragraph, Kant underlines the original aspect of his reflections on the synthesis of apprehension, namely that 'the imagination is a necessary ingredient of perception itself' (Kant 1998: A 120). If one starts from the premise that in the senses themselves impressions are only received but not able to be combined, the imagination is not restricted to its reproductive performance. Apprehension carries out its job neither in the mere reception of sense, nor in a synthesis that combines perceptions previously made ready in consciousness. The perceptions which are put in relation to one another in the reproductive imagination are namely themselves already the product of a precombinatory and imaginative synthesis. If Kant says that apprehension of the manifold as manifold implies that the given impressions are synthesised into a temporally differentiated 'unity of intuition', he is making clear that on this level the succession of impressions as such is in no way realistically presumed. Appearances (indeterminate objects of empirical intuition) can only come to consciousness or be apprehended as perceptions, so that an act of synthesis corresponds to the synopsis of the manifold in the intuition, an act that makes possible for the first time empirical relations of simultaneity and succession. The manifold aspect of sensations, which stands in a relationship to possible consciousness, must be subordinate to the formal necessity of the inner sense. Empirical synthesis of apprehension therefore presupposes a pure synthesis of apprehension: the empirical manifold can only then be perceived as such a one if it is taken up in a pure manifold form, which makes possible the temporally differentiated unity of the manifold as something that incorporates the manifold. Kant proceeds in all three cases (apprehension, reproduction, recognition) in such a way that he first presents the syntheses in their empirical form, after which he goes one step further and infers their silently presupposed transcendental form.

Kant's thoughts about the transcendental concept of apprehension, as developed in the context of the deduction of the concepts of understanding, reveal their special relevance when confronting Hume's scepticism and his theoretical foundations of perception. As Waxman can argue plausibly in his book *Kant's Model of the Mind*, it is precisely through his newly conceived doctrine of imagination that Kant succeeded in surmounting the Humean position and mastering his philosophical embarrassment as expressed most eloquently in the appendix to the third book of the *Treatise*. Crucial in this regard is that Kant, in distinction to Hume, has at his disposal the concept of a pre-reflective and pre-associative imagination, which revises Hume's realist assumptions of an immediate succession of empirical facts available to consciousness. Waxman's analyses again clarify that the essential power of the arguments that Kant uses in his critique of empiricism can only come to the forefront where the intellectualised standard-interpretation is evaded.

> Clearly, unless Kantian imagination can reach all the way down to the appearances themselves and lay claim to the flux of inner sense, his entire effort to surmount the challenge of Humean skepticism will be brought to nought. (Waxman 1991: 196)

The problematic core of Humean scepticism shows up in the incompatibility of the realist principle of succession with the atomist principle of difference and the associationist principle of connection. That means that the assumption of a real sequential progression of perceptions stands in conflict with the fundamental empirical premises which Hume cannot relinquish. In contrast, Kant opens up another way to solve the problem of time by conceiving of apprehension itself as a synthetic mode that codetermines the form of the inner sense. Anticipating Husserl's terminology, we could say that in the synthesis of apprehension Kant conceives of a retentive consciousness that has the singular role of comprehending manifold impressions as something, to run through them and to unify them within one moment. It follows that the succession of distinct perceptions are not given pre-imaginatively in consciousness, but rather can be brought to consciousness as a given only if the necessary, imaginatively driven, synthetic processes of apprehension run their course in the intuition.

> Kant's claim is that, without such a synthesis, the manifold offered in synopsis would not be the manifold of any representation; there could be no representation in us which contained an actual manifold. Since this is just to say that no manifold would ever be given in representation, the implication is that the manifold given via synopsis is a manifold only potentially. If, apart from synthesis of apprehension, there can be no representation of which impressions are the manifold – no consciousness in which any are gathered together – then how could one still speak of an actual manifold in synopsis? What is it we could characterise as manifold, when everything manifold-containing that is representational in nature is excluded? (Waxman 1991: 188)

Waxman extracts from the Kantian doctrine of the apprehension the decisive consequences for the criticism of empiricism. If, namely, it is true that consciousness of something is always also retentive consciousness, in which case there can quite simply be no pre-imaginative consciousness of something, then, contra Hume, it isn't possible to assert the actual existence of atomist and non-real interconnected perceptions. In addition, the association qua synthesis shifts into the genesis of perceptions itself and thus functions within the constitution of the given – the same given that is given for the reproductive imagination and its ability to make combinations. The manifold aspect contained in a representation can only be defined as virtual or potential manifold, whose partial moments are subrepresentationally connected in a rather special way. Deleuze will pick up on these transcendental implications, as we will later see. The fundamental proposition regarding the interiority of manifoldness, as it is held in transcendental empiricism, will reinscribe itself in essential ways onto the time-theoretical revolutions in Kantian thought as interpreted above.

Perceptions, according to Kant, are not sense-data but appearances which are brought to consciousness. No consciousness exists apart from apprehension. Thus it would be possible to understand the manifold as it is given in the synopsis, as well as the sensations given in sensibility, as 'moments of experience without consciousness' (Waxman 1991: 210). As Leibniz says in the *Monadology*, 'Here it is that the Cartesians especially failed, having taken no account of the perceptions of which we are not conscious' (Leibniz 1951: 535). In his refutation of Mendelssohn's proof of the persistence of the soul, Kant, for example, returns to this Leibnizian idea of 'dark perceptions' and thus inserts himself into a traditional lineage which runs counter to the corresponding Cartesian tendencies (the presumed inability to get behind the self-certainty of consciousness), even in classical empiricism. 'For even consciousness always has a degree [meaning intensive quantity; MR] which can always be diminished; consequently, so does the faculty of being conscious of oneself. [. . .] So there are infinitely many degrees of consciousness down to its vanishing' (Kant 1998: B 414–15).

Here Kant talks about 'obscure representations'. Their 'degree of consciousness [. . .] is not sufficient for memory' (Kant 1998: B 415). It is therefore important to introduce steps of difference into the simple scheme of 'conscious-unconscious'. Consciousness of perception results from the melting together of indistinct sense impressions produced by the productive imagination. That does not mean, however, that the perceptions produced in this way presume a conceptually regulated reproduction synthesis. Consciousness need not in principle be equated with consciousness of objects. Borrowing from the conceptual vocabulary of Kant's *Dissertation* (1770), the immediate object of sensed intuition, *apparentia*, can be distinguished from the object that corresponds to the sensed intuition, *phaenomenon* (for an example, see Longuenesse 1998: 25). As long as apprehension is only taken as pre-conceptual synthesis, which is sublated in a (threefold organised) whole of experience, as long as it is seen as the fundamental layer of apperception, both abstract and subject to extension, it is from the beginning subordinate to the intellectual model of recognition. If instead it can be considered separated from the categorially determined synthetic unity of experience, it is possible to claim for it an independent existence. The question of the unitary structure of the synthesis is posed here for the time being in the context of the 'inseparable combination' of apprehension with reproduction (Kant 1998: A 102).

According to Kemp Smith and most of the commentators of the A-deduction (Kemp-Smith 1918: 245; Paton 1936: I 361ff.), including Heidegger (Heidegger 1990: 116), the synthesis of apprehension presumes that of reproduction because otherwise the 'gathering together' of the manifold in a representation would not be explainable: the individual representations could not be held in consciousness, but would disappear one after the other as abruptly as they appear. If, on the other hand, the productive imagination with its effective temporal formation is harboured within apprehension, so that the perceptions always fill up a conscious presence and contain combinations among potential representations, then these perceptions take on a certain self-sufficiency, even though they can be understood as secondary to the object of reproduction. To the standard-model of the encapsulation of the syntheses from above, which stems from the original apperception, there is therefore an opposing conceptual model from below, which stems from the synopsis, that does not immediately unify the three syntheses, but arranges them in an asymmetric conditional entailment. That would mean that only the higher level syntheses presume the lower ones, not, however, the reverse. The two interpretive possibilities shall be explicated in what follows based on Kant's presentation of the reproductive synthesis in the A-deduction.

On the way to a completely determined concept of experience, Kant points out that the presentation of whole series of perceptions – necessary if we are to take into account their empirically detectable coherence – requires a reproductive ability of imagination. The synthesis of reproduction in imagination must therefore first follow the empirical law of association, because otherwise it would become arbitrary which representations place themselves in relation to one another. Kant's discussions become interesting when he begins to argue for an objective basis for association as a necessary requirement for its possibility. Kant's decisive argument against Hume asserts that the empirical reproductive imagination presumes the regularity of appearances, if it shall 'get to do anything suitable to its capacity' (Kant 1998: A101). To put it another way, the empirical law of reproduction can only claim founded objective validity if we can declare that the appearances themselves are subordinate to it. 'There must therefore be something that itself makes possible this reproduction of the appearances by being the *a priori* ground of a necessary synthetic unity of them' (Kant 1998: A 101). Otherwise, the associationality of perceptions would not be guaranteed, insofar as they might not be subordinated to the general rules of a thorough-going linking in their reproduction.

At first glance Kant presents two different 'strategies' by thinking about the objective ground of association or about a connection of the manifold based on *a priori* principles, either of which make the empirical synthesis of reproduction possible (see Longuenesse 1998: 38–44). In the first effort he refers to a pure synthesis of reproduction, in analogy to the empirico-transcendental double structure of the synthesis of apprehension. It is this pure synthesis 'which grounds even the possibility of all experience (as that which the reproducibility of the appearances necessarily presupposes)' (Kant 1998: A 101–2). This synthesis of reproducibility posits an original memory that must necessarily be presupposed so that empirical reproduction of representations is at all possible, for otherwise the representations which are supposed to be reproduced are not necessarily reproducible or necessarily retainable (in memory). The transcendental synthesis of reproduction therefore guarantees first that the apprehended perceptions can be retained.

> Now it is obvious that if I draw a line in thought, or think of the time from one noon to the next, or even want to represent a certain number to myself, I must necessarily first grasp one of these manifold representations after another in my thoughts. But if I were always to lose the preceding representations [...] from my thoughts and not reproduce them when I proceed to the following ones, then no whole representation [...] could ever arise. (Kant 1998: A 102)

Very few interpreters of the *Critique of Pure Reason* have been able to do much with this answer that Kant gives to the problem of the objective foundation of factual regularity in the nature of things. There even seems to be evidence that Kant himself gives little weight to his reflections, in A 100–2, on the transcendental synthesis of reproduction. In section A 119ff., for example, where he once again works through the 'connection of the understanding with the appearances' 'from beneath' with a recapitulating reference to the construction of the three syntheses as described just a bit earlier, the objective ground of association is placed under the concept of the *affinity* of appearances, which is in turn easily identified with the principle of the unity of apperception. With this second version Kant guides his venture in the criticism of association into settled tracks, insofar as the presupposition of the regularity of the world of appearances need only be justified by means of the proof of the objective reality of the concepts of understanding. The primacy of the second reading is endorsed by the B-deduction when, without the detour through the reproduction problem, it leads directly from apprehension to its synthetic unity in apperception.

Following Heidegger's interpretation of the transcendental synthesis in the mode of reproduction as pure imitation, 'to the extent that it opens up in general the horizon of the possible attending-to, the having-been-ness, and so [...] "forms" this "after" as such', Deleuze also lingers at first at that point in Kant's train of thought where the transition into the synthesis of recognition is still in abeyance (Heidegger 1990: 125, Deleuze 1994: 78–9, and below: Chapter 8). What he's looking for is a way to think of a transcendental-virtual memory in connection with the formation, in the synthesis of reproduction, of the temporal horizon of the past, a memory that, as time-theoretical 'foundation', comes into play not only with respect to association or empirical reproduction but also – as we shall see – with respect to apprehension and recognition. To get there Deleuze can glean support from Husserl and, above all, Bergson, who obtained fruitful results by observing how Kant, counter to classical empiricism, went deeper into the problem of the constitution of experience in the name of a 'critical empiricism'. These connections will be explored more rigorously in the following chapters. Right now it will have to suffice to say that although Deleuze picks up essential motives of the Kantian doctrine of the synthesis, he also criticises emphatically their structural framework. Blatantly, for example, the integrated arrangement of the three syntheses, that terminate in the 'last and highest' synthesis of recognition and 'that make possible the formal unity of experience' (Kant 1998: A 125), represent an epistemologically predetermined ideal image of experience to which even Heidegger, in his analyses in his book on Kant, still remains committed. That is very clear when he adopts without question the Kantian method of doubling transcendentally the presupposed empirical syntheses. In this regard he misses completely the truly transcendental structures that can be arrived at phenomenologically only by means of bracketing the natural setting. As Heidegger self-critically admits in later years, the natural setting asserts itself with particular force in the banal acts of recognition relating to 'representational thought'. But in his Kant book he still follows the Kantian procedure all the way into the region of 'recognosis'.

> It has thus been shown: what emerged as the third synthesis in the characterisation of the empirical genesis of conceptual development is in fact the first, i.e., the synthesis which in the first place directs the other two characterised above. It pops up in advance of them, so to speak. [. . .] It explores in advance and is 'watching out for' what must be held before us as the same in order that the apprehending and reproducing syntheses in general can find a closed, circumscribed field of beings within which they can attach to what they bring forth and encounter, so to speak, and take them in stride as beings. (Heidegger 1990: 127)

According to Heidegger, the first two syntheses are 'already oriented in advance toward the being as something which has presence in sameness', since 'a unifying (synthesis) of the being with respect to its sameness' lies at their foundation (Heidegger 1990: 126). To this empirical synthesis of recognition within the concept corresponds, therefore, a pure synthesis which, as expected by Heidegger, is responsible for the formation of the horizon of future. He interprets the future horizon of pure identification as a conceptual 'horizon of being-able-to-hold-something-before-us in general' with respect to which being lets itself be reproduced and identified (Heidegger 1990: 127). Deleuze, in contrast, will conceive of the active syntheses of reproduction and recognition as derived empirical forms and will situate them on the foundation of the previous passive syntheses of apprehension and memory. Thus the third time synthesis will completely escape the model of representation: it refers to a chancy, aleatoric future, and summarily dumps the notion of the past as foundational instance based in a logic of reflection which, together with its categorial framing requirements, is supposed to accompany all my representations and essentially is able to anticipate.

To close this section, we will again make clear, based on the synthesis of recognition within the concept, how Kant finds the transcendental ground of reproduction in the original apperception and in this way allows the three syntheses to be completely absorbed in a single unified form. We have noted that the representations which are supposed to be empirically reproduced are only then reproducible if they are on the one hand appropriately held in memory and on the other hand stand in certain ordered relationships, relationships which make possible the application of the reproductive imagination. However, according to Kant, individual representations that are to be reproduced can only be put in series if they can be identified as reproductions of something = X.

> Without consciousness that that which we think is *the very same* as what we thought a moment before, all reproduction in the series of representations would be in vain. For it would be a new representation in our current state, which would not belong at all to the act through which it had been gradually generated, and its manifold would never constitute a whole, since it would lack the unity that only consciousness can obtain for it. (Kant 1998: A 103, italics MR)

Within the concept of the object, individual representations can be combined with one another and can be brought into one synthetic unity, which corresponds to the formal unity of consciousness. Cognition of an object therefore happens when the synthesis of the manifold of intuition is regulated conceptually in a single consciousness, and that means the reproduction takes place from the beginning with respect to a possible, conceptualisable object. The transcendental requirement of the necessary synthesis of representations into an object as thought in a concept is the numerical unity of an original consciousness, 'without which it would be impossible to think of any object for our intuitions; for the latter is nothing more than the something for which the concept expresses such a necessity of synthesis' (Kant 1998: A 106). Consciousness of the generic identity of the representations reproduced in a series does not result from their empirical conformity to regulations but only from their conceptually regulated and object-related summation. This act of conceptualisation presupposes a pure consciousness of the unity of the synthesis carried out within itself. As we know, Kant characterises this non-empirical, self-identical consciousness as the transcendental unity of apperception. But we must realise that the transcendental consciousness doesn't produce itself, but only wins unity with itself on cognitive completion of the connection of the manifold, as far as it constitutes itself as identical within the synthetic act.

> Thus the original and necessary consciousness of the identity of oneself is *at the same time* a consciousness of an equally necessary unity of the synthesis of all appearances in accordance with concepts, i.e., in accordance with rules that not only make them necessarily reproducible, but also thereby determine an object for their intuition, i.e., the concept of something in which they are necessarily connected; for the mind could not possibly think of the identity of itself in the manifoldness of its representations, and indeed think this *a priori*, if it did not have before its eyes the identity of its action, which subjects all synthesis of apprehension [. . .] to a transcendental unity [. . .] (Kant 1998: A 108, italics MR)

It is therefore evident that Kant subjects the synthesis of reproduction to the epistemological programme of recognition as it keeps up with its given task of representing a totality of experience. Actually one can say that the reproduction of a series of past representations can only take place if it lines itself up from the beginning with its prescribed goal of making possible the cognition of objects. Hoppe therefore rightly speaks of the 'prognostic sense' of the synthesis of recognition, which, through its thematic prescience, makes necessary the conceptual regulation of the synthesis of reproduction (see Hoppe 1983: 186). The objective ground of association that Kant champions in the section on the synthesis of reproduction can thus first be defined with finality on the plane of recognition, namely dependent on a transcendental synthesis which borrows from the categories the *a priori* laws of reproducibility. In the end, therefore, we see again that Kant plays out his reflections in opposition to empiricism against the backdrop of a dogmatic and intellectualised concept of experience, so that one has to agree with Paton when he asserts: 'We are dealing with only one synthesis, and not with three' (Paton 1936: I 376).

PART II

From Phenomenon to Event

The systematic construction of transcendental empiricism is carried out from the double perspective of a transcendental critique of empiricism and an empiricist critique of transcendentalism. Decisive impulses for a fruitful compression of these perspectives come from Husserl and Heidegger. In line with his new conception of *genetic* phenomenology, Husserl, in a positive inspiration, reaches back to the Kantian concept of the transcendental synthesis, which – as we have seen – stands in the problematic centre of a critical empiricism. Husserl's *Analyses of the Passive Synthesis* are appropriated quite literally in the second chapter of *Difference and Repetition*. The characteristic passivity of the syntheses expresses Husserl's empiricist motivation. For him the active synthesis, as the production of understanding, rests on earlier associational syntheses that are not regulated categorially. Husserl's thoughts on the *genealogy of logic* reflect his relationship to Humean philosophy.

In contrast, Heidegger loses sight of the empiricist context when, in connection with Husserl's analyses, he treats the ontological underpinnings of experience. Heidegger's anti-empiricist predilection corresponds to his secret alliance with a 'Being' that withdraws from experience's plane of immanence. Nevertheless, in the following discussion I will try to develop with and against Heidegger the problem of thought's temporalisation. The insights in Heidegger's critique of metaphysics and subjectivity cannot be ignored. It will turn out that Heidegger's late philosophy should be taken seriously in its attempts to be self-critical and that it announces a philosophy of difference that distances itself from the ritualising character of his allegiance to Being. Deleuze has been particularly influenced by Heidegger's analyses, in his book on Kant, regarding the temporal character of the transcendental syntheses of imagination, as well as by his later critique of the onto-theological determination of representational thought which is supported by a 'post-metaphysical' ontology of difference.

In this Part, the phenomenological preparation for transcendental empiricism will be reconstructed in two steps. First Husserl's efforts in the field of transcendental phenomenology will be examined with an eye to their influence on Deleuze's concept of experience. I follow with a discussion of Heidegger, first looking at his much debated interpretation of *transcendental aesthetics* and *analytics* in the *Critique of Pure Reason* in the 1920s, and then at his critique of representational and onto-theological thought, undertaken in later years, culminating in the 'leap forward' into the event.

4

Husserl's Concept of Passive Synthesis

> A passive synthesis is a contradiction in terms if the synthesis is a process of composition, and if the passivity consists in being the recipient of multiplicity [...] What we meant by passive synthesis was that we make our way into multiplicity, but that we do not synthesise it. Now temporalisation satisfies by its very nature these two conditions. (Merleau-Ponty 1962: 496)

The fact that none of Gilles Deleuze's many books promises in its title a study of phenomenology should not lead to over-hasty conclusions. Clearly Deleuze had strong opinions about Heidegger. There are plenty of connections to Husserl as well that are just as adequately documented. We could start by distinguishing two groups of texts that refer directly to Husserl. First, at the end of the 1960s, Deleuze presents his position regarding Husserl's philosophy above all in *Logic of Sense* (see for example Series 14 and 16), but also in *Difference and Repetition*. Then, in the mid-1980s, he undertakes an examination of Foucault's critical relation to phenomenology (Deleuze 1988b: 110ff.), which leads, finally (together with Guattari), to a 'prospective' conceptual analysis of phenomenological thought in *What Is Philosophy?*

At first glance Deleuze's connection to Husserl's phenomenology seems to lean in the direction of disapproval, for Deleuze sympathises fundamentally with Heidegger's critical considerations regarding *representative thought*, considerations that can also be directed at phenomenology itself. Foucault demonstrates this in exemplary fashion for Deleuze when, following Heidegger, he finds the mark of logical reflection of representative thought in the '*empirico-transcendental doublet*'. The *prima facie* rejection of phenomenology, especially evident in Deleuze's later texts, will have to be relativised. Often it is the implicit affinities that provoke critical distance. Deleuze stresses his negative judgement of phenomenology because, *in spite of all points in common*, he wants to stress where he differs. Therefore it is not surprising that Deleuze, in his book on Foucault, is rather more interested in how phenomenology self-critically radicalises itself –

and thus bumps into its own *difference philosophical* boundaries. The origin of a structuralist philosophy of difference is, to be precise, essentially related to (post-)phenomenological reflection. So the first impression of a general disapproval, as suggested in the work of Deleuze, needs to be specified. Phenomenology possesses through and through, already with Husserl, self-critical tendencies as well as concrete benefits of research in the area of 'transcendental experience' that do not harmonise with its dogmatic image. Deleuze is well aware of this ambiguity in Husserl's thought and has expressly helped put it into words, especially in the earlier texts. In the *Logic of Sense* Husserl functions as the exemplary transcendental philosopher, pretty much taking over the role that Kant plays in *Difference and Repetition*, which is why one can perfectly well speak of the *ambiguity of phenomenology* in this context.

Deleuze is therefore quite prepared to attest to Husserl's having descended into the transcendental regions of sense. In fact, in the *Logic of Sense* Deleuze adopts the intentional analysis that leads to the determination of the *noema*. In what follows I will sketch out what this theoretical appropriation looks like. Husserl's intention to determine experience immanently calls for the method of *phenomenological reduction*, which problematises the natural view of the world by making it the object of philosophical reflection. This alienation technique makes it possible to describe experience as such with respect to its structural origination. Following critically the Kantian model of transcendental cognition, Husserl attempts to demonstrate the conditions of normal acts of recognition in the experiential process itself. In this way he undermines the subjective logic pertaining to acts that bestow meaning and takes away from them the 'sense' that from now on is effected on a pre-egoistic plane. When in *Ideas 1* Husserl speaks of sense as 'the noematic "object in its modal setting"' (Husserl 1999: 367), then he talks about the intentional mode of consciousness in general. This transplanting of sense marks the transition from the natural stance into the transcendental: the perceptual *noema* results from a process of 'becoming phenomenon' or from the reduction to 'immanent' experiences, as otherwise required only in empiricism (see Murphy 1980: 10). It is true, however, that the *noema* characterises a *quasi-objective* status of sense's Being (*Seinssinn*), for consciousness, which sustains itself in the catharsis of pure evidences, is originally only consciousness of something. Thus sense lies in a precedential identity which grounds the natural experience and its subsequent explanation. Husserl finds himself in twilight when he questions the positive components of experience regarding their self-constitution, and he does so specifically by declining to make use of uninvestigated opinions on the issue. This shifting of sense into the transcendental which Husserl attempts had to please Deleuze. For in this way the variable genesis of experience can be determined without danger of confusing the transcendental constitutional process with the empirical results.

> When Husserl reflects on the 'perceptual *noema*', or 'the sense of perception', he at once distinguishes it from the physical object, from the psychological or 'lived', from mental representations and from logical concepts. He presents it as an [...] incorporeal entity, without physical or mental existence [...] – pure 'appearance'. The real tree (the *denotatum*) can burn [...] This is not the case, however, for the *noema* 'tree'. [...] When therefore Husserl says that the *noema* is the perceived such as it appears in a presentation, [...] we ought not understand that the *noema* involves a sensible given or quality; it rather involves an ideational objective unity as the intentional correlate of the act of perception. [...] Is the *noema* anything more than a pure *event* – the tree occurrence, [...] a surface effect? (Deleuze 1990b: 20–1)

Deleuze considers the noematic sense to be 'something' that precedes as phenomenon the object of consciousness; it cannot be identified with the external object, nor can it be pure psychic experience. Husserl's conjecture of a *neutral* and *inscrutable* sense, that is neither absorbed by propositions nor merged with things but functions *in between*, is integrated by Deleuze into his theory of sense paradoxes (see Deleuze 1990b: 94–108). On the other hand, Deleuze notes – in spite of all the advantages of the phenomenological position – Husserl's definitive tendency to understand the noematic nucleus as the formal *identity pole* of an object-in-general. In this Husserl himself is subject to essential postulates of representative thought as analysed by Deleuze: idealist tendencies pacify, as it were, his radical philosophical departures. Thus Husserl conceives intentionality along the lines of Kantian *apperception*, which sets in advance a transcendental object that, as isolated opposite, unifies the subject's powers of comprehension.

> Henceforth, the relation between sense and object is the natural result of the relation between noematic predicates – a something = x which is capable of functioning as their support or principle of unification. This thing = x is not at all therefore like a [...] point zero presupposing nothing of what it necessarily engenders. It is rather the Kantian object

= x, where 'x' means 'in general'. It has in relation to sense an extrinsic, rational relation of transcendence, and gives itself, ready-made, the form of denotation, just as sense, as a predicable generality, was giving itself, as ready-made, the form of signification. (Deleuze 1990b: 97)

According to Deleuze, although Husserl comes upon the genuine domain of the transcendental, he makes it – as Kant did before him – dependent on impermissible empirical presuppositions which are borrowed from the element of common sense. The model of perception at the base of Husserl's scientifically ambitious methodology corresponds to his consciousness-directed philosophical background. But if phenomenology raises natural perception and its conditions to the norm, then, says Deleuze, they remain caught up in the scheme of recognition that handicaps their ability to construct concepts in a corresponding way.

In *What Is Philosophy?* Deleuze takes up again this dogmatic side of phenomenology's ambitious programme when he treats their concepts – and particularly *doxa* and *protodoxa* (*Urdoxa*) – as *functions* whose variables are experiences immanent to consciousness, that is, perceptions and affections. In this case phenomenology makes itself at home in the life-world (*Lebenswelt*), which is supposed to become the foundation and 'ground floor' of the sciences.

> It is necessary therefore to discover at the very heart of the immanence of the lived to a subject, that subject's acts of transcendence *capable of constituting new functions of variable or conceptual references*. [...] Numerous phenomenological concepts [...] are not only experiental contents that are immanent to the solipsist subject but references of the transcendental subject to the lived. [...] They are not merely empirical judgements or opinions but proto-beliefs, *Urdoxa*, original opinions as propositions. (Deleuze 1994: 142, trans. mod.)

Deleuze stresses that the phenomenologically conceived immanence of the stream of consciousness is immanent to a transcendental subject that expresses itself in three essential transcendent functions: in the constitution of the object world, of the intersubjective world of others, and of the scientific culture world. Precisely the *traversing* of immanence, which should be immanent only to itself, characterises, according to Deleuze, a deformation of life or the life-world which becomes evident in the hierarchisation of differential structures. Only by putting real ordering and power relationships in parentheses can pre-predicative, everyday-intuitive experience make up that fundamental experience which – modelled epistemologically – is capable of bearing the foundational schematic of a philosophically grounded science. Yet, working parenthetically, Husserl's phenomenology cannot succeed in carrying through its radical intuition in an unambiguous way. In the eyes of Deleuze, it remains a complex construction with many dogmatic trapdoors and blindfolds.

However, these dogmatic aspects do not govern Husserl's whole phenomenological project. For the formulation of the question that we are undertaking here, namely how phenomenology contributes systematically to the development and critique of empiricism, it is of particular interest to reconstruct the fruitful impulses that began the project. According to the already expressed suspicion that for Deleuze phenomenological themes operate mainly tacitly, our task is to get at the systematically relevant questions, independent of explicit comments to be found in his books. Nevertheless, the following examination of Husserl remains oriented on Deleuze and his philosophical intentions. The theory of the passive syntheses, which gives contour to the Deleuzian concept of repetition, already points by its name in the direction of Husserl's familiar *Analyses* and their implicit transformation of the Kantian doctrine of synthesis. Deleuze's often undertaken parallelisation of the concepts of manifold or multiplicity in Husserl and Bergson, with its distinctly affirmative tone, falls into this context as well.

So in what follows I will *first* examine the empiricist relevance of phenomenological discoveries by presenting Husserl's initial steps regarding *genetic phenomenology* together with a re-evaluation of the problem of passivity. Husserl's positive use of the concept of transcendental synthesis since that time leads *subsequently* to a re-examination of Kantian philosophy to see what effect Husserl has on it with the formation of *his* concept of the transcendental. In this part I will make the ambiguity of transcendental cognition understandable using the methodological difference between reconstructive and intuitive procedures. *Third*, Husserl's relationships to Hume and empiricism will try to get at the profits of scepticism, which result from the critique of rationalist premises of transcendental-philosophical thought. Hume's theory of association gives Husserl the possibility to extend the investigations of his *genealogy of logic*, although with reservations thanks to his non-acceptance of the empiric-psychologistic viewpoints of science. Under the rubrics 'activity' and 'passivity' we will treat the phenomenological formation of two kinds of syntheses which the characteristic of intentionality precipitates. Thus, *fourth*, it will become clear that the dichotomous partition (passive-active) will have to be differentiated, insofar as temporality, as form of synthesis, is not yet available to passive syntheses. *Finally*, the conceptual determination of the three syntheses points in the direction of Husserl's theory of affection, which gives a plausible argument that the non-synthetic model of receptivity needs critical modification. With his reflections on the gradation of affection, Husserl passes onto the transcendental terrain of an empiricist philosophy.

Beginnings of Genetic Phenomenology

In the case of Edmund Husserl, the 'work on the phenomenon' took on prodigious dimensions. In the archives in Louvain his remnant manuscripts total more than 40,000 pages, written in Gabelsberger shorthand and not yet fully transcribed, to say nothing of being published. This huge mountain of material throws a long shadow over the research landscape: as a memorial to phenomenology it recalls the provisional nature of its results. Considering the wealth of Husserlian works, we will have to be content here to focus on very limited excerpts, namely on the beginnings of genetic phenomenology, as documented above all in volume 11 of the German collected works, in English as *Analyses Concerning Passive and Active Synthesis* (Husserl 2001).

It was around the year 1918 that Husserl began to develop and practice genetic analysis to correct deficits in his previous studies, using a completely new research perspective. This new approach makes visible the *marginal* status of passive genesis, which precedes the abstract division of the inner and outer worlds or of spontaneity and receptivity – allowing Husserl to question his own Cartesian habits of thought. Elmar Holenstein, in his book *Phenomenology of Association*, makes the point that, together with the development of genetic analysis of intentionality, Husserl also raises the theme of association as a passive kind of constitution – and he does so by introducing that strangely paradoxical-sounding term 'passive intention'.

> Although passive pre-givens are not proffered in the manner of acts, they nevertheless present a genetic event and are not simply singular contents or static relations received by consciousness. Passivity cannot be reduced to statically available givens. Instead, it refers to a genetic process of constitution. Husserl speaks expressly of a 'passive production'. (Holenstein 1972: 216–17, see also Husserl 2001: 276)

Husserl's Concept of Passive Synthesis

Passivity should clearly not be confused with receptivity. Genetic phenomenology differentiates itself from a merely static one by making itself at home in a new problem area, namely one in which passivity is understood as constitutive 'substratum' for all occurrences of consciousness. This is how it mediates the processes of becoming and habituation of those parts of experience which are not treated in the static description of simple apperceptions.

As soon as Husserl awards passivity an internal *synthetic* role, he discovers the transcendental verticality of a 'hidden process of understanding'. In this connection Husserl is reminded of Kant and transcendental synthesis. It is the genetic perspective that allows Husserl to affirm the *productive* character of the Kantian synthesis, as shown by Iso Kern in his standard work, *Husserl and Kant* (see Kern 1964: 259). It almost seems as though Husserl recalled Kant and his doctrine of the productive imagination to establish his new position in the first place. Husserl writes the following in the first edition of his lectures on genetic logic:

> It is of historical interest to recall here Kant's brilliant insights that are expressed in his profound but obscure doctrine of the synthesis of productive imagination, above all in his transcendental deduction from the first edition of the *Critique of Pure Reason*. When Kant [...] speaks of a productive synthesis, in our view that is nothing other than what we call passive constitution. (Husserl 2001: 410)

As we shall see, Husserl attempts to interpret with greater clarity the 'profundity' of Kantian transcendental philosophy from inside the framework of his research into genetic constitution. Precisely the productive character of passive 'output', which cannot be explained in a purely static way, grounds representational activity, which then bears 'the output's gain' – as Husserl puts it – 'as ready-made havings'. In this way genetic phenomenology proves to be a truly transcendental phenomenology. The doubtfulness of what is present, as revealed in the phenomenological reduction, brings the genetic dimension of experience to the fore. What is statically present as a resultant is seen in genetic reflection as the product of passive syntheses. In his *Cartesian Meditations* Husserl writes:

> In any case, anything built by activity necessarily presupposes, as the lowest level, a passivity that gives something beforehand; and, when we trace anything built actively, we run into constitution by passive generation. The 'ready-made' object that confronts us in life as an existent mere physical thing [...] is given, with the originality of the 'it itself', in the

synthesis of a passive experience. [. . .] It is owing to an essentially necessary genesis that I [. . .] can experience a physical thing. With good reason it is said that in infancy we had to learn to see physical things, and that such modes of consciousness of them had to precede all others genetically. (Husserl 1960: 78–9)

Reconstruction and Intuition

The fundamental problem relative to transcendental philosophy consists in the proof (or evidence) of an immanent logic of experience. Transcendental reflection, which tries to come up with this proof, finds itself in the dilemma of a double dependency – it faces empirical findings as well as intellectual self-production of experience – and must for better or worse reconcile this conflict. It seems the dilemma can be handled methodically if philosophy takes on the task of letting experience come round to itself: the circularity would then be scientifically legitimate insofar as the experience from which one starts must subsequently and essentially be determined. With this in mind, however, already *Kant*, in his transcendental analytics, takes recourse in the unity of experience, which has to be presupposed as the guiding thread of the deduction. The imposition of unity suspends the possibility of prior, tacitly occurring cognitive processes that would have to be described using the vocabulary of a transcendental psychology and signals that the matter to be mediated in the area of synthesis and schematism is undertaken after the fact based on abstract justification. All this has tempted many interpreters of Kant's revision of the deduction chapter to see it as a self-critical reworking of the structure of the three syntheses to rid it of suspected psychologisms. Husserl, who, just like Kant, rejects any kind of mingling of the transcendental and the empirical, believes nevertheless that he can detect in Kantian thought an insidious dependency on the psychology of Locke and Hume. In his opinion Kant regards the empirical all too traditionally (following classical empiricism) – and abruptly makes an about-face into the field of pure reason, putting his faith in the standards of scientific claims to truth.

> Because he [Kant] understands inner perception in this [. . .] psychological sense and because, warned by Hume's skepticism, he fears every recourse to the psychological as an absurd perversion of the genuine problem of the understanding, Kant gets involved in his mythical concept-formation. He forbids his readers to transpose the results of his regressive procedure into intuitive concepts, forbids every attempt to carry out a progressive

construction which begins with [...] self-evident intuitions and proceeds through truly self-evident individual steps. (Husserl 1970a: 115)

Thus the naturalist preconceptions of psychology cause even Kant rashly to give up searching within experience for structural characteristics that might not be categorially preordained. Husserl demands instead – to put it sharply – a reorganisation of the transcendental method: it should no longer rest in the categorial unity of experience, which just barely allows its genetic foundations to be reconstructed regressively as *pre-subjective* and abstract moments, but rather it should orient itself toward elucidating these foundations intuitively and phenomenologically as concrete *experience of experience*.

Kant's precept, to demonstrate the validity of scientific findings based on experience, is dependent on its adequate rationalisation. This results from the regressive analysis of the necessary conditions for any possible experience, which thereby are divested of any *genetic* relevance. But as we have seen, we need a concept of experience that allows it to be thought as emergent. The processes of becoming precede their results, which in turn distort them, which is why the results as such need to be made thematic and questioned regarding their origin. Husserl reflects this *questionability* of experience by 'bracketing' the natural attitude in a philosophical way. It is the phenomenological method of *reduction* that characterises Husserl's concept of the transcendental, opening new paths from reconstruction to intuition. It remains to be seen whether on these paths the *paradox* of transcendental reflection, that is to say, the circular procedure of founding cognition, can be sublated in a good – not ruinous – ambiguity. Husserl's persistence in avoiding under all circumstances the mixture of the transcendental and the empirical anticipates the commandment of difference to impugn the correctness of any fabrication of empirico-rational conceptual doublets.

Husserl conceives of the phenomenological reduction 'through and through' as falling back to transcendental subjectivity. The phenomenological version of transcendental philosophy begins with the famous change in attitude, the methodologically founded suspension of the natural-objective valuation of Being, which connects with the Kantian version insofar as it deepens and radicalises the latter through an immanent critique of how consciousness experiences the world. The promised radicalisation shows many faces, but they all focus on the Kantian inability to really suspend every empirical presumption. Husserl repeatedly asserts that the leftover dogmatic presuppositions of Kant's critique of reason come from the natural attitude toward the world. The essential function of the transcendental reduction is protecting the work of philosophy in principle from the destructive consequences of a *metabasis eis allo genos* – that is, from the contamination of transcendental experience with positive assumptions of objective-natural knowledge. Phenomenology guarantees this protection thanks to the *epoché*, that is to say, by getting involved in experience to the best of its knowledge without any reservations, thus describing it in all its peculiarities. 'According to Husserl, it is through the *epoché* that we first attain the world as a phenomenon' (Zahavi 2001: 6). Husserl reaches the decisive point of his Kant-critique when he calls for a method of intuitive exhibiting (*intuitiv-aufweisend*) to replace Kant's practice of mere regressive reconstruction.

> Kant's critique of reason remains far removed from a transcendental philosophy as a final founding and final founded science. [. . .] The regressively methodological practice plays for him the greatest role: how is pure mathematics possible, how is pure science, etc. [. . .] [This] is a constructive thought process [. . .] and not a way of making clear the constitutive achievements of consciousness by starting from the bottom in a step by step intuitive progression of exhibiting, and moving in all directions available to reflection. The innermost sides, so to speak, of constitutive consciousness are hardly touched by Kant; the sensible phenomena which concern him are already constituted units, with a very rich structure that never undergoes systematic analysis. [. . .] No doubt there is much to be seen in the way of shapes in pure subjectivity and important layers are uncovered in it, but everything floats in a mysterious milieu, the product of still mythic, transcendental powers. (Husserl 1956: 197–8)

The 'innermost sides' mentioned by Husserl refer in particular to the constitution of the sensible life-world as exhibited in genetic research and the immanent consciousness of time which still lies ahead regarding the problems of scientific objectivity. Husserl rejects critical *aprioristics* and its regressive approach insofar as it contains speculations about concepts and procedures that cannot be intuitively justified. The latter brings some interpreters to suggest that Husserl's phenomenology should not be classified as transcendental.

This strategy, based on simple solutions, falls short, however, because it is a one-sided view of Kant's philosophy and/or attributes to Husserl's project a misconceived connection with tradition. Yet we learn precisely from Husserl that Kant's transcendental philosophy is ambiguous – and Husserl himself runs the risk of standing in its shadow if he should fail to elucidate this ambiguity completely. Husserl refers often to Kant's investigations, which 'in fact take place on the absolute ground of transcendental subjectivity' (Husserl 1956: 197). These concrete analyses are certainly in line with phenomenological interpretations, but, says Husserl, they are not systematic and by right should be treated as such. As we have already seen, Husserl not only forces Kant's verdict on empirical psychology, but also considers his conception of the transcendental synthesis as a positive draft 'of certain syntheses carried out in immanence' which are assumed for 'constitutive world problems' (Husserl 2001, 171). Husserl discovers the unavoidable ambiguity in the doctrine of the synthesis, which Kant presents 'from beneath' and 'from above' with a view toward its figural and intellectual type.

With this in mind, Husserl turns to the chapter on the *transcendental deduction*, which he acknowledges as the path to the systematic disclosure of the conditions regarding the possibility of experience. The importance for Husserl of this chapter of Kantian metaphysics consists in the fact that it implements for the first time the necessary fallback to transcendental consciousness – 'particularly under the title "subjective deduction" (in the A version of the *Critique of Pure Reason*)' (Husserl 1956: 281). Following up on the *transcendental question* raised by Kant regarding the conceptual ingredients of experience, Husserl reaches for the ontologically *a priori* aspects of the life-world in terms of the conditions of possible cognition, or, more generally, seeks the ontological structures of experience in terms of their relation to the constitutive subject and its productive syntheses. In this regard it has been said that Husserl takes the discovery of the synthesis to be Kant's actual Copernican stroke of genius. Husserl himself puts it this way in a lecture on Kant's relation to German idealism:

> Luckily, Kant's theory is better than Kant himself knows. [. . .] Just one example: Kant comes across the intentionality that builds up in steps in consciousness [. . .]; he doesn't merely designate this as 'synthesis', but already tries to classify the steps, which represents a theoretical beginning that will turn out to be seminal for an entire science. (Husserl 1956: 404)

However, the phenomenological reach of the Kantian doctrine of synthesis won't be seen as long as the regressive formulation of the following question dominates the project of transcendental philosophy: 'How must a subject be constituted *a priori* if nature is to be objectively determined?' On a path 'from above', in the objective realisation of the deduction, the foundational task of concrete descriptions of consciousness cannot be carried out, which is why it remains in the 'mythical' darkness of speculative concepts. 'The transcendental deduction's path "from above" for deducing ontological laws is contrasted by Husserl to "the path from below", which he calls the direct, most obvious and best way. It is for him the path to phenomenology' (Kern 1964: 161). The path 'from below' begins by opening up the world of experience with genetic analyses, so that the constituent syntheses and laws become intuitively accessible. Husserl prefers this Kantian perspective in analysing the lowest levels of what constitutes experience, that is, the apprehending perception and its reproductive aspects, rather than casually 'deriving' the objectivity of experience from the uppermost unity of apperception. That is why Husserl also refers specifically to the *figural* synthesis and not to the *intellectual* one, since the former is capable of composing a manifold of given space-time representations in view of their objective unity (see Husserl 2001: 212).

Husserl repeats these synthesis-related ambivalences in his lecture on the 'doubly functioning understanding':

> An example of a great discovery – a merely preliminary discovery – by Kant is the 'doubly functioning understanding' in respect to nature: on the one hand, understanding interpreting itself, in explicit self-reflection, as normative laws, and, on the other hand, understanding ruling in concealment, i.e., ruling as constitutive of the 'intuitively given surrounding world' ['anschauliche Umwelt'] as always already developed and always further developing meaning-configuration. This discovery could never be actually grounded or even be fully comprehensible in the manner of the Kantian theory, i.e., as a result of his merely regressive method. In the 'transcendental deduction' of the first edition of the *Critique of Pure Reason* Kant makes an approach to a direct grounding, one which descends to the original sources, only to break off again almost at once without arriving at the genuine problems of foundation which are to be opened up from this supposedly psychological side. (Husserl 1970a: 103–4, trans. mod.)

Husserl's concept of the 'doubly functioning understanding' makes it possible to think proto-logical structures in the pre-representational region of passive syntheses. Particularly in the empiricist field of immanence one has to assume a synthetic performance by the functioning understanding, even if it escapes notice, so that the life-world experience can be structured. For the mere occurrence of sensed data and data collections does not explain our immediate perception of things. Husserl therefore requires a doubly functioning understanding based on Kant to show that pre-predicated constitution relies on the same categorial functions that work in actual conceptual thinking. In this way philosophically exhibited structures of the pre-scientific life-world can be set out beforehand that their *fundamental* scientific status will later guarantee. It is this phenomenological tendency of the Kantian theory of synthesis, which announces itself in the hidden operations of transcendental understanding, that is so attractive for Husserl. Nevertheless, a line of development leading to the *genealogy of logic* in Husserl's sense emerges only vaguely within this tendency.

Kant has to disregard systematically the possibility of passive syntheses because the general and necessary conformities to natural laws can only be justified through spontaneous sources of understanding – and on no account can be perceived as intelligible evidences. His rigorous rejection of empiricism tips the scales. Husserl, on the other hand, moves in the explicitly ontological forefield of cognition by taking as his theme the problem of genesis on the plane of habit, in the area of associations and affections, and this plane precedes the simple alternative of passive sensibility and active force of understanding. In his critique of the *transcendental aesthetic*, Husserl makes much of the subject of passive synthesis. Accordingly, the syntheses that Kant treats in the analytic must be carried over into the (transcendental) aesthetic. For both temporality as well as the capability of being affected are internally synthetic in nature and reveal pure receptivity as a fictional limit. If anywhere, then here is the place where Deleuze saw possibilities of jumping in, possibilities which can equip particularly his concept of *repetition* with phenomenological qualities (see Deleuze 1994: 68, 57–8, 98).

For Husserl succeeds in penetrating into that transcendental forefield of representation by analysing the 'lower', preliminary achievements of *passive subjectivity*. He manages this philosophical descent because he can accentuate the awe produced by the question, 'Why is there something, and not nothing?' in such an epoch-making way that the loss of objective preconceptions becomes radical enough to sight phenomenological events 'behind' traditionally existing conditions. In this way the self-evident belief in world and cognition becomes problematic and thereby forces rethinking of the genesis of this belief. However, even the genetic analyses undertaken by Husserl remain relatively caught up in the wholeness of experience as they intend it, caught up, that is, in the model of recognition. In this model the syntheses of reproduction are subordinate from the beginning to the form of identity of an object's assigned regulation in consciousness, as even in the background of the 'tendency to affection' a polarisation of ego shines through. One could assert that Husserl follows two heuristic maxims that are in 'conflict' with one another. On the one hand the concrete experience should be *abstractly* examined as to its constitutive parts; on the other hand, however, in such a way that the reconstructions satisfy in detail the phenomenological *criteria of evidence* as well. Thus Husserl tries to approach experience in its innermostness so that whatever remains unnoticeable from the natural perspective is now made visible. But in this manner he reconstructs pre- and subordinate areas which lose their intuitive independence within experience as a whole. The phenomenological 'enlargement effect' of certain moments of experience then disappears in favour of their belonging to the whole. The intuitive method does not hereby escape reconstructive ambiguity: the method allows Husserl to describe subrepresentational processes, but it ultimately does so within the framework of the terminology of a philosophy of consciousness.

That leads, finally, to the problem of *pre-predicative* experience and its philosophical *description*. Just as basic experience – basic because it precedes conceptual speculation as rightful source – must first be presented conceptually as such so that Husserl can instrumentalise it (*as basic*), this is exactly how he describes those passive pre-givens of the wholeness of experience that precede the latter, or at least ought to. The pre-reflexive experience then has to be reconstructed as such while simultaneously satisfying the requirements of evidence. But how can the difference between the pre-linguistic phenomenal givens and their necessarily reflexive comprehension be made thematic? How can the immanent difference of experience, its ambiguity, be conceptualised? There are two alternative possibilities. Either the *homogeneity* of self-consciousness circumscribes *by right* every thinkable piece of experience. 'In this case one has first to be clear in one's own mind that any and every 'reflexion' has the character of a modification of consciousness which in principle can be experienced by every consciousness' (Husserl 1977: 148). This implies that it is therefore part of the essence of pre-ego and passive lived experiences to be comprehended as pre-forms of the wholeness of experience. Or, alternatively, the logical circularity of reflection loses its closed foundational coherence: then there would no longer be any talk of a pre-reflective experience, since it is only a question of a reflected one. Bernhard Waldenfels, who insists resolutely on a *good* ambiguity, argues therefore in favour of the transition from the *eidetic* to the *structural reduction* (see Waldenfels 1983: 177). In this sense the transcendental formalism of necessary conditions will have to be criticised, because the latter are not sufficient to make precise the real genetic factors of experience. Rather, these *a priori* invariances come from specific idealisation processes that present the likenesses taken from experience as originals. But as soon as the transcendental dimension becomes visible within the work of structuration itself, for which nothing precedes or is transcendent, the idealist totalisation projects become dispensable. The structural differential will then have to shift with each single actualisation, so that the formal scales of the structure are subject to changes that result only from their self-organisation. Just as the structure doesn't allow the actualisations to be *anticipated*, because thinking itself emerges out of the structuration processes, so also the passive forefields cannot relate to the active regions in a one-sided way. Thus the transcendental difference remains unsublatable and the opacity of genetic passivity can never be dissolved into the active achievements of the (Hegelian) Spirit. Deleuze reflects these methodological difficulties by insisting that the genetic conditions of experience as well as the unthinkable conditions of thinking must be thought *as such*, as 'forefield', which draws its meaning not out of its circular self-founding, but rather out of its transcendental 'abyssmality' (*Abgründigkeit*).

Passive Intentionality? Husserl and Hume

Husserl's transcendental method is realised in recourse to the immanence of phenomenal events and their material *a priori* structures. His method absorbs the anti-dogmatic dissolution strategy of scepticism insofar as it aims for an absolute grounding that tests every cognition against the standard of pure evidence. The minding of the immanence of perceptions, as required in empiricism, is repeated by Husserl as minding the phenomena. 'Impression is truly a name for consciousness of evidence in general or, in the widest sense, self-intuition in general, as possible substrate for any kind of making evident, for any kind of probation [*Bewährung*]' (Husserl 1956: 165). And that is why it is Hume who delivers starting points for a phenomenological reduction, starting points that cannot be found by Kant. Hume's perspective allows both scientific rationality as well as everyday consciousness of the world to become 'incomprehensible', so that for the first time – as Husserl asserts – a science of the life-world and the subjectivity functioning within it begins to emerge (see Husserl 1970a: 69, 91–2, 99–100, and Murphy 1980: 3, 39, 83–8).

Husserl's efforts at a philosophical prehistory of phenomenology, to be found primarily in Kantianism and empiricism, are intended to work out historical relations that can sustain his own philosophical postulates. Terminological agreements with the tradition can thus act as signposts that problematise the corresponding concepts in its light. Take for example the case of the expression 'immanence' in the Husserlian vocabulary: as soon as Husserl uses it within the framework of genetic analysis, he is using it in a new way; it obviously doesn't mean a naturalist horizon of experience, as we hear in the following:

> [Even Kant] only had in mind there the higher lying problem of the constitution of a spatio-worldly object [*Gegenständlichkeit*], of an object that transcends consciousness. Thus, his question is only this: what kinds of syntheses must be carried out subjectively in order for things of nature to be able to appear, and thus a nature in general? But lying deeper and essentially preceding this is the problem of the inner, the purely immanent objectlike formation and the constitution, as it were, of the inner world, that is, precisely the constitution of the subject's stream of lived-experience as being for itself. [. . .] It is clear that the constitutive problems of the world presuppose the doctrine of the necessary, most general structures and the synthetic shapes of immanence that are possible in general. (Husserl 2001: 171)

Husserl's dropping of the dualist scheme of hyletic data and noetic acts corresponds to his change of perspective from the static investigation of intentional structures of consciousness to 'regard everything immanent in a constitutive manner' (Husserl 2001: 634). It is not meaningless sense-data as the stuff of experience that are immanent, but impressions that organise themselves and become noticeable. The analyses that Husserl admires in Hume's *Treatise of Human Nature* are not those concerned with sense atomism or the copy theory, but the attempts at genetic description of immanent regularities of experience.

> Hume is the first one who, without letting up and by way of concrete immanent analyses and real, consequential study of the immanent sphere, looked for a rational understanding of the way transcendent objects can be constituted within the framework of pure consciousness, while asking

how this kind of cognition is possible [...] For the moment, then, his reflexive relating of the development of all objective apperceptions back to associations is not a blemish for Hume, it is in fact a great discovery. (Husserl 1956: 348)

For Husserl the question, already anticipated by Hume, is as follows: how does the supposedly self-evident perception of transcendent objects or their relations come about, that is to say, what immanent genesis do they presume? Hume's explanation of the belief in the reality of the exterior world gives a paradigmatic answer to this question: according to him, we cannot avoid associating a given presentation with its usual concomitants. The succession of events is subject to the principle of association, so that the imagination affects itself, after a repetition of similar cases, insofar as it is led by *habit* to go from one impression to its habitually determined correlate. Husserl is interested in this idea with respect to the problem of a pre-scientific order. For the active categorial acts of judgement must let themselves be grounded in a life-world manner, without becoming submerged in flowing temporal relations. Husserl wants to show that typical perceptions already refer pre-predicatively to objective units, that is, they involve passive syntheses. In this regard Husserl also figures on associative forms of relations between successive or coexisting experiences in the forefield of thematically directed reflections. In *Experience and Judgement* Husserl writes the following, with a view toward Hume and his 'belief in the world:'

> The act of judgement in this broadest sense of ego-activity of higher or lower levels should not be confused with that of Hume's passive belief [...] Every pregiven object which affects us from a passive background has its passive doxa. [...] Even the passive constitution of a datum standing out of the background as a unity in immanent temporality has a passive doxa. This is nothing other than the certainty of belief belonging to the passive agreement of intentionalities in a synthetic unity. This certainty of belief, as modified, enters into all reproduction, but always as passive certainty. [...] To this extent, all passive consciousness is already 'constitutive of objects' – more precisely, it is preconstitutive. But only the activity of objectifying, of cognition, the ego-activity of lower and higher levels, which is not merely passive doxa, creates objects of judgement and cognition. (Husserl 1973: 61–2)

Husserl expressly notes the phenomenological achievement of the older theory of association, which needs only to be transferred into an intentional analysis to be freed from its naturalist baggage. Husserl takes over its concrete development in the 'doctrine of association as an all-important and absolutely universally functioning form of passive genesis' (Husserl 2001: 76), which is how it appears for the first time as an integral part of his work on the *Analysis of the Passive Synthesis*. To be sure, association is herewith also firmed up as a label for (passive) intentionality.

In the *Logical Investigations*, while discussing Hume's theory of abstraction, Husserl already points to genetic-psychological questions that anticipate his later treatment of association (see Husserl 1970b: 35–7). Perhaps one can say that Husserl understands the doctrine of *distinctio rationis* – at least in its 'moderate' interpretation – as a phenomenological pre-form of eidetic variation (see Murphy 1980: 87). And does not Hume in the *Treatise* conceive of an *immanent a priori* in the form of epistemic-internal *relations of ideas*, which are distinguished intuitively from mere analytic relations of representations as presented by Hume in the *Enquiry* (see Husserl 1956: 351)? Husserl makes it his project to apply the 'eidetic' concept of the *a priori*, as developed by Hume, also to *matters of fact*, hoping in this way to outsmart Hume's ruinous scepticism (Husserl 1956: 352). Accordingly, the laws of association can be grounded in essence, without squandering empirically in an infinite regress their scientific claim to validity.

> We actually need only show that consciousness is self-evidently a locus for immediate insights into essences of pure generality and necessity; we would even dare to demonstrate this for the laws of association, which would only require a correct, purely immanent conception. (Husserl 1956: 171–2)

Nevertheless, the phenomenologically necessary intentional character of the laws of association reflects back on Husserl's fundamentally critical stance when it becomes a question of consolidating Hume's nominalist principles. His doctrine of abstraction is untenable for Husserl thanks to its radical, sceptical prerequisites. The empiricist *proton pseudos*, he notes, allows immediate experience only of individual particulars, but not of conceptual generalities. Hume's *forking* of analytical and empirical necessity reduces the latter to merely 'natural' external relations that cannot be legitimised. Husserl describes the all too importunate alternative as follows:

> Reason has its solidly limited sphere of influence, its boundary marker is engraved: absurd. Within this sphere of legitimacy there are only ideas and relations between ideas, but nothing of a real world. The latter belongs

in the realm of another faculty, that of 'imagination', which, according to immanent-psychological laws, brings forth experienced nature as its fictive creation by allowing itself secret, illegitimate, yes, absurd, boundary breaches. (Husserl 1956: 179)

This is the point where Husserl sees the sceptical tendencies in empiricism gain the upper hand, so that its *fictionalist* essence, as he puts it, comes to the fore. This exceeding of the given in the direction of what is not given, necessary for the cognition of facts, is, according to Hume, only possible by way of association and is predetermined by way of habit, but in no way can it be grounded by right. Thus typical or 'eidetic singularities' can at best be attributed to facts only as *faked units of representation*, not to mention categorial *a priori* constitution. The essential laws that Hume derives from experience all possess a *problematic* status: they are namely related as abstractions to the experience they are supposed to regulate. Therefore they do not belong in a foundational explanatory form, but rather only in a genetic one regarding theoretical practice; one cannot use them to determine ontologically the *life-world's apriority*.

In Husserlian terms we may characterise data positivism as a naturalist working hypothesis relating to an empiricist *reductionism* that from a phenomenological perspective is passé. The principles of association are descriptive concepts of the habitual and self-regulated courses of life-world experience. It is misleading to use these principles for the ordering of a still deeper lying, atomistic layer of the experiential, more likely accessed methodologically as a probationary control. The primary fact of experience belongs to a referral-structure of associative syntheses: contrasts, similarities, spatio-temporal relations of neighbourhood. It is within the concept of *transcendental association* that the oft-discussed empirio-rational ambivalence of phenomenology can be resolved, an ambivalence that cannot be elucidated in terms of the fondness of some interpreters in citing their preference for either Kant or Hume as predecessors of the phenomenological movement. Husserl leans neither toward a pure *sensualism* that avoids intentional essential laws, nor inversely toward a *formalism* that has to turn away from the empirical field of immanence to validate its logical principles.

Transcendental association is understood by Husserl as the characteristic mode of passive synthesis. It is essentially different from the active connective functioning of the understanding: this is its most obvious feature. Associations take place (self-actuating) and structure the field of experience without actively forming or affecting the material that at the moment is present in receptivity. Rather, the affection itself already organises itself 'proto-associatively'. From this perspective the Humean analyses prove to be very valuable. They show that the associations of cognition produce experiential-genetic substrates by being carried out in a *pre-self-aware* (*vorichlich*) and *pre-objective* realm. Yet it is still questionable whether these passive chainings of perceptions – as Husserl suggests – are from the beginning objectively *directed*, so that they would be understandable only as pre-forms of subjective identifications.

If now Husserl praises Kant for having realised the *transcendental* necessity of association, this is incomprehensible only at first glance. For Husserl bases his opinion on his interpretation of the deduction chapter and on Kant's doctrine of the three syntheses as given there. His point is to peel *passive intentionality* out of the concept of the transcendental synthesis. Kant would never speak of transcendental association, because association is only subjectively necessary and therefore must be grounded in the principle of *affinity*; this allows the passive developments in the act of recognition to be sublated. On the other hand, Husserl can rightly claim (at least two) *pre-apperceptive* syntheses that Kant also characterises as transcendental. In this way Kant's doctrine of the synthesis aids Husserl in breaking up the psychologist antinomies that still adhere to the classical concept of association. For this purpose Husserl distinguishes between two forms of association: the *reproductive* referral of objects to one another and the *apprehensional* merging of homogeneous impressions within a field of presence. For Hume, the differences are still unclear and blurred between associations of individual impressions that, when constantly bound together, evoke the belief in external objects, and associations of complete objects that call attention to themselves in a reciprocal manner. Husserl, by relying on the transcendental synthesis, manages to illuminate the pre-objective processes (some of which run unnoticed) that first generate the facts of consciousness as such, and which evade the parameters of sense atomism. His genetic analyses assume the imbeddedness of associations in the original temporal consciousness, which allows their phenomenological grounding. In the next section we will therefore investigate the syntheses of temporality as the substrate of association, syntheses which themselves make possible the active achievements of, for example, recollection. In the concept of passive intentionality a pre-form of act intentionality is articulated, whereby passivity here is perhaps only an index of its preliminary status. Nevertheless, this sober assessment by Thomas Seebohm has merit:

> If we distinguish sharply between passive and active synthesis and intentionality is an 'act' of consciousness, or even is supposed to be essentially an act of an ego, then passive synthesis is not intentional. [...] On the other hand, there is no real difficulty in recognising an intentionality specific to the passive synthesis if from the start the concept of intentionality is not completely bound to an activity driven by the subject or the ego. (Seebohm 1994: 77)

Phenomenology of Time and Association

The modern tendency toward *subjectification* and *universalisation* of time, namely to understand Being only within a temporal horizon, already moves forward with Kant's critical glance at the *finitude of human cognition* and finds its full expression in phenomenology. Husserl himself construes the synthetic character of time in such a way that it enters into the processes of experience as a pure form of the inner sense. This *consciousness of time* functions as the original 'ground level' of pure passivity in a synthetically constituted form in which all other possible syntheses must participate. In *Experience and Judgement* Husserl stresses its *primordial* status:

> Thus, the sensuous data [...] are themselves also already the product of a constitutive synthesis, which, as the lowest level, presupposes the operations of the synthesis in internal time-consciousness. These operations, as belonging to the lowest level, necessarily link all others. Time-consciousness is the original seat of the constitution of the unity of identity in general. (Husserl 1973: 73)

This 'original seat' of a *living present* cannot simply be located on the tape measure of objective time calculation if one wants to get on its phenomenological track. Husserl pursues the *temporal data* or *temporal signs* in the way they are produced out of the experiental immanent time. Accordingly, a duration has to be ascribed to the present because every proto-impressional Now is always provided with an immediate horizon of past and future. In this regard, Husserl speaks of 'protentions' and 'retentions' which determine the *pre-associative stretching* of each particular present time. Contrary to Franz Brentano, Husserl argues against the need to have to express demands for a reproduction synthesis to guarantee the continuation of the past. The metaphors 'stretching' or 'field' indicate that the three dimensions of time permeate one another in the present as if in a zone of *indistinguishability*. The inner differences which play within time-consciousness cannot be *extensively* separated. Rather, it is question of *continuous* transitions within the stream of consciousness, which retentionally modify a present moment (and its concomitant retentions) (see Stevens 1974: 40–6). The incessant displacement of the Now, which, within the framework of prescribed lines of expectation, creates ever new – and thus in turn transitory – presents that immediately retreat into memory, determines time as the unchangeable form of change or the unvarying form of becoming. The caesura that separates the 'just now' (*soeben*) from the 'at once' (*sogleich*) marks the empty place of Now that distributes itself to infinity on the before and after of the stretched-out present. On the other hand, Husserl speaks of the *proto-impressional* Now-point, to designate a centre of *actuality* within the given field of time, quasi the pure unmodified 'source of evidence' without protentional-retentional murkiness.

The flowing self-differentiation of time-consciousness is made concrete as a continually transitional *manifold of sensation* insofar as each momentary impression only affects because it modifies all that has come before. Only 'sensed temporality' can be phenomenologically analysed into purely formal structures, as indicated by Husserl's favourite example, the melodious sequence of notes. The immanent objects of material syntheses are subject to formal temporal conditions, so that relations of succession and coexistence begin to emerge as fundamental forms of possible sensation complexes. Thus it becomes clear that temporality is already presupposed on the level of what Husserl calls *proto-association*, a temporality – imbedded in an 'affective relief' – capable of specifying the circumstances of empirical associations and of clarifying the type of Being of the association's relata.

Husserl's doctrine of association, which is structured as a whole on the formal proto-synthesis of temporality, refers to the genesis of reproductions and expectations that precede the objectively directed identification syntheses of apperception. However, certain particulars already extracted from the reproductive associations (and which *imply* a manifold) are presupposed which as static givens are genetically constituted – something that can only be clarified by recurring to proto-associative merging processes within the 'hyletic sphere' of the present. Thus it makes sense to treat association phenomenology from this perspective. Husserl draws the decisive difference not between reproductive and anticipational associations, but between continuous and discontinuous ones.

The reproductive association presupposes, as we see, extracted 'objects' which are proto-associatively constituted as implicit multitudes. This passive 'proto-constitution' (Husserl's *Urkonstitution*) is carried out within the temporal course of homogeneous overlap syntheses, at first only within a specific field of sense. Sensations thus show an *inner temporal continuity* insofar as they cannot be given in isolation but merge with others like themselves. By means of continual affective arousal (*Weckung*) of retentionally declining sensations in the present, they build up that *implicit unity of sense* in a pre-objective covering synthesis. Where Bergson refers to the peals of a bell, Husserl describes the temporality of the living present with the help of recurring hammer blows.

> When the second hammer blow strikes, how does the synthesis with the first come about, which by this time has been emptied of intuitiveness or even completely vanished below consciousness? [. . .] In the evolvement of the retention the identical objective sense has nevertheless been preserved, and the same sense content, once in the mode of an impression and again in the mode of an emptily presented apprehension, grounds the synthesis. [. . .] As incomplete as such an objective sense may be, affectively speaking, it is still there as the first, toned down, hammer blow and can thus still step into a sense relation with the new hammer blow. From the latter's affective force, thanks to this kinship, an affective arousal now retrieves the sameness of the sense. (Husserl 2001: 225 and see Bergson 2001: 68, 94–6)

Let us keep in mind that here the scarcely vanished impression is apprehended immediately in a hyletic field of presence and is in no sense intuitively reproduced, which would require a discontinuous arousal of a now past, no longer present-connected, domain. The continuous synthesis is carried out along the proto-associative 'propagation' of affection 'exclusively within a particular field of sense' (Husserl 2001: 151). Regarding content, the homogeneous connections stand in an ordering relation of coexistence and succession: Husserl speaks of *configurations* of sensed moments insofar as hyletic 'data' associated with one another concretise and contrast against a background, whether they be ink spots or light signals (see Husserl 1973: 72ff.). Thus the impressional presence-sphere constantly modifies according to the mergings and dissociations of hyletic object phases.

This continuously found consciousness in the present, which drags a 'retentional tail' along with it, is not only suffused with a horizon of emptiness that presages new experiential possibilities, but is also infiltrated by affective surpluses and arousal tendencies that discontinuously radiate back into the retentional background. The model case for a normal association is given when a present perceptional situation is spontaneously 'reminded' of a past experience (see Husserl 2001: 120). The connection in the mode of *'something refers (on the basis of something) to something'* is here based as well on the affective motivational foundation of passive synthesis, and the associational parts stand quite generally to one another in relationships of similarity, contiguity or contrast. The arousal of a past emptily presented apprehension is aimed, in normal association, at the *reproduction* of what is aroused; this reproduction is associated in a passively intentional way with the actual experience. So one easily sees that the reproduction presupposes time structures: retentionality grounds the associational agency of past representations; and only in view of the future can a reproductive arousal be motivated. The phenomenological idea of temporality (or, more precisely, reproducibility) lends association a foundation that Kant correctly found missing in Humean empiricism. The past, which is not simply ineffectual history or 'over', *insists* in the present by structuring the very referential contexts that make possible relationships of similarity, etc. When a present passes along, it does not just visibly give up its evidence at the affective zero point, but rather it becomes sedimented in the accustomed corpus of multiple habits which strengthen themselves in repetition and which predetermine actual associational horizons.

'Similar reminds of similar, but also allows anticipation of similar' (Husserl 2001: 185). Cases of reproductive association that pervade the protention-horizon with an explicit *anticipation* complicate the 'pairing model' of passive referrals. A representation aroused in the retention continuum is not reproduced as singular, but is itself associated with further representations which are concurrently aroused as such. Husserl describes these cases according to the pattern of Humean belief – and aims to achieve thereby also the reconstruction of experience oriented on the primacy of objective perception. Hume's analysis had shown that we only postulate a causal relationship between two events because we generalise the habitual experiential contexts (founded only 'subjectively') by anticipating (as effect) what has always followed a certain event (as cause). Hume's association scheme, which Husserl adopts, goes as follows: if P' comes about and I then expect Q', then there is the presupposition that 1) P' reminds me of P and 2) P and Q are associated because they have always (or often enough) appeared together in my experience (Husserl 2001: 186). The solidity of belief is measured with the frequency of repetitions or the invariable nature of the connections. Anticipations that are based on reproductions are strengthened when they are repeatedly realised, or diminish when they are thwarted.

The association proves to be a complex theme when the passivity of the processes are carefully investigated. Husserl stresses in his *Analyses* that it is quite possible we only notice the final link of an otherwise inconspicuously flowing chain of associations. Then it could be a matter of an apparently sudden memory whose motivation can nevertheless eventually be reconstructed.

> For instance, the thought of a magnificent seascape occurs to us during a talk. If we reflect upon how it came to us, we will find for instance that a turn of phrase immediately reminded us of something similar that was uttered during a conversation last summer at the sea. The beautiful image of the seascape, however, completely monopolised our interest. (Husserl 2001: 167)

The analysis of problems of affection will enable Husserl to make plausible the belated uncovering of associative representations that at first remain inconspicuous. The 'foggy retentions' are bound up in structures of order and can coherently be revived to some extent. Although, of course, the past, sinking away into nothing, encompasses with its implicit layers of sense not only associations with their backs to the future. It is just as possible that one anticipates something (willynilly) without knowing why. Occasionally an effort is made to decipher the backgrounds after the fact – even if it is only approximately successful. As Husserl himself admits, the association processes take place more than half the time below the perceptible plane and thus have only an unconscious existence: that of genetic conditions for the consciousness of extracted objects. Associations, however clearly they are grasped, involve passive processes that differ essentially from that which later calls attention to itself. Sensations which persist in time or even *pre-affective* processes simply must be conceived in such a way that they do not appear as mere preliminaries of representations.

Husserl's tendency to orient the construction of the association doctrine on the concept of apperception becomes tangible in the transition from reproduction to the recovering of memories in recollection. For the passively reproduced representations, although discontinuously aroused 'out of emptiness', remain at first extremely vague, until they are made the object of active efforts to remember again, that is, to recollect.

> When awakening progresses, only individualised, especially strong sense-moments of the distant present in question will come into relief in the emptiness, just like rough contours in a dimly illuminated fog. An even more favourable case is when awakening passes over into remembering. Of course, this transition is carried out as the synthesis of identity; the synthesis of identity is the accomplishment of intuitive remembering, the accomplishment of the re-constitution of the objectlike formation. (Husserl 2001: 232)

The passive life of consciousness does not control its objects, which, 'are first constituted as identical with the help of recollection' (Husserl 2001: 182). Not for nothing does Husserl, in his *Cartesian Meditations*, characterise identification as the 'ground form of synthesis'. In this way, that reflection-logical self-relation, as 'Being related intentionally back on itself', now becomes transparent as it finds its boundaries in the pre-reflexive cogito of time consciousness. Every passing present experience can by right be determined in its objective truth because it not only reproduces, but repeats as the same – which means it can be recollected.

> Examining this more closely, we will see however that immanent perception is only a perceptual self-giving with reference to possible immanent rememberings. Certainly it originally constitutes a self [of the object], but a self that is identical and identifiable for the ego only by virtue of the manifold possible rememberings. [. . .] A self, an object, we already said earlier, is only there with reference to the active ego, 'available' for it as something that remains at its disposal, something identifiable again and again. And precisely for this reason, we already speak of a constituted self in the passive sphere because the conditions for something freely at our disposal are already prefigured there. (Husserl 2001: 254)

So even Husserl's concept of transcendental philosophy is essentially determined by the model of recognition and its corresponding fundamental scientific claims (see Husserl 2001: 210).

Affection versus Reception

Husserl's affection theory is an indispensable part of the more general doctrine of association: the recapitulation of the former will make it possible to give the latter another look. The theory's original achievement arises at first out of a comparison with the equation of affection and reception, as done in exemplary fashion by Kant. Kant stands in the classic tradition of epistemology, which sees sensations as the necessary objective foundation for 'higher level' forms of knowledge. He insisted that (empirical) cognition only takes place when objects are given to us, that is when we become affected by them. This capacity of the '*Gemüt*' or mind to receive presentations insofar as it is in some way affected is defined by Kant as the *receptivity* of our cognitive capacity or our sensibility (see Kant 1998: A 19/B 33, A 44/B 61, A 51/B 75). The exterior sense guarantees, in complete passivity and openness, the purity and reliability of the empirical material that streams in from the outside in an affect-neutral way. The non-representational character of affections shows only its abstractive epistemological side, namely its status as material ground of all reality-related presentations. Thus, although we do require sensations that vouch for the reality of our concepts, they are nevertheless nothing in themselves if they must be apprehended in consciousness, 'through which the representations of a determinate space or time are generated' (Kant 1998: B 202). The receptively presented affections, of which we know 'nothing except our way of perceiving them' (Kant 1998: A 42/B 59), are therefore subject to the *a priori* forms of our intuitions, so that their objective determination is possible in principle. Sense impressions appearing in the passive ego without any synthetic operation are nevertheless related to the homogeneous representational forms of space and time, so that sense-data always qualify an identifiable object just when they become ordered by the understanding.

A complementarity exists between the assumption of sensations that receptively affect us from the outside without being conceptually synthesised in advance and the theory of pure forms of intuition. The rigorous separation of sensibility and understanding, basic to the design of transcendental philosophy, can only be made plausible according to Kant if space and time relations determine empirical consciousness *a priori*. Forms of intuition set in advance, which mark out the finite boundaries of possible recognition of objects, correspond to the given sensations that come from an existing exterior world. Space and time, if they do not enter into the genesis of sensations but only structure formaliter their intuition, make possible the doubletalk regarding mere data material delivered by the senses and the spontaneous act of synthesis that is to be undertaken for the sake of understanding. If on the contrary, as Kant himself intimates in his complicated discussions on transcendental synthesis in the *Analytic*, sensations are indeed temporally synthesised, then it is hardly a stretch to assume, with Husserl, passive syntheses in the realm of the previously so-called 'receptivity'. And this is exactly how Husserl speaks of *affection* – in opposition to the Kantian idea of a non-synthetic passivity that has the thoughts of affection run parallel with the sensed impressions of reception. As Husserl explains in his genetic analyses, sensations can only come into consciousness if they, already passively organised, overstep a specific grade level of affection that allows them to become noticeable. Givens that can affect us have to stand out in a field of experience: they have to extract themselves from a background, which means they have to have undergone passive constitution. Husserl understands by affection a 'stimulus appropriate to consciousness, which trains an object onto the ego' (Husserl 2001: 196) to the point where it demands to be perceived by the ego. The *gradation* of affection is measured by the contrastively regulated claim of the phenomena to become perceived. The affection is realised by arousing notice, which simultaneously eases the affective tension by turning toward the affecting object, as it 'continues to draw intuitional attention toward greater revelation of its self-giving, objective nature' (Husserl 2001: 196).

This tension stands, then, with the way objects extracted from sensations take shape as they raise interest in themselves or become 'virulent'. Husserl wants to say that extracted data affect in exactly the degree to which they flaunt themselves as phenomena among phenomena. Affections jump out of the horizontal, expansionary scope of actual experiences insofar as they, for example, motivate observation of concurrent boundary or side affects. Affections assume empty horizons, both temporally and spatially hollow, that make room for the ego to be able to receive signals from facts beyond its present situation, facts it hasn't (yet) heeded. This leads regularly to being affected by something that we haven't yet perceived. As Husserl stresses, we are not only affected by clearly extracted objects that we – reacting to their arousal – take a look at and identify, but also by others which have not motivated us strongly enough for us to notice them at all.

> In this respect we must distinguish between the actual affection and the tendency toward affection, the potentiality of affection that is not empty, but that is rooted materially in essential conditions. Sensible data [...] send, as it were, affective rays of force toward the ego pole, but in their

weakness do not reach the ego pole, they do not actually become for it an allure that awakens. (Husserl 2001: 196)

The already mentioned gradation of affection means that some objects that are not seen affect below notice, which opens up the pre-affective domain that Husserl distinguishes from actual affection as tendency or potential for affection. In more general terms, it follows, from the way that Husserl defines affection, the fundamental fact that passive pre-givens that are never or not yet given can also affect. What is pre-given are implicit objects that are not explicitly given and hence not perceived.

Husserl is here thinking of hyletic mergings and extractions running pre-affectively in the impressional present domain, dependent on further affective conduction or transfer of force, but only unconsciously effective in the genetic forefield of static givens. These pre-affective overlap-syntheses take place proto-associatively in the homogeneous realm of a field of sense. The corresponding configurations of manifold sense impressions build a steadily changing, high/low 'affective relief' of more or less emphatic sensory facts.

> I am alluding here to the differences of freshness in which all present objects [. . .] gain (or in the opposing case, lose) something of the vivacity of consciousness, of affective force. But at the same time within every present there are relative differences of vivacity, differences of more or less affectively efficacious data. Hence the discourse of affective relief. (Husserl 2001: 216–17)

Husserl speaks in this regard about a 'perceptibility relief' that characterises each living present, insofar as a few facts always stand thematically in the foreground and extract themselves from a background of imperceptible things.

The problem of implicit sense gets more concrete when Husserl focuses on the temporal nature of the experience that grounds the associative function of affection. Accordingly, each impressional phase not only sinks into the retention continuum but also loses thereby concomitantly its affective power. The retentional loss of affection from passing presents is offset by a constant, affect-laden Now that makes possible its associative revival. This possible revival refers to an identical objective sense that is implicit in the 'non-lively form of the unconscious' (Husserl 2001: 179).

> In the continuity of this process [of retentional modification], the sense remains identical, it has only become veiled, it has shifted from an explicit

sense to an implicit one. What else can awakening mean here than this: What is implicit becomes explicit once more. (Husserl 2001: 223)

The affective conduction, which goes out from the proto-impression and bolsters the passive syntheses, makes possible the reproductive and discontinuous revival of appropriate past presentations, which in the meantime haven't lost their implicative sense. Before that, in any case, the transference of affection within the framework of the living present sets up a continuous connective bond between actual impressions and past, but still 'fresh', ones. Thus the atomistic idea of isolated sense-data streaming in upon us from the outside is driven *ad absurdum* by way of the phenomenological insight into the continuity of affection. 'Within the streaming living sphere of the present there can be no isolated intuitions' (Husserl 2001: 175). Husserl achieves, we might say, phenomenologically the radicalisation of classical empiricist theory of perception contemplated by William James, as is supported by possible critiques of sense-data theory from this perspective. The elementary, inseparable 'object phases' of experience of which Husserl speaks are in no sense separable, independent happenings following upon one another successively. The immediate facts of consciousness are not to be understood as fundamental building blocks of higher-order cognitions. Rather, in their case it is a matter of 'mediated' units, because they assume genetic processes that remain for the most part beneath the threshold of consciousness. In this sense Husserl speaks of the gradation or relativism of affection:

> If we reflect upon the essential character of affection which is obviously relative, whereby something noticeable can become unnoticeable, and something unnoticeable can become noticeable, then we will hesitate in interpreting something unnoticeable as something that does not exercise an affection at all. (Husserl 2001: 211)

Second thoughts are necessary regarding 'not really' being affected. The problem of the affective tendency which is nevertheless sensed pre-self-centred and pre-objectively corresponds to the problem of the degrading of affection in the ever-darkening retentions which, far removed from this or that present, assert themselves only in its substratum. The gradual sinking of retentions in affective ineffectiveness testifies to a steadily modifying null domain that is carried along by every living present. This virtual domain of the past is structured by the pre-affective happenings in the field of experience. Why shouldn't the blind spot of forgetfulness, which afflicts temporal consciousness to its core, recur within imperceptible exteriorities? The manifold impressions that teem unnoticed in the background of consciousness affect us only below the threshold, and therefore they should not be counted as belonging to the affective null-horizon, but rather to the intuitive null-horizon. In this they resemble the impressions sinking away in the retentional process. The 'gradation of liveliness' varies with the retentional modification of the proto-impression. Husserl characterises the proto-impressional moment of the Now as the high point of 'most intensive intuitability'. 'After that, intuiting loses ever more satiation with respect to the past to the point of null intuiting' (Husserl 2001: 218). The evidential character or intuition of a present degrades and vanishes in time long before it completely loses all affective value. 'As intuiting approaches null, the affective power is by no means null' (Husserl 2001: 169). This then constitutes a zone of 'imperceptible becoming' or of 'sense thresholds' between the pure affective null domain and the originary givens of intuition.

Experiences imply a genetic substratum of passive syntheses that can themselves be experienced. To put it another way, along with every consciousness there coexists a threshold that makes itself noticeable in so-called threshold experiences which tend toward the dissolving or expansion of that consciousness. Thresholds correspond to the 'narrowness of consciousness' and mark its inability to ground itself. Varying here a phrase by Deleuze: thresholds have the attribute not to be where they are sought but are therefore to be found where they aren't (see Deleuze 1998: 275). A deregulation of the senses sets in. Thresholds of sense are genetic conditions of natural experience and remain invisible behind the order of senses that they define. Husserl observes in this regard a 'modal alteration of affection' when pre-affective happenings are just about to be grasped. Accordingly, at a specific level of intensity, an ever louder noise

> [. . .] has already become detected in its peculiarity even though [the ego] does not yet pay attention to it by grasping it in an attentive manner. This 'already become detected' means that in the ego a positive tendency is awakened to turn toward the object. (Husserl 2001: 215)

The theory of the gradation of affection makes it possible for Husserl to consider the phenomenon of threshold experiences, that is, 'something becoming roughly audible'. In this way perceptibility as such turns up below the static order of perception. No longer do the givens of perception (affections) now draw thought's interest, but rather that through which the given is given (= pure affects). According to

Deleuze and Guattari, pure percepts lie 'below and above the threshold of perception [. . .], a threshold that can operate only as a function of a perceptible form and a perceiving, discerning subject' (Deleuze and Guattari 1987: 281, trans. mod.). Yet these subrepresentative percepts must also somehow be simultaneously perceived, for 'the imperceptible is also the percipiendum' (Deleuze and Guattari 1987: 281). The default visibility of what is visible cannot be overlooked insofar as it is a precondition of every seeing. One cannot get around the integration into experience of the tiny perceptions below the threshold that, determined only virtually, ally themselves passively to one another, because these minute perceptions constitute what can only just be perceived – even before they allow themselves to represent something.

> And these are minute, obscure, confused perceptions that make up our macroperceptions, our conscious, clear, and distinct apperceptions. Had it failed to bring together an infinite sum of minute perceptions that destabilise the preceding macroperception while preparing the following one, a conscious perception would never happen. How could a pain follow a pleasure if a thousand tiny pains or, rather, half-pains were not already dispersed in pleasure, which will then be united in conscious pain? However abruptly I may flog my dog who eats his meal, the animal will have experienced the minute perceptions of my stealthy arrival on tiptoes, my hostile odor, and my lifting of the rod that subtend the conversion of pleasure into pain. [. . .] The tiny perceptions are as much the passage from one perception to another as they are components of each perception. (Deleuze 1993: 86–7)

Sensations that gather force at the threshold do not fall into line with the order that reigns in front of or behind the threshold. These non-referential and sense-specific sensations are 'ego-alien' or – as Husserl says – only available 'without ego-participation', because they testify to an affectivity that precedes consciousness that first consolidates itself in relations to things. Even though Husserl tends to restrict himself to reconstructing only the unified experience structured throughout by a transcendental consciousness, his genetic investigations nevertheless lead him to the concept of sensations that organise themselves in passive syntheses insofar as they continuously undergo differentiation. In this way a certain mobility of experience can be seen that Deleuze seeks to construe in the concept of *intensity*. He finds necessary clues in the history of concepts. At this point it is enough to mention that Fechner – following in Herbart's footsteps – uses the Kantian definition of intensive magnitudes to draw a horizontal threshold across the vertical gradation that allows one to speak of imperceptible sensations that constantly modulate (see Fechner 1860: 74, 94). These differences of quantity are, however, not measurable – contrary to Fechner's speculations – because no unitary base measure of intensive magnitudes can be defined. Nevertheless, it is a matter of *quantities*, although they do not result from successive syntheses in a homogeneous milieu of countable differences. Instead, they come from passive syntheses of 'pre-affective forces' or 'tiny perceptions', as Deleuze suggests in his book on Leibniz. These connections of the phases of sensations correspond to the extractive-genetic processes (*abhebungsgenetische Prozesse*) we have just been treating, processes we will return to in what follows next.

5

Heidegger's Metaphysics of Finitude

> Being shrouds itself in the enowning event [*Sein verschwindet im Ereignis*]. (Heidegger 2000b: 22, trans. mod.)

It is a fact that Heidegger's radicalisations of Husserl's phenomenology were greeted in a productive way, especially in France. The 'primary works' of French phenomenology, Sartre's *Being and Nothingness* (1943) and Merleau-Ponty's *Phenomenology of Perception* (1945), are strongly influenced by Heidegger and inconceivable without *Being and Time* (1927). In addition, Heidegger's critique of subject-centred reason, presented after his 'turning away' (*Abkehr*) from metaphysics, has led to important new developments in the course of phenomenological thinking. I need only mention *The Visible and the Invisible* (1964) by Merleau-Ponty, *Totality and Infinity* (1961) by Levinas, *Speech and Phenomena* (1967) by Derrida and *The Order of Things* (1966) by Foucault. These works put a stop to the indiscriminate dismissal of Heidegger's late works. To be sure, we also see in them the beginning of a more nuanced, mostly less than favourable and usually politically motivated critique of his philosophy as a whole. To put it somewhat simply, the aforementioned authors take from Heidegger the insight that the recently dominating image of representational thinking rests in a subjective logic of recognition that 'overlooks' ontological difference. But they all contend that the *negligence of difference* as such cannot be inserted into the 'grand narrative' of the history of Being in a way that would allow Heidegger to regain for philosophy its full measure of authority.

Gilles Deleuze also expresses this ambivalent attitude. On the one hand he links the necessary radicalism of difference directly to Heidegger's insistence on leveraging out (*ausheben*) the negation-theoretical basis of the Hegelian dialectic, while on the other hand he traces Heidegger's 'good pages' back to his latent Nietzscheanism (Deleuze 1994: 201). Yet from his assertion that 'Heidegger is Nietzsche's potential, but not the other way around' (Deleuze 1988b: 113), one can conclude not only that Heidegger's critique of

Nietzsche is highly questionable in Deleuze's eyes, but that in any case Heidegger's all too rapid assignment of technology to an inattention to Being will need overhauling. Clearly the decisive points that make Heidegger's metaphysics of finitude interesting for Deleuze and his working out of the philosophy of difference need to be discussed. First it is important to learn how Heidegger introduces temporality into the understanding of Being as such, thus infiltrating transcendental philosophy ontologically by way of the productive imagination and its synthetic function. Then, in a second step, later texts of Heidegger need to be dealt with that seek to reveal the onto-theological roots of representational thinking by laying claim to an idiosyncratically Heideggerian onto-experience of difference called 'Ereignis', the 'enowning event'.

Before we go into these matters, let me insert here a note on Deleuze's early understanding of Heidegger's conception of time. I recently became aware of a lecture called 'What is Grounding?' that Gilles Deleuze gave at the Lycée Louis le Grand during winter semester 1956–7. Reading Pierre Lefebvre's transcript was an exciting experience (see Deleuze 2015). The school's students found themselves confronted with a young Deleuze developing his own philosophy – later to be labelled 'transcendental empiricism' – over against tradition. Central to his explication is Kant's critical stance, leading to the fundamental questions that play a role in the (German) post-Kantianism of Fichte, Maimon, Schelling, Novalis and Hegel. Later positions are also represented through Kierkegaard, Nietzsche, Bergson, Freud and Heidegger, who all have something to say about 'repetition'. No other text by Deleuze shows better how his philosophy got started and how his thinking operates regarding the often still raw or unrefined ideas and only partly solved problems. On the other hand, it isn't necessary to overburden the text with conjectures or make of it a key for gaining access to yet unreachable reserves of thought.

As I see it, one shouldn't overinterpret Deleuze's confrontation with post-Kantianism in this context. No doubt he works out an idea of transcendentalism that originates in the Humean version of empiricism. Taking his cue from Heidegger, he works through the synthesis theory of the transcendental analytic in the *Critique of Pure Reason* so as to set up the systematic demand for a transcendental synthesis in the form of a genetic methodology which leaves the Kantian dualism behind (Deleuze 2015: 24ff., 138ff.). For this purpose he connects, among others, with Salomon Maimon and his adaption of the Leibnizian differentials as genetic principle: 'Maimon's demand is thus excellent' (Deleuze 2015: 161). But as a matter of fact the theme of repetition (see Kierkegaard and Nietzsche) already circumscribes how the question regarding the ground – according to Kant: *quid juris?* – is to be answered. *Not* in the sense of Fichte, Schelling or Hegel. Rather, Deleuze passes from post-Kantianism and the demand 'to replace the Kantian method with a genetic and synthetic method' (Deleuze 2015: 138) directly over to the problem of time (à la Heidegger). Time becomes autonomous: it is the essence of finitude and repetition. At this point Deleuze has not yet completely managed to get rid of transcendental subjectivity. Nor has he yet thought through the alleged connection of the systematic question of grounding, as posed by the post-Kantians, with his understanding of repetition. In this sense, for example, his reliance on Fichte, Schelling or Hegel must still be regarded as problematic and not as an expression of a higher correspondence with 'speculative experience', 'new realism', 'absolute difference', and so on (compare Christian Kerslake, *Immanence and the Vertigo of Philosophy: From Kant to Deleuze* (Edinburgh: 2009)). Whoever claims that creates for himself a quasi 'fundamental-ontologist' or even a 'dialectic-existentialist' Deleuze. The same holds for Deleuze's relation to Heidegger.

In the lecture in 1956–7, Deleuze has not yet studied the late Heidegger's onto-theological critique or his theory of difference. These subsequent examinations will foster the possibility of thinking grounding as immanence (and thus also as abyss) and will allow the scrutinising of Dasein's transcendence – or what amounts to the same thing, the careful dissecting of the transcendental imagination in Heidegger's 1929 interpretation of Kant. A consequence of Deleuze's reading of the later Heidegger is thus to avoid mixing together the transcendental analytic of finitude (based on Maimon) with a speculative and idealist interpretation of self-consciousness as a grounding principle.

Reinhold and Fichte countered Maimon, Schulze, Fries and others by searching for a way to sublimate rationally the paradox of the thing in itself and thereby 'spiritualised' experience as a whole. In opposition to this fundamental interpretation of Kant, which aims for something absolute, the Leibniz-inspired post-Kantianism from, for example, Maimon to Fechner takes a more empiricist or experimental approach. As Deleuze puts it, 'the finite takes on a constituent power for the infinitely small' (Deleuze 2015: 163). This philosophical psychology remains for Kierkegaard or Nietzsche a strategic reference to an empiricist thinking that encloses within the empirical domain a transcendental dimension (like the unconscious). This transcendental dimension is definitely not simultaneously and speculatively 'super-elevated' so as to empower in its interior or in its essence assumed underlying intelligible structures that have (always and *a priori*) been there.

More on this in the corresponding passages in *Difference and Repetition*. Or to put it in other terms, Nietzsche's idea of repetition can finally be worked out philosophically and systematically – in the sense of transcendental empiricism – when Deleuze succeeds in rejecting the *transcendence* of finitude (using Heidegger's critique of representational thinking, or using Bergson's idea of a virtual manifold). This results, for example, in producing a temporal philosophical concept of immanence and in finding a means of differentiating difference that is not centred in subjectivity.

The Ontological Foundation of Transcendental Philosophy

In the Preface to *Difference and Repetition*, Deleuze readily acknowledges 'Heidegger's increasingly pronounced orientation towards a philosophy of ontological difference' (Deleuze 1994: xix). With this emphatic reference Deleuze does not merely state that the theme he treats in *Difference and Repetition* is currently in fashion. He also wants to point to the necessity of an adequately radical thinking that does justice to the 'failure of representation' in 'modern thought'. Thus it is all the more astonishing that Deleuze, in the body of this book – but also in his other works – refers only very occasionally to Heidegger. For doubtless he welcomes Heidegger's beginnings of a critique of metaphysics as he himself moves further in that direction. His most important texts dealing with Heidegger to any extent consider the questioning of ontology by the early Heidegger to be a promising start (see Deleuze 1994: 64–6, 1988b: 107–13, 1997: 91–8). Above all, they make it very clear that the critique of onto-theology developed by the late Heidegger also applies to Heidegger's own fundamental ontological papers before his so-called *Kehre*, or turn. Deleuze goes one step further when he asserts that the supremacy of the *same* for Heidegger – the belonging together of what differs – prevents, right up to the end, his intended 'surmounting' of metaphysics from truly succeeding. Particularly meaningful in this context is Heidegger's critique of Nietzsche's eternal return and his psychology of the will to power, which clearly signals for Deleuze that Heidegger doesn't fully 'effectuate the [empiricist] conversion according to which univocal Being [*Sein*] can only be expressed in terms of difference and, in this sense, necessarily encompasses all individual beings [*das Seiende*]' (Deleuze 1994: 66, trans. mod.). According to Deleuze, Heidegger's critical position regarding *metaphysical representation* affects Heidegger's philosophy *in toto*, at least if it is worked through in all its consequences.

We begin with a detailed look at the book Heidegger published in 1929, *Kant and the Problem of Metaphysics*, because it opens a new way of getting at transcendental philosophy. His approach influenced Deleuze more than one can say, even if its influence is rarely mentioned, though admittedly it is hard to read the book using Deleuzian bifocals and *not* lay it aside. Deleuze made extensive use of it, in part to fire up his own anti-Hegelianism. For Heidegger tries to reconstruct precisely those of Kant's pages that Hegel never liked: the ones on sensuality, temporality, finitude and so on. Heidegger brings to light the ambiguity of Kantian thought, even if his primary intention is to find a way into its wellsprings. Both Heidegger and Deleuze try to radicalise Kant's critical project by introducing temporality into thought, and in this manner encroach upon a transcendental realm that precedes all empirical knowledge.

In his 1929 book on Kant, Heidegger suggests reading the *Critique of Pure Reason* as a groundlaying of ontology – that is, as a historical preparation for fundamental ontology. This predecessor role assigned to Kant is a result of the 'wellspring-oriented' (*ursprünglichen*) interpretation that Heidegger intends to undertake, especially of the deduction and schematism chapters. To carry through this interpretation it suffices, according to Heidegger, to re-energise the buried potential of Kantian thinking. We've heard this hermeneutical imperative before: try to understand the philosophers better than they understand themselves! Heidegger insists that the critique must continue to be forced until the *finitude* of humanity is plainly presented. To do this, Heidegger distances himself 'first and foremost' from Kant's other 'possibility', namely from the speculative variant of interpretation that treats metaphysics as pure science. Of course Heidegger in his Kant book also opposes for other reasons the neo-Kantian interpretation of the *Critique of Pure Reason* as a 'theory of experience' or as a 'theory of positive science'. Yet we won't deny that Heidegger, precisely at the end of the twenties, also understands fundamental ontology as *the* paradigm of a scientific philosophy, that is, as the science of Being. In the end, however, it is more important that the 'existential concept of science', which he advocates, has nothing in common with the 'concept of pure science' held by German idealism.

At any rate, Heidegger discovers two essential tendencies in systematic transcendental philosophy – and thus points out (provisionally) the decisive alternative which post-Kantian philosophy as a whole proposes: either the art of dialectical argumentation sublates human shortcoming within the infinite element of spirit, or else metaphysics originates on the (infirm) ground of a death-permeated existence. In his lecture series on the *Phenomenology of the Spirit* (1930–1), Heidegger considers the dispute with Hegel 'to be framed by this crossroads of finitude and infinity' (Heidegger, GA 32: 92). To prevent Kant's 'own' interests from being corrupted dialectically, Heidegger feels he must break the power of (Hegelian) logic (that is of pure thought) *onto-logically* – which means, in this context, based on prior-occurring existential structures. As Gadamer emphasises, 'Heidegger's historical self-awareness signals the most extreme counterthrust against the thrust of absolute knowledge and of freedom's total self-awareness in grounding Hegel's philosophy' (Gadamer 1987: 94).

All too seldom is the importance of Hegel recognised when it is a question of tracing the principal features of Heidegger's history of theory. Not only do Heidegger's reflections on Being's destiny point to Hegel as the great adversary – at a time when Heidegger considers Kant's representationalism (*Vorgestelltheit*) as the epochal expression of general decline – but so do Heidegger's proposals for a metaphysics of finitude *before* his so-called turn, which also bear negatively upon Hegel. These circumstances make it imperative to read Heidegger's interpretation of Kant with an eye toward Hegel. It is characteristic of Heidegger's project that he remarks on the ambiguity of Kantian thought in terms of the divergent orientation of the deduction chapter in the A and the B edition. It is also in this connection that his central critique of 'German idealism' is formed, insofar as German idealism – for Heidegger – takes the wrong fork in the road.

> Because the transcendental power of imagination, on the grounds of its indissoluble, original structure, opens up the possibility of the laying of a ground for ontological knowledge, and thereby for metaphysics, then for this reason the first edition remains closer to the innermost thrust of the problematic of a laying of the ground for metaphysics. Regarding this most central question of the whole work, therefore, the first edition

deserves a fundamental priority over the second. All re-interpretation [...] – a re-interpretation which 'German Idealism' even accentuated subsequent to the second edition of the *Critique of Pure Reason* – misunderstands its specific sense. (Heidegger 1997: 134–5)

The variance between the speculative and the onto-phenomenological interpretations of the synthesis doctrine, and in that connection also of Kant's concept of experience, can be seen in preliminary fashion if one looks at the two approaches to a critical judgement of the *thing-in-itself*, that perhaps most idiosyncratic construct of the Kantian philosophy.

Notably, the earliest of Kant's critics take special aim at the thing-in-itself. Thanks to its conspicuity it makes an obvious target for a critical investigation. It not only presents a perplexing problem, but is also systematically relevant and not merely a bit of nonsense on the fringe. The 'thing-in-itself' belongs to the essence of Kant's transcendental philosophy and whoever 'smothers' it is no longer grounded in that philosophy (see Hintikka 1989: 243–57). This merely thinkable but not recognisable 'something' stirred up opposition from Maimon, Jacobi, Fichte and many others. Yet starting from this state of affairs one can also develop Hegel's and Heidegger's Kant-critique: it so happens that here they both agree: the critical interpretation of some kind of *being-in-itself* (*Ansichsein*) must lead to whole new philosophical regions.

Kant's problematic being-in-itself was interpreted in exemplary fashion by Friedrich Heinrich Jacobi (1743–1819). According to Jacobi, Kant gets stuck 'halfway' on the road to true science because he 'dogmatically' restricts the power of recognition. The fulfilment of knowledge forbids the bracketing of an ontological no-man's-land because knowledge has as its goal the 'merciless' conquest of reality as a whole. The 'thing-in-itself' has to be understood as a product of reflexive thought and as such cannot be left out of the theory of knowledge. Consequently the 'thing-in-itself' reveals itself as a symptom of 'weakness', as the placeholder for anything unrecognisable. According to Kant, the boundaries which reason must self-critically set for itself will mirror – says Jacobi – only the limitations and insufficiency of this philosophical construction, which necessarily must be dismantled in a system-immanent way (Jacobi 1815: 303–5). That documents the thesis that the 'thing-in-itself' acts as *exterior* cause of sensory affections. After all, according to Kant, experience requires in advance a 'genetic forefield' of which no empirical knowledge is possible (see Kant 1998: A 141/B 180–1). Inversely, the origin of spontaneous acts of understanding also remains in the dark. Understanding's inscrutability corresponds to its *finite* state (see Jacobi 1815: 303–4). Reason as judge is biased insofar as it is placed in the role of defendant. This bias is reflected in the *paradox of transcendental recognition*, for with its limitations, recognition loses simultaneously its authority to determine limitations, that is, to limit itself. Even Hegel refers to this paradoxical situation in the *Critique* in order to overcome it, for 'as limit, a lack or defect can only be known or felt when one is suddenly above and beyond it' (Hegel 1991, §60).

As can be seen in works of the next generation, Jacobi's sceptical remarks about the foundations of critical philosophy anticipate various idealist attempts to get around these problems. Hegel's thinking in terms of system consolidates around 'the liberation from opposing elements of consciousness [like appearances and the 'thing-in-itself'], a liberation process which the theory of knowledge must be able to undertake' (Hegel 2010: 45). In this process, the 'thing-in-itself' proves to be the telltale characteristic of a metaphysics of finitude: it unpropitiously impedes the dialectical movement. This interruption marks the limit of finite recognition. In his logic of essence (*Wesenslogik*), where Hegel treats the 'thing-in-itself' as a form of *existence*, its complex logical structure – its conceptual consistency – is presented in an especially fruitful way. This presentation acts as a critique insofar as it results from a thoughtful consideration of the movement of concepts in general (from which the origin or formation of the 'thing-in-itself' is demonstrated) and thus carries within itself a reflexive potential in such a way that, by means of its (anticipated) further realisation, this persistent logical product becomes immanently transformed. Concretely, this means that in the logic of existence Hegel introduces the 'thing-in-itself' as abstract product of exterior reflexion, a product which this reflexion assumes to be unreachable. The relationship of logical reflexion that rules the 'thing-in-itself' is configured out of three parts: thing-in-itself, manifold and exterior form of reflexion. The 'thing-in-itself', caught reflexively out of bounds, doubles as the 'indeterminate material' of *appearance* because exterior reflexion has also (dialectically) become exterior to itself, not only regarding the essence from which it has been reflexively separated. In addition, the persistence of the 'thing-in-itself' is proven again when, in the following mental step, it is presented as the essential substratum of properties that are externally distanced from it.

> The thing-in-itself (and under 'thing' is embraced even Mind and God) expresses the object when we leave out of sight all that consciousness makes of it, all its emotional aspects, and all specific thoughts of it. It is easy to see what is left – utter abstraction, total emptiness, only described still as an 'other world' – the negative of every image, feeling, and definite thought. Nor does it require much penetration to see that this *caput mortuum* is still only a product of thought, such as accrues when thought is carried on to abstraction unalloyed: that it is the work of the empty 'Ego', which makes an object out of this empty identity with itself. (Hegel 1991: §44)

For Hegel, the actual philosophical step forward beyond Kant consists in the recognition that the 'in-itself' (*Ansichsein*) of existence can be picked up or sublated as the *negative* aspect of reflexion insofar as the 'in-itself' continues to play a prescribed role behind the scenes. As Jacobi already put it, the 'thing-in-itself' is just the logical obverse of the Kantian concept of appearance. The unreflected, straightforwardly given immediacy of empirical reality exhibits only the finitely apparent side (*Schein*) of a reflexion which darkens in the same measure as it is unable to think how it looks from behind. With the 'thing-in-itself' Kant pays tribute to the rationalism of orthodox school metaphysics because he, as Hegel explains, limits experience (with biased criticism) to *empirical* knowledge, without taking the further step of unmasking all unreflected exteriority as only apparent, that is to say, sublating all this in philosophical reflexion to get the complete picture.

The 'thing-in-itself', which Hegel conceptualises as 'empty abstraction from all determination', thus holds its place in the self-finding process of the spirit (Hegel 1990: 135). Hegel's critical interpretation of pure *being-in-itself*, which opens up the way to the absolute appearance and manifestation of the spirit, becomes for Heidegger an exemplary object of criticism.

> What does the struggle against the 'thing in itself', which started with German Idealism, mean other than the growing forgetting of what Kant struggled for: that the inner possibility and necessity of metaphysics, that is its essence, are at bottom brought forth and preserved through the more original working-out and increased preservation of the problem of finitude? (Heidegger 1990: 167)

In the fifth subsection of his book on Kant (1929), Heidegger gives his own view on the status of the 'thing-in-itself' in the *Critique of Pure Reason*. Essentially he characterises the 'thing-in-itself' as the (fictive) correlate of an infinite relationship of understanding. From it arises a finite knowledge that depends on the ('receptive') intuition of a being already available, and in that sense 'derivative' (*intuitus derivativus*). Heidegger agrees with Kant that only appearances can be possible 'objects' of experience. Nevertheless he radicalises the problem: 'The term "appearance" means the being itself as object of finite knowledge' (Heidegger 1990: 20). Heidegger says that 'the being itself' (*das Seiende selbst*) appears without it having to be subsumed or 'projected' under the thought of a thing 'in-itself'. For Heidegger, objectivity epitomises the concept of being: only objective presence, that is, what stands before us (*Gegenstehendes*) affects us in such a way that we can have experiences. 'German Idealism' for its part speculates about an 'originary intuitive understanding' (*intuitus originarius*), not derivative, that brings forth being essentially as itself. This amounts to that logical construct of an infinite knowledge which allows the real genesis of being as such. Heidegger can therefore reserve the term 'thing-in-itself' for the being that absolute knowledge itself gives to itself. In this case the (designated) being reveals itself as generated or produced: the 'thing-in-itself' would be 'pro-ject' (*Ent-stand*), but in no way can it be 'ob-ject' (*Gegen-stand*).

Kant's critique of metaphysics doesn't go far enough to suit Heidegger's purposes. Of course knowledge must be restricted to the world of appearances, but according to Heidegger there is no other world in any case. The conditions of every possible experience are therefore no longer to be misunderstood as restrictions. Objects are only possible on the 'subjective basis' of apprehensions and apperceptions: that is the only way *a being* can be experienced through its Being (*in seinem Sein*). Heidegger's radicalism consists precisely in working out metaphysics anew based on finitude, thus making finite the understanding of Being itself.

That is also why the most telling criticism that Heidegger directs at Kant in the context of *Being and Time* concerns the inadequate analysis of time in the *Critique of Pure Reason*. Heidegger asserts that the *transcendental aesthetic* produces the 'essence of time' only in a raw and preliminary manner. Thus Kant comes to speak only indirectly about actual (*eigentliche*) temporal truth, namely in the chapter on schematism and in the A-deduction. Actual time, however, reveals itself in the *ontological synthesis* which the transcendental imagination accomplishes. That opens the way for ontological knowledge to be the condition for possible ontic enlightenment. In Heidegger's way of thinking the clarification of synthesis finally sets the stage for laying the ground of metaphysics.

Before any experience, the unification of sensibility and understanding *happens* in the ontological self-design (*Selbstentwurf*) of Dasein. Heidegger persistently circles around these 'unknown roots' of the two 'branches' of cognition and discovers the transcendental imagination as the fundamental mediating faculty of synthesis. The imagination, which Kant (especially in the first edition) introduces as third faculty of the soul, enables, as 'formative mediator of ontological knowledge', the *a priori* interplay of sense and understanding. The pure veritable synthesis builds the structure that lets a being confront itself as a being and thus forms the horizon of objectivity as such. This 'formative move' does not bring forth what is at hand but rather produces the (intuitive and conceptual) framework within which what is at hand can be confronted. The framework, the structure of 'letting become present' (*Anwesenlassen*), is systematically set up in a schematic sensualisation of pure concepts and sets down in advance the conditions for each possible experience. Heidegger says in this context that ontological knowledge – which relates not to what is (objects) but to the Being-constitution in general of what is (objectivity) – *constructs transcendence* insofar as it locates itself in *nothing*. In this way ontological knowledge widens the scope of human experience conclusively so that the difference between Being and being can be made thematic. This also means that ontological knowledge relates primarily to that 'non-empirical, that is, transcendental object = X', which in turn shows where the 'thing-in-itself' crops up for Heidegger – assuming that infinite knowledge is finally excluded.

> The X is 'object in general'. This does not mean: a universal, indeterminate being which 'stands-over-against' [objectively]. On the contrary, this expression refers to that which permits in advance the rough sizing up of all possible objects [...], the horizon of an objectification. This horizon is indeed not object but rather a Nothing, if by object we mean an apprehended being which can be treated thematically. And ontological knowledge is not knowledge if knowledge here means the treating of apprehended beings. (Heidegger 1990: 84)

Heidegger orients his interpretation of the 'transcendental object' on his attempt to illuminate the subliminal structures of experience. Here, if not already about a being, it is at least about 'something'. This transcendental something cannot be intuited empirically, but, as Heidegger says, 'this terminal point of the preliminary turning toward something [...] includes the necessity of its immediate distinguishability in a pure intuition' (Heidegger 1990: 83). And that brings us back to Heidegger's version of time.

Time as pure intuitional form delivers for Heidegger the horizon of what can be empirically intuited. However, this interpretation demands that time be determined from the perspective of transcendental schematism, which means, first, that time must be brought into a relationship to pure imagination. As the fundamental ability of synthesis, imagination 'provides' for time an internally synthetic character. Heidegger makes this thought plausible by recourse to the Kantian theorem of self-affection, which can be transferred to the *a priori* synthesis of apprehension. Pure intuition thus achieves the *synopsis* of multiplicity – implying, from Heidegger's perspective, transcendental functions of imagination – in an intuition (a 'beholding' in the double sense) in which, before all else, time relationships are established. The pure form of time is distinguished essentially from what is present at hand, which stands in a temporal order. As Kant says, 'time itself does not elapse, but the existence of that which is changeable elapses in it' (Kant 1998: A 144/B183). However, the impressions of the inner sense are set off against one another and reproduced back and forth *a priori*, so that it is possible to order points of time or fragments of presence in relationships of subsequence, simultaneity or persistence. Clearly determining time as *succession* (now and next now) is not satisfactory, precisely because *synopsis* (as non-conceptual unity of synthesis) implies a 'duration', according to which a now-point (*Jetztpunkt*) cannot be perceived in isolation. 'The taking-in-stride of pure intuition must in itself give the look of the now, so that indeed it looks ahead to its coming-at-any-minute and looks back on its having-just-arrived' (Heidegger 1990: 119). Heidegger connects this trio with imagination's three syntheses, within which actual time constitutes itself as 'threefold-unified' (Heidegger 1990: 125).

Not only is pure intuition rooted in the productive imagination, but so is pure thought. If we follow Heidegger's argument, imagination's original synthesis more or less stretches itself into the two transcendental branches of logic and aesthetics. The pure synthesis of apprehension unlocks the essence of pure intuition, just as the pure synthesis of apperception (*synthesis speciosa*) unlocks the essence of pure schematism. In this way Heidegger draws up two conditions for the possibility of experience that at the same time make up the two moments of transcendence: aisthesiological openness in general and the (compatible) conceptual formation of objectivity as such.

Heidegger grounds the ontological synthesis in productive imagination by how it acts within transcendental schematism. Since conceptual schematism determines the inner sense as *figurative synthesis*, various pure types of 'objectification' (*Vergegenständlichung*) regarding categories lie at hand. Categories have objective reality because in general they make available a self-expressive rule (*Selbstdarstellungsregel*) which produces the possible 'image' of objectification. Within schematism the categories gain influence on the pure 'transcendental horizon' of time by prepping the inner sense insofar as they instil an intention toward objectivity. The categories exhaust themselves in this purely schematic regulation of the temporal horizon. Pure concepts of understanding thus function as transcendental determinations of time and yet determine only the possibility of experience. They are authoritatively set down (*unterstellt*) in anticipation of any particular empirical application, so that the actual phenomena appear in the light of the *already given* (*vorgegebenen*) conceptual schemata.

To sum up, the schematism of the pure concepts of understanding specifies the possibility of experience before all experience. In the Heideggerian sense, it pre-forms the ontological horizon of time. The imagination successfully brings about the agreement of understanding and intuition because it schematises the form of the inner sense. For Heidegger, the transcendental structures are thus systematically set out (*herausgestellt*) so that human existence or '*t/hereness*' (Dasein) has the possibility to open itself up in principle to whatever is around (*Seiendes*) to be intuited and understood.

The mediational intention that Heidegger looks into 'by springing back' (*ursprünglich*) proves to be the ontological test of the legitimacy of epistemological validity claims. It is part of human destiny to determine whatever is (*das Seiende*). Then when Heidegger after his '*Kehre*' focuses on the problem of metaphysical representation, he also tosses away the 'subjectivist' tendencies of his own fundamentally ontological starting points. The disputation with Hegel clearly contributed to the fact that Heidegger in later years structured his onto-theological analyses in such a way that a radicalisation of the ontological interrogation becomes unavoidable. When Heidegger in *Time and Being* challenges us to think Being without beings, that means above all that the thought of thinking Being (as highest of beings) in advance as the ground of whatever is in general – so that objects are presented, that is to say represented and conceived, with respect to their ground – must be dismissed as profoundly metaphysical.

Onto-Theology and Thinking the Event

> That Being is defined as ground has until now been considered most self-evident; and yet it is most open to question. (Heidegger 1998: 340)

Ever since his work on *European nihilism* (see *Nietzsche II*, published in 1940) Heidegger fits Kantian philosophy quite clearly into that history of increasing forgetfulness of Being which begins with Plato's interpretation of Being as *idea*, receives its distinctive modern form with Descartes, and comes to a head in Nietzsche's thought. Already in *Being and Time*, in 1927, Heidegger had reproached Kant for conceiving the ego in the phrase 'I think' ontologically as subject, that is 'as always already at hand'. Heidegger characterises this transcendental subject as an *unworldly* and *isolated* ego, one that tries to reach over to innerworldly beings through the categorial functions of understanding, which is why 'from the ground up, the ontological problematic of Dasein has been mis-leading (*ver-kehrt*)' and 'the real ontological problem has been mis-taken if not *skipped* altogether' (Heidegger 2008: 497, trans. mod.). To these assertions there correspond the ones in the Kant book regarding Kant's 'retreat' from the transcendental imagination, a movement in philosophising that for Heidegger 'reveals how the bottom has fallen out of the floor, leaving metaphysics with no firm ground' (Heidegger 1997: 146). For not only does the bottomlessness of finite existence appear in the 'retreat', but clearly Kant in general is quite far from grounding subjectivity in the practical self-relational understanding of human Dasein.

> In the second edition of the *Critique of Pure Reason*, did Kant not give mastery back to the understanding? And is it not a consequence of this that with Hegel metaphysics became '*logic*' more radically than ever before? (Heidegger 1997: 166)

Heidegger works out the 'radical' metaphysical horizons of thought in Hegel and Nietzsche in the following years. This coincides at the latest with his nihilism studies, leading as well to the condemnation of the practical dimension of subjectivity. When Heidegger locates in the technical realm the practical essence of that scientific knowledge which sets up being (*das Seiende*) as the thing at hand, the analyses regarding the temporal deep structure of practical subjectivity in particular also cannot any longer satisfy him. Rather, to stand up to difficulties relative to both theory and practice in the technical realm, it becomes necessary to consider 'on its own' (*eigens*) the essence of the giving of Being and in this way to forestall the representational nature (*Vorgestelltheit*) of the given. Heidegger's lecture entitled *Identity and Difference*, published in 1957, tries to recapitulate the *onto-theological critique* which applies to the questionableness of the ground, as found in the metaphysical tradition, for the modern rule of the subject. Such a project must indeed refer to a kind of thinking that gets around the limits of reflexive philosophy, but this does not mean that we are speaking of a 'flight into the immediacy of mystical ecstasy', however much Heidegger himself may be tempted by this flight (see Habermas 1987: 137).

In the lecture on *Identity and Difference*, which 'makes an attempt to begin a conversation with Hegel' (Heidegger 2000a: 42) Heidegger prepares his interpretation of the 'onto-theo-logical constitution of metaphysics' with his thought-provoking interrogation of the principle of identity. Accordingly, the 'highest principle of thought' does not express equality (of something with something else), but rather proclaims the sameness of something that is same *with itself*. This thinking of identity as a reflexive unity which mediates itself first appears, says Heidegger, in speculative idealism, and finally reaches its fitting formulation in Hegel. Let us not forget that the principle of identity has not only a logical significance, but also an ontological one, which says that every being as such bears a unity with itself.

> The grounding contention [*Grundton*] of the principle of identity is exactly what the whole of Western European thinking has in mind – and that is: the unity of identity constitutes a grounding feature [*Grundzug*] in the Being of beings. (Heidegger 2000a: 26, trans. mod.)

Heidegger counters this metaphysically grounded identity with a pre-Socratic assertion that reads as follows in Heidegger's own version of the Greek: 'For the *same* is perceiving [*Vernehmen*] (thinking) as well as Being' (Heidegger 2000a: 27). This assertion by Parmenides, says Heidegger, delivers an 'excessive' and 'baffling' sense. Parmenides does not say that identity belongs to Being, but that Being belongs in an identity (the '*same*'). For Heidegger, this change marks the decisive difference between metaphysical thinking and pre- or post-metaphysical thinking. What does it mean that Being and thinking *belong to one another in the same*? Heidegger first answers this question by intending identity as a belonging-together, not in the sense of an assignment (*Zuordnung*) of thinking to Being, but as a reciprocal give and take (*Übereignung*). The human being exists only because, as thinking creature, it is open to Being and responds appropriatively to Being, whereas Being can only be 'as it concerns man through the claim it makes on him' (Heidegger 2000a: 31). The identity of their mutual belonging precedes Being and thinking and cannot be established or explained 'either in terms of man or in terms of Being' (Heidegger 2000a: 30). Heidegger plays with the possibility of experiencing the realm of the Same, an experience in which man owns up to Being (*dem Sein vereignet*) and Being owns over to man (*dem Menschen zugeeignet ist*). 'We must experience directly this belonging together [*eignen*] in which man and Being long for each other [*einander ge-eignet sind*], that is, we must return home [*einkehren*] into what we call "*Ereignis*" or the "*enowning event*"' (Heidegger 2000a: 36, trans. mod.). (Translator's note: For *Ereignis* and 'enowning' see Heidegger 1999, as construed by Parvis Emad and Kenneth Maly.) This enowning, appropriating experience sets aside the stance of representational thinking by springing away from Being taken as or represented as the ground of being. But '*Ereignis*', this 'enowning' event, which Heidegger also sees as the '*essence of identity*', is still beset with an ambiguity. For within the enowning event there persists a lesser claim of Being embedded in the essence of technology, that is, in the technologically framed systematic setup (*Ge-stell*) with its own structure of give and take (*Übereignung*), raising the hope or possibility that in some preliminary way the enowning event 'may transmute the mere prevalence of the frame into a more inceptive eventuation' (Heidegger 2000a: 37, trans. mod.). With the 'frame' Heidegger means the systematic belonging together of man and Being in our *actual* technologically stamped world. However, says Heidegger, the technological world envisaged as a totality is necessarily blind to the essence of technology from which the frame *stems*, for although the latter determines the horizon of Being and thinking in the technological age, yet as frame it is not something that can be grasped as some kind of being *within* this horizon of absolute functionality, that is, within the system. The frame cannot *properly* be encountered 'within the purview of a representation which allows us to think the Being of beings as a *property*', rather than as an *appropriateness* (Heidegger 2000a: 36).

Heidegger therefore speaks of a necessary listening for a certain 'cryptic' innuendo in the framing setup, a subtly problematical element that, when tracing Being and thinking, in the way they are related to each other as calculable and calculating, as on hand and on order, back to their framing out of the 'intrinsic aspect' original to both, enigmatically makes possible the experience of a *foreshadowing* with respect to the enowning event as such. This foreshadowing is still part of technology, but it prepares for passing beyond technology by suggesting a spring from Being as the ground of beings into the ungroundedness of the event. Ungroundedness is possible in this case, says Heidegger, because the *actuality* of the representational view of the technical world is not the only *reality* – and requires a thinking that impulsively withdraws from the prevalent domination of calculation and planning. Identity, which has nothing to do with the representative view of the Being of beings, can suddenly lead from the understanding of Being as promulgated within the horizon of feasibility directly back to the enowning event, so that what is in a state of having been given can now be related to the process of becoming-given (enowning as such). This, then, characterises the *turning point*, performatively carried out by Heidegger's remarks, which reveals the springboard-nature of identity. (*Satz* in German means both 'the set of a jump' and 'a set of words'.) 'The "principle of identity" (*Satz der Identität*) now emerges as the springboard for an assertive leap, demanded by the essence of identity because it needs that jump if the belonging together of man and Being is to overcome the technological hurdle and shine intrinsically within the enowning event' (Heidegger 2000a: 39, trans. mod.).

In the second section of *Identity and Difference* Heidegger concentrates more directly on Hegel, to present more rigorously the onto-theological conception of metaphysics insofar as Hegel treats the principle (*Grundsatz*) of identity in the manner of a representational logic, and to confront this conception with the thought of ontological difference. 'For Hegel, what needs to be thought out is the Idea as the absolute concept. For us, [. . .] the matter of thinking is difference as difference' (Heidegger 2000a: 47). Heidegger further distances himself from Hegel right at the beginning in two ways. Counter to the prevalent philosophical way of doing history, he seeks the force of earlier thinking not in what has already been thought but in *what has not yet been thought* (*das Ungedachte*). Instead of Hegel's progressive sublation (*Aufhebung*) of traditional knowledge as it has been acquired and understood, Heidegger advocates *stepping back* into that murky region of the unthought. Heidegger's preliminary definition of the unthought, that is what has been unquestioned in the history of philosophy, is the *difference* between Being and beings. Therefore the task of thinking becomes the thinking of the *forgetting* (*Vergessenheit*) of that difference, since forgetting is in this case unavoidable.

In his attempt to think identity and difference beyond metaphysics, Heidegger intends to expose the onto-theological essence of metaphysics, so that on the one hand we learn to see certain influential structures in the epoch-making character of the understanding of Being in our modern, technologically determined world, and on the other hand we begin to catch sight of a related problem, namely, the ever-increasing forgetting of a crucial difference. Heidegger orients himself on Hegel's logic to bring out the essential double character of the metaphysical disposition. This appears in its twofold endeavour to define being (*das Seiende*) as a whole as well as in general.

> Because Being appears as ground, beings are what are grounded; the highest such being is what counts in the sense of a grounding first cause. When metaphysics thinks of a being in terms of the general grounding that is common to all beings as such, then it is logic as onto-logic. When metaphysics thinks of that being as a whole, however, as the single grounding being of everything, then it is logic as theo-logic. (Heidegger 2000a: 70, trans. mod.)

In the case of Hegel, this means that the Being of being is thought as ground (of being), carried by a thought that both finds its ground only in itself (in the unity of the most general) and grounds what it finds only in itself (in the unity of the whole and the highest): 'Being manifests itself as thought', as Idea (Heidegger 2000a: 57). From this Heidegger concludes that the *indeterminate* nature of relations between the two metaphysical ways of thinking, articulated in the unquestioned unity of being as such and as a whole, corresponds to a distortion of ontological difference. 'What differs shows itself [within the essence of metaphysics; MR] as the Being of being in general, and as the Being of being in the highest' (Heidegger 2000a: 70). Difference consists at this point only in the fact that the formula 'Being of being' (*Sein des Seienden*) can be grasped once as *genitivus obiectivus* and once as *genitivus subiectivus*. This allows Being and being to be thought as related to one another differently in different historical constellations. Thus again, within the 'conflictive perdurance' (*Austrag*) of Being and being, which rely on each other in alternation, it is the 'Same' that becomes noticeable as a preordained '*Being/being-action*' (*Seinsgeschehen*). 'For Being in the sense of manifestation [Entbergung] and being in the sense of manifold reality are different thanks to their encompassing sameness, i.e. differentiation' (Heidegger 2000a: 65, trans. mod.).

Starting from the philosophical perspective on difference attained so far, Heidegger now looks more closely at 'conflictive perdurance' (*Austrag*), that is the structure of give and take (*Übereignungsstruktur*) regarding Being and being, a perspective that with its inherent circularity marks the onto-theological character of metaphysics. Not only do we see Being-as-ground relative to being as something grounded, but also that being, as highest being, grounds, or causes, the ground. 'Grounding itself begins to appear [. . .] as something that *is*, thus itself as a being that requires the corresponding grounding through being, that is, causation [. . .] by the highest cause' (Heidegger 2000a: 69–70, trans. mod.). Heidegger, as we see, does not only determine the theological aspect of metaphysics by answering the question regarding being-as-a-whole insofar as he draws attention to the case where the unity of being is grounded by a causa prima, thereby granting God a highly privileged position. What is more important, the two ways of questioning being (as such/as a whole) interpenetrate. Therefore it becomes necessary to pay attention to the enowning-structure (*Ereignisstruktur*) of their belonging together. The ontological method of determining being as being-in-general is based on a 'grounding relationship' – to use Hegel's words – that is anchored in the unity of the Absolute. Considering Hegel's remarks leading into the logic of Being – 'How shall we get to the beginning of knowledge?' – Heidegger describes the circularity within the onto-theological grounding context, where the First grounds the Last and the Last the First. 'Speaking in terms of difference, this means that conflictive perdurance [*Austrag*] is a circling, the circling of Being and being around each other' (Heidegger 2000a: 69).

The theoretical view of difference may thus reveal the essence of metaphysics. However, the essence of difference escapes metaphysical thinking, which 'stems from the prevalence of that difference' (Heidegger 2000a: 71). When Deleuze criticises the circularity of the representational grounding structure because it fails to recognise its own linguistic-differential foundation, he is certainly standing within Heidegger's 'range of influence'. That is clear also when, according to Heidegger, the inaccessible forgetting of difference is reflected in the standard premises of ontology, where clearly Being is not to be thought as difference but as generality. Thus – in the context of the present-day oriented interpretation of Being by metaphysics and technology – the singular constellations among so much order and repetition 'that pop up as given' (Heidegger's *'es gibt'*) or 'that are the case' (Wittgenstein's *'was der Fall ist'*) are from the beginning simply misjudged.

> Even when we speak merely of a general meaning, we have thought of Being in an inappropriate way. We represent Being in a way in which IT, Being, never gives of itself. The manner in which the matter of thinking – Being – comports itself remains a singularly enigmatic state of affairs. (Heidegger 2000a: 66, trans. mod.)

Deleuze correctly situates Heidegger's thinking of Being in a tradition counter to the metaphysics of *equivocity*, namely one constituted instead on the primal ontological principle of *univocity* (see Deleuze 1994: 66). Nevertheless, Deleuze has not allowed himself to be unnecessarily influenced by Heidegger. Instead, he is busy unlocking the 'cryptic' concealment of Being through a philosophy of immanence, while distancing himself from the Heideggerian idea that only a very few thinkers might be able to express the essential framing fabric that makes up 'Being's fateful history' (*Seinsgeschichte*). The limits of Deleuze's Heideggerianism are found where Heidegger (against his intentions) falls short of 'thinking original difference', or when he refers to a largely indeterminate 'fateful moment in history' (*Geschick*) that keeps withdrawing from its own 'boundless disclosure' (see Deleuze 1994: 64–6). The 'ownness' of the enowning event might better be resolved in the living – and not at all selfless – play of differences, rather than in so-called 'dis-ownment' (*Ent-eignis*). No doubt Heidegger succeeds in conceptualising the implicative nature of Being in the withdrawal mode of 'allowing presence' (*Anwesen-lassen*).

In the well-known lecture *Time and Being* (held in 1962), Heidegger makes the temporal structure of the event his theme. Nevertheless, he succumbs to a strong tendency to push the concealed aspects of the fateful moment into the foreground because they can be expressed in an all too direct way, in the history of philosophy. That is to say, there seems to exist a dogmatic agreement between thinking and Being that is not, to be sure, regulated conceptually, but nevertheless comes about in such a way that the formations of Being find expression in the classical canon of great thinkers. The point at which Deleuze distances himself from Heidegger can be grasped more systematically if we keep an eye on the peculiarly *transcendent pre-existence* of the epoch-making character of Being, a kind of objectivity of Being which is not dependent on a process of becoming in the course of its actualisation. Deleuze makes use of his transcendental-structural method to find for Being as difference a truly immanent determination.

In the curious article on 'An unrecognised Precursor to Heidegger: Alfred Jarry', Deleuze approaches Heidegger's antipathies (*ressentiments*) in three steps (see Deleuze 1997: 91–8). First, in connection with the question regarding the essence of phenomenology, he finds fault with the fact that Heidegger withdraws the Being of the phenomenon not only from consciousness, but also from life, which appears as its decay (Deleuze 1997: 92). In a second step, he asserts that Heidegger – probably because of his rejection of will – connects the dominance of technology all too impulsively with the forgetting of the 'forgetting of Being' and demands, as does Jarry, 'a profound reconciliation of the Machine with Duration', that is of technology and 'Being (Dasein or [Jarry's] Super-man)' (Deleuze 1997: 95). Finally, Deleuze more or less agrees with Heidegger that the *transition from technology to art* consists of 'unfolding' the signs of phenomena, that is of expressing the 'showing-itself-as-such' (*Sich-Zeigen*) of the phenomenon that is veiled behind its present appearance. But again, says Deleuze, Heidegger is moving on extremely questionable paths in line with highly suspect political motives because he fails to notice the extent of the already mentioned transition 'in the play of the world' (Deleuze 1997: 95–6). We will have to be satisfied here with this hint: Deleuze, *after* Heidegger, returns to the Nietzschean 'Will to Live' not only to 'reconcile' himself with machines but to find for them an entirely new conceptualisation.

We turn now to Heidegger's text *Time and Being*, which opens the fourteenth volume, *The Matter of Thought*, in the German edition of his *Collected Works*. In this text Heidegger endeavours 'to think Being without being' (Heidegger 2000b: 2), that is to say, 'without regard to metaphysics' (Heidegger 2000b: 24), to get at the distinctive temporal character of Being. In this way he attempts a springing away from representative thinking 'verbally' (*sagend*), withdrawing himself – along with those humans who pay attention to Being through listening – into that clearing, that light, in which the essence of Being-itself (*Selbstsein*) is no longer metaphysically set aside (*ent-stellt*) and thus distorted. Here Heidegger does not develop the 'ownness of Being' (*Seinsvereignung*) on the basis of the essence of technology, but instead he orients himself solely on that aspect of *a-letheia* that precedes, behind the scene, the enowning structure of the systematic setup (*Ge-stell*). It remains true for Heidegger that an un-settling (*nicht vor-stellbare*) relationship between Being and thought is enclosed in the essence of technology, and furthermore that a potential turning point takes root in the progress of modernisation processes – but it is not sufficient to analyse only this metaphysically grounded grasp of Being, to be followed by 'springing away' from this grasp: it is a direct springing *into* the event that ultimately brings mankind back to a confrontation with its radical forgetting of itself. Heidegger must take it upon himself to think the event-structure on its own terms without regard to metaphysics, that is, not only by setting aside the onto-theological stumbling block, but by making concrete the temporal nature of time, which cannot be reached and determined by metaphysics.

The text of the lecture begins by setting time and Being in a relationship. Being is not a being that is in time – and yet it is determined as 'proprietary presence' (*Anwesenheit*) by time. Time is just as little a (transient) being – and yet it is determined, relative to Being, as 'steadfast in its passing away'. 'Being and time determine one another alternatively, but in such a way that the former – Being – cannot be addressed as temporal, nor can the latter – time – be addressed as being' (Heidegger 2000b: 3). Heidegger expressly refuses to treat this problematical 'relational context' dialectically. Such a possible 'way out', which 'evades' the issues, may not be followed if only because it doesn't consider whether Being and time are produced out of the (antecedent) relationship, or whether on the contrary the relationship in question is first constituted through a juxtaposing of Being and time. Using the rhetorical style of circumspect suggestion, Heidegger, 'through an unforeseen twist [*unversehens*]', arrives at a fortuitous linguistic move involving two superficially equivalent German idioms, '*es ist*' and '*es gibt*'. The way one talks of the Being of some being, namely that 'it is', won't work with Being itself or time itself, because neither one 'is' a being. But in German we can also say that 'it gives' time and Being instead. The 'it gives' (*es gibt*) replaces 'it is' (*es ist*), and with this supposedly harmless substitution Heidegger has found a new non-dialectical or post-metaphysical way to proceed. For by now emphasising the normally insignificant 'it' in the idiom, Heidegger 'through an unforeseen twist of accent' comes upon the sought-after relational context expressed in the (German) formulation 'it gives Being and it gives time' (*es gibt Sein und es gibt Zeit*). By saying 'it gives' Being and 'it gives' time, the 'it' in some new way – like the springboard of identity – apparently gives of its self.

Having established *what gives* as different from the Being-nature of beings, Heidegger has found an entry point for pondering Being and time on their 'own' terms (*eigens*). This point of departure leads to reconsideration of the historically binding determination of Being as 'proprietary presence' (*Anwesen*) – and thus also consideration of that 'allowing-into-presence' (*Anwesen-lassen*) that Being properly allows by its disclosing, bringing into the open, or *giving*. For Heidegger insists that although Being has exhibited itself in epoch-making 'fateful tidings' ever since the early Greeks in various forms as proprietary presence, never has the giving on its own or the gift as gift been treated thematically.

> In the beginning of Western thinking, Being is thought, but not the 'it gives' as such. The latter withdraws in favour of the gift as given, so that the gift is carried forward, thought, and conceptualised from then on exclusively as Being with regard to beings. (Heidegger 2000b: 8)

To allow for the rightful retrieval, philosophically speaking, of forgetting, which belongs intrinsically to the withdrawal temper of giving-of-its-own, demands a 'destruction of the history of ontology, with the problematic of Temporality as our clue' (Heidegger 2008: 63 and 2000b: 9). For the epoch-making givens of Being are fated to conceal more and more the unrestrained giving of Being. To put it another way, the historically sequential forms of Being lead to increasingly lose contact with the self-concealing Being that *inherently and proprietarily* owns them (*innewohnt*). Heidegger chooses time as guideline for what follows to allow a better understanding of the now formulaic 'IT gives Being'. After all, as already indicated, Being as proper presence is determined by time. 'This gives rise to the supposition that the IT which gives Being [...] might be found in what is called "time" in the title *Time and Being*' (Heidegger 2000b: 10).

If what is distinctive of Being, its 'owning' nature, is not revealed in the characteristics usually attributed to it, we might expect that, in the case of time, we have a similar situation. The normal or 'vulgar' idea of time has been oriented since Aristotle on the present in the sense of Now. Accordingly, past and future 'are' not, that is, they lack the necessary presence and are represented only as 'no longer now' or 'not yet now'. In this way, time receives its one-dimensional and calculable determination as 'succession in the sequence of nows' (Heidegger 2000b: 11). Heidegger distinguishes time's 'own' nature from this all too technical idea of time by allowing it to show itself in the present in the sense of the sway of presence. 'The sway of presence' (*Anwesenheit*) does not come into its own in the time period from one Now to another, but rather holds together the three dimensions of time in the unity of 'withstanding' (*Währen*) and 'withholding' (*Weilen*). It is decisive in this regard that this unity of 'time-space' or 'biding nearness' (*Nahheit*), as he calls it – Heidegger never tires of creating new concepts for 'matter to be thought' – incorporates the absence (*Abwesenheit*) of past and future into his temporal structure of 'allowing presence' (*Anwesen-lassen*). Time as no longer or not yet simply present (in the narrow sense) is, after all, not nothing: the past that was and the future which is still to come somehow abidingly *involve* us.

> If we heed still more carefully what has been said, we shall find in absence – be it what has been or what is to come – a manner of presencing (*Anwesen*) and approaching which by no means coincides with presencing in the sense of the immediate present (*Gegenwart*). Accordingly, we must note: Not every presencing is necessarily the present. A curious matter. But we find such presencing [. . .] in the present, too. (Heidegger 2000b: 13)

The unity of the three dimensions, their give and take, their enowning-event structure, cannot all be attributed to a one-dimensional present. On the contrary. Their (*four*-dimensional) unity is determined by 'it gives time', that is, by the 'overreaching' of future, present and past. According to Heidegger, time on its own terms is four-dimensional because it consists in an integrated byplay of three dimensions where the integrating element cannot be reduced to one of these dimensions and hence is that 'biding nearness' (*Nahheit*) which 'gives' time in its integrated sense in the first place (Heidegger 2000b: 15). Thus we see that when presencing or the unity of the sway of presence is not fixated on a simple present, it opens up or clears time-space by *withstanding* the simple present of the past and by *withholding* the simple present of the future. Then all of a sudden the 'strange' presence of absence becomes noticeable precisely in that abiding withstanding and withholding. 'The giving that gives time is determined by the biding that withstands and withholds' (Heidegger 2000b: 16, trans. mod.). Within these determinations of giving, there is expressed the enowning-event character of both time and Being, which belong together in the 'allowance of proper presence' (*Anwesen-lassen*). 'Accordingly, the "IT-that-gives" in "it gives Being" and "it gives time" proves to be the enowning event itself' (Heidegger 2000b: 19, trans. mod.). Heidegger calls attention to the self-withdrawal of giving in the epoch-making fateful history of Being, as articulated in withstanding and withholding, a self-withdrawal that testifies to the event-character of fate. If it is the sole intention of the lecture *Time and Being* 'to bring before our eyes Being itself as the enowning event' (Heidegger 2000b: 21), as Heidegger says, then he is truly attempting to think Being 'without re-gard' (*ohne Rück-sicht*) to metaphysics.

Clearly, this 'no-looking-back' stance (*Rücksichtslosigkeit*) – which nevertheless is not based on the assumption that the tradition of metaphysics is of no importance or trivial, but rather on the suspicion that a counter-position is still held captive (more than necessary) by that against which it asserts itself – this no-looking-back stance also singles out Deleuze's approach to metaphysical criticism from that of all of Heidegger's other successors. Nowhere are the connections between Deleuze and Heidegger so close as where the fundamental onto-theological conception of metaphysics is undermined with the thinking of the event. This shows up all the way into the phenomenology of withdrawal that Deleuze, in the *Logic of Sense*, puts into concrete terms with the concepts of *aion* and *counter-actualisation* (*contre-effectuation*).

> Always already passed and eternally yet to come, Aion is the eternal truth of time: pure empty form of time, which has freed itself of its corporeal content and unwound its own circle. [...] Upon this straight line there is also an eternal return [...] of pure events which the instant, displaced over the line, goes on dividing into already past and yet to come, [...] forming what must be called the counter-actualisation. Nothing other than the Event subsists, the Event alone, *Eventum tantum* for all contraries, which communicates with itself through its own distance and resonates across all of its disjuncts. (Deleuze 1990b: 151, 165, 176, compiled by the author)

Deleuze has recourse to the Stoic form of time called *Aion* to rebuff the 'Chrono-logical' collection of past and future in the living present. The present is truly alive only *in the sense of the instant* (*Augenblick*), in the moment when the non-given of future and past are immanently experienced in their withdrawal from the present, that is, when they are counter-actualised.

Although great significance is attributed to Event in Deleuze's empiricist philosophy, it is nevertheless, contrary to Heidegger's convoluted wordplay, determined immanently. The dissimilarity between the two is clear when we note the kind of borrowing from *negative theology* with which Heidegger lets his lecture die away at the end. Thus 'we are still faced with the enigmatic IT that we named in the expression: it gives time, it gives Being' (Heidegger 2000b: 16). Heidegger's dealings with the enigmatic nature of his *own* lecture are revealing. He suggests – in view of the growing danger that 'when we speak of IT, we arbitrarily posit an indeterminate power which is supposed to bring about all giving of Being and of time' (Heidegger 2000b: 16–17) – that we remain focused on what characterises the process of giving itself. For Heidegger, this points to the *preliminary status* of the interpretation of IT as giving. This preliminary aspect results, says Heidegger, from the insufficiency of the grammatically sedimented logic of language. For 'contrary to all appearances, in saying "it gives Being" or "it gives time" we are not dealing with statements that are always fixed in the sentence structure of the subject-predicate relation' (Heidegger 2000b: 18–19). Nevertheless, Heidegger cannot get over the fact that his lecture 'has spoken merely in propositional statements' (Heidegger 2000b: 24). So where's the problem? The problem is that the interpretation of giving (time, Being) does not, ultimately, go far enough in determining the crucial IT, because although time and Being are given, IT is not given but foreruns them as *the Same, the Identical*. This IT merely names 'the presence of absence, at least in the interpretation *available to us for the moment*' (Heidegger 2000b: 18). Thus, in spite of his own assurances to the contrary, Heidegger is nonetheless content to posit IT as an (transcendent) 'undetermined power' – even if not arbitrarily. 'The IT of which we speak when we say "it gives Being", "it gives time" presumably indicates something distinctive which we shall not discuss here' (Heidegger 2000b: 18). Why does Heidegger not want to discuss the matter any further? Certainly not because it is not his theme, the one and only matter of thought. Heidegger suggests rather that IT, which presents itself as the enowning event, cannot be further discussed.

> Could it not be that we might suddenly be relieved of all the difficulties [...] by raising and answering this simple and long-overdue question: what is the enowning event? At this point we must be permitted an interim question: What is meant here by 'answering' or by 'answer'? Answer means the Saying that co-responds to the matter at stake which we must think here: the enowning event. But if the matter at stake prohibits our speaking of it by way of a statement, then we must give up the declaratory sentence that is anticipated by the question we have raised. (Heidegger 2000b: 19–20, trans. mod.)

Heidegger not only refrains from answering the question concerning the status of the event, he not only rejects – as a second step – the way the question is formulated (because what essence and Being mean should derive from the event and not the other way around), but he goes on to take refuge in a negative ontology that can hardly be free of theological ulterior motives. Heidegger notes specifically that something unsayable and unrepresentable in the current meaning of the word 'compels us to say how enowning must *not* be thought' (Heidegger 2000b: 20). Heidegger's attempt to derive the meaning of the event in a positive way by determining the giving of time and Being should not, in his opinion, deceive us about the essential weakness of such an attempt. '[For] do we by this road arrive at anything else than a mere thought-construct? [. . .] What remains to be said? Only this: the enowning event eventuates on its own. Saying this, *we say the Same in terms of the Same about the Same*' (Heidegger 2000b: 24, trans. mod.). But is this version of univocity really enough?

Taking the critique of identificational thought and the metaphysics of the subject to its absolute and ultimate end turns it into a plain and tame confirmation of *the Same* as that which determines the run of things abstractly as well as incontestably. Whereas Heidegger for his part subsequently gives up his attempts to find within Kantian philosophy ways out of the dilemma of representative thinking because the problem of temporality and transcendence he treated in the Kant book must appear to him all too 'subjectivist', Deleuze on the contrary still has the possibility of returning to the Kantian doctrine of synthesis with a different concept of temporal subjectivation, without in the process retreating behind an onto-theological criticism as practiced by Heidegger. In so doing, we see that Deleuze does not at all speak of a concomitant expropriation or 'dis-owning' (*Enteignung*) of the subject, as presented in Heideggerian thought. Instead, his empiricist position allows for the description of the subjectivation of the subject '*from the bottom up*', which now means in terms of *immanence*.

PART III

Deleuze's Transcendental Empiricism

In *Difference and Repetition*, Gilles Deleuze's 'major' systematic work, difference philosophy reaches its culmination. The title alone indicates both an intensification of Heidegger's ontological position and flight from the seductive profundity that actually wants to keep what is unique and original out of the repetition-event in immanence. Heidegger's negative interpretation of the notion of eternal return thus gives Deleuze cause to make a clean break with Heidegger's concept of repetition. His own concept, inspired by Nietzsche, is related directly to difference. That is why Deleuze cites his lifelong allegiance to empiricism, since there is no other philosophy that so vehemently questions the metaphysical image of thought – and why he defends immanence so vigorously against transcendence. Deleuze begins his philosophising with Hume, and his very last text still revolves around empiricism.

> We will speak of a transcendental empiricism in contrast to everything that makes up the world of the subject and the object. There is something wild and powerful in this transcendental empiricism that is of course not the element of sensation (simple empiricism), for sensation is only a break within the flow of absolute consciousness. It is, rather, however close two sensations may be, the passage from one to the other as becoming, as increase or decrease in the strength of virtual quantity. (Deleuze 2001: 25)

Deleuze constantly thinks of himself as an empiricist, even if, over the years, his concept of empiricism does not remain the same. During the second half of the 1950s, at a time marked by a curious inactivity as an author, a fundamental shift in his conceptual coordinate system takes place. In retrospect, this gap in publication after his book on Hume (1953) appears to Deleuze himself as 'a gap in my life, a gap of eight years. That is for me something interesting about life, the gaps they contain. [. . .] Maybe movement occurs in these gaps' (Deleuze 1995: 138). Michael Hardt has already drawn attention to this 'critical' phase, in which Deleuze works out his philosophical convictions: 'This eight-year hole in Deleuze's intellectual life does in fact represent a period of movement, a dramatic reorientation of his philosophical approach' (Hardt 1993: xx). As the Deleuze quote suggests, his reorientation can be related directly to the distinction between plain empiricism and virtual-transcendental empiricism. His 'plain' empiricist position catches Deleuze in a 'crisis' – and only with great difficulty is he finally able to reconceptualise the newly surfacing problems. It is not unreasonable to suppose that his philosophical 'discovery' of Nietzsche helps him get over the crisis. Remarkable, however, is the continuity with which Deleuze formulates his position from the beginning of the 1960s. That continuity is only obscured by the sheer number of subjects he treats and his constantly attempted regrouping of concepts. Deleuze develops his very own philosophy in the 1960s by publishing one book after another on various 'classical' authors. That already gives *Difference and Repetition* special importance, since it 'systematically' bundles the multiple themes and 'results' of the earlier works. Nowhere else do we find the promised answers given in a more concise and accessible way to the problems of empiricism – as here conceived starting with Kant and Husserl. In what follows, the theory of differential empiricism will be developed in the context of the transcendental and phenomenological critiques presented so far. By turning primarily to *Difference and Repetition* it is possible to explicate in a positive way what has been gained through the philosophical-historical approach taken so far, although from time to time other books or texts by Deleuze will be consulted as well to work out in a consistent way the overall presentation of a coherent empiricism that includes the difference-oriented repetition of themes and problems already covered.

6

The Paradoxical Nature of Difference

> In any case, difference in itself appears to exclude any relation between different and different which would allow it to be thought. It seems that it can become thinkable only when tamed. (Deleuze 1994: 262)

With the philosophy of *difference*, rationality as such once again goes on trial. In its appeal to Nietzsche, this philosophy promises a critique of reason that doesn't hold back, even with respect to Enlightenment foundations. So one might suspect that a radical critique of reason ceases to be reasonable: it has to cut off the branch on which it sits. Will it therefore speculate on the 'Dionysian event', on the 'abyss of Being'? Jürgen Habermas, who declares Nietzsche to be the 'hub' of postmodern ways of thinking, sets the course of the polemic:

> With Nietzsche, the criticism of modernity dispenses for the first time with its retention of an emancipatory content. Subject-centred reason is confronted with reason's absolute other. And as a counterauthority to reason, Nietzsche appeals to experiences that are displaced back into the archaic realm – experiences of self-disclosure of a decentred subjectivity, liberated from all constraints of cognition and purposive activity, all imperatives of utility and morality. A 'break-up of the principle of individuation' becomes the escape route from modernity. (Habermas 1990: 94)

Surely no one will dispute that Nietzsche plays an essential role in the advent of post-structuralism. But it is worth asking why Habermas relates Nietzsche's critique of Romanticism only to Richard Wagner and his religious ideals, and not to Schopenhauer's metaphysics ('the principle of individuation'). This emphasis is strategically motivated: Habermas wants to interpret Nietzsche's aversion to romantic reconciliation as his final farewell to modernity and its potential for freedom. Ignored is the fact that his genealogy of truth also undermines the will to nothingness, to romantic indifference or to the 'absolute other'. Deleuze, as one of the few who demonstrate Nietzsche's *philosophical* relevance in France, clearly distinguishes between the romantic-Dionysian indifference of the *Birth of Tragedy* and the later conception of difference in the doctrine of the *Will to Power*. 'That groundlessness should lack differences, when in fact it swarms with them, is the ultimate [. . .] illusion' (Deleuze 1994: 277). Habermas does say that a new era of French Nietzsche-reception dawns with Deleuze's interpretation; nevertheless he subsequently ignores this interpretation as such (Habermas 1990: 127). It is easier to talk globally about 'reason's Other' and relegate this Other to the 'romantic' darkness of the Counter-Enlightenment. Manfred Frank, for one, appropriates Habermas's strategy when he willy-nilly consigns Deleuze to the right wing of Nietzsche scholars (see Frank 1983: 412ff. and 1989a: 566f.).

In fact, Nietzsche tries to discover the immanent efficacy of the will to power by analysing the moral presuppositions of the belief in truth. This belief carries nihilistic traits which hinder the will's ability to affirm itself because it adapts to *absolute* truths that disown their constructive or genealogical character. Accordingly, metaphysical habits of thought impair life by striving to compensate for an apparently natural shortcoming with the help of universal commandments that transcend the finite boundaries of mind-body faculties.

> Henceforth, my dear philosophers, let us be on guard against the dangerous old conceptual fiction that posited a 'pure, will-less, painless, timeless knowing subject'; let us guard against the snares of such contradictory concepts as 'pure reason', 'absolute spirituality', 'knowledge in itself': these always demand that we should think of an eye that is completely unthinkable [. . .] (Nietzsche 1967b: 118)

It may be possible to use a pragmatic theory of language to sober up Nietzsche's criticism of theological reason and its absolutely valid categories, as presented so forcefully in the famous chapter on the meaning of *ascetic ideals*. It must be said, though, that the will to power, as the differential principle of becoming, defines the critical perspective of genealogy. Deleuze unearths *difference* in the midst of Nietzsche's philosophy. But it is still unclear whether or not this difference lapses into a lack of discernibility, acting simply as a metaphysical leftover which balks at identification as such.

Deleuze cites Nietzsche in order to denounce the *dogmatic* presuppositions of doing philosophy, presuppositions that are reflected in the view that concepts are universals. Might it be possible that the project of Enlightenment rests on implicit premises that themselves need clarification? Philosophy of difference must allow itself to be judged in terms of the rationality of this double enlightenment. With

The Paradoxical Nature of Difference

regard to the *problem of starting point,* whose unique solution for any philosophy betrays its conceptual foundations, Deleuze formulates the thesis that no philosophy begins without presuppositions, which is why it is essential to explore those presuppositions thematically. All onsets claiming no presuppositions, or promising to catch up with them through a logic of reflection, or quietly and secretly carrying them along as obviously self-evident, are problematic. In all three cases Deleuze diagnoses pre-philosophical assumptions drawn from common-sense opinions, which tend in the last analysis to concoct philosophy the way we prepare to enter into a debate or a marketing campaign. These assumptions form an image of thought that coincides in key respects with the principles of the *Discourse on Method.*

When Deleuze, in his book on *Nietzsche and Philosophy,* demands that we break with the form of representation, it is primarily in order to question the presumably natural tendency of thought to seek truth. The Cartesian assertion that human reason possesses truth by right and is merely hampered by lack of the proper method to cultivate it scientifically manifests itself in the indubitable certainty of 'cogito ergo sum'. Descartes proposes the general rule 'that things which we recognise as clear and distinct are all true'. This axiom defines the concept of illusion as well as that of methodological doubt, in order to bring them under control. Although Descartes gets rid of all objective presuppositions in order to avoid any opinions and concepts not personally examined, his method regarding the correct use of reason nevertheless implies presuppositions of another kind. 'It is presumed that everyone knows, independently of concepts, what is meant by self, thinking and being. The pure self of "I think" thus appears to be a beginning only because it has referred all its presuppositions back to the empirical self' (Deleuze 1994: 129). Descartes assumes that everybody by right has at his/her disposal a natural knowledge of universal truths which can be discovered and – under threat of his/her divestment as a reasonable being – cannot be denied. Deleuze will assert that the form of representation finds its element in common sense:

> This element consists only of the supposition that thought is the natural exercise of a faculty, of the presupposition that there is a natural capacity for thought endowed with a talent for truth or an affinity with the true, under the double aspect of a *good will on the part of the thinker* and *an upright nature on the part of thought.* It is because everybody naturally thinks that everybody is supposed to know implicitly what it means to

think. [...] The implicit presupposition of philosophy may be found in the idea of a common sense as *Cogitatio natura universalis*. On this basis, philosophy is able to begin. (Deleuze 1994: 131)

These implicit presuppositions, inscribed within common sense, allow Descartes to pass directly from the certainty of thought to the existence of the thinking ego. To be sure, Deleuze is hardly interested in discovering logical inconsistencies in the proof, so as to 'liquidate' the fundamental foundational claim that is bound with the concept of the 'cogito'. When Deleuze criticises Cartesianism, it is directed at the representation of a pure interiority of thought which – to speak in Husserl's terms – perfectly illustrates 'the shortcomings of the transcendental shift'. That means, first, that thought never consists in the natural practising of a faculty: that 'thought cannot think by itself, any more than it can find truth by itself' (Deleuze 1983: 104). It is not incited simply by forces remaining on its outside, but must be *excited* from within to move itself at all. Thought must be confronted with problems and signals which force it to think. Thought is *after*-thought. 'There is nothing more false than the idea of "founts" of truth' (Deleuze 1983: 110). Since an experience is first required to give *cause* for (philosophical) reflection, Deleuze says that the *abstract* generality of concepts, regarded as universals, derives precisely out of ignorance regarding *concrete* motivations of thought. He demands that the relationship which sustains thought vis-à-vis the 'outside' also find its place within thought, with the proviso that thought understands this relationship as one of its *essential*, and not marginal, features: the one danger inherent in this venture is possible confusion of the necessary interiorisation of the outside with the sublation (*Aufhebung*) of the outside's uniquely characteristic dimensions.

When Deleuze asserts that the Cartesian presuppositions of thought are anchored in the element of common sense, his critique is directed fundamentally at the unquestioned assumption of the natural validity of the objective world. Deleuze explicates this stubbornly promoted experience by citing the Kantian model of recognition, which infers from common sense – as 'the most equally distributed of all things in the world, [...] by nature equal in all men' (Descartes 1998: 81) – its definition as *concordia facultatum*. The Cartesian concept of error can be analysed in terms of this inference. Accordingly, the errors of thought display a *de facto* dysfunctional or disturbed coordination of the faculties, whereas the coordination is *by right* guaranteed by

The Paradoxical Nature of Difference

the good nature of thought. Making such a division between factual and rightful is a selective hallmark of every philosophical orientation.

> The image of thought implies a strict division between fact and right: what pertains to thought as such must be distinguished from contingent features of the brain or historical opinions. *Quid juris?* – can, for example, losing one's memory or being mad belong to thought as such, or are they only contingent features of the brain that should be considered as simple facts? (Deleuze and Guattari 1994: 37)

If error characterises by right the negative of thought, then all things factually deplorable can be reduced to error insofar as they are ascertained to be mere empirical cases which do not diminish the rightful image of thought. It isn't enough, then, to confront the rule of common sense with clinical or aesthetic facts in order to change the pre-philosophical image of thought: instead the participating division of the empirical and the transcendental must undergo an immanent critique.

It is clear that Deleuze criticises those presuppositions inherent in the experiential concept of recognition which support the postulate of a natural affinity of thought and truth. The philosophic starting point beginning with homogeneous experience as objective recognition reveals its unexamined presuppositions when its essential structures are reconstructed. In this context, Deleuze characterises Kant's transcendental method as a 'tracing method', which – as was discussed earlier in this book – consists in reduplicating the general requirements of a corresponding presupposed experience. The various faculties of recognition, working together under the supervision of the understanding, line themselves up with one and the same object, whose form of identity finds its ground in the unity of a thinking subject. Decisive is the fact that this conception is contradicted by the primary empiricist intuition of the immanence of pure experience, an intuition expressed in the radical impulse to criticise metaphysics.

> Something in the world forces us to think. This something is an object not of recognition but of a fundamental *encounter*. [. . .] Its primary characteristic is that it can only be sensed. In this sense it is opposed to recognition. In recognition, the sensible is not at all that which can only be sensed, but that which bears directly upon the senses in an object which can be recalled, imagined or conceived. The sensible is referred to an object which may not only be experienced other than by sense, but may itself be attained by other faculties. It therefore presupposes the exercise

of the senses and the exercise of the other faculties in a common sense. The object of encounter, on the other hand, really gives rise to sensibility with regard to a given sense. It is not an *aistheton* but an *aisthetéon*. It is not the given but that by which the given is given. (Deleuze 1994: 139–40)

This, then, constitutes the rationalist illusion: the spontaneous objectification of the real and immanent content of experience by means of a conceptual regulation. The representations of independent objects exterior to us have, for the most part, an unexamined relationship to common sense's habits of thought, habits with which we have made ourselves at home in the world. Nowhere does Deleuze deny the factual presence of everyday acts of recognition, but he tries to discover, behind their positive actuality, genetic and non-representational conditions that *by right* define the experience. This leads to a new division of transcendental and empirical, which amounts to a lasting change in the image of thought. That is why Deleuze characterises his philosophy as 'transcendental empiricism, [. . .] the only way to avoid tracing the transcendental from the outlines of the empirical' (Deleuze 1994: 144). In contrast to their merely empirical application, the faculties in their *transcendental* practice exercise their incomparable potential: they each direct themselves only toward those phenomena in the world which are their exclusive concern. Thus, for example, affects, which can only be sensed, are not to be confused with sensible qualities of distinct objects which can also be perceived, remembered or conceptualised. The transcendental form of a faculty is purely immanent, since it cannot be governed by any *transcendent* instances which are guaranteed by the regime of senses in common sense. In order to think a communication of the faculties not dependent on the form of common sense, Deleuze draws on Kant's theory of the sublime: the inability of imagination to synthesise perceptions asks reason to think an idea that is likewise objectively unrealisable (see Deleuze 1994: 144 and 148). Difference circulates in the literally paradoxic interplay of the faculties by transmitting itself from one to another among them all. No matter how experience comes to represent itself, it must surely first be thought starting from its immanent reality.

Clearly experience doesn't result solely from the actively driven collaboration of the faculties, but simultaneously implies passive-synthetic processes that easily slip from view. Deleuze verges on the method of phenomenological reduction when he makes visible, beneath the natural habits of perception, the transcendental experi-

The Paradoxical Nature of Difference

ence of signs and simulacra. In this sense, the difference that subtly influences everything lies *between* the transcendental and the empirical: there, where the self-organising process of experience makes something (empirically) visible that arises from a (transcendental) background it cannot shake off. In contrast, the abstract reduplication of a presupposed experience misses this crucial difference because the universal concepts, abstracted from the image of empirical facts, appropriate, as transcendent factors, the whole field of experience to themselves. They not only miss the real, genetic process at work within experience, but deny in addition their own immanent origin. 'The first principle of philosophy is that Universals explain nothing but must themselves be explained' (Deleuze and Guattari 1994: 7). Deleuze is especially concerned about consciousness-oriented representation in philosophy, which always forms the immanent events conceptually by assuming a reflective, logical, subjective unit which defines itself in the process of grasping the given. 'The error of all efforts to determine the transcendental as consciousness is that they think of the transcendental in the image of, and in the resemblance to, that which it is supposed to ground' (Deleuze 1990b: 105). It follows, therefore – as shall be developed more fully in the next section – that the concept of difference can neither be reduced to empirical *diversity* (*Verschiedenheit*), nor can it be defined *negatively* and conceptually innate as opposition or contradiction.

Deleuze endeavours to give his thought an empiricist orientation because 'only empiricism knows how to transcend the experiential dimensions of the visible without falling into Ideas' (Deleuze 1990b: 20). That means that only empiricism is capable of constructing the plane of immanence *as* virtual idea. In this way it is possible to think pure experience of singularities without rashly categorising them in terms of their universal features. We are talking about an empiricism that happily plays with concepts in order to unlock their genetic dimensions. Deleuze uses concepts of difference and repetition to unfold the becoming in the realm of immanence. This procedure proves to be *rational* insofar as it can grasp conditions of experience that in no way drown in the milieu of indifference (or the unproblematic), but rather let themselves be defined structurally, both in their virtual state as well as in their mode of actualisation. Transcendental empiricism opposes the power of the universal by localising and explaining it within its theory. Its critical achievement is to elucidate the adaptation of experience to epistemological requirements and also to relativise their speculative truth claims. Thus a new theory comes into view which works with a novel, up-front understanding of the philosophical concept. Deleuze draws in an uninhibited way from the antipodes Nietzsche *and* Hegel, who come in contact with one another at the *extremities*.

In what follows, the essential features of Deleuzian empiricism will be broken down piecemeal. In the next chapter, the critique of representational thinking takes the floor, especially in the framework of the analyses, in *Difference and Repetition*, of concept blockage and equivocal Being.

7
Virtuality of Concepts

Empiricism is generally confronted with the preconceived notion that it carelessly disregards actual thought processes. The rejection of *a priori* sources for concepts, unanimously ascribed to empiricism by Kantian and Hegelian tradition, appears as general denial of philosophical reflection and its claims regarding a categorial mediation of experience. This classic condemnation of empiricism has rooted itself so deeply in continental thought that the non-positivist critique of metaphysics from Schopenhauer to Derrida, while no doubt making use of empiricist theorems, does so only with negative intent and careful delimitation (see Derrida 1988: 127). It seems paradoxical to this critique to conceive pure experience conceptually: therefore sensible immediacy functions merely as a non-identical corrective that sheds light on the deficient or abstractly subsumptive character of philosophical concepts. Nietzsche has formulated this critical aspect of empiricist abstraction theory in a particularly effective way in his treatise 'On Truth and Lies in a Nonmoral Sense'.

> Let us [...] consider the formation of concepts. Every word instantly becomes a concept precisely insofar as it is not supposed to serve as a reminder of the unique and entirely individual original experience to which it owes its origin; but rather, [...] insofar as it simultaneously has to fit countless more or less similar cases – which means, pure and simply, cases which are never equal and thus altogether unequal. Every concept arises from the equation of unequal things. Just as it is certain that one leaf is never totally the same as another, so it is certain that the concept 'leaf' is formed by arbitrarily discarding these individual differences and by forgetting the distinguishing aspects. This awakens the idea that, in addition to the leaves, there exists in nature the 'leaf': the original model according to which all the leaves were perhaps woven, sketched, measured, coloured, curled and painted – but by incompetent hands, so that no specimen has turned out to be a correct, trustworthy and faithful likeness of the original model. (Nietzsche 1979: 83, see also W. James 1987: 735–6, 739)

This instrumental character of the concept, as described by Nietzsche, defines its pragmatic truth value. Concepts are set up in the empirical milieu of singular events, to which they are related genetically – through a reduction of complexity. At the same time they take on a nihilist tendency as soon as they are freed from the status of their genesis and claim validity as pure logical predicates. The *Critical Theory* of the Frankfurt School also makes use of this figure of thought in order to reflect especially on the unavoidable impairment and distortion of the given within the concept. Nevertheless, that theory fixes the concept's traditional form using historical-philosophical means.

> What we differentiate will appear [...] negative for just as long as the structure of our consciousness obliges it to strive for unity: as long as its demand for totality will be its measure for whatever is not identical with it. (Adorno 1981: 5–6)

The negativist conception of difference corresponds, says Adorno, to the constitution of consciousness in the blinding context of capitalist working conditions. His analysis presupposes the factual incapability of contemporary thought to affirm differences, a hopeless situation that can at best receive only critical reflection.

Deleuze counters this forlorn fettering of thought with his unguarded statement that 'modern thought is born of the failure of representation, of the loss of identities' (Deleuze 1994: xix). In presenting this failure, Deleuze does take up motives of the empiricist critique of 'identificational thinking', but he possesses at the same time a conceptual foundation for his procedure which can be explicated positively. Deleuze appeals to the faculty of thought to sublate its limitation in terms of the logic of identity – but not at all in the sense of a mere reflection on the unavoidability of rational failures. The programme of metaphysical critique with respect to an empiricist philosophy of immanence is carried out in *Difference and Repetition* by treating the problematic of Being's *equivocity* in the context of an analysis, with respect to concepts, of so-called natural and artificial blockages. This critical presentation of equivocity is grounded in the conception of the *univocity* of Being. Deleuze unfolds it in the fourth chapter on *ideas and the synthesis of difference* and anticipates his later outline of the plane of immanence with the introduction of Idea as differential structure. Virtually determined concepts make possible the structural description of the idea of difference, without letting themselves be reduced to the equivocations of representative thought

Virtuality of Concepts

or be listed as propositional functions on the tablet of judgement. In this sense Deleuze counters the categories with so-called 'phantastical concepts'.

> For categories belong to the world of representation. [...] Philosophy has often been tempted to oppose notions of quite a different kind to categories, notions which are really open and which betray an empirical and pluralist sense of ideas. [...] Such notions [...] are distinguished from the categories [...] They are conditions of real experience, and not only of possible experience, [...] not universals like the categories, nor are they the *hic et nunc* [...], the diversity to which categories apply in representation. (Deleuze 1994: 284–5)

In this way it becomes clear that the philosophy of empiricism is compatible with a theory of concepts that is neither reductionist, that is, built up on a sense-atomistic foundation, nor derived from there. Deleuze suggests that great empiricist concepts like 'habit' and 'association' are already exempted from the classical self-image. In their case it is not a question of specific combinations of abstract representational elements but of concrete *autopoietic* acts of thought whose subject matter is inherent. (There are hardly any references in the secondary literature on the necessary transformation of the classical-empiricist theory of concepts within Deleuzian thought (see Balke 1998: 86)). The theory of concepts that Deleuze, together with Guattari, unfolds in *What Is Philosophy?* supports once again his often posited thesis regarding empiricism's capability for the 'free and wild creation of concepts' (Deleuze and Guattari 1994: 105). In the programmatic foreword to *Difference and Repetition* Deleuze speaks of 'the secret of empiricism'.

> Empiricism is by no means a reaction against concepts, nor a simple appeal to lived experience. On the contrary, it undertakes the most insane creation of concept ever seen or heard. Empiricism is a mysticism and a mathematicism of concepts, but precisely one which treats the concept as object of an encounter, as a here-and-now, or rather an Erewhon from which emerge inexhaustibly ever new, differently distributed 'heres' and 'nows'. Only an empiricist could say: concepts are indeed things. (Deleuze 1994: xix)

The virtuality of the concept defines its truly empiricist status: 'Real without being actual, ideal without being abstract'. This short definition of the virtual anticipates – in Hegel's terminology – an 'essential immediacy' with respect to the concept which is neither actually given, nor does it have to be seen as an abstract form of possibility.

'Hegel showed that the concept has nothing whatever to do with a general or abstract idea, any more than with an uncreated Wisdom that does not depend on philosophy itself' (Deleuze and Guattari 1994: 12). It will become apparent that – at least according to the self-evidence of their usage and their conception – only the concepts of subsumption result from the abstractive generalisation of certain characteristics of actually given representations, so that they establish an ambiguous relationship of representation between perceptions and understanding.

In what follows, the motivation of the empiricist critique will reveal itself with respect to the experience-transcending truths of speculative thought, insofar as the latter express themselves in their categorial claims to a higher and all-embracing objectivity. Evidently, the universality of (equivocal) concepts results from a specific self-blocking, which corresponds to their step-wise subdividing and distribution of the world of experience. This leads to a reconstruction in a positive way of Deleuze's theory of conception. Clearly the traditional notion of an empirical foundation for the construction of concepts won't hold: concepts can perhaps be analysed as to their components, but cannot be reduced to elementary constituents of actually different sensibilia. Deleuze demonstrates how a concept must be conceived without regressing to abstract features. This, then, allows thematic treatment of the interchangeable relation that exists between concepts and the situations in which they actualise themselves. The inability of phantastic concepts to manifest themselves completely in actuality defines the 'reserved' character of their eventuation. Nevertheless they determine experience in remarkable fashion by defining notable singularities (like perception perspectives) and bring about a corresponding affective sensibility that give things and acts a new fit. And that is why Deleuze measures 'the greatness of a philosophy [. . .] by the nature of the events to which its concepts summon us or that it enables us to release in concepts' (Deleuze and Guattari 1994: 34).

Metaphysics and Difference Philosophy

Non opposita sed diversa. (Spinoza)

Only when difference in itself is thought can 'the reconciliation of the singular with the general' be carried out (Deleuze 1994: 25). Here we have Deleuze's fundamental thesis when criticising metaphysics

Virtuality of Concepts

(in Hegelian style). Traditional metaphysics misses this 'reconciliation' because 'assigning a distinctive concept of difference is confused with the inscription of difference within concepts in general' (Deleuze 1994: 32). For then the requirements of representation mediate difference, which seems unable on its own to show any relation of different to different allowing it to be thought. The mediation overwrites difference into the interior of the concept, which within the framework of its indeterminate identity anticipates the limits of its determinability. Again and again Deleuze denounces the fourfold displacement of difference through its subordination to *identity* in the form of the concept, to *analogy* of judgement, to *opposition* of predicates, and to *resemblance* of perception. The analysis of determinations of Being blocked by equivocity will pursue these aspects more closely. As a first step, it is enough to establish the correlation of difference with negation in the form of (Being-logical) limitation or of (essence-logical) opposition. This correlation has as a consequence – as exemplified in Hegelian logic – that a positive and immediate reality is opposed to its negative determination. Hegel adds to this critical diagnosis that indeterminate reality takes on – if anything – only conceptless external differences, which get their essential definition when they are filtered in a negation-theoretical way. So those differences which do not seep through the spiritualisation process can be weeded out. Therefore, on the level of a logic of reflection, Hegel passes Being off as Appearance: Being actualises, as negated immediacy, its appearance (*Schein*) in terms of the essential form provided by negation. To put it another way, in appearance the non-identity of presented being and concept is reflected, an opposition that has to be mediated on the ground of absolute negativity.

Deleuze agrees with Hegel that in metaphysical thought the solidly anchored either/or alternative between essence and appearance is unacceptable, precisely because both sides stand in an abstract relationship to one another: to put it in Hegel's terms, essence is incapable of fully unfolding its conceptualisation potential because it remains related structurally to external appearance. But in clear contrast to Hegel, Deleuze denies the possibility of resolving this problematic alternative *one-sidedly*, namely to the advantage of the conceptually comprehensible truth of essence. The negation-theoretical comprehension of difference *unifies* the differences as long as 'accidental Being' is not immediately affirmed but is defined immanently only *per negationem*. Thanks to this negativity, the finite gets caught in the slipstream of the general. 'The non-being [*Nichtsein*] of the finite [*des Endlichen*] is the being [*Sein*] of the absolute' (Hegel 2010: 385). In contrast, Deleuze insists on the radical singularity of events, because every change immediately gives expression to difference, which thus evades the conceptual standards of its dialectical reflection in the Hegelian sense. Nevertheless, Deleuze does not simply argue in favour of irretrievable or unbounded differences which do not correspond to their concepts and merely renew thoughts of the indeterminate positivity of Being. Rather, the whole metaphysical alternative must be rejected as a badly posed ontological question:

> *Either* Being is full positivity, pure affirmation, but undifferentiated Being, without difference; *or* Being includes differences, it is Difference and there is non-Being, a Being of the negative. [. . .] [In contrast to these alternatives] we must say both that Being is full positivity [. . .], and that there is (non)-Being which is the Being of the problematic, of problems and questions, not the Being of the negative. (Deleuze 1994: 368–9)

With the idea of a positivity of '(non)-Being', Deleuze refers to a concept of difference that is precisely not conceived dialectically, in a negation-theoretical manner.

The 'alternative' either/or proposals mentioned above have a certain interdependence. Deleuze asserts that the *inner* differences which determine the self-differentiation of the concept are necessarily confronted with external, non-conceptualised differences which, 'ceasing to be thought, [. . .] [are] dissipated in non-being' (Deleuze 1994: 262). This necessity belongs to representation-based logic. Stated provisionally, such a logic has to have objects of intuition to put in order. The ordering procedure produces the discursive truth of immediate presentations, which as such appear gross and uncoordinated, unconnected and unthinkable. As pure differences they either blur in 'an ocean of dissemblance' (Plato's *Politikos*) or swim in representational indifference (see Deleuze 1994: 262). The conceptual work applied to the mediation of difference systematically draws the external phenomena under the logical forms of judgement – and pretends to articulate their essence. In the face of this idealist procedure of truth-finding, Deleuze raises the suspicion that the initial commotion is not erased and revoked in a proper way, but rather simply shoved aside and ignored. To put it another way, empirical indifference is nothing but a constitutive fiction of certain types of selective and exclusionary ordering acts. (In the course of this work it will always be a matter of drawing correctly the boundary between an initial experience that is merely abstractly technical and one that

Virtuality of Concepts

is concretely empiricist. Here I want to make especially clear that an epistemological orientation with respect to the experience of objects does not rule out the possibility of regressively investigating the different constituent layers. But in this case, to the 'arbitrariness' of the initial experience corresponds an intellectuation of the grounds of experience.) The integration attempted by representation-based logic, which only operates with a fictive (negativist) reproduction of difference, functions in a smooth but also (unconsciously) dismissive way: it expels what it can't digest.

Problems in the Tradition of Ontology – Aristotle

Deleuze's difference-based critique of metaphysics, to which I now turn, cannot be treated exhaustively within this framework. Only a few aspects will be discussed, namely those which are important with respect to the empiricist problem of the theory of concepts. The fundamental concepts of representation I am exposing within empiricism as abstractions derive, accordingly, from a perceptual positivism which itself is conceptualised in terms of its model. This circular procedure of doubling an already assumed *complementary* experience skips over from the beginning – in the tacit drafting of its basic axioms – the empiricist immanence of pure perceptions.

One of the fundamental critical thoughts in *Difference and Repetition* says that the representation of difference *inside* the concept corresponds to the representation of repetition *outside* the concept, so that things which are conceptually identical differ numerically in time and space and thus repeat themselves. Deleuze first turns to Aristotelean metaphysics, in order to investigate the *blockage* of universal concepts which limits the determining function of difference to constructing types. Concepts are therefore *artificially* or logically blocked when they receive *by right* an infinite content, or universality, that cannot correspond to any existing particular thing.

> In so far as it serves as a determination, a predicate must remain fixed in the concept while becoming something else in the thing. [. . .] But this is also why each determination remains general or defines a resemblance, to the extent that it remains fixed in the concept and applicable by right to an infinity of things. (Deleuze 1994: 12)

Whereas in the *logical* application of the concept its differentiating predicates remain unchanged because it must allow itself to be related to an infinity of things, they 'unfix' (*verändern*) themselves in the *real* application on these things and determine their specific kind of resemblance. This 'unfixing' of the concept points to the productive defining process which Deleuze attributes to the Aristotelian difference in kind: 'Animal becomes something other in man and in horse' (Deleuze 1994: 12). Deleuze refers to the concept's 'inverse relation of content and extension' (ibid.), which cuts across the scope of resemblance among perceived individual things in line with the Aristotelian definition of difference in kind for classification of species. Similar things are qualitatively indistinguishable from one another, which is why their non-conceptual difference merely reflects how the concept is blocked or makes explicit the negative interpretation of repetition. One could practically speak of a *generalised Aristotelianism* which expresses itself clearly in the (biological) ideal of classification, where the definition of kinds necessitates a continuous taxonomical scaling of resemblances.

As is well known, Aristotle develops his metaphysics of substance with the 'critical' intention of finally surmounting the Parmenidian problem of Being, stated but 'unsolved' by Plato. Heidegger, for example, calls attention to Aristotle's reopening of this ontological question in the first pages of *Being and Time*:

> The 'universality' of 'Being' is not that of a *class* or *genus*. [...] In medieval ontology 'Being' is designated as a *'transcendens'*. Aristotle himself knew the unity of this transcendental 'universal' as a *unity of analogy* in contrast to the multiplicity of the highest generic concepts applicable to things. With this discovery, in spite of his dependence on the way in which the ontological question had been formulated by Plato, he put the problem of Being on what was, in principle, a new basis. (Heidegger 1962: 22)

Being, Parmenides alleged, cannot be defined, because that would require a distinction that necessarily expresses the idea of non-Being. Aristotle gets around this aporia by assuming independently detachable singular things which can remain identical with themselves in spite of changing characteristics (see Strawson 1992: 55ff. on 'good old-fashioned Aristotelian essentialism', as well as Wiggins 1980). The expression 'Being' can therefore take on different meanings: on the one hand in relation to the persistent something (*ousia*), on the other hand in relation to its changeable accidents (*symbebekota*). Pierre Aubenque describes the ontological foundation of the Aristotelian doctrine of categories in two succinct sentences, completely in tune with Deleuze:

1) That which is [*das Seiende*] is not a genus, that is, it cannot be subsumed under a single concept thanks to which we could determine and define a restricted field of application. 2) [...] The term 'Being' [*Sein*] is not a univocal term, but has multiple meanings. The sense of Being carries the primary inference that it consists of a multiplicity of senses. (Aubenque 1993: 167)

To this Deleuze adds, 'Being [*Sein*] cannot be supposed a common genus without destroying the reason for which it was supposed thus; that is, the possiblility of *Being* for specific differences' (Deleuze 1994: 38).

The equivocity of Being makes explicit its a-generic character since only a multiplicity of categories can express the necessary equivocation which makes possible the scientific procedure of specifying *a single* genus. Deleuze will say that it is precisely the collaboration of genus and differences in kind in Aristotelian metaphysics that overcomes the Parmenidian problem of Being – but at the cost of a lengthy founding of representational thinking. That would mean, however, that the Aristotelian suggestion for solving ontological indeterminacy itself creates new indifferences: a situation that has to do with the fixing of difference as difference in kind.

Under what circumstance does difference in kind appear to Aristotle as the greatest difference? Clearly, difference in kind formulates a contrast *within* the assumed identity of a concept: 'Contrariety in the genus is specific difference' (Deleuze 1994: 30). In distinction to mere difference (*Verschiedenheit*) or otherness (*Andersheit*), two things differ essentially when they are not indifferent, not unproblematic, to one another, but contrarily – in terms of a common and stable foundation – opposed (see Deleuze 1994: 64). The concept of genus is partitioned into corresponding kinds by the differentiating predicate. Thus difference in kind, says Deleuze, characterises a particular Greek moment of reconciliation between difference and concept, since the former acts only as a predicate within the content of the concept. This ideal of reconciliation stands under the sign of metaphysical axioms that need to be specially treated in order to avoid a threatening repetition of indifference.

We have to keep in mind that difference in kind is surrounded above and below by too small and too large differences on which it has to rely structurally. On the one side, the order of difference relative to genera is different from those of kind. On the other side difference of kind is different from the equality or inequality of similarities. The little individual differences tend just as much toward an indistinct otherness of disconnected parts as the large, generic distinctions which cannot be related to any presupposed conceptual identity. Nevertheless, in both cases Aristotle integrates them into his procedure of specification. In the case of similarity, the different qualities of perceived things reflect only the concept's ability to define according to theoretical characteristics. In his book on Spinoza, Deleuze shows that the abstract ideas of Aristotelian biology only take into account sensory and apparent differences among things (see Deleuze 1990a: 278). Thus difference can be 'experienced only on condition that there is an assimilation of diversity taken as raw material for the identical concept' (Deleuze 1994: 266).

Whereas the individual differences are represented in the model of similarity, the generic differences are defined in terms of a judgement by *analogy*. That means that categorial difference is also based on a concept held in common.

> This concept of Being is not collective, like a genus in relation to its species, but only distributive and hierarchical: it has no content in itself, only a content in proportion to the formally different terms of which it is predicated. [. . .] The two characteristics of the concept of Being – having no more than a distributive common sense and a hierarchical primary sense – show clearly that Being does not have, in relation to the categories, the role of a genus in relation to univocal species. They also show that the equivocity of Being is quite particular: it is a matter of analogy. (Deleuze 1994: 33)

The Thomistic tradition with respect to the *pros-hen* relation of the categories, which express themselves in proportion to a single sense, stipulates that the scheme of generic assignation associated with difference of kind be carried over to the mode of categorial relations of Being. But as Deleuze stresses, this analogy of proportionality should not be interpreted in the mathematical sense of *equality* of proportions (see Deleuze 1994: 308–9, footnote 5). The differences of genera are not to be understood as differences of kind since they cannot be derived from a common uppermost genus, but rather express the diversity of a-generic Being and thus make possible the regionalisation or 'categorial' limitation of different sciences. The genera formulate in each case a unitary principle with respect to their binding specification, whereas Being in its diversity cannot be grasped in terms of a logic of predication. Thus Heidegger speaks of Being's *indefinability* (see Heidegger 1962: 23). Obviously the thought of the equivocity of Being is precisely what prevents its dif-

Virtuality of Concepts

ferentiation: difference distributes itself only on the most universally definable concepts (genera) and on the empirically derived concepts (kinds), but it is not related in an 'immediate' way to Being.

The uppermost genera all participate equally in Being, although they express it differently. Thus the concept of Being is distributive and hierarchical: the categories are all related immanently to the One, which guarantees their coherence. 'In the *pros-hen* the unique term is not only Being as common sense but already substance as first sense' (Deleuze 1994: 309). According to Heidegger, this ambiguity is reflected in the composition of 'first philosophy': 'It is both "knowledge of beings as beings" and also knowledge of the most remarkable region of beings out of which the being as a whole determines itself' (Heidegger 1990: 5). The undefined relationship of categories to one another is explicated by judgement insofar as it relegates determinations of Being either to an essence (*ousia*) or to a 'dialectical' idea (*epekeinea tes ousias*) and thereby adopts one of the regulative functions of cognition. However, the repetition of ontological indifference can be grasped both in the process of the definition of essence as first category as well as in the negative utopia of transcategorial Being.

The empirically given being functions *in the first case* as objective auxiliary identity of Being, *in terms of which* the categorial determinations are stated. The independent unity of an existent (*tode ti*) is presumed and is mediated by means of a handful of concepts. This mediation of the singular with the universal (for example, the concept of its kind) lends the individual object its essential identity. In this manner 'the individual is from now on understood as that which bears differences in general' (Deleuze 1994: 269–70). For it is the categories that relate 'inwardly' to Being, which is why analogy falls into an unresolvable difficulty:

> It must essentially relate Being to particular existents, but at the same time it cannot say what constitutes their individuality. For it retains in the particular only that which conforms to the general (matter and form), and seeks the principle of individuation in this or that element of the fully constituted individuals. (Deleuze 1994: 38)

The concepts of representation are not able to distinguish individuation from individual and thus make themselves ineligible to get rid of a remainder of indifference in their determinations.

In the second case, Being withdraws from its categorial grasp, refuses translation into substance as first category, and renews its univocal status – beyond the Being of beings. When Heidegger, in *Time and Being* (p. 2), requires us 'to think Being without beings', and Adorno, in his *Negative Dialectics*, replies, 'No Being without Beings', then, from Deleuze's perspective, both must be accused of still orienting themselves on the concept of beings or existents. To be sure, Deleuze allows himself to be inspired by Heidegger's considerations of ontological difference. Nevertheless he turns toward an immanent description of the process of becoming and never in any way lets himself be distracted by a negative theology.

This distraction arises from reflection on an unresolvable inadequacy of representative thought and from the abstract wish to resolve it. In spite of its digression into the nebulous, it correctly points to fundamental problems going back to the Enlightenment, having to do with the control of difference and the way it is put into practice when carrying out the negativist determination of Being. The decisive point is that the representation of difference operates within the blockage of concepts, and thus the empirical manifold caught up in the concept of repetition degrades to non-essential material of beforehand regulated determinations. In this sense, Deleuze states, 'It is the inadequation between difference and repetition which gives rise to the order of generality' (Deleuze 1994: 25). The existence of an uncountable number of things for one identical concept proves the inability of representation to ground itself, because it is dependent on a power of repetition that does not merge with generality and can be interpreted in terms of the latter only negatively, in a form without concept. The metaphysical penchant for order and structure meets its undoing in finite representation, insofar as it wants to shelter itself from life's continuous processes of change instead of considerably expanding the variability of its structures by bestowing fundamental meaning to temporality.

The general dilemma of metaphysical representation – the fact that the positivity of Being, that is, a positivity that doesn't let itself be influenced by any definitions and therefore is definable, if at all, only at the price of categorial differentiations that for their part generate new undifferentiated entities – articulates itself in diverse ways in the 'heretical' traditions of philosophy, but also within the various alterations of representational thinking itself. The philosophy of representation is no unified theory, but comes to an agreement only with respect to a few fundamental postulates which Deleuze analyses as decisive characteristics of a non-immanent way of philosophising. Up until now they have only been considered under the aspect of their artificially blocked concepts within the framework of their finite form. With the transition to *natural* blockage of finite *and* infinite representation, Deleuze's deliberations become more directly critical of Kant, Hegel and Freud. In some central points of their doctrine, these three stand together within the Cartesian tradition regarding the quest for certainty. The repetition which results from natural blockage points in turn to the limits of representation, and these limits are indeed exceeded by various Romantic movements. Thus begins, with Schopenhauer and Schelling, a tradition of nature or life philosophy based in intuition as a type of cognition, with which one can forge forward into the dark, sub-representative regions of the world of appearance: its Being-in-itself. The appeal to 'life', 'nature' or 'will' articulates defects in theoretical reason, but it still remains caught in the tracks of indifference. Thus it is important to investigate more closely certain pronouncements of recent representation in the light of Deleuze's critical perspective. But first let us check over a few fundamental goals connected with this critique that can be applied to representation as a whole taken as the philosophy of equivocity.

SINGULARITY OF SUBSTANCE AND ULTIMATE MULTIPLICITY – SPINOZA

Deleuze counters the concepts of representation, which confine themselves to preforming a *possibility* of experience, with concepts that determine the experience in *virtuality*. In *Difference and Repetition* 'ideas' or 'structures' have the necessary virtual status to transfer the general conditions of possible experience to genetic conditions of actual experience. Instead of relating the possibility of experience to abstract features of its external givenness, Deleuze suggests grasping 'structurally' the virtuality in the processes of self-actualising. The logic of representation ignores these processes and thereby abstractly simplifies from the outset the real conditions of an experience which does not *terminate* until it factually coincides with conceptual possibilities. In the following passage, written with an eye on natural blockage and cited in its entirety, Deleuze explicates the whole problem in terms of the spatio-temporal individuation of existing things.

> Every time we pose the question in terms of possible and real, we are forced to conceive of existence as a brute eruption, a pure act or leap

which always occurs behind our backs and is subject to a law of all or nothing. What difference can there be between the existent and the non-existent if the non-existent is already possible, already included in the concept and having all the characteristics that the concept confers upon it as a possibility? Existence is *the same* as but outside the concept. Existence is therefore supposed to occur in space and time, but these are understood as indifferent milieux instead of the production of existence occurring in a characteristic space and time. Difference can no longer be anything but the negative determined by the concept: either the limitation imposed by possibles upon each other in order to be realised, or the opposition of the possible to the reality of the real. The virtual, by contrast, is the characteristic state of Ideas: it is on the basis of its reality that existence is produced, in accordance with a time and a space immanent in the Idea. (Deleuze 1994: 211)

It may be that the reality of every experience presupposes that it is possible. But this possibility is usually restricted to formulating a few very general requirements. Between the real and the possible there develops a relation of resemblance which allows the things to become likenesses of their possibility – a possibility which has to block itself in order to realise itself. *Realisation* is thereby completed 'disjointedly' while *actualisation* takes place in genetic syntheses which are determined virtually. The virtual, in contrast to the possible, has *reality* throughout, a reality that differentiates itself in the course of its actualisation. This *different/ciation* has a double meaning, by means of which the complexity of Deleuze's theory of experience announces itself. The actual does not only differ from the virtual, but the virtual differential structures as such undergo a permanent process of differenciating. In the next chapter I will analyse these interrelations more exactly. There is neither a relation of resemblance or imitation between (transcendental) idea and (empirical) actuality, nor are ideas to be understood as *a priori* conditions which remain exterior to whatever is conditioned by them. This non-exterior difference points to THE determination of experience to differentiate itself from itself. Experience is not reducible to internal differentiations of the general or to the diversity (*Verschiedenheit*) of empirical givens.

What Deleuze wants is to conceive of a non-negative concept of difference, which is why he is constantly trying to produce exterior relations between differences, that is, relations that manage without any conceptual mediation. 'Thinking *with* AND, instead of thinking IS, instead of thinking *for* IS: empiricism has never had another secret' (Deleuze and Parnet 1987: 57). 'Nature is not attributive, but rather conjunctive' (Deleuze 1990b: 267). The demand to substitute 'and' for 'is' in order to escape the traps of the verb 'to be' points to connective syntheses or enchainments of differences that cannot be traced back to their constitutive parts and cannot be localised within the framework of a predetermined whole. These informal multiplicities characterise the 'secret' of empiricism, namely that there is – as Foucault once said – '"something altogether different" behind things: not a timeless and essential secret, but the secret that they have no essence or that their essence was fabricated in a piecemeal fashion from alien forms' (Foucault 1977c: 142).

The accidental configuration of singularities may indeed actualise itself in empirical cases – for example, in noticeable perceptual objects which stand out against an undifferenciated background, whether with preconceived attention or not – but it remains behind the consequences it produces and defines itself according to its virtual character. These virtual ideas do not stand *before* all experience as prescriptive possibilities, but are effective as conditions *within* experience. The 'and' stands for the egalitarian distribution of Being among the manifold of events and singularities and sets aside the hierarchical structures or qualitative gradations that supposedly allow the ontological participation of beings. In this sense, metaphysics transmutes into difference philosophy when it partakes of the univocity of Being in order to hinder the blocking of the concept in its form of possibility.

But how is the idea of the univocity of Being supposed to overcome the non-differentiation that was incorporated in the implicit blockage of equivocal determinations of Being? Isn't it precisely the multiple meanings of Being in contrast to its abstract identity that is supposed to be affirmed and defended? Deleuze answers these questions in his theory of expression, which actualises the thought of univocity. Accordingly, the univocity of Being does not make difference disappear, but rather establishes novel formal and modal distinctions that end the transcendent restraint of sense. With an eye on letting the ontology in the doctrine of the 'eternal return' emerge, Deleuze firmly asserts the 'one and only ontological proposition': 'The essential in univocity is not that Being is said in a single and same sense, but that it is said, in a single and same sense, *of* all its individuating differences or intrinsic modalities' (Deleuze 1994: 36 and see Deleuze 1990a: 165).

Deleuze intends to unfold the temporality and perishability of Being as it is incorporated in modern philosophy. Being loses itself in becoming or dissolves itself in the immanence of the 'flux of experience': that, it seems, is *de jure* philosophy's situation from the beginning. In the Scotistic tradition Deleuze finds first starting points for an ontological grasp of difference that can replace thinking in terms of analogies and essences. Duns Scotus grounds the doctrine of univocity with the thesis that 'Being is predicated in the same sense of everything that is, whether infinite or finite, albeit not in the same "modality"' (Deleuze 1990a: 63). Duns Scotus relates the univocity of Being to the (essential) difference between substance and mode, or *natura naturans* and *natura naturata*, as Spinoza puts it. It is important that the univocity of Being implies the univocity of attributes, which find application in the same sense to both God and creations. 'The same attributes are predicated of God who explicates himself in them, and of modes which imply them – imply them in the same form in which they are congruent with God' (Deleuze 1990a: 48). The ontological identity consists in the fact that the attributes or irreducible formal grounds express the Being of substance and modi in the same sense. Duns Scotus counters the problem of a diversity of attributes belonging to the simplicity of God by means of the concept of formal difference (*distinctio formalis*). Accordingly, the attributes act like qualitatively different meanings which relate to substance as one and the same entity. 'There are here as it were two orders, that of formal reasoning and that of Being, with the plurality in one perfectly according with the simplicity of the other' (Deleuze 1990a: 64). The singularity of substance is in no way affected by the real difference of names or attributes. 'Real and yet not numerical, such is the status of formal distinction' (Deleuze 1990a: 64).

Spinoza, as is well known, changes the sense of the real difference, which no longer – as by Descartes – is used to divide two substances. Spinoza conceives of a concept of difference that is without negation and non-numeric, so as not to distinguish substance from something else, but rather within itself. This differentiation takes place first in the attributes, which are not understood by Spinoza in theological terms as *propria* or qualities of God, but as definitions which express the nature of God, all with one and the same ontological sense. The monistic singularity of substance, which has to define itself through the medium of expression, turns the univocity of Being into the hallmark of a philosophy of immanence. In terms of their formal equality, the attributes implicitly express these definitions in the modes. Michael Hardt, who has astutely analysed the relationship between Deleuze and Spinoza, gets right to the point.

Virtuality of Concepts

> Univocity means precisely that Being is expressed always and everywhere in the same voice; in other words, the attributes each express Being in a different form but in the same sense. [. . .] On the one hand, by means of the attributes, God is absolutely immanent (fully expressed) in the world of the modes; and on the other hand, through the common forms of the attributes, the modes participate fully in divine substance. Immanence and participation are the two sides of the expression of the attributes. (Hardt 1993: 65–6)

The formal distinction is augmented by the modal distinction that exists between substance (or attributes) and the finite modes, that is, the intensive variations it is capable of. Deleuze's Spinozism is essentially dependent on the idea of immanent causality making a coherent picture of the formal identity of substance and mode. 'God is said to be the cause of all things *in the very same sense (eo sensu)* that he is said to be cause of himself' (Deleuze 1990a: 67). If the real distinction is never numeric, then inversely the numeric distinction is never real, but only modal: the production of modes has recourse to the *quantitative* differentiation of substance. This quantitative expression has two possible forms: 'intensive in terms of the essence of the modi and extensive when the modi cross over into existence' (Deleuze 1990a: 186 and see 196f.). As Deleuze states, Spinoza's genetic method distinguishes itself from Descartes' regressive, analytic method insofar as it makes explicit the effective cause (*causa efficiens*) that is expressed by every finite mode of Being in terms of the strength or capacity of its intensive quantity (see Deleuze 1990a: 135f.). The individuation comes about for Spinoza quantitatively in terms of the intensive graduality of a capacity to affect or become affected – and does not in any sense run from the general to the particular or from the genus to the specific. In this sense Deleuze sees in Spinozist thought a circumvention of hierarchical structures derived from a literal de-preciation (*Ver-urteilung*, condemnatory judgement) of Being.

> The essences of finite modi [. . .] do not form a hierarchical system. [. . .] They are not more or less remote from the One. But each depends directly on God, participating in the equality of Being, receiving immediately all that it is by its essence fitted to receive. (Deleuze 1990a: 184, 173)

The modes are expressive because they imply the same attributes that constitute the essence of substance. Substance is expressed equally by all modes in line with their capacities. 'Being is the same for all these modalities, but these modalities are not the same [. . .] – just as white includes various intensities, while remaining essentially the same white' (Deleuze 1994: 36). When univocity is thought consistently, there aren't various meanings of Being, but rather Being expresses itself univocally in terms of all its individuating differences. 'Univocity signifies that Being itself is univocal, while that of which it is said is equivocal' (Deleuze 1994: 304).

The philosophy of difference gains from univocity an empiricist concept of Being. Deleuze talks of the 'nomadic' distribution of things in an infinitely open space, a distribution not dependent on the mediation of categorial determinations. This 'self-distribution' in space is the very opposite of the hierarchical partitioning of a preconceived space that is conceptually structured in accordance with the rules of analogy. 'There is a hierarchy which measures beings according to their limits, and according to their degree of proximity or distance from a principle' (Deleuze 1994: 37). Decisions stemming from ontological characteristics of distribution directly affect the immanent and transcendent relations of order which Deleuze is trying to separate. Transcendent relations of order are by definition blocked in an onto-theological way, because they consider Being to be a higher entity that is supposed to ground the development, structure and organisation of subjects. That is why a *plane of transcendence* always has at hand a higher additional dimension, which 'stays hidden, that is never given, that can only be divined, induced, inferred from what it gives' (Deleuze 1988c: 128). On the other hand, the *plane of immanence* coexists with the nomadic distribution of things. 'The process of composition must be apprehended for itself, through that which it gives, in that which it gives' (Deleuze 1988c: 128).

The philosophy of univocity prepares the ground for the immanent description of the self-organisation of experience, once it has destroyed the ontological illusions of metaphysically infiltrated common sense. It doesn't iron out the ambiguity of Being, it radicalises it. Of course Being always expresses itself in the same manner, yet changes incessantly occur, which is why Being expresses nothing but difference. When Deleuze asserts, with an eye on Nietzsche, 'Returning is Being, but only the Being of becoming' (Deleuze 1994: 41) he makes visible the temporality which covers Being as a whole. On the basis of his concept of *intensity*, which I will examine more closely in Chapter 8, Deleuze unites his thoughts on individuation – as they were already sketched out in the context of Spinoza's definition of the modes – and univocal Being's form or manner of distributing itself. But after the *Logic of Sense* (1969), Deleuze drops the concept of univocity, because certain historically sedimented connotations prevent a complete resolution of this ontology in favour of a philosophy of difference. This 'inertia of thought' is already expressed in *Difference and Repetition* insofar as the theme of univocity is 'filtered' through three stages: as thought out by Duns Scotus, as affirmed by Spinoza and as realised by Nietzsche. The point here is that the ontology of univocity, when used critically, helps bring to the fore a concept of difference that can be understood as a response to the fundamental questions of metaphysics and its representational presuppositions.

INFINITE AND ABSOLUTE REPRESENTATION – HEGEL

So far, what has been said regarding Deleuze's critique of metaphysics has been based on a small-scale analysis of concepts collected under the rubric 'artificial blockage' in the introduction of *Difference and Repetition*, leading to a theme which is developed in the section on the metaphysics of equivocity. Accordingly, the concepts of *organic-finite* representation are blocked insofar as they think repetition in terms of the concept of universality. By reaching back to the theory of univocity, Deleuze succeeds in breathing life into a counter-tradition of metaphysical speculation, which problematises the abstract determinant power of ontologically privileged categories. Especially in his treatment of Spinozism, he shows clearly that the ontological backgrounds of single entities can only be determined immanently. In what follows, Deleuze's critique of the metaphysical foundations of representational thinking is now made concrete by analysing naturally blocked concepts, which will allow a look at *orgiastic-infinite* representations.

According to Deleuze, natural blockage characterises transcendental logic (as opposed to 'simple' Aristotelian logic) and develops in a threefold manner: in the realm of nominal concepts, of natural concepts and of concepts of freedom. Kant lays the cornerstone for the transcendental procedure on determining concepts when, in the *Critique of Pure Reason*, he relates logic to aesthetics as the doctrine of subjective conditions of perception. Natural blockage differs from the artificial since 'it forms a true repetition in existence rather than an order of resemblance in thought' (Deleuze 1994: 13). It represents in all three cases repetition as non-conceptual difference: 'repetition is attributed to elements which are really distinct but nevertheless share strictly the same concept' (Deleuze 1994: 15). In what follows, it will be enough if we consider the negativity of concepts of nature and freedom which individually refer to the separate regions of practical and theoretical reason but in terms of their dialectical interaction anticipate the Hegelian version of infinite representation.

Kant defines nature as 'the quintessence [*Inbegriff*] of all objects of sense' which can be subsumed under the concepts of human understanding (or e.g. Newtonian physics). These concepts of nature have, says Deleuze, a *virtually* infinite content. They apply in some vague way identically to all kinds of different reference objects, so it hardly suffices to individuate an object with conceptual means. As is well known, Kant used the paradox of symmetric objects to motivate the development of transcendental aesthetics – and to ground his objection to the Leibnizian principle of indistinguishability.

> By contrast with the actual infinite [in the case of artificial blockage; MR], where the concept is sufficient by right to distinguish its object from *every* other object, in this case the concept can pursue its comprehension indefinitely, always subsuming a plurality of objects which is itself indefinite. (Deleuze 1994: 13)

The virtual infinity of the concept 'reflects' the real existence of non-conceptual differences among things not completely specified conceptually. It is precisely the *power of intuition* (*Macht der Anschauung*) which defines an indefinite region of Being that cannot be immediately accessed by the determinations of understanding. The distinction between intuition and understanding attempted from the standpoint of finitude receives in the *transcendental aesthetic* a new form of mediation. Kant's question concerning the formal capacity of the subject to be affected by objects determines the transcendental framework of perception theory. Deleuze constantly points out that Kant criticises the Cartesian theory of consciousness by introducing the temporal dimension: indefinite existence (I am) can only be defined by 'I think' with the help of time. 'This third value suffices to make logic a transcendental instance' (Deleuze 1994: 86). The revolutionary element lies therefore in the subjectivation of space and time, whereby a region of non-conceptual yet inner differences opens up. The interiority of time relates Being and thought *a priori* to one another. Existence determines itself in time as a passive 'self', but the activity of determination (I think) doesn't imply a subject that is identical with this determinable, sensible existence. The easily misunderstood thesis of the 'death of the subject' meant exactly that. But Kant, who is responsible for the discovery of the transcendental difference between determination and that which is determined, renewed the identity of the subject by subjecting the pure activity of synthesis to a unified self-consciousness, 'while passivity is understood as simple receptivity without synthesis' (Deleuze 1994: 87). This division, which is grounded in the impossibility of passive synthesis, necessitates the blocked application of concepts of nature on given exterior things. The sensible givens in intuition are no more than indeterminate repetitions which coexist or succeed one another in the non-conceptual form of space-time relations.

The 'impotence of nature' which, says Hegel, expresses the furthest absence of the Spirit, corresponds to what Kant found to be nature's singular power, namely to be fundamentally prior to human powers of cognition. Deleuze draws a parallel between the nature concepts of Kant and Hegel in so far as their blockage in each case brings to the fore a material repetition that 'obstinately' withdraws from conceptual difference. Repetition thus appears as pure externality, partes extra partes. As Merleau-Ponty puts it, 'in the extreme boundary region of the Spirit, one finds at most a *mens momentanea seu recordatione carens*, or in other words, actually nothing' (Merleau-Ponty 1952: 90). When Hegel characterises nature as 'self-alienated Spirit', this not only expresses nature's abstract immediacy as marking the real *boundary* of finite cognition, but also its radical dependency insofar as it is in the last analysis nothing but the Other of the absolute Spirit, which sets itself over against itself as its own otherness.

The concepts of nature relate to objects 'without memory', whereas the concepts of freedom are blocked only when they have a memory but no self-consciousness. Thus the freedom of practical reason is real *de jure* and is only subject to factual restraints or pathological determinations of the will.

> The comprehensive representation is indeed in-itself, the memory is there, embracing all the particularity of an event [. . .] What is missing, however, for a determinant natural reason, is the for-itself of consciousness or recognition. (Deleuze 1994: 14)

So also in the case of concepts of freedom, the natural alienation of the Spirit points to the shortcoming of the concept in not being there in-itself. 'Repetition here appears as the unconscious of the free concept, of knowledge or of memory, the unconscious of representation' (Deleuze 1994: 14). Deleuze treats the theme of freedom in this connection very generally and aspires especially toward criticising the negative interpretation of repetition which is bound to an abstract concept of freedom. According to this interpretation, as long as knowledge cannot reach knowing itself as a free entity, *speculative unrest* rules existence or requires repetition in the opaque milieu of the process of self-discovery. Even if actual truth as such is retained in memory or in conscience, it still has to be made *present* in order to win closure in the light of cognition: it needs to be repeated until understood. Deleuze shows that Freud gives this Hegelian model of blockage a natural ground in terms of *repression* (*Verdrängung*). Thus it is not only true, as the saying goes, that I really don't recognise as long as I have to repeat – but also that I have to repeat to avoid recognition. This results in the playful and unconscious element of a repetition carried by a theme that can't be presented directly but is constantly alluded to.

The many problems that Deleuze raises in his treatment of 'freedom concepts' need not here be pursued further. Suffice it to say that the dialectical bringing together of practical and theoretical reason is a trait of infinite representation, as it is used in Hegel's metaphysics. The natural blockage thus no longer denotes the restriction of a form but the internal contradistinction of essence or the dynamic correlation of ground and grounded. The finite entity (*Seiende*) is indeed set over against its essential definition, but that setting finds its ground in the infinite negativity of the concept. Here we have the *idealist* aspect of Hegelian philosophy allowing itself to be localised in the transition from finite to infinite. It is not very difficult to rediscover this idealist theme in the reconciliatory process of sublation (*Aufhebung*) of the Spirit's split with itself (*Entzweiung*). The reconciliation is described by Hegel as the return of Spirit to itself from 'nature's estrangement', insofar as Spirit *remembers* itself – as *living* Spirit, having survived the death of the individual.

Remarks on Hegel in *Difference and Repetition* are in short supply and concentrate mainly on the grounding of infinite representation. They are not based on the natural blockage of concepts but on the extreme forms that cannot be represented in finite cognition (see Deleuze 1994: 42–3). Representation becomes infinite when it tries 'extending itself as far as the too large and the too small of difference' (Deleuze 1994: 262). Hegel therefore takes it upon himself to ground the categorial or largest differences in terms of an infinite principle wherein the determinations of Being and their dissimilarities are first produced as a whole out of the absolute movement of Spirit and are then resorbed back into it. The unified essence of reflection manifests itself in antagonism (*Widerspruch*) insofar as the opposed moments mutually exclude and include each other. By losing their finite independence they collapse (*zugrunde gehen*) or find in reconciled and sublated contradiction their negative unity, which contains and carries their determinations. Deleuze emphasises several times that Hegel allows differences to culminate in contradiction so that they can be grounded in terms of infinite reflection. 'Difference finds its own concept in the posited contradiction: it is here that it becomes determined as negativity' (Deleuze 1994: 45). Essential difference in Hegel's sense continues to assume a foundation in identity, although it is no longer the differences in species as related to a common genre but categorial differences as related to an infinite foundation (*unendlicher Grund*). 'Mediation itself has become foundation' (Deleuze 1994: 49). The concept systematically dismantles its identity and asserts a substantial immediacy that manifests itself in the mediation of absolute negativity. Being becomes categorially differentiated insofar as it arrives at itself within the movement of the concept.

But Deleuze is not satisfied with explaining Hegel's dialectical method by the example of contradiction as the one ideal type of infinite representation. Rather, he presents two variants, according to whether the infinity expresses itself as infinitely large or infinitely small. In this way he skilfully disputes the systematic claim of Hegelian logic to represent the only possible movement of the concept. This 'duality' which the thinking of infinite representation cannot shake off marks a blind spot in its unbounded effort to allow nothing outside of itself to be.

> When the infinite is said of the finite itself under the conditions of representation, there are two ways in which it can be said: either as infinitely small or as infinitely large. These two ways, these two 'differences' are by no means symmetrical. Thus duality is reintroduced into orgiastic representation, no longer in the form of a complementarity or a reflection of two finite assignable moments (as was the case for specific difference and generic difference) but in the form of a choice between two infinite unassignable processes – in the form of a choice between Leibniz and Hegel. (Deleuze 1994: 44)

With this alternative, which need not be further worked out here, Deleuze not only draws attention to the limits of dialectical representation. One should particularly note that Deleuze sees in Leibnizianism another kind of possibility to relate infinity to finite consciousness. When in fact Leibniz appears in *Difference and Repetition* as the second philosopher of infinite representaion, this after all communicates through him a substitution with respect to the paradigm of represenation based in a non-speculative and non-idealist post-Kantianism. 'It cannot be said that Leibniz does not go as far as Hegel: there is even a greater depth in his case, more orgiastic [. . .]' (Deleuze 1994: 49). By acknowledging above all the small differences, perspectives open up on passive incidences and occurrences which precede their representation. But it remains to be examined – as in the case of natural blockage in general – to what extent this preliminary field of non-conceptual repetitions is only presented in the form of transitory and factual indetermination.

The consequent elimination of difference or its infinite sublimation in the Being of the negative marks the decisive point in the Deleuzian rejection of Hegel's dialectical method. Deleuze sees its negativist dissolution realised in paradigmatic fashion in the sublimitive destruction of contradiction (*Zugrundegehen des Widerspruchs*), since Hegel takes contradiction to be the purest expression of difference. Yet difference 'cannot be reduced or traced back to contradiction' (Deleuze 1994: 51). When Deleuze plays out Nietzschean 'affirmation' against Hegelian 'negativity', it means that the logic of representation reaches its last nihilistic culmination with Hegel.

> The spirit of the negative made an appearance out of the sensible; and linked the intelligible to the One or the Whole. But this Whole, this One, was but a nothingness of thought, just as the appearance was a nothingness of sensation. (Deleuze 1990b: 279)

Deleuze accuses Hegel of affirming the Being of the sensible only indirectly since it is negated or fitted out with a tentative appearance (*Schein*) whose nothingness potentially contains all by itself the whole of conceptual truth and the ability to unfold it. For the affirmation of difference *as* difference Hegel substitutes in effect the negation of the differentiator – or for self-affirmation he substitutes the negation of the thoughtless otherness or exteriority. Deleuze interprets in a similar manner the beginning of the *Phenomenology of the Spirit*, which takes the here and now of sensible consciousness as a set of abstract universals and ignores their implicit difference from the start. 'The whole of *Phenomenology* is an epiphenomenology' (Deleuze 1994: 52). Singularities do not result from the mediation of opposed determinations or whenever one tries to compensate one insufficient generality with another (see Deleuze 1994: 182 and Deleuze 1988a: 44).

Deleuze points out the theological implications that hide in the

Virtuality of Concepts

nature of real contradiction 'in so far as it distinguishes a thing from everything that it is not' (Deleuze 1994: 45, 49). This 'logically monstrous' non-being implies the setting up of a beings-taken-all-together (*Seiendheit im Ganzen*), an *ens summum*, that corresponds to the identity principle of absolute negativity. Alluding to the critique of Hegel by Althusser, Deleuze speaks of the threadbare monocentrism of the circle that characterises Hegel's dialectical project (see Deleuze 1994: 310–11). It is certainly unnecessary to follow blindly Deleuze's generalised anti-Hegelianism. But 'difference' and 'negation' must be strictly separated from one another. A philosophy that makes itself at home in negativity loses sight of difference, and with it the problems and questions which are preordained in reflection. In Deleuze's challenge to think dialectically in a good way one cannot miss hearing approval of Merleau-Ponty, who in *The Visible and the Invisible* characterises the dialectic as thinking of a Being 'that is not simply positivity, not in-itself and also not the setting up of a thinking, but expresses self-manifestation, disclosure, and continuous genesis [...]' (Merleau-Ponty 1968: 125). When Deleuze insists that the actual positivity of the thesis cannot be mediated with its antithesis, which has anyway been extrapolated with regard to their synthesis, Merleau-Ponty on the other hand argues inversely that every thesis – as antithesis of an opposing thesis – presents an idealisation that must be critically examined. Both develop a 'dialectic without synthesis' which gets involved in concrete differential relations and problematical constellations since it concentrates on the description of their ideal structures and uncovers and criticises the emptied meanings when the proposed solutions, in the guise of clarity, precision, objectivity or truth, push into disappearance the problem areas. 'In other words, what we exclude from the dialectic is pure negativity and what we look for is a dialectical definition of Being [...], quick, fragile, unstable definitions' (Merleau-Ponty 1968: 95). Merleau-Ponty's so-called 'hyper-dialectic' can accomplish this task if it creates unique virtual concepts and ideas, so-called 'concepts without equivalence', that find expression for the invisible *of* the visible (Merleau-Ponty 1968: 151).

Thinking can therefore only be understood as 'realisation of something invisible that is precisely the backside of the visible, the strength of the visible' (Merleau-Ponty 1968: 145). Merleau-Ponty admits that he doesn't get around to working out this 'doctrine of ideas', but his hints and suggestions will be picked up by Deleuze in his conception of 'problem-ideas' and phantastic concepts. The phenomenological insight that concepts get their specific reality from their self-reference and nevertheless relate to the visible world, whose very *visibility* they determine, without becoming detached from it, proves to be implicitly Deleuzian. In this way Deleuze takes it upon himself, as will be more precisely shown in what follows, to immunise empiricism against Hegel and his verdict on abstraction. Bruce Baugh has pointed out that 'the empirically actual is not a bare paticular, a "this" like any other "this", but a singularity that has a determinate content in virtue of its actual genesis' (Baugh 1993: 24). And that is why the simple difference between empirical givens can be expressed as positive difference with specific content, thanks to the immanent causal processes of their givenness.

Structuralism of Ideas and Concepts

The reality of the virtual is structure (Deleuze 1994: 209)

Difference must be thought, even if it cannot be recognised. Deleuze therefore adopts the concept of the transcendental Idea to which Kant draws attention at the beginning of his dialectic (see Deleuze 1994: 168f). It is a peculiarity of these Ideas, which Kant lumps together as concepts of reason, that they cannot be restricted to the 'possibility' of experience and can only be thought in *problematic form* (see Kant 1999: A 320/B 377, A 328/ B 384, A 335/ B 392, A 286/ B343). 'The object of an Idea, Kant reminds us, is neither fiction nor hypothesis nor object of reason: it is an object which can be neither given nor known, but must be represented without being able to be directly determined' (Deleuze 1994: 169). 'Difference' is such an idea: it is problematic because, although neither given nor known, it 'gives one to think'.

Transcendental Dialectic – Kant

Kant repeatedly says that no object in experience is *congruent* to or adequate to the dialectical Idea. Nevertheless, *reason*, as 'the faculty for posing problems in general' (Deleuze 1994: 168), can be used meaningfully in matters of speculation, even if it introduces inescapable illusions and must be carefully limited to its immanent usage. Only ideas lend systematic unity and widest application to various acts of the understanding, although they are problematic 'without resolution' and in no sense merely hypothetical or probable, 'since

Virtuality of Concepts

we can never envision [*im Bilde entwerfen*] such a thing [that is, the idea in the form of a cognitive whole (MR)]' (Kant 1999: A328/B384). Problems of reason are grounded or ungrounded according to their legitimate or illegitimate usage. Deleuze draws on the objective as well as indeterminate status of the transcendental idea as expressed in its legitimate or regulative function, because thanks to it, 'the constitution of a unitary and systematic field [is made possible] which orients and subsumes the researches or investigations [of the understanding] in such a manner that the answers, in turn, form precisely cases of solution' (Deleuze 1994: 168). Thus indeterminance would be a positive and objective structure which binds together the concepts of understanding in a *focus imaginarius* – from outside the limits of possible experience. Deleuze places special value on the establishment of the transcendent-immanent double character of the Kantian idea, which retreats behind experience although it organises this experience in a *quasi*-virtual way as focal point or horizon. Clearly the 'transcendental' character of the idea should therefore not be confused with its transcendent application. The former signifies only the non-empirical status of the idea, which makes it necessary to distinguish between its legitimate and illegitimate application (according to immanent and transcendent principles [*Grundsätze*]).

Indeterminance signifies merely the first objective moment of the transcendental idea. Going one step further, Kant defines the object (*Objekt*) of the idea indirectly, relative to the objects (*Gegenstände*) of experience. The systematisation of the act of understanding finds expression in the material *similarity* of appearances, so that the transcendental idea can be determined in *analogy* to their reciprocal relations. In the last analysis, its object (*Objekt*) possesses the ideal of a continuous or infinite determination insofar as it makes possible the increasing specification of concepts of understanding (see Deleuze 1994: 169). It is important for Deleuze that within the dialectical idea the three moments, namely indeterminance, determinability and determination, converge in a genuine problematic way. That shows to advantage again and again in the construction of the chapter on *Ideas and the Synthesis of Difference* (Deleuze 1994: 168–221). For example, Deleuze asserts that the idea picks up the three aspects of the Cogito: 'The *I am* as an indeterminate existence, *time* as the form under which this existence is determinable, and the *I think* as a determination' (Deleuze 1994: 169). This parallelisation shows that Kant derives the ideas from temporally determined experience and its self-organisation: the temporal order of succeeding perceptions thus opens up the unavoidable question of its beginning, its wholeness and its end.

For Deleuze, as we shall see, the temporal status of ideas gains importance insofar as the ideas determine in a positive and problematic way the form of inner sense. However, according to Kant, two of the three moments of the idea remain extrinsic: 'If ideas are in themselves undetermined, they are determinable only relative to objects of experience, and bear the ideal of determination only relative to concepts of the understanding' (Deleuze 1994: 170). As expected, Deleuze isn't satisfied with this extrinsic determination of the idea, because representation will not really be bypassed as long as pure thought remains undetermined and/or dependent on empirical propositions of consciousness. At this point Deleuze suspects not only that Kant's true motive is to hold fast 'to the point of view of conditioning' (Deleuze 1994: 170), but also that the post-Kantians want to extend the *Critique* to the point of genetic questioning. Thus the three moments of the dialectical idea have to be interpreted as three interdependent principles pertaining to a single adequate ground (principle of sufficient reason).

To support his argument Deleuze uses Salomon Maimon, who strives to overcome through idealisation the extrinsic relationship, postulated by Kant, between determinable phenomena and spontaneous determination. That means that determinability is overtaken in the direction of a principle of reciprocal determination, so that determinable facts experience their determination in reciprocal syntheses or differential relationships. According to this *Salomonic* view, the relationship between determinability and determination has to be interiorised in the idea, by means of which its indeterminate positivity attains a fully adequate structural distinction (see Deleuze 1994: 173f.). All objects in its specific sphere of influence are supposed to be immanently or sufficiently grounded: the idea determines, as a dialectical problem, the real conditions of its corresponding resolutions. Deleuze in no way intends to understand the idea as speculative essence that altogether sublimates the difference between the concepts of reason and the finite representation of things (see Smith 1997: 85). Instead, philosophically speaking, the difference idea describes the *real* genetic structures of experience without interacting with the *actual* results conditioned by them. The problematic element of the idea has nothing to do with its unconditioned status resulting from the negative judgement of finitude, but rather with the temporal dissociation of the transcendental subject, which affects thinking as such.

From the perspective of classical German philosophy it is difficult to understand this shift of the problem. After all, it seems either the idea can be limited to its regulative function or else it ignores the finite boundary of possible experience and manifests itself in the absolute. In the first case, reason abstains from legislating experience. In the second case, reason makes itself concrete by lifting experience to its own level or by sublimating in itself the achievements of the understanding. But in contrast to these alternatives, Deleuze creates a dialectical idea that distinguishes itself *essentially* from empirical propositions, although it completely determines the latter. This conception of the idea is not inconsistent if it can be shown that in it the interplay of understanding (faculty for concepts) and reason (faculty for ideas) is completely overhauled.

Deleuze has recourse to at least two directions in modern philosophy to unfold in a difference-philosophical way his reflections on transcendental Ideas: first toward 'structuralism' from Saussure to Lacan and Foucault (see Stivale 1998: 251–82) and second toward the phenomenological ontology of Heidegger and Merleau-Ponty. The economic, biological or linguistic structures, which Foucault, in *The Order of Things*, presupposes in principle with respect to the foundational actions of finite subjects, are transposed by Deleuze into the ontological realm of questions and problems which necessarily emerge without getting final answers. This 'problematic' character of structures can be defined conceptually, even though the ideal problem cannot be solved with a limited number of scientific propositions nor can it be traced to a subjective source that only seems to be able to get around the problem.

> It must be remembered to what extent modern thought and the renaissance of ontology is based upon the question-problem complex. This complex has ceased to be considered the expression of a provisional and subjective state in the representation of knowledge in order to become the intentionality of Being *par excellence,* the only instance to which, properly speaking, Being answers without the question thereby becoming lost or overtaken. On the contrary, it alone has an opening coextensive with that which must respond to it and can respond to it only by retaining, repeating and continually going over it. (Deleuze 1994: 195)

This phenomenological discovery of the 'problematic' character of experience is explicated by Deleuze in concepts of structure. By going back to the ontological interrogation, he lends to structural thought a virtual dimension. Emphasis should be placed on the an-hypothetical constitution of the pure potentiality of the dialectical or structural idea, which in no way is to be reduced to one or more unproven theses whose truth content could in principle be expressed in one or more apodictic propositions. Ontological questions and problems do not carry any preliminary deficit that can be cast aside by giving correct answers. Their virtual constitution ought not to be confused with a possibility that is not yet realised but could be realised. They plainly possess no shortage that would have to be compensated for by means of teleological models. Deleuze refers to the mathematicians Abel and Lautman, who have demonstrated that the truth of a problem is not defined by its solution, but rather that every possible solution results from the form of the problem (see Vuillemin 1962: 213ff.). The progressive determination of the conditions of a problem articulates itself in correlative attempts at solution. In the first place, the problem is essentially different from the solutions. In the second place, the solutions are produced immanently in terms of internal conditions of the problem. And third, solutions have a tendency to alter or disguise the problems they are supposed to solve, so that the problems withdraw from them or fall behind, more or less unresolved. Problems do not reveal themselves in the solutions: distinguishing them one from another makes it possible to determine the genesis of solutions structurally or to regard solutions as the process of actualising the problem. As will be demonstrated more precisely later, the decisive difference between actual and virtual makes it impossible to base variable appearances on laws of structure construed as static laws of form.

Questions that inevitably impose themselves and unfold in thought as problems mark the blind spot in the self-images of the grounding reflection. Unlike Heidegger, Deleuze carefully avoids a homology between what must be thought and what thought itself is, especially when thought supposedly thinks about itself (see Deleuze 1994: 321, note 11). Deleuze speaks with Blanchot of that 'aleatory original point which designates "the impossibility of thinking what thought is"' (Deleuze 1994: 199). This impossibility contests the self-satisfaction of reason, which is driven by an essential unrest: thinking is irrelevant as long as it circles, self-contained, within itself and becomes meaningful only when it reacts to objective problems and knows how to interpret them. Questions which arise in an imperative way result from ontological repetition, as Deleuze asserts in concert with Heidegger. 'Not that it is sufficient, however, to repeat a single question which would remain intact at the end, even if this question is "What is Being?"' (Deleuze 1994: 200). Repetition itself must be understood as the empiricist 'cause-in-itself' (*Ur-Sache*) which always comes up with new questions: the Being of the sensible which sets in motion the process of thought.

> Thinking only thinks insofar as it is forced and necessitated to do so in the face of that which 'gives one to think', that is, the questionable – and the questionable is at the same time the unthinkable or the unthought, that is, the constant fact 'that we don't yet think' (in accordance with the pure form of time). It is true that on the path which leads to that which is to be thought, all begins with sensibility. From the intensive to thought, it is always an intensity that hurls thought at us. (Deleuze 1994: 144, trans. mod.)

Nonrepresentable perceptions and sensations throw out questions that make us remember, dream or construct concepts. Deleuze speaks occasionally of 'climes' or zones of 'non-sense' that cannot be determined from the outside because their relation to a transcendent authority would mean standing in direct contradiction to the statutory conceptual self-identity of a pure subject. The questions which are taken up by thought have to explicate themselves as problems or ideas: in the course of their philosophical determination they lose none of their non-expressible characteristics as genetic phenomena or subrepresentative signs. When Deleuze says that the philosophy of transcendental empiricism has to relate in an essential way to the nonphilosophical realm, then we should expect that it can give expression to the unconscious of thought as structure or structuralising process using conceptual means (see Deleuze and Guattari 1991: 218 and 40f.). 'Nonphilosophical' are the pure sensations and so forth that raise nonpropositional questions which in turn develop 'prephilosophically' in thought by delivering the internal conditions required for their conceptual determination. The 'origin of ideas' lies in thought, not because it comprehends or grounds the various faculties, but because the exclusive object of thought is to have ideas as conceptually structured ideas – and indeed, at best, those that have internalised difference with regard to faculties and their genetic potential (see Deleuze 1994: 192ff.).

Deleuze defines the immanent structure of experience as virtual *multiplicity* – and draws on the Bergsonian meaning of the word, rather than the Kantian (see Deleuze 1988a: 38ff.). For the time being, let's keep in mind that with his concept of multiplicity Deleuze thinks the continuous *self-organisation* of the many. The structure which characterises empiricism is not primarily language, but time – as Deleuze has shown by introducing the idea as a 'time-problem' in accordance with Kant's transcendental dialectic. With inimitable 'flexibility', time pulls the virtual-actual *differenciation* process into a never-ending becoming. In the next chapter I will give a more detailed account of Deleuze and temporality. But first it is advantageous to outline the structure of multiplicity in light of Deleuze's reading of Bergson.

Idea of the Virtual – Bergson

The concept of *virtuality*, one of the hallmarks of the Deleuzian philosophy, issues above all from Bergson's philosophy of memory and consciousness, and characterises in a decisive manner Deleuze's dialectical idea – that is, the problematic structure or transcendental field of multiplicity. *First*, Deleuze adopts from *Time and Free Will* (1889) Bergson's distinction between continuous (virtual) and discrete (actual) multiplicity. In reaction to psycho-physiological parallelism, in particular with respect to Fechner's application of Weber's law, Bergson argues against the possibility of determining, in the realm of temporal consciousness *(durée)*, homogeneous minimal differences of intensive states of consciousness that guarantee their divisibility and measurability. But if the differentials of sensation cannot be reduced to smallest, simple and equal intervals, then they also cannot be equated with physiological units of stimuli. Bergson insists that it is always the objective symptoms that accompany sensations that can be measured. The heterogeneous diversity of duration has no uniform basic unit of measurement that could bring its differences in intensity to a common denominator, because 'the metric principle varies with every step of division' (Deleuze 1988a: 40). Deleuze adopts the distinction Bergson makes between types of multiples on the basis of a pair of concepts regarding intensive and extensive magnitude. Thus the essential differences within the concept of duration have to be understood as virtual differences of intensity, which are neither extensive nor numerically quantifiable.

> In reality, duration divides up and does so constantly: That is why it is a *multiplicity*. But it does not divide up without changing in kind, it changes in kind in the process of dividing up: this is why it is a non-

numerical multiplicity, where we can speak of 'indivisibles' at each stage of the division. [...] The subjective, or duration, is the *virtual*. To be more precise, it is the virtual insofar as it is actualised, in the course of being actualised. It is inseparable from the movement of its actualisation. For actualisation comes about through differenciation, through divergent lines, and creates so many differences in kind by virtue of its own movement. (Deleuze 1988a: 42–3)

Duration is a virtual multitude because it is not put together out of simple and separated parts, but implies passive syntheses of objective indeterminate elements, that is processes of becoming 'which permeate one another, imperceptibly organise themselves into a whole, and bind the past to the present by this very process of connexion' (Bergson 2001: 121). The 'qualitative' unit, which comes and goes continuously in the temporal stream of consciousness, cannot be traced back to rudimentary discrete particulars. Radical empiricism, as advocated by Bergson no less than by William James, dispenses with logical atomism in sense-data theory. Nevertheless, Bergson himself later corrects his rigorously dualistic thinking, as reflected in the citation above from Deleuze, whereby the virtual 'is inseparable from the movement of its actualisation'. Deleuze worked out this connection, which is so important for his concept of structure, for the first time in his presentation of Bergson's theory of memory. Bergson himself first defined philosophically his concept of the virtual in *Matter and Memory*. The deepening of consciousness through recollection makes it possible to designate pure memories, which are both unconscious and real, as virtual memories.

With the introduction of the *pure past*, Bergson attempts to found ontologically the continuous syntheses of the present. Deleuze emphatically greets this new development in Bergson's theory, especially its implications for the theory of time. To put it concisely, the distinction between present and past as found in *Matter and Memory* marks the *second* important point in Deleuze's *Bergsonism*. The 'living present' of duration 'empties' itself to a certain extent because it rests on a transcendental synthesis of the past which, under the rubric *mémoire souvenir*, is the self-sustaining or subjectivation form of Being. In an important passage, Bergson elaborates:

> You define the present in an arbitrary manner as *that which is*, whereas the present is simply *what is being made*. Nothing *is* less than the present moment, if you understand by that the indivisible limit which divides the past from the future. When we define this present as going to be, it exists

not yet, and when we think it as existing, it is already past. (Bergson 1988: 149–50)

Deleuze will follow up on Bergson's suggestion in the *Logic of Sense* when he investigates the (Stoic) *Aion* (Deleuze 1990b: 162ff.). Of immediate importance is to establish the intriguing *pre-existence* of pure past, which is not constituted after being present. Bergson says again and again that we jump 'all at once' into the past or into the 'region of sense' (see for example Bergson 1988: 135 and Deleuze 1988a: 58). The mode of being (*Seinsmodus*) of the past, which *insists* in the present without ever being present, is characterised by Deleuze, in concert with Bergson, as 'virtual'. Thus we have the non-representative character of pure recollections: 'To picture is not to *remember*' (see Bergson 1988: 135f). Only the present allows itself to be represented as an earlier or actual present, whereas the pure past initiates the representation. When Deleuze refers to Proust (see Deleuze 1988a: 96 and Deleuze 2000: 58), in order to resurrect the virtuality in the transcendental or involuntary use of memory, then it is precisely not a question of the re-presentation (*Vergegenwärtung*) of a previous present (*Gegenwart*), but of a counter-actualisation (*Gegenverwirklichung*) of a pure past that in singular fashion expresses its virtual richness. Or, to put it another way (see Deleuze 1990b: 160–1), the present as immediate troubling event is doubled by counter-actualisation, 'the identification with a distance', which 'gives thought time' to explore what is troubling and hence escape getting caught in the event as a 'crack-up'.

Memory recall is therefore a system of unconscious Being, containing multiple coexisting layers of the past which repeat and differenciate themselves *simultaneously* with the progression of the present precisely because new time segments are continually being added. In the cone of memory the virtual contents permanently shift about as they repeat themselves and connect with one another in passive syntheses, so that thought can take from them the determinations which are available for a particular situation needing interpretation. These layers of recollections, which in their totality underscore and undercut every present, turn up, says Bergson, in a more or less countervailing capacity, depending on the degree to which they determine the actual situation. And here we arrive at the *third* important moment, the movement of actualisation which completes the recollection when it is called up to adapt itself to a presently vexing context in order to help interpret it.

Virtuality of Concepts

> Whenever we are trying to recover a recollection, [...] we become conscious of an act *sui generis* by which we detach ourselves from the present in order to replace ourselves, first, in the past in general, then, in a certain region of the past [...] But our recollection still remains virtual; we simply prepare ourselves to receive it by adopting the appropriate attitude. Little by little it comes into view like a condensing cloud; from the virtual state it passes into the actual; and as its outlines become more distinct and its surface takes on colour, it tends to imitate perception. (Bergson 1988: 133–4)

This process of actualisation is inaugurated by a discontinuous sign in the field of perception that won't allow itself to be assimilated by the senso-motoric schemata. The 'disruption' calls upon memory to explicate the sign. Deleuze characterises the plunge into the past – alluding to Heidegger's thinking the event – as a 'leap into ontology', which must first be accomplished so that memory can re-present itself. Those actualisations which often repeat themselves are then habituated or made automatic within contractive memory. – But enough for now! It makes no sense to consider Bergson's doctrine of memory in more detail at this point (but see Rölli 2004b). The three moments I have presented suffice to make Deleuze's concept of structure more tangible. The virtual multiplicity of the 'memory-idea' precedes and helps determine actual givens (in this case, the factual 'mixture of images' of a perception suffused with memories). Nevertheless, this determination takes place immanently, that is, *in* the actualisation process of the self-determining idea. Every actualisation means that the structural relations or the virtual conditions of the idea simultaneously undergo a process of differentiation. The structure can be understood as a complex, self-adjusting system because it integrates the ideal factor of time as its constituent element.

The 'structuralist' evaluation of Bergson's time and memory theories can be summarised (in anticipation of the next chapter) with the help of Deleuze's presentation of the three paradoxes of pure past (see Deleuze 1994: 81f). The first paradox has to do with the *contemporaneity* of the past and the present it once was, so to speak. Deleuze wants to say that a present can only pass by and 'be past' if, simultaneously with its construction, it already possesses a past-dimension. This leads to the second paradox of the *coexistence* of the complete past with every new present relative to which it is the past, 'whence the Bergsonian idea that each present is only the entire past in its most contracted state' (Deleuze 1994: 82). Pure past is called by Deleuze the *a priori* element of time, which, because of its simultaneity with the present, is not constituted thereafter, and therefore has never been present, but coexists with every present as non-present. The third paradox, that of *preexistence*, signifies this precedence of the past with respect to the fleeting present. The 'counter-sense' (*Widersinn*) of these three 'counter-opinions' (*Gegenmeinungen*) is aimed at that representational logic pertaining to present and past which Bergson, especially in *Matter and Memory*, criticises so astutely. It is no longer a question of starting from the individual givens of the present and to reflect these – by way of memory – in the general medium of the concept. Bergson goes in the opposite direction. He begins with the singular relations of recollections and tries to discover in the process of their actualisation the conditions for their generalisation. Although Deleuze is in many respects reserved toward Bergson, with his challenge to go beyond the synthesis of the past and get to a concept of *future* and *becoming* in a more Nietzschean sense (see below, Chapter 8), the three paradoxes just named mark essential structural characteristics of the problematic idea. Their virtual multiplicity does not, indeed, rest on a priority of recollection over the other faculties (and not at all on the abstract homogenisation of space), but addresses the sensual differences of intensity and their synthetic relations with respect to the realm of temporal subjectivation processes. Nevertheless, the *pre-existence* of pure past points to the precedence of the problem with respect to its solution, its *coexistence* with the present points to the continued virtual existence of the 'overdetermined' problem behind its solutions, and its *simultaneity* with the present points to the curious immanence of the problem within its solutions.

What is a Structure?

In a short article on structuralism in the many-volumed *Histoire de la philosophie* edited by his friend François Châtelet, Deleuze states that 'structuralism is not to be separated from a new transcendental philosophy' (Deleuze 1998: 263). He substantiates his thesis by reiterating that in structuralism symbolic conditions (places and relations) are defined in a pre-extensive topological space, that is, are ordered before empirical things take these structurally defined positions and attitudes. The actual 'novelty' consists in the fact that the structures define a (transcendental) realm that is prior to the finite knowledge foundations of human understanding. The determination of structures will have to be understood in epistemological terms as determination that must be comprehended from assumptions no reflectional logic can catch up with. This demand can only be fulfilled because, in the train of the structuralist procedure, the model of subjectivity, in which traditionally the faculty for concepts is situated, also undergoes changes. The transcendental presuppositions do not define a formal *a priori*, but rather characterise concrete conditions of experience that are effective within experience but cannot be empirically or actually given.

Deleuze defines the universal structure of experience as a multiplicity that integrates the three principles of sufficient ground, that is, arranges a complex correspondence relationship between the three dimensions of quantitability, qualitability and potentiality. What does that mean? Deleuze first introduces into the definition of structure *undetermined elements* which are not derived from the realm of given empirical determinations. These elements, which come from the *structural reduction*, do not signify anything: they possess neither sensible form nor conceptual meaning. They do not actually exist, but belong exclusively in a virtual context. 'In this sense they imply no prior identity, no positing of a something that could be called one or the same' (Deleuze 1994: 183). Take, for example, the phonemes in the linguistic model, which cannot be traced back to the vocal or semantic units of the speech in which they realise themselves. Phonemes do not exist outside the phonemic contexts in which they define one another. Or, for another example, Deleuze borrows from the interpretation of the calculus by Bordas-Demoulin: when dx and dy are equal to zero, 'dx is strictly nothing in relation to x, and dy is nothing in relation to y' (Deleuze 1994: 171). Nonetheless these *zeros* do not annihilate the differential quantities as such, but only the particular values of the intuition and the general values of the concepts of understanding. This pure *quantitability* of symbolic elements of structure describes, for a start, the ideal source (*ideelle Ursache*) of the continuity of an experiential totality 'which must not be confused either with certain fixed quantities of intuition *(quantum)* or with certain variable quantities in the form of concepts of the understanding *(quantitas)*' (Deleuze 1994: 171).

It is precisely the undefined and non-differenciated ('chaotic') elements that enter into specific relations by means of which they define one another. In the case of structural relations, it is a question of differential relationships which are characterised by the fact that their relata have no defined individual value in themselves and show no independent or non-relational existence. 'Each term exists absolutely only in its relation to the other' (Deleuze 1994: 172). Within the idea of the sensible, the virtual state of these genetic elements, definable in reciprocal syntheses, allows them, as 'minute' (molecular) sensations, to have at their disposal only an intensive quantity, corresponding to quantitability. As we have seen, Deleuze relies on the transcendental critique of classical empiricism's theory of representation, as when Kant conceives of intensive sensations as non-extensive, non-referential and sense-specific affections. But now it is important that the continuous synthesis, which every intensive quantity implies, does not simply add homogeneous parts, but keeps on producing continuous quantities which by definition can be diminished infinitely, without ever reducing to equal, discrete, fundamental components. Intensity is only a quantity because it 'constantly' implies a change in the condition of the sensation, a change that cannot be quantified extensively. This is, to speak with Bergson, a difference of 'essential' rather than 'gradual' nature, since it cannot be traced back to a base scale that allows measurement. Only time differentiates *itself* continuously while constantly running through processes of becoming. Snippets from these reciprocal processes can be objectified when their flowing syntheses bring about shifts of accent that cross the threshold of consciousness. In many places Deleuze speaks of the special conditions of the *transcendental experience* taking place 'primarily' in the sub-representative realm (in the paradoxical mode of the faculties): these are intensive 'smooth' spaces and times, which are treated (for example, in his interpretation of Bacon's paintings) as 'zones of indiscernibility' (see Deleuze 2004: 20ff. and Deleuze and Guattari 1987: 488).

The 'synthetic function' of structure, which Deleuze finds in the reciprocal determination of symbolic elements in a differential relationship, transmutes the *principle of determinability* into the *principle of interchangeable determination*, whereby the indeterminate differential elements become determinable in qualitative form. 'The reciprocal synthesis of differential quotients as the source of the production of real objects – this is the substance of ideas insofar as they bathe in the thought-element of *qualitability*' (Deleuze 1994: 173). At this point it is important to understand reciprocal syntheses as non-localisable connections within the idea, connections that characterise the multiplicity intrinsically without recurring in a uniform, homogeneous space. The interrelationally determined 'pure qualification' expresses a structural genesis that covers the extension as well as the objects over which the extension extends. Thus times and spaces are immanent to the structures as forms of actualisation: they are the inner dynamics which the differential relationships unfold and thus 'completely' determine the structure. So now we have reached the third aspect of structure, *potential* determination, which Deleuze formulates rather dryly as 'distribution of singularities'.

> Corresponding to the determination of differential relations are singularities, distributions of singular points. [. . .] In this way, the determination of phonemic relations proper to a given language ascribes singularities in proximity to which the vocalisations and significations of the language are constituted. *The reciprocal determination* of symbolic elements continues henceforth into *the complete determination* of singular points that constitute a space corresponding to these elements. (Deleuze 1998: 265)

The *singularities* define the special, flexible positions in a structural field or provide the flexible objective conditions for a problem that in no way can be reduced to mere prior obstacles, mistakes or fictions raised by a provisional or approximate knowledge. For example, discernible *dimensions* of structure can be characterised by means of the concrete order of singularities within that structure: say, different languages with respect to their phonological peculiarities. Clearly Deleuze uses the concept of 'singularity' to mark a fact as non-representable: the unique, non-identically repeatable, and not generally classifiable pre-individual event. The singularity designates the singular rather than the regular, the notable rather than the commonplace, the important rather than the unimportant. From the perspective of the differenciation of structure, Deleuze gives the concept a very precise meaning: the singularity does not mark the empirical case of a conspicuous occurrence that stands out against a dark background, but rather the *conditions of conspicuousness* are defined in the concept, which is to say, the singularity presents an accentuated element of organisation in the self-organisation process of structure that defines immanently the structuration that is happening – without being a stable marker in a formal framework that would be abstractly prior to the happening. The division between the commonplace and the distinctive works itself out at first in the virtual space of structure, whereas the notable empirical object presents the result of the structurally defined actualisation. Nevertheless, there are naturally many structural models with an essentially limited variability of basic definitions. The complete definition that takes place with the distribution of singular points defines the potentiality of structure – whereby their specification is immanent to the various solutions in which the structure incorporates itself. The structure in its totality doubles itself in a field of actualisation that sets in advance the exclusive directions of its differenciation: the multiple relations manifest themselves in the corresponding extensive bodies or quantities.

Yet this determination of structure by means of undefined elements, reciprocal connections and singular points remains rather schematic. Further characteristics of the *ideal syntheses of difference* can now be brought to light using the example of language. However, explanations of time and intensity aspects of Deleuzian philosophy, undertaken in Chapter 8, will be needed to illuminate his thoughts on structure, because they treat the actualisation processes that decisively define the occurrence of 'structuration'.

In the structuralist movement in France, Ferdinand de Saussure showed conclusively that the differential determination of the sign cuts apart the accustomed bond between things and their linguistic representations: the sign's ambivalence (*signifiant/signifié*) marks its arbitrariness. Only the placement of the sign within a language system, that is, its relation to the other signs from which it distinguishes itself, regulates its meaning. This meaning is never completely fixed because, at the very least, the linguistic set of relations, that is to say their differential, again shifts within the individual speech acts, and this production of new or unanticipated linguistic meanings can only be explained by the introduction into the structural occurrence of an *ideal time*. Structural determination is open in principle because 'we must carefully distinguish the object insofar as it is complete and the object insofar as it is whole. [. . .] What the complete determination lacks is the whole set of relations belonging to actual existence' (Deleuze 1994: 209). The potentiality of structure designates the virtual (complete) totality of what can be said, which (never wholly) actualises itself in linguistic expression. The process-character of the virtual marks the simultaneity of structure and genesis: ideal relationships determine *once and for all* the way actualisation can happen, just as a particular throw of the dice determines once and for all that throw. Even though the virtual determines the actual, it does not encompass the latter wholly, because it must constantly work to carry out or *fulfill* that determination (in a process of actualisation). This fulfilment – not 'realisation', for the virtual is fully real in itself – completes itself over time and leaves behind its traces in the *different/cial* relationships of structure. 'For the nature of the virtual is such that, for it, to be actualised is to be *differenciated*' (Deleuze 1994: 211). (For the notion *different/ciation*, see Deleuze 1994: 209f.)

Virtuality of Concepts

To be sure, the actual representations result from genetic processes of structuration, but these processes are simultaneously distorted or misplaced – which gives the impression that the representations merely concern an abstract, preset form of possibility instead of potentiality. Actualisation tends (in its results) to unify virtual differences. Deleuze speaks of the *unconscious* of structure to designate the unavoidable exclusion, thanks to the logic of representation, of the genetic backgrounds, which can be seen happening in the realm of the already constituted objects. The structuralist position reverts to *formalistic* thinking, which operates by means of a *contradictional* logic, whenever it conceives the conditions between structure and its 'realisation' in an atemporal way. In this sense the concept of structure can only be construed immanently if in its inner consistence the hypothetical element of concept and the form of the negative are not registered or inscribed (see Deleuze 1994: 203). The actuality itself must be determined in a difference-philosophical way, so that the structural process which underlies it comes into view. Only then is it possible to emphasise the conditions and limitations of representationalism.

A further aspect of structure is that it actualises itself in (at least two) series, which relate to one another in the process. Deleuze develops this fundamental parallelism above all in *Logic of Sense*. There, the heterogeneous series converge in the direction of the structural element of sense, which constantly distributes itself over and circulates within the two rows of signified and signifiers. In other words, 'in an assemblage there are, as it were, two faces, or at the least two heads. There are the *states of things*, states of bodies [...]; but also *utterances*, regimes of utterances' (Deleuze and Parnet 1984: 70). The sense attributes itself on the one hand to the state of things and insists on the other hand within the sentences. At the same time it neither dissolves completely into the words that express it nor into the bodies and qualities that realise it. Deleuze's theory of sense-paradoxes, which he develops on the basis of the stories of Lewis Carroll, combines the genetic and expressive potential of structure with the impossibility of its complete actualisation, which instead refers to an empty field within its serial arrangement, a field which constantly shifts about in the process of differenciation. The attempt to localise on either one of the two sides the explanatory ground implies the loss of that third field, as a pre-existent as well as genetic dimension.

The *philosophical* concept of structure developed by Deleuze can be defined by means of a number of criteria: elements, relations, singularities, temporality, seriality, unconsciousness. 'Structure' can be defined as the problematical, differential or virtual idea of multiplicity. Or to put it another way, the idea is characterised by a threefold internal determination, which organises itself serially and has at its disposal a temporal mode of actualisation which is not exhausted in a linear transition from one actual state to another. These conceptual explanations of the dialectical idea and its immanent criteria culminate in a final mark of structure: the so-called *'empty field'*, *'blind spot'*, *'aleatorical point'* or simply *'object X'*. What mystery is expressed by this ominous empty space, the differential that circulates within the structure: *'la différance'*, as Derrida calls it? The transposition of the letter calls attention to the difference that Deleuze captures between the concepts 'differen*t*iation' and 'differen*c*iation' when he says that a structure 'is still undifferen*c*iated, even though it is totally and completely differen*t*iated' (Deleuze 1998: 268). The empty space is not the abyss of radical indifference, but a virtual potential that allows the heterogeneous series to communicate with one another. It cannot be represented in its totality because it contains a superfluity of actualisable relationships and singularities: each actualisation is partial and restricts itself to one chosen structural regime, while other regimes become actualised at other times or in other places. The constitutive lack of sense, its *unpresentability*, corresponds exactly to this superfluity. It is the transcendental field of events that does not allow itself to be presented empirically as such and which cannot be brought to its essential resolution (see Deleuze 1990b: 102f.). As we have already seen, the genetic differential undergoes change in the process of structuration because the virtual relations shift around as they actualise themselves: the non-empirical difference of the singularities can only be thought when at the same time the dividing line between the virtual and the actual remains in force without cuts or concessions. The passive syntheses which steer the actualisation processes, or rather (as I shall discuss later) the various processes of individuation, each reveal something that makes *itself* distinct with respect to an undifferen*c*iated background, but which is completely differen*t*ially determined and shifts about in subsequent repetitions, without ever allowing itself to be identified objectively. The genetic self-differen*c*iation processes of the notable with respect to the commonplace slip from view as soon as the productive syntheses as a whole are submitted to the active act of understanding.

With the introduction of a logical time into the internal multiplicities of structure, the epistemological break in structuralist thought is complete. It is easy to object that one cannot meaningfully speak of 'structure' if in fact one is alluding to a groundless virtual reality which does not exactly coincide with its (always abstract) formalisation. But why should the inscrutability of problematic experience not be structured? Why should it not be determinable – without necessitating general and formal conditions of knowledge for the task? According to Deleuze, the restriction of the horizon undertaken by positivistic or neo-Kantian models of structure leads precisely to the reduction to the form of possibilities which actual resolutions or specifications can take. This reduction expresses itself in the choice of differential elements and in the logic of their relations. Thus for them a structure can be formalised or else a problematic multiple can be transformed into a field of resolution when the undetermined elements are coordinated according to formal laws and thereby uniformly specified. In this way the genetic and temporal aspects of the structure are neatly excluded from further investigation into their true nature – and their mathematical logic remains bound by the paradigms of Euclidian geometry. Tim Clark, in his thoroughgoing comparison of the structure thinking of Piaget and Deleuze, has extracted from Piaget three mathematical principles regarding formal structures: the principle of *reversibility*, the principle of *equifinality* and the principle of *invariance*, where the latter is implied by the two former. It follows that the beginning and end points do not change and thus withdraw from the *play* of structure whenever they ground or centre the structure in the name of an origin (*arché*) or a goal (*telos*). According to Clark, Deleuze subverts these three principles and folds them over, insofar as his structuralist position is marked by a *logic of virtual time* which corresponds in an appropriately different way to handle the temporality of actual (formalised) systems.

> It is a correspondence, [. . .] in which, starting from a set of arbitrarily specified initial conditions, development is *irreversible* and the development paths are *multifinal*, that is, the end state or final condition of the system will be dependent upon the path taken. If there is then a logical correspondence between the time of structure and the times of actualisation it is nonetheless a correspondence without resemblance. (Clark 1997: 68)

There is no resemblance between the concrete transcendental structure and the empirical givens, because these givens result from unpredictable genetic processes which are not 'actually' determined. Inversely, the definition of the 'transcendental' *form* as the possibility of that which can be 'really' given means that just the general features of the already constituted individual objects can be conceptually understood.

The 'reification' of virtuality, which results whenever there is an equation of the virtual and the possible, is reflected in the *hypothetical* element which permeates the representational formalisation of structure. The problem that can supposedly be resolved by a series of possible propositions thereby appears to be reducible to one or more hypotheses which are (*de jure*) to be verified. Deleuze would say that the hypothetical form of the concept is negatively blocked.

> Once the problem is translated into hypotheses, each hypothetical affirmation is doubled by a negation, which amounts to the state of a problem betrayed by its shadow. [...] Whether the One is, whether the One is not... [...] The complicity of the negative and the hypothetical must everywhere be dissolved in favour of a more profound link between difference and the problematic. (Deleuze 1994: 202–3, see also 206)

The betrayal of the problem shows up in its tailoring to the alternatives of various possible solutions. For in this case only the possible opposes the real (and must be realised), whereas the problematic, in comparison, has at its disposal a positive reality of its own which cannot be derived from a dialectic of Being and non-Being. But this reality cannot be appropriately reconstructed as long as one finds oneself on the level of a philosophy of final actualisation through consciousness, a philosophy that situates space and time, as homogeneous forms of intuition, outside of structure, in the open, factual world and operates with the tools of a logic of contradiction. Cut off from diverse and preconscious processes of actualisation, the necessary conditions of actual givens can only be established regressively, starting from natural opinion and their apparently unproblematic basic assumptions.

As expected, Deleuze turns against the determination of structural combinations as oppositional relations, as well as against the presentation of structure using the dialectic terminology of negation, because in this way the genetic micro-processes with their subrepresentational differences are stereotypically simplified and made coarser. 'The oppositions, conflicts, and contradictions in the concept appear such crude and rough measures by contrast with the fine and differential mechanisms which characterise the Idea [that is, the structure; MR]' (Deleuze 1994: 203). Deleuze finds residues of such oppositional thinking even in the linguistic analyses of Saussure

Virtuality of Concepts

and Trubetzkoy (see Deleuze 1994: 204) and in Chomsky versus Labov (Deleuze and Guattari 1987: 90ff.). The duplication and overdetermination of opposition will therefore not suffice to overcome the forms of negation. Nevertheless, Deleuze is of the opinion that, thanks to the structural insight into a large number of coexisting oppositions, the next step in the problematic realm of differences is *in the offing*. Seen from that perspective, the negative and the oppositional betray their deceptiveness, which consists in their hidden derivative character.

> One cannot pluralise opposition without leaving its domain and entering the caves of difference which resonate with a pure positivity and reject opposition as no more than a shadow cavern seen from without. (Deleuze 1994: 204)

The criticism of formalistic models of structure undertaken by Deleuze has shown that the analysis of structure inspired by immanence philosophy demands that their conceptual status be investigated. So it is now necessary to explain in more detail the conceptual state of the concepts that Deleuze introduces to determine his own model of structure. Implicit assumptions regarding the *conceptuality* of the concepts used for the construction of philosophical systems are reflected in the design of structural planes as well as their specific arrangement. The relational constitution of concepts as well as their operational differences are grounded in a more or less explicitly presupposed 'principle' of immanence. But if this presupposed *structurality* cannot be reached conceptually, then this unreachability must – according to Deleuze – precipitate in terms of the consistency of the concept. The suspicion that the use of concepts is carried by implied presuppositions that cannot be completely explicated makes it meaningful to first distinguish the concept from the structural plane on which it has settled and where it maintains relations with other concepts. (Nevertheless the plane can and must be thought conceptually, if only to counter the dogmatic image of opinion. That is why Deleuze says that the prephilosophical – 'image' or 'plane' – cannot be localised outside of philosophy (see Deleuze and Guattari 1991: 41). Or to put it another way, the plane of immanence is (pre) philosophical because it is preconceptual. But that does *not* mean that it is simply unintelligible.)

Admittedly the concept gets its consistency from its relational character, but the plane of thought remains the same for all concepts that are grouped on its level. A concept does not have the same comprehensive status as the plane because each concept is constituted of only a small number of components, which themselves are distributed on the plane as concepts in their own right with other component relations, so that a concept is never immediately bound together with all the others on that plane.

For Deleuze, the strict distinction between concept and 'conceptual plane' locks the door against any disastrous and metaphysically troublesome attempt to ground the conceptual *systematics* of a philosophical theory on a final and original principle. The implementation of blocked or abstract concepts leads, as Deleuze emphasises, to the flattening out of any *difference*, because these concepts *assign* the planes to themselves – like transcendent instances – without interiorising their prephilosophical and preconceptual peculiarities. Nonetheless, philosophical concepts *as such* always imply a plane on which they distribute themselves and which 'registers' their relations, even when specific assignments of concepts reflexively reproduce their immanent conditions on an 'ideological' level, thereby losing sight of their genealogical affiliations. Deleuze is particularly anxious that concepts be made to display in their construction as much as possible their immanent position, that is, that they do not distort, eliminate or transcend their genetic relation to the non-conceptual problems they answer.

These *preliminary remarks* regarding the theory of concepts suggest that not only is the idea of structure developed by Deleuze in *Difference and Repetition* sufficient to meet the demands of a philosophy of immanence, but so also are the concepts implemented in this idea. In this sense, Deleuze speaks of the concepts as 'categories of the dialectical Idea' (Deleuze 1994: 190). Here it is a question of *open* and *descriptive* concepts which testify to an 'empirical and pluralistic sense of Ideas' (Deleuze 1994: 284) and should therefore not be understood as *categories* in the strict sense. Deleuze gives a number of examples taken from his investigations into the determination of structure: 'differential and singularity; differentiation-individuation-differenciation; question-problem-solution, and so on' (Deleuze 1994: 284). One might add that the concepts used in *Difference and Repetition* to describe the structural synthesis of difference are clarified as to their conceptual status in the reflections on the theory of concepts in *What Is Philosophy?* At any rate, in both books the empiricist 'essence' of (difference-)philosophical concepts is worked out.

In the Preface to *Difference and Repetition* Deleuze places himself firmly in the tradition of empiricism, 'which is in no way a reaction against concepts, nor a simple appeal to lived experience' (Deleuze 1994: xix), in order to accentuate the *problematic coherence* of his concepts. Precisely the rejection of metaphysical sources provides empiricism a rarely worked out potential for creating concepts. The empiricist-friendly concept-oriented formulations coined in *Difference and Repetition* find in *What Is Philosophy?* their equally exact and enthusiastic supplementation.

> Wherever there are habits there are concepts, and habits are developed and given up on the plane of immanence of radical experience: they are 'conventions'. That is why English philosophy is a free and wild creation of concepts. (Deleuze and Guattari 1991: 105)

With the classical empiricist concept of 'habit' Deleuze denotes his model of subjectivation, which I will treat in the next chapter. Here it is important to note that the empiricism of the concept which Deleuze expressly advocates in *What Is Philosophy?* is subjected to a new investigation or interpretation. More than twenty years after *Difference and Repetition*, the midpoint of his philosophical exertions, Deleuze returns again to his concept of philosophy. Supported by Félix Guattari, he picks up again the questions concerning the concept and the structure of Being (immanence). This resumption of philosophical work 'in its own name' (and not detouring by way of an interpretation of other philosophers) signals that Deleuze is considering changes or deepenings with respect to the fundamental ideas he unfolded in *Difference and Repetition*, in addition to bringing the latter up to date. These changes need not be taken as revisionist. In the Introduction to *What Is Philosophy?* Deleuze seems to give an answer to the question of the status of the book:

> The question *what is philosophy?* can perhaps be posed only late in life, with the arrival of old age and the time for speaking concretely. [...] It is a question posed in a moment of quiet restlessness [...] when there is no longer anything to ask. It was asked before; it was always being asked, but too indirectly or obliquely; the question was too artificial, too abstract. [...] Those who asked the question set it out and controlled it in passing. [...] There was too much desire to *do* philosophy to wonder what it was. (Deleuze and Guattari 1991: 1)

A few pages further on, Deleuze indicates what the problem was, what remained unsatisfactory, even with respect to his own earlier queries: 'Philosophers have not been sufficiently concerned with the nature of the concept as philosophical reality' (Deleuze and Guattari

1991: 11). Philosophy's tool for thinking, which distinguishes it from other forms of thought, is the concept. However, philosophy has to *construct* its concepts: the self-evidence of the concept is not served by taking it as a finished historical product that can merely be picked up or appropriated. 'The concept as a specifically philosophical creation is always a singularity. The first principle of philosophy is that universals explain nothing but must themselves be explained' (Deleuze and Guattari 1991: 7). Universals are artificially or naturally blocked concepts based on implicit representationalist presuppositions embedded in contemplative, reflexive or communicative thinking. On the other hand, Deleuze makes it clear that even universals are intellectual creations that provide answers to submitted questions. This fact is developed from a concept-oriented philosophical perspective in the first chapter of the first part of *What Is Philosophy?* There it is shown that the concepts lead to a differential structural plane, at least when their conceptuality is *adequately* brought to expression. Construction does not insist on producing new concepts, but means above all *rearranging* the relational systems of historically determined concepts so that they can work together and consequently redefine each other in new and unexpected ways.

Whereas the first chapter is largely concerned with working out the 'essence' of the concept, the theme of the second chapter is the so-called *plane of immanence*. There the emphasis is not so much to revise or correct the still all too 'abstract' or 'forced' discussions concerning the idea of structure, and even less to explicate the implications of the already lightly touched upon usage of concepts. Rather, the second chapter focuses on the relation between the concept and the plane of immanence and produces a complex image of implicit presuppositions of thought. Thus we come to see that Deleuze's concept-oriented investigations are accompanied by an original understanding of the relation between philosophy and science. In *Difference and Repetition* he still puts his idea of structure in concrete terms with the help of scientific models which are in use in the various directions of structuralist research. These concrete examples are presented by Deleuze as genuine philosophical interpretations. This can be read out of the thesis he advocates in that context that the problems are intrinsically *philosophical* and only the solutions are specifically *scientific* in nature. But as long as scientific problems are not distinguished from the philosophical ones, a noticeable argumentational gap remains to be closed. In *What Is Philosophy?* Deleuze places the three 'disciplines' of philosophy, science and art next to one another by distinguishing their structural planes with respect to the characteristics of *immanence*, *reference* and *composition*. As a consequence, philosophy can only then retain its 'autonomy' if it does not relate itself to the sciences in forbidden fashion in order to justify its existence. Deleuze's theory of concepts is therefore directed against the semantic reduction to be observed in the newer analytic philosophy of language which accompanies the logical functionalisation of the concept. In this sense Deleuze also distances himself from the importunate questions regarding the naturalist end of philosophy. 'Today it is said that systems are bankrupt, but it is only the concept of system that has changed' (Deleuze and Guattari 1991: 9). Although in the last century many more scientific aspirants than ever before have come forth with the claim to replace philosophy, there still remains for it a singular and incomparable task, namely to forge *concepts* that produce immanent ways of being alive and processes of becoming or know how to diagnose them and their political implications (see Hardt 1993, Negri 1995 and Patton 2000).

It seems now plausible at first glance to conclude that Deleuze sets his thoughts regarding the plane of immanence – known as 'a pure stream of asubjective consciousness' or as 'a qualitative duration of consciousness without a self' (Deleuze 2001: 25) – in relation to *radical empiricism*. This would bring to mind not only William James but also the so-called 'empirio-critical' positions who stand together in the psycho-physiological tradition of the nineteenth century and who can be ascribed back to the classical English 'association psychology' while also having close, non-accidental ties to the so-called 'life-philosophical' tendencies at the end of that century. Less clear in contrast are the genuine *empiricist* motives that Deleuze marshals for his theory of concepts. Wasn't empiricism always defined by giving immediate experience a priority that at the same time founded the secondary or derivative status of the philosophical concept? Even the 'critical' empiricism of William James, Ernst Mach or the young Nietzsche couldn't keep its fingers off the tempting theoretical abstractions promulgated by Locke or Hume. But empiricist reductionism is unsatisfactory as long as it speculates on sense-data or immediate experiences that are one-sidedly distorted or coarsely sorted out in the process of producing concepts. Concepts, on the other hand, that are uncoupled from their propositional reference function and, speaking imprecisely, are constituted coherently in a *virtual thought constellation* cannot be analysed down to single empirical perceptions.

The empiricist motive with respect to 'speculative' concepts consists therefore precisely in thinking the im-mediate (*un-mittelbar*) experience, which of course cannot serve as the foundation for more complex, conceptually mediated experiences. Thinking in concepts is essentially different from pure sensations and perceptions, but it is capable of construing precisely this non-hierarchical state of affairs. This is what precipitates out of Deleuze's theory of concepts, because concepts refer to genetic conditions that are precursors of their conception: affects and percepts. This *non-philosophical* foreground designates, however, also the 'subject matter' (*Gegenstand*) of philosophical thinking – and must therefore be defined as the *pre-philosophical* plane of immanence. It is the job of thinking to explore immanence 'down to the ground of its repetitions' (Deleuze 1994: 220). These determinations are only then adequate in immanence-theoretical terms when they internalise the difference that separates concepts from their non-conceptual conditions.

Curiously, Deleuze refers in his introductory remarks on the question of philosophy to Hegel and his 'powerful definition' of the concept. This seemingly strange reference – one is aware of his usual disapproval of Hegel – becomes clearer when one considers that Hegel situates the concept in the milieu of the Absolute, which means that he tolerates no empirical dependence in its truly idealist composition. This 'quasi-virtual' *withdrawal* of the concept is attractive for Deleuze for two reasons. On the one hand Hegel is against an external determination of the concept: against its *empirical derivation* and against its *a priori discovery*. On the other hand, Hegel gathers the consistency of the concept solely out of its relations, both internally and externally, to other concepts: the object of the concept is the concept itself, and consists solely in order to configure 'objective thought processes'. Its formations and reformations result from an inner logic of self-positing and self-relating and are in no way dependent on external reference points.

> Hegel showed that the concept has nothing whatever to do with a general or abstract idea, any more than with an uncreated Wisdom that does not depend on philosophy itself. (Deleuze and Guattari 1991: 12)

Deleuze appropriates from Hegel that the meaning of concepts is not to be sought in its empirical confirmation. Not only the empiricists but also Kant miss consequently the 'absolute subjectivity' of the concept when in the deduction chapter Kant tries to prove the reality of the categories by asserting that only they communicate to the prof-

Virtuality of Concepts

fered *empirical intuition* the necessary objective form of experience. To put it another way, Deleuze disputes along with Hegel the legitimacy of equating recognition with experience. Nevertheless, Deleuze does not throw overboard his critical opinion of Hegelian logic as a theory of *infinite representation*. To put it briefly, the representationally logical core of Hegelian thought, says Deleuze, consists in the fact that Hegel uses his negation-theoretical basis to inscribe the 'plane of immanence', that is, the non-conceptual field of intuitions and sensations, into the sublimational movement (*Aufhebungsbewegung*) of the concept. Although Hegel does give a 'definition of philosophy' that can be supported up to a point, he nevertheless misses the immanently assumed problematic regarding why and *for what purpose* concepts are constructed in the first place. Deleuze would say, in agreement with Nietzsche, that the inner conditions of concept construction are subject to a never-ending becoming, which is why they found a *pragmatist kind* of thought that no longer revolves around *the* truth – and these conditions seem to lose their sting only in the *imaginary* realm of thought, which is to say within the framework of a second, exclusively spiritual (*vergeistigt*) reality.

But how can Deleuze reconcile this problematic value of the concept with the Hegelian motives of a self-referential and autopoietical conception of concepts? (The regress to Hegel is supposed to make possible a powerful definition of the concept that skips with a pragmatic intention over the usual empiricist derivations.) This question can only be answered stepwise by following up the virtual definition of the concept as promulgated in *What Is Philosophy?* Accordingly, concepts are not only related to the questions regarding their presuppositions; and they do not only differ essentially from the empirical givens in terms of which they actualise themselves. Concepts possess for Deleuze a *necessity* that yet in no way excludes their *contingency* and singularity. The *absoluteness* that belongs to them in no way erases their *relativity*. The *wholeness* and complete self-containment of a concept does not contradict its singular *fragmentariness* – and the *becoming* or the movement of a concept does not fully grasp or determine its *history*. One must always count on an ideality of the concept that is not monistically centred upon *one* hinge or pivot. In what follows, the grounds for these assertions will be more carefully looked into.

On the Logic of Concepts

Deleuze starts his discussion on the essence of concepts with the statement that there is no simple concept, but rather that every concept is a multiplicity (*Mannigfaltigkeit*) (Deleuze and Guattari 1991: 15). Conceptual multiplicity introduces a special kind of magnitude (*Vielheit*). Nevertheless, thanks to the analyses carried out so far, we can expect to find certain characteristic features. Thus concepts have formless and functionless elements which organise and constantly determine themselves in reciprocal relationships. Deleuze calls these elements concept components; they do not – *as* components – exist independent of the concept's internal operations, to which they contribute. These relational operations define themselves in terms of the *inseparability* of their components. To be sure, the components can be clearly distinguished from one another – if for no other reason than that they can each be taken as concepts in themselves – but as participants in the inner workings of a concept, the components relate to one another and constitute a common field that is not clearly differenciated, that is, where the relational parts cannot be seen as abstract isolated entities. 'There is an area *ab* that belongs to both a and b, where a and b 'become' indiscernible' (Deleuze and Guattari 1991: 20). The inner-conceptual relations that are constitutive of a concept distinguish themselves from extra-conceptual relations simply by making inseparable some other concepts that have been downgraded into dependent components and genetic factors. That is why Deleuze speaks of the *internal* consistency of a concept when referring to the composition of its components, and of its *external* consistency with respect to other concepts. The two fields of consistency communicate with one another: 'Having a finite number of components, every concept will branch off toward other concepts that are differently composed' (Deleuze and Guattari 1991: 18). Here it suffices to note that the self-initiation and self-determination of a philosophical concept consists in placing selected components next to each other in such a way that they begin to resonate and thus converge toward a common conceptual juncture. It follows that every concept must be seen as the accumulation point of its own preconceptual singularities, in such a way that they become totalised, that is, become locked together into a conceptual whole. The concept and its constellation of conceptual particles become the locus of a potential for thought that must be activated by a process of attunement. Concepts must literally be attuned (*bestimmt*); they must be regarded

Virtuality of Concepts

as 'centres of vibration' (*Schwingungszentren*) for the non-discursive resonance relations of their own components.

Take, for example, the Cartesian concept of the cogito, which Deleuze analyses in detail. The cogito has three components: doubt, thought and Being. Suffused by the common conceptual point, they are arranged in two neighbouring zones. 'The first zone is between doubting and thinking (myself who doubts, I cannot doubt that I think), and the second is between thinking and Being (in order to think it is necessary to be)' (Deleuze and Guattari 1991: 25). In addition, all three components of the concept support a 'phase space' (*Phasenraum*) implying internal differenciations ('phases'). For example, memory, imagining, grasping and so on are variations or modes of thinking, whereas infinite Being, or finite thinking Being, or extended Being are variations of Being. Often the exclusive use of only one phase of a conceptual component marks the concept as self-enclosed – leaving spontaneous bridging (on the same plane) as the only means of establishing external relations to other concepts (for example, to the remaining phases of Being). 'Zones and bridges are the joints of the concept' (Deleuze and Guattari 1991: 20). Thus in the course of Cartesian proof, the sentence 'among my ideas I have the idea of the infinite' marks the sudden transition that throws an arch from the concept of the cogito to that of God (see Deleuze and Guattari 1991: 25–6).

Deleuze's phenomenology of thought stands and falls on grasping the components of a concept as *intensive features* or *singularities* that cannot be made to function *as such* or be coordinated in space-time. Deleuze is here opposing the logic of concepts developed by Frege on the basis of mathematical functions, whereby the concept is characterised as a propositional function through its *reference* to objects (as well as to other propositions). Precisely the intensional consistency of the concept gets lost, says Deleuze, when its components are assigned various independent values on the one hand or constant functions on the other. The eventfulness of the philosophical concept consists in its relation to the close-knit inseparability of different variations or in its self-referential consistency, which gets lost if the concept is objectively *actualised* or *blocked*. At this point it is helpful to shed a cursory glance at Frege's lecture on 'Function and Concept', which formulates the fundamental position in conceptual theory that Deleuze is fighting.

Frege begins his remarks with the distinction between functions and numbers. Functions are *unsatisfied or unsaturated* (*ungesättigt*) calculational expressions in need of supplementation (*ergänzungs-bedürftig*) which build a complete totality only with the addition of the (mathematically conceived) argument.

> For instance, if I say 'the function $2 \cdot x^3 + x$', x must not be considered as belonging to the function; the letter only serves to indicate the kind of supplementation that is needed; it enables one to recognise the places where the sign for the argument must go in. (Frege 1970: 25)

Thus the *value* or the *string of values* of a function for a particular argument results from its corresponding insertion into the function, and the *generality* of an equation with respect to values of a function can be considered – axiomatically – as an equation with respect to the string of values. In a further step Frege adapts the equal sign for the purpose of constructing the expression of a function, so that from now on one can speak of a *truth value* (true or false) of the function for various arguments. Sense and meaning (or denotating and denotation) can now be easily distinguished, because although $2^3 = 8$ and $4 \cdot 2 = 8$ express (denote) different thoughts, their referential meaning (denotation) is identical. The expansion of the 'symbolic language of arithmetic [...] into a logical symbolism', which Frege promotes, leads to the definition of the concept as 'a function whose value is always a truth value' (Frege 1970: 30). Thus the set of positive truth values for the string of values of a function makes up the extension of the concept.

When converted to the linguistic form of propositional sentences, *objects* (instead of numbers) are warranted for which *in every case* a truth value must be assignable to the corresponding concept, 'which must be regarded as the reference of the sentence, just as (say) [...] London is the reference of the expression "the capital of England"' (Frege 1970: 31). Frege's proof that concepts are a special class of functions rests on the premise that concepts can also be thought of as split into two parts, of which the incomplete part encloses the placement of an independent variable, whereas the other part is an encompassed object that can satisfy the empty place. The reference that is thereby inscribed into the concept downgrades the latter – at least in Deleuze's eyes – to merely a kind of possibility that must be realised empirically.

> The relation of the propositional function to the independent variable or argument defines the proposition's *reference*, or the function's truth value for the argument: John is a man, but Bill is a cat. [...] The concept's objects occupy the place of variables or arguments of the propositional

Virtuality of Concepts

function for which the proposition is true, or its reference satisfied. Thus the concept itself is the function for the set of objects that constitute its extension. (Deleuze and Guattari 1991: 136)

The logical or propositional 'concepts' derive all their power from reference and lose thereby the genuine philosophical characteristics of conceptual consistency. Modern logic peddles the correspondence theory of truth: as long as it 'considers empty reference in itself as simple truth value' it restricts itself to positively constituted falsifiable facts that define its information value (see Deleuze and Guattari 1991: 138). Even though it dreams of finally leaving the empiricist's field of psychological processes behind, it nevertheless retains psychology's abstract form of recognition. From this perspective the limits that characterise logical empiricism's understanding of concepts become obvious when for it the philosophical concept 'appears only as a proposition deprived of sense' (Deleuze and Guattari 1991: 22).

On the contrary, transcendental empiricism operates with concepts deciphering the ideal or problematic structures of experience, the very structures which determine the immanent genesis of that experience. In no way do the philosophical concepts depend on the empiricist meaning criterium; rather, they have a *pragmatic* value that is measured against the problems and questions that are posed by them and answered by them. Concepts serve to think the virtual potential of experiences. By reaching out to the genetic processes of differenciation already involved in the *formation* of concepts, the usual assignments among the visible and the articulable become problematised so that the implicit strategic presuppositions dictating their epistemic homology come into view. Deleuze has always turned against the image of thought that has wanted to deceive itself for moral reasons with respect to the nature of these presuppositions.

The critique of the belief in truth from empiricist scepticism up to Nietzsche shows an essential change in the design of the prephilosophical plane. In the course of this work I have often pointed out that Nietzsche, with his critique of theological implications within the fundamental logic of scientific discourse, makes a clean break with the multiple attempts to patch over the voids and fissures inherent in the finite faculties of thought. Nietzsche's pathos states that we have to live with these fissures – and that we can manage to live with them all the better the less we need to deceive ourselves about them. Nietzsche (with a gnashing of teeth) demands the affirmation of fleeting life and speaks against its devaluation in the name of 'higher' expectations of belief. If there is a need for belief, then it must be a belief in this world, an empiricist's *will to belief* issuing directly from that affirmation.

> It may be that believing in this world, in this life, becomes our most difficult task, or the task of a mode of existence still to be discovered on our plane of immanence today. (Deleuze and Guattari 1991: 75)

The conversion to empiricism is a conversion to the immanence of difference-and-repetition-processes. These processes are not given but are instead the *givenness* of the *given*, or that *through which* the given is given. The *allusion* to the event which oscillates in tune with this conversion in no way reflects vitalist utopias which are satisfied with the mere deterritorialisation, liquification or relaxation of the self-evident, never questioned empirical given – as if one could simply break through to the origins of life. Rather, the modern distancing from the 'meaning of life' leads to indifference with respect to oneself or others, to a detachment that sometimes shows pathological symptoms. From that perspective it is worthwhile to regain or bring forth a belief in the world in which the fleeting intensities are taken over by more or less stable habits that prevent new disbeliefs from taking effect. 'Whether we are Christians or atheists, in our universal schizophrenia *we need reasons to believe in this world*. This amounts to an unalloyed conversion' (Deleuze 1989: 172, trans. mod.).

But the philosophical 'conversion' to empiricism, which can be paraphrased as the substitution of believing (only in this world) for knowing, corresponds to the construction of absolute immanence, 'immanent to every thinkable plane that does not succeed in thinking it' (Deleuze and Guattari 1991: 59). Nevertheless, every philosophical construction requires that the conditions of experience produce images of themselves on the prephilosophical plane and thereby show the normative contents that make up the implicit definition of whatever should legitimately belong to experience. Conceptual thinking rests on a preliminary understanding of the problem, which is made concrete by dividing up factual and legitimate definitions, that is, by allocating what is empirical and what is transcendental. The various allocations correspond to different philosophical planes. They answer such questions as to what is important and what is unimportant (see Deleuze and Guattari 1991: 82–3). Now it happens that empiricism is singled out to construct a plane that legitimately manages without the *a priori* determination of transcendent instances. In this way Deleuze shows that empiricism, as a philosophy of immanence and becoming, is best realised when it appropriates the critique of metaphysical truths, as Nietzsche does in exemplary fashion (see Deleuze and Guattari 1991: 49–50). As I have shown in Chapter 2, the image of thought changes radically when Platonic-Cartesian error no longer incorporates all transgressions of truth in its concept but allows stupidity, craziness, illusions and the 'power of falsehood' to usurp its place legitimately, by right, thereby making forthright and frank certain aspects of the unconscious of thought. If thought is fundamentally 'bothered' – inhibited, crazy, apathetic, withdrawn – then this situation can be understood by the fact that a particular world of signs has legitimately presented itself to thought which moves it, toward which it reacts and for which it tries to find solutions and answers. Philosophy becomes an empiricist adventure when it focuses on experience in this sense: percepts which can only be perceived, sensations which can only be sensed.

Radical empiricism's plane of immanence is nothing else but the transcendental field that distinguishes itself *by right* from the empirically actual givens. From a philosophical perspective it is created at first as a *non-conceptual* plane that predetermines the construction of concepts. Thus Deleuze also calls it the *prephilosophical* plane of immanence as soon as the relation of philosophy to *non-philosophy* becomes the theme. This latter relationship to an *exteriority* (*Außen*) is mirrored in every philosophical construction whose prephilosophical partitions are not sufficiently grounded conceptually, enough so that their particular features can be more or less reflected upon or (conceptually) explicated. 'The "prephilosophical" plane is only so called because it is laid out as presupposed and not because it preexists without being laid out' (Deleuze and Guattari 1991: 77–8). Nevertheless, the non-philosophical field of sensible signs, which to some extent has to be considered the absolute plane of immanence, is steadily sieved or filtered within the various philosophical layouts and their selective determinations. So it always remains questionable to what extent the prephilosophical distinctions that show up can be converted into concepts. Transcendental empiricism must in any case carefully observe and reflect upon the line of division between prephilosophical planes and conceptual constructions in its general considerations regarding the theory of concepts. It follows that concepts presuppose a plane of immanence which is in principle distinct and separate from those concepts: only in that way can they confer on that plane its necessary consistency. But precisely the allocation of a privileged conceptual position to immanence leads to the metaphysical distortion of differential structures. 'Movement takes in everything, and there is no place for a subject and an object that can only be concepts' (Deleuze and Guattari 1991: 37–8). On the other hand, it is through conceptual consistency that immanent determination itself moves ahead to uncouple the concepts from functioning as references for transcendent entities and instead commits them to problem fields from which they derive their objective meaning. 'A concept lacks meaning to the extent that it is not connected to other concepts and is not linked to a problem that it resolves or helps to resolve' (Deleuze and Guattari 1991: 79).

Descriptive concepts are designed by Deleuze to describe a problematic structure of experience, whereby of course this structure is already prephilosophically created, that is, normative distinctions are already presupposed that predetermine the concrete allocation and distribution of the conceptual network. There is no simple concept, which is why every 'concept creation' is not only related to a conceptual *history*, but also and above all to a systematic 'preunderstanding' of conceptual coherence. Deleuze speaks in this regard of *trans-historical becoming* or of the *virtual consistency* of the concept. This preunderstanding cannot be completely recovered or explicated because it first makes possible the setting of the concept: it is a matter of a *problem horizon* that occurs prior to its conceptual solution.

The virtual complexity of philosophical thought consists in the conceptual cross-references which 'give consistency without losing anything of the infinite' (Deleuze and Guattari 1991: 42). Concepts do relate only to themselves and their internal variations – they actually cut themselves off by totalising their conceptual moments – and yet they point beyond themselves because the components can only function as determinations interior to the concept if they themselves allow themselves to be created as concepts along with other components. That leads to the fragmentary and relative character of the philosophical concept: always a finite number of components that fit the concept with its misshapen pattern and still leave open the possibility that something can be added or taken away from it. 'As fragmentary totalities, concepts are not even the pieces of a puzzle, for their irregular contours do not correspond to each other' (Deleuze and Guattari 1991: 23). They get their coherence only from the problems to which they react: they build no discursive unity and do not follow the appropriate logical rules of correspondence. Therefore the importance of a more or less antiquated philosophy is measured by how it can be actualised with respect to the currently circulating problems or what kind of potentials for problem-solving it has at its disposal.

The fact that concepts belong on a plane of immanence is explained in terms of their virtual consistency, so that a concept on a certain plane always stands in special relation to other concepts that in no way allow merely the revival of its historical formations. An 'old' concept is newly conceived if, in a particular systematic context, it deviates from its historical version – and gets new contours precisely from this deviation. That is why a difference-theoretical history of concepts will make use of historical presuppositions which prevent the various historical results of philosophical investigation within a particular theory to be arranged according to a developmental logic that allows that historical aspect to be inscribed into the consistency of the concept. Constellations of concepts on a particular plane can be characteristic for this plane in a way that one of these concepts in a constellation, when applied on another plane, makes deep and lasting changes necessary. Alternatively, it is sometimes sufficient to introduce one single new concept in order to disquiet a major referential system enough so as eventually to pave the way to letting a quite different new plane become visible.

> Concepts pave, occupy, or populate the plane bit by bit, whereas the plane itself is the indivisible milieu in which concepts are distributed without breaking up its continuity or integrity: they [...] are distributed without splitting it up. The plane is like a desert that concepts populate without dividing up. [...] The plane has no other regions than the tribes populating and moving around on it. It is the plane that secures conceptual linkages with ever increasing connections, and it is concepts that secure the populating of the plane on an always renewed and variable curve. (Deleuze and Guattari 1991: 36–7)

The distribution of philosophical concepts on a plane of immanence is carried out nomadically in accordance with the law of univocity. In no way do they cross the land in order to divide it up and occupy it. They set up their tents only temporarily and restrict themselves to a specific problematic task, from which they gain their full-blown concreteness.

8

Subjectivity and Immanence

The unfurling of immanence as the field of structure undercuts modern rationality insofar as the latter's unlimited claim to subjective autonomy and objective transcendence is concerned. On the plane of immanence no trace remains of the old presumption that one can profit from divine thought. The idea of immanence is critical of metaphysics and stands for a radically new empiricist beginning regarding experience. Clearly there isn't anyone who can feel or see or think as long as feeling, seeing and thinking are solely situated on the plane of immanence. Does Deleuze's conception make it necessary for us to wallow in abstractions or to assume unconscious events which must remain hidden from us – as subjects? Forces that we cannot recognise because we perceive only the surface of things? Hardly. The ideal synthesis of difference, that is to say, the structural constitution of purely immanent moments of experience, entails a coterminous second step involving the spatially and temporally determined actualisation processes of virtual constellations. There is no differential unconscious without disclosure or articulation, as Deleuze learned from Bergson or Lacan. In other words, world and expression cannot be considered in isolation from one another. Therefore the analyses on the idea of immanence are incomplete as long as its modes of actualisation are not addressed. That I will do in detail in the next subsections. Subjects are not simply given; they are produced or produce themselves. They result from multiple determinable processes of actualisation, called by Deleuze processes of 'subjectless subjectivation'. Thus it is possible to work through the genealogy of subjectivity using an immanence-theoretical approach. I will first elucidate the ways of relating oneself to another, of becoming 'subject' or of having experiences by reflecting on the philosophical minefield of temporal structures. After that, in the second part of the chapter, I will introduce the category of intensity as the fundamental concept of empiricist philosophy, with whose help the temporal and spatial determinations of individuation can be made more concrete.

The Ideal Constitution of Repetition: Temporal Structures

> Difference lies between two repetitions. Is this not also to say, conversely, that repetition lies between two differences [...]? (Deleuze 1994: 76)

'Empiricism does not raise the problem of the origin of the mind but rather the problem of the constitution of the subject' (Deleuze 1991: 31). Deleuze wrote this in 1953, in *Empirisme et subjectivité: Essai sur la nature humaine selon Hume*. Accordingly, the destiny of empiricism does not turn on the question of atomism of ideas, but on the question of the doctrine of association. It is not the theory of sense perception but rather the theory of reflection that leads David Hume to the concepts of habit and belief that Deleuze adopts for his own purposes. Thus Deleuze stresses that the characteristic duality of empiricism is one between simple givens and relations, not one between what is sensible and what is intelligible. The blueprint regarding external relations, a thesis which does not allow relations to internalise their relata representationally or assign to them any kind of objective qualities, characterises a mode of connection or chaining that does not spring from the activity of legislative understanding but rather precedes that understanding.

> The coherent paradox of Hume's philosophy is that it offers a subjectivity which transcends itself, without being any less passive. Subjectivity is [...] an impression of reflection. (Deleuze 1991: 26)

This paradox is reformulated by Deleuze at the beginning of the second chapter of *Difference and Repetition* as the 'paradox of repetition', which will become the cornerstone of my argument in what follows. Normally one speaks of repetition in at least two cases, of which the one is the repetition of the other (previously existing). This objective repetition of two independent cases is governed by the rule of discontinuity: 'One instance does not appear unless the other has disappeared' (Deleuze 1994: 70). Here Deleuze presents repetition as natural or conceptless difference, which makes it possible to see the cases of repetition as identical and yet not the same. Repetition that is extrinsical, bare or material like could also be called repetition *in itself* (*an sich*), says Deleuze, and 'disappears even as it occurs: hence the status of matter as mens momentanea' (Deleuze 1994: 70). No doubt this identity model of repetition corresponds to the natural blockage of thinking: the blocked thought cannot reach any positive consideration of the difference which every repetition implies and effects *for itself* (*für sich*). However, what is this difference all about which repetition expresses?

LIVING PRESENCE

In a preliminary answer to this question, Deleuze refers to David Hume's own explications regarding the problem of empiricism by starting the chapter on repetition with this sentence: 'Repetition changes nothing in the object repeated, but does change something in the mind which contemplates it' (Deleuze 1994: 99). The subjective modification happens because repetitions occasion habits or leave traces in memory that contribute significantly to horizons of expectation or futurity. Hume assigns to imagination the faculty of allowing itself to be affected by habit or custom and thus 'by a secret operation, and without being once thought of, [...] we can draw an inference from the appearance of one object to the existence of another' (Hume 2001: 72–3). Imagination affects itself when a sudden circumstance makes it anticipate immediately, based on its disposition, a certain future. This tacit transition comes about 'without the assistance of memory: custom operates before we have time for reflection' (Hume 2001: 72). Hume says that we sense a determination or propensity to move from one object to its usual attendant circumstances. That is, we perceive inner sensations of reflexion that result from the inner observation of enough similar instances or repetitions.

> These instances are in themselves totally distinct from each other, and have no union but in the mind, which observes them, and collects their ideas. Necessity, then, is the effect of this observation, and is nothing but an internal impression of the mind, or a determination to carry our thoughts from one object to another. (Hume 2001: 111)

Deleuze calls this non-cognitive act, by which the imagination puts together or contracts single and separate ideas 'in the mind', the start of a new paradigm of subjectivation. In this reflexive observation, which Deleuze pins down terminologically as contemplation, not only are the individual elements united together into a new impression, but this passive process is accompanied by effects of subjectivity: 'for it is through contemplation that one contracts, contemplating oneself to the extent that one contemplates the elements from which one originates' (Deleuze and Guattari 1994: 212). In *Difference and Repetition* the idea of self-affection (*Selbstaffektion*) through custom gets applied to the problem of temporal syntheses.

Subjectivity and Immanence

The imagination traverses all three time dimensions when it associates a present impression with a past situation and thereby develops the future-oriented belief in the repetitive arrival of that which is to be expected. The contraction of the imagination fulfils itself not in active memories, but is a synthesis of time which, 'in every respect, must be called "passive synthesis"' (Deleuze 1994: 71). To put it more exactly, it is a question of the synthesis of the present, taken with the repetition of logically independent successive moments or instants.

> It is in this present that time is deployed. To it belong both the past and the future: the past in so far as the preceding instants are retained in the contraction; the future because its expectation is anticipated in this same contraction. The past and the future do not designate instants distinct from a supposed present instant, but rather the dimensions of the present itself in so far as it is a contraction of instants. (Deleuze 1994: 70–1)

With this exposition of repetition for itself (*pour elle-même*) on the plane of a consciousness continuum oriented to the present – thus bringing about an immediate condensation of the time dimensions wholly similar to Bergsonian duration or Husserl's living present – this empiricist concept of experience has now been raised to a standard that can be applied critically to other notions. In the passive synthesis the present forms itself from individual successive moments of time now apprehended as a whole, and that whole encompasses the immediate past of retention and the immediate future of anticipation.

Starting with this synthetic conception of experience, Deleuze criticises implicitly the all too abstract, technical or artificial sense-data or perception theory of classical empiricism, which not only comes down to sensualist impressions quantified in extension – something we will return to later in connection to the problem of intensities – but also wants to determine time as succession. 'A succession of instants does not constitute time any more than it causes it to disappear; it indicates only its constantly aborted moment of birth' (Deleuze 1994: 70). For Deleuze, who diagnoses a threefold 'paradigm change' in the theory of time from Plato through Descartes to Kant, the classical empiricists, including Hume, remain more or less on the Cartesian level as to their ideas of time. Kant revolutionised these ideas by conceptualising time as an immutable form of interiority which can no longer be defined as mere succession. Time as subjective form *a priori*, to be affected (by itself), is taken by Deleuze to be a form of self-determination through passive syntheses of apprehension regulating processes of individuation. However, Deleuze does conceptualise what Hume put at the centre of his analyses on knowledge and probability: namely, custom or habit as passive subjectivity, which leads to temporal determinations that lie on the plane of the first passive synthesis of the present, and even go beyond that to force the transition to the second passive synthesis. Deleuze calls custom the 'groundwork' or foundation (*fondation*) of time, which on no account should be confused with the 'ground' (*fondement*) of time. But in the descent to the ground and its transcendental syntheses the virtual structures of custom will also be discovered.

Before Deleuze steps into this region of pure past, he works with Hume's model of repetition, on whose basis the distinction between passive and active synthesis will be introduced. Accordingly, we will take up custom or habit when the individual cases of repetition we are considering are contracted (*contracter une habitude*). These individual cases remain separate in memory and can become the object of active remembering or material for carefully-thought-out prognoses.

> Hume forcefully distinguishes the union or fusion of cases in the imagination – a union which takes place independently of memory or understanding – and the separation of these same cases in the memory and the understanding. (Deleuze 1994: 313)

The passive syntheses of the present make up a presence whose temporal space ranges from the past to the future, whereas the active syntheses of deliberate memories or calculated predictions make up reflexive forms of the past and of the future, cut off from the present. 'In other words, the active syntheses of memory and understanding are superimposed upon and supported by the passive synthesis of the imagination' (Deleuze 1994: 71). One could say that the rational reconstruction of experience, which derives empirical truths from self-evident principles, and theoretical truths from undisputed observational propositions, operates by means of abstract concepts which are taken from the natural consciousness – philosophically speaking – of active syntheses. Thus concrete and complex experiences are investigated for their objective meaning by setting out the determinations relevant to their validity: the logical conformities of the understanding, which can be recognised in the object of scientific observation, and the passively available (and therefore unconnected and unmanipulated) material of sensuous intuition, which in the act of cognition reveals its objective relations of order. This model of recognition exists in almost infinite variety, all of which are based

Subjectivity and Immanence

on representationalist assumptions. These assumptions, with their seemingly foundational meaning, distort the passive syntheses, which present the onset of structuralisation processes. We will go into this matter later along with the paradoxical undermining of common sense. At this point it suffices to make a connection between the status of passive syntheses and this turning away from traditional epistemology.

The implicit pragmatism of difference-thinking comes down to the special standing of custom or habit. With a nod to Samuel Butler and Etienne B. de Condillac, Deleuze asserts 'that we have no other continuities apart from those of our thousands of component habits [. . .], from which all other psychic phenomena derive' (Deleuze 1994: 74, 78). Perhaps a few readers will be surprised that Deleuze takes on the role of apologist for habit. After all, he fights tooth and nail against opinions, which are not entitled to claims of knowledge in philosophy – and in the Pyrrhonic school it was customary to attack this entitlement by pointing to the ubiquity of habit. Nevertheless Deleuze can lean on the moderate scepticism of David Hume, who uses the concept of habit to place a practical subjectivity at the centre of his philosophy, one that not only unmasks such rationalist categories of 'substance' and 'causality' as concepts of relation based on impressions of reflection, but understands these ideas as necessary illusions that must be explained 'psychologically' and must be made useful, which is to say that they must be adequately grounded in pragmatic terms. Deleuze searches for and finds in Hume's work an empiricist 'subject' that decomposes into a plurality of habits and whose identity had better be constituted from below rather than be regulated from above – and yet (as the theory of temporal syntheses will also show) it encloses a transcendental dimension which brings together the inability to ground itself on the one hand with the immanent micrological givenness of structures on the other. The concept of habit is not really at the disposal of a theory of empirical behaviour: instead the self-constitution of the subject lives in it, only to end in clichés and perseverations, in parochialisms or 'myths of everyday life'.

Deleuze contests the behaviourist idea that, mainly, habits are acquired through activities. Habits are primarily contemplations. The passive superjects, as Deleuze says alluding to Whitehead, exist only as contemplators while they synthesise where they came from or what they consist of (see Whitehead 1929: 406). They fulfil themselves narcissistically with the self-enjoyment of their own becoming, depending on the amount of intensity with which they 'prehend' or seize the repetitive elements from which they assemble themselves. 'All our rhythms, our reserves, our reaction times, the thousand intertwinings, the presents and fatigues of which we are composed, are defined on the basis of our contemplations' (Deleuze 1994: 77). The sensory-motor schemata of activity that structure the care-laden being-in-the-world are constantly accompanied in secret by the primary habits and their tricky forms of repetition. Grouped activities coexist with passive processes of subjectivation which become known as such when the sensory-motor flow is cut off or disrupted. However, the two series show interference patterns and communicate in many ways, insofar as each passive synthesis broadcasts a sign that can be interpreted in the active syntheses: for example, an expectation or a need that results from the acceptance of a (primary) habit. The need emerges at first as a completely positive phenomenon of expectation out of the passive synthesis, whereas with the active syntheses and activities it appears as a lack. Thus it delivers an example of signs or questions that in their negative interpretation are only grasped incompletely, insofar as their immanent determinations are simply ignored. 'Need expresses the openness of a question before it expresses the non-being or the absence of a response' (Deleuze 1994: 78). The immediate perception of such questions indicates the beginning of thinking, which feels itself called upon or forced to unfold its implicit meaning. Thereby it gets caught up in a never-ending process of learning, in an apprenticeship of signs, whereby it draws out of the signs' virtual potential its own immanent features. The signs are properly explicated when one investigates the causes that allow them to flash as surface phenomena. With the fanning out of its implicit referral structures, thinking becomes sensitised to the problematic regions of experience – and with the increase in viewpoints, it intensifies its ability to be affected. Deleuze advocates an empiricist position which not only originates from sensory signs which give something to think, but in addition unfolds their differential structures, so that philosophy becomes involved more deeply in the transcendental regions of experience – instead of skimming over them heavenward in search of immutable essences. With the concept of habit Deleuze rejects ideas of a susceptible and passionate subject of reception and a spontaneous and active subject of reflection, whose incommensurability can only be 'sublimated' within a prerequisite 'intermediary', a superject of affectation.

> These thousands of habits of which we are composed – these contractions, contemplations, pretensions, presumptions, satisfactions, fatigues; these variable presents – thus form the basic domain of passive syntheses. The passive self is not defined simply by receptivity – that is, by means of the capacity to experience sensations – but by virtue of the contractile contemplation [...] This self, therefore, is by no means simple. [...] Selves are larval subjects; the world of passive syntheses constitutes the system of the [diffused] self, under conditions yet to be determined. [...] There is a self wherever a furtive contemplation has been established, whenever a contracting machine capable of drawing a difference from repetition functions somewhere. (Deleuze 1994: 78–9)

The dissolution from the conception of the experience of original simple sense perceptions which precipitate in the nature of pure receptivity brings empiricism to the idea of a passive subjectivity which has constitutive meaning for the forming of the immediate facts of consciousness. Deleuze moves often and vehemently against the Kantian dichotomy of activity and passivity, where the latter appears as mere receptivity without synthesis. In contrast, the transcendental aesthetic can be conceived in a new way with the concept of habit as its centre, letting the intensive element of sensation lead to primary processes of binding and individuation which ground the status of enjoyment (*Lustprinzip*). In what follows I will make more precise the 'system of the diffused self' in reference to the other syntheses of time.

Pure Past

In the first section of the chapter on repetition, Deleuze introduced the first passive synthesis of time, the synthesis of the present. Accordingly, the present has variable intratemporal boundaries which depend on habits to contract in an expectant way repeating successive moments or elements of repetition. Thus one can say that a present lasts variably long, insofar as more or less past and future is constitutive for its formation. The present in no way coexists with time, but rather it passes in time and constantly reforms itself. Past and future are considered to be internal dimensions, although they do not exhaust themselves in the living present – unless the present were inflated to eternity. 'This is the paradox of the present: to constitute time while passing in the time constituted' (Deleuze 1994: 79). From this passing of time derives the necessity of a further determination.

Deleuze asks for the ground regarding the passing of time because in its concept this continuous disappearance could not be sufficiently thought. The synchronicity of the synthesis of the present must be changed to account for the diachronic nature of the structure of time. With this in mind, Deleuze refers to Bergson and his concept, developed in *Matter and Memory*, of a pure past that was never present. The transition from the actual plane of the present to the virtual plane of the past can best be managed here by making a detour through the active syntheses of memory. These constitute themselves, to be sure, on the basis of habit, but in the process they assume a memory that precedes every phase of the present. An earlier present can only be reproduced if the particular passively contracted present field can be transcended within the element of a general past (see Deleuze 1994: 80). This is how Deleuze poses the question regarding the ground or the conditions of the possibility of representation which comes forth in connection with the description of the process of remembering in all its ambiguity.

In anticipatory remarks I have more than once pointed out that Deleuze carries out his doctrine of the three passive syntheses according to the model of the Kantian analyses in the deduction chapter of the first edition of the *Critique of Pure Reason*. This model is mediated through Heidegger's time-theoretical interpretations; Heidegger sees the synthesis of apprehension as synthesis of the present, the synthesis of reproduction as the synthesis of the past, and the synthesis of recognition as the synthesis of the future. It makes sense here to remember the distinction, so important for the interests of those who criticise empiricism, that Kant makes between the empirical and the transcendental synthesis of reproduction. The possibility of regular empirical association of ideas must accordingly be grounded before all experience in *a priori* principles, 'and one must assume a pure transcendental synthesis of this power, which grounds even the possibility of all experience (as that which the reproducibility of the appearances necessarily presupposes)' (Kant 1999: A 101–2). Deleuze adopts and transforms the Kantian thought on *reproducibility*. In spite of his rejection of Kant's transcendental doubling of the empirical synthesis – and in this connection Heidegger follows the Kantian model – he understands the transition from the first to the second synthesis of time as a transition from the empirical synthesis of the present to the transcendental synthesis of the past.

> Far from being derived from the present or from representation, the past is presupposed by every representation. In this sense, the active synthesis

of memory may well be founded upon the (empirical) passive synthesis of habit, but on the other hand it can be grounded only by another (transcendental) passive synthesis which is peculiar to memory itself. (Deleuze 1994: 81)

This transition changes not only the understanding of time, but also the concept of repetition, which is no longer primarily related to the present. Following Kant's construction of the syntheses, Deleuze will be able to say that 'the synthesis of apprehension [...] is inseparably combined with the synthesis of reproduction' (Kant 1999: A 102). But the question that distinguishes between two paths of post-Kantianism will then be how this combination can be conceived. The defining characteristic of idealist post-Kantianism over against an empirically inspired one is the thought of letting reproducibility, with which Kant seeks to guarantee the associability of ideas, be absorbed into the objective principle of the *affinity* of appearances. With the concept of transcendental affinity Kant designates the *a priori* necessity of a concomitance between the empirical and the original consciousness that must accompany all my ideas. In this way the objective ground of reproduction reveals itself as the objective unity of apperception, which makes possible the formal unity of the experience of objects in general. Deleuze refers to the homogeneous union of the syntheses of reproduction and recognition, as undertaken by Kant, when he locates the principle of representation in the active synthesis of memory. Accordingly, an earlier present can be represented in an actual present only when the latter controls an additional dimension or a form of reflection in which the former (as former) can be remembered and determined.

> It is of the essence of representation not only to represent something but to represent its own representativity. [...] The present present is not treated as the future object of a memory but as that which reflects itself at the same time as it forms the memory of the former present. Active synthesis, therefore, has two correlative – albeit non-symmetrical – aspects: reproduction and reflection, remembrance and recognition, memory and understanding. (Deleuze 1994: 80)

The active synthesis of representation implies the reproduction of an earlier present within the framework of actual self-reflection. This reflective structure of recognition corresponds to Kant's presupposed fact of experience, namely that an actual perceived phenomenon can only be recognised if it is reproduced as such or made present in an identical manner. The objective reality of empirical givens becomes determinable, therefore, during its subjective representation. The objects of recognition refer to a ground insofar as they are grasped in consciousness as something, thanks to the pure functions of the understanding. Their comprehension takes time, even if the iterability qua determination is integrated into the synthetic unity of apprehension and that unity proves thereby its conformity with the repetitive form of recognition.

The immanent background of the paradox of the inner sense, in line with the ambiguity of the Kantian philosophy as worked out by Deleuze, opens up a different way of seeing the pure synthesis of reproduction as it sets out the structural conditions for empirical association. The representationally founded unity of apperception disintegrates precisely when we consider the transcendental difference between passive existence as determined within time and the spontaneous determinations by the understanding that affect the passive subject from the outside. The dissolution of the apparently self-evident identity relation which prevails when I think of *my* experiences, dissociates the categorial forms of thought from the memory which precedes the active syntheses of recognition. The attempted separation of sensibility and understanding *de jure*, which for Deleuze is 'one of the most original points of Kantianism' (Deleuze 1984: 22), presents a reductionist method, critical of metaphysics, that not only makes possible a subrepresentational start with perceptions, but just as much modifies thought's self-control in the direction of Lichtenberg's formulaic 'it thinks' (*Es denkt* vs *ich denke*). The transcendental synthesis of reproducibility is therefore interpreted by Deleuze as the virtual storage of the past, in line with Bergson's memory of recollection (*mémoire-souvenir*), thereby functioning as passive synthesis of memory, which fundamentally precedes voluntary memory. 'In short, what we live empirically as a succession of different presents from the point of view of active synthesis is also the ever-increasing coexistence of levels of the past within passive synthesis' (Deleuze 1994: 83). With this step into the virtual order of repetition, Deleuze succeeds in giving to relations of association that are based in habit a time-theoretical grounding as conditions of reproduction.

The three constitutive paradoxes of the pure past, which Deleuze – as shown above – draws together with a glance at Bergson's theory of memory, uncover the 'noumenal character' of the second passive synthesis. The past, which does not preserve itself in the present with which it is past, delivers the element in which the present transpires, that is to say, in which the presents become embedded. Deleuze topples the one-dimensional understanding of time: the past does not form itself only after it was present, so that it exists only in its possible recollection. Rather, the present can only pass along if it is transitional (*vergänglich*), that is, if its passing nature, its past (*Vergangenheit*), is simultaneous with it. This simultaneity does not refer to the similar character of the time syntheses of present and past. Instead it shows that the total past coexists with every new present, that it insists in every present. The pure past, which does not constitute itself after it was present, 'forms a pure, general, *a priori* element of all time' (Deleuze 1994: 82). These determinations of time possess a paradoxical form, because as a whole they express the impossibility of presenting the ground of representation in the present itself. What is represented is always the present, but not the general past *a priori*, in which one intends an earlier present as something particular. This opens up a transcendental field that can explain the origin of the relations of association out of the integration or embedding of presents in the passive synthesis of memory. For their part, these relations determine the actual parameters of reproduction and recognition syntheses.

If the synthesis of the present defines itself on the contraction of successive, indifferent and independent moments, to elicit from them a difference, then the synthesis of the past is defined through the contraction of planes or levels of the total past that coexist with one another. In this regard it is the past that as synthesis of time subordinates present and future as its two asymmetric dimensions. The present appears now as the moving tip of a rotating cone of memory insofar as it always repeats anew the whole past or 'the same life', doing so in a degree of contraction that deviates from the immediately preceding present 'by a hair's breadth'. Deleuze develops the repetition form of mnemosyne primarily in the fourth section of the second chapter of *Difference and Repetition* (Deleuze 1994: 96–116), which again presents in detail the three already covered syntheses of time as found in the psychoanalysis of Freud and Lacan. But in the second section (Deleuze 1994: 79–85), which we are here negotiating, he distinguishes between the psychic (*geistig*) and the material repetition, whereby the latter, in its bareness, 'following the Bergsonian hypothesis, [. . .] must be understood as the external envelope of the [psychic or] clothed' (Deleuze 1994: 84). While the psychic repetition develops in the memory which encloses difference in the totality of the virtual planes of the past, the material repetition grounds itself in single, independent elements or cases from which one can gain a difference only on the basis of an assumed memory. Deleuze has in mind here a noumenal and an empirical order of repetition, whereby the latter takes in the non-psychic forms of the 'actual' and 'horizontal' synthesis of the present, which relates to the succession of parts and not to the coexistence of the whole, as well as to its active means of representation.

> What we call the empirical character of the presents which make us up is constituted by the relations of succession and simultaneity between them, their relations of contiguity, causality, resemblance, and even opposition. What we call their noumenal character is constituted by the relations of virtual coexistence between the levels of a pure past, each present being no more than the actualisation or representation of one of these levels. (Deleuze 1994: 83)

Now it is important to see that habit – as empirical synthesis of reproduction – is not solely opposed to the noumenal memory and thereby discredited, but gains a new value when the present is understood as the form of actualisation of the past. Even if Deleuze, in the text sections I am discussing here, refers to observations regarding 'memory and spirit', as covered in the third chapter of *Matter and Memory*, and thus sees habit more in terms of a senso-motoric pattern, it will nevertheless be evident, in the fourth section of his chapter on repetition, that habit, in the sense of the consideration of virtual objects, is in force as a truly transcendental instance of subjectivation.

The whole conception of the psychic (noumenal) repetition, presented by Deleuze as an explication of the second synthesis of time, refers to that famous metaphor of the cone that Bergson uses to illustrate the memory of recollection and its actualisation processes. The cone SAB touches the present only with its extreme tip S, whereas the various cuts A'B', A"B", and so forth correspond to 'floors', one on top of the other, that designate all the potential intervals or degrees of contraction of the pure past coexisting with the present. In his study on Bergson, Deleuze writes, 'with coexistence, repetition must be reintroduced into duration', that is to say, into the coexistence of all the levels of the past, which, more or less contracted, 'measure the degrees of a purely ideal proximity or distance in relation to S' (Deleuze 1988a: 59–60). Whenever a sign is sent out from the present requiring an answer, memory is mobilised to choose one of its various possible interpretations (a certain level of contraction) and to apply it to the given situation.

'Freedom lies in choosing the level' (Deleuze 1994: 83), says Deleuze

Subjectivity and Immanence

laconically, referring to Bergson. Bergson makes it clear that dissolving the processional aspect of the present in the ontological repetition of the pure past does not sacrifice the claim of the present to influence the actualisation of virtual memories or the gaining of 'psychological' (conscious) existence, although the present is 'nothing else, in fact, than [memory's] actual and acting extremity' (Bergson 1988: 168).

> This amounts to saying that between the sensomotor mechanisms figured by the point S and the totality of the memories disposed in AB there is room [...] for a thousand repetitions of our psychical life, figured by as many sections A'B', A"B", etc., of the same cone. We tend to scatter ourselves over AB in the measure that we detach ourselves from our sensory and motor state to live in the life of dreams; we tend to concentrate ourselves in S in the measure that we attach ourselves more firmly to the present reality [...] (Bergson 1988: 162–3)

Bergson illuminates the genetic processes that engage the past in various degrees in every present, whereby this past must admittedly lose its virtual status in the train of its actualisation. However, this loss never affects the past as such, which simultaneously coexists with its partially becoming present.

Referring to Marcel Proust, Deleuze asks at this point the question whether it is possible to force an entry into the virtual region of this passive synthesis: 'The entire past is conserved in itself, but how can we save it for ourselves [...]?' (Deleuze 1994: 84). Deleuze sees Proust as furthering Bergson's ideas on memory by reaching back to the Platonic model of anamnesis regarding ideas established in some sphere of the pure past. Accordingly, involuntary remembering designates a virtual event that lost time doesn't actualise (in a memory-image), but recovers, counter-actualises, as lost (in a time-image). Nevertheless, the problem of time synthesis on the level of reminiscence cannot be adequately solved, because reminiscence – as the Platonic doctrine of anamnesis shows – becomes infiltrated by an essential ambiguity. That is to say, the pure past grounds time as it 'arranges the order of presents in a circle according to their decreasing or increasing resemblances to the ideal [...]' (Deleuze 1994: 88). In this way it gets from identity a feature of the idea and from resemblance a feature of its copies. The pure past governs the ordering of representation and grounds the circular arrangement of successive presents, so that it 'is itself still necessarily expressed in terms of a present, as an ancient mythical present' (Deleuze 1994: 88). Platonic anamnesis introduces time as pre-temporality (*Vorzeitigkeit*), which is why the ideas can be constituted without difficulty as archetypes that preexist any becoming. Time would thereby be subordinated to the contents and events that transpire in it. That leads to the conclusion that the transition to the third synthesis of time becomes necessary insofar as memory, speculating on a transcendent ground of time, cannot really be freed from its ambiguity, which means from its onto-theological implications, on the level of the second synthesis. In the depth of the ground lurks the inscrutable.

> The shortcoming of the ground is to remain relative to what it grounds, to borrow the characteristics of what it grounds, and to be proved by these. It is in this sense that it creates a circle: it introduces movement into the soul rather than time into thought. Just as the ground is in a sense 'bent' and must lead us towards a beyond, so the second synthesis of time points beyond itself in the direction of a third which denounces the illusion of the in-itself as still a correlate of representation. (Deleuze 1994: 88)

Before finishing this chapter by delving into the third synthesis of time, we must deal with the already mentioned section of *Difference and Repetition* on psychoanalysis, in which Deleuze summarises the various syntheses and their transitions again – with corresponding variations and additional requirements.

It will not be possible here to investigate in detail the complex connections between Deleuze and psychoanalysis. However, the observations on the passive syntheses and the differential forms of repetition in *Difference and Repetition* have fundamental relevance for his later extensive disputes, especially in *Anti-Oedipus*, with various schools of psychoanalytical research. This is particularly obvious when Deleuze, in critical reference to Freud and Lacan, distinguishes between a negatively blocked and a positively virtual repetition. In the section we are treating here, Deleuze reformulates first the problem of the empirical reproductive synthesis of habit, insofar as he refers to the erotic binding processes of libidinous excitations, as conceived in exemplary fashion by Freud in *Beyond the Pleasure Principle*. Setting up pleasure as an empirical principle that organises psychosomatic life in the Id (*Es*) assumes that the floating differences of intensity as free excitations will be uniformly bound or invested, so that their systematic resolution will be possible. These bindings or integrations of individual differences are nothing other than ways of looking at things (or contemplations), populating the Id's primary field of individuation with small, immediately narcissistic subjectivities, habits or lively presents.

Subjectivity and Immanence

> In all these senses, binding represents a pure passive synthesis, a Habitus which confers on pleasure the value of being a principle of satisfaction in general. Habit underlies the organisation of the Id. (Deleuze 1994: 97)

Repetition in habit therefore lies beyond the pleasure principle and should in no way be subsumed under it. Acts that for example are intentionally carried out to reproduce an earlier state of pleasure assume the pleasure principle and the reflected temporal concepts, although they rest in the passive synthesis of Habitus. 'Pleasure then exceeds its own instantaneity in order to assume the allure of satisfaction in general' (Deleuze 1994: 97). Using the distinction between primary and secondary habits, as defined above, one could say that it is the secondary habits, at most, that are governed by the pleasure principle.

In a further step, and in exact correspondence to the argument of his first passage through the time syntheses, Deleuze describes two lines of development that go beyond the passive synthesis of habit. On the one hand, there is the active synthesis of recognition that consists 'in relating the bound excitation to an object supposed to be both real and the end of our actions' (Deleuze 1994: 98), and on the other hand, there is the deepening of the passive synthesis that results from the contemplation of virtual objects. In the first case the ego tries actively to unify itself in relation to a real object. Thus the reality principle does not oppose the pleasure principle, but complements and amplifies it by further energising the scope of activity it has created. In the second case, the sequence of real objects is accompanied by an asymmetric and correlative sequence of virtual centres which draws attention to the singular continuation of passive syntheses beneath the activities regulated by the ego. In the context of psycho-genetic discussions on the pre-genital sexuality of the child, Deleuze shows clearly what this sexuality's virtual-real double structure is all about:

> The child who begins to handle a book by imitation, without being able to read, invariably holds it back to front. It is as though the book were being held out to the other, the real end of the activity, even though the child seizing the book back to front is the virtual centre of its passion, of its own extended contemplation. (Deleuze 1994: 99)

The correlative dimensions of real and virtual relations to objects that simultaneously cross the passive synthesis of the present in two different directions stand together in a complementary relationship, in spite of their dissimilarity. 'We see both that the virtuals are deducted from the series of reals and that they are incorporated in the series of reals' (Deleuze 1994: 100). Deleuze makes use of Freud's distinction between self-preservative and sexual drives insofar as partial objects of pre-genital sexual relations, in their qualitative isolation from real total objects, are produced as virtual objects. Lacan's virtual object 'a' lacks its own identity because it is split into two parts which can never be put together as a whole: the father is simultaneously serious and playful but never where he ought to be. Isolation corresponds inversely to the incorporation of virtual objects in real objects: the former do not lose in the latter their partial status, nor are they absorbed as real, but rather they act as inserted foreign bodies (*Fremdkörper*) which nevertheless see to it that sexuality can be integrated into the realm of real satisfactions.

With these thoughts on the bilateral objective concretisation of habit, Deleuze follows the descriptions he has set in advance on the transition into the transcendental synthesis of reproduction. Again a continuing passivity of memory is made mandatory by way of the introduction of active syntheses of reproduction which realise themselves when actively collected subjects are obsessed with the reality of past-desired or future-threatening objects. This 'process of becoming' of the pure past weighs constantly upon its conceptual formation and requires a further transition beyond it (almost in the Hegelian sense), a transition meant to eliminate the formation's latent fundamental theoretical ambivalences. At first, however, Deleuze treats these ambivalent structures according to how they show up on the problematic level of the second synthesis of time. As expected, and with Bergson in mind, virtual objects will again be qualified as 'essentially past', whereas the real objects, perceived as actual in the temporal order of successive presents and in the extensive milieu of a homogenised space, can be uniquely localised and dated. Virtual objects – Deleuze reminds us of Lacan's interpretation of Poe's tale about the purloined letter – are not where we look for them and are found where they aren't. They are of a symbolic nature and are missing in their place, whereas what is real always carries its place as if stuck to the soles of its feet. Virtual or symbolic objects allow themselves to be experienced only in the erotic mode of the pure past, as Deleuze says, alluding to his comments on Proust's *mémoire involontaire*.

The ambiguity of the synthesis of the past diverges into two models of repetition: into the so-called bare (straightforward) and clothed (disguised) forms of repetition. The former runs from one actual present to another, so that a first or original state is to be assumed, one that is repeated or must be repeated in a successive and derivative way. In Freudian theory the concepts 'of fixation and regression, along with trauma and the primal scene' (Deleuze 1994: 103) express this first element. Thus a counter-investment is automatically or compulsively built up around the primary psychic crack or lack, in such a way that this investment (*Gegenbesetzung*) must hold out against the crack with the help of constant repressions (*Verdrängungsleistungen*), as if the secondary repetitions could otherwise clothe or disguise the truth only until it were to break out and bare itself. As Deleuze says, 'repetition is subjected to a principle of identity in the former present and a rule of resemblance in the present one' (Deleuze 1994: 104). In this negative interpretation of repetition we have a case of natural blockage, insofar as the original idea is captured in memory but its 'processing' (*Durcharbeitung*) with self-possession has yet to occur. From this perspective one appears to repeat only because one neither understands nor remembers, but instead represses. For Deleuze, Freud complicates his model of repetition with the introduction of the death instinct – and yet it remains fundamentally materialistic, realistic and representationalistic. (I will later say a few words about Deleuze's reinterpretation of the opposition between the drives of Eros and Thanatos.)

In distinction to the bare repetitions, which develop from one present to the next and are teleologically connected to the original state, Deleuze conceives of clothed repetitions, which are primarily directed toward virtual objects. 'Repetition is truly that which disguises itself in constituting itself, that which constitutes itself only by disguising itself. It is not underneath the masks, but is formed from one mask to another' (Deleuze 1994: 34). Whereas, for example, according to the first model of thought the adult series follows the infantile series – and in a relatively unexplainable way is supposed to be determined by the latter – the second model makes clear in a desirable way that both series coexist in dependence on a virtual object that continually circulates in them. Thus the repetition no longer travels from an (earlier) present to another (actual) present – as it did in the series of real objects – but moves between both heterogeneous series, which coexist in the symbolic field: 'Neither of these two series can any longer be designated as the original or the derived' (Deleuze 1994: 105). It is rather a case of actualisation-lines in which the structural element continuously displaces itself because it can never be represented but always differs from itself. 'The displacement of the virtual object is [. . .] the principle from which, in reality, repetition follows in the form of disguised repetition' (Deleuze 1994: 140). This is how Deleuze adjusts the concept of repetition to his structuralist requirements: the empty field circulates in time within at least two series which are immanently determined. The structural relations and reciprocal syntheses find their virtual and genetic concretion in the repetitive element of the passive syntheses. Deleuze draws attention to the connection of the fourth and fifth chapters of *Difference and Repetition* to the second chapter by commenting that the ideal static genesis 'may be understood as the correlate of the notion of passive synthesis, and [. . .] in turn illuminates that notion' (Deleuze 1994: 183).

The ideally constituted repetition cannot be represented by the identity form of the concept, which allows only superficial differences between normal specimens of a genus to subsist within the homogeneous milieu of experience. No matter in what monotone the repetition may present itself, it always involves a passive subject that is affected in silence by the repetition's redundancies. As Deleuze shows with numerous examples in the area of aesthetics, a vertical repetition always rumbles along that runs from one conspicuous point to the next below the horizontal surface of reiterative occurrences, a rhythm that underscores the metre. Repetitions disguise the structural potential that displaces itself, actualises itself, conceals itself within them. They unfold in dynamic processes because they communicate through differences that circulate within them. They imply the intensive structures of their own genesis, which can only be explicated in further repetitions. Therefore they are marked by an essential inequality which characterises the positivity or origin of continuous actualisations. Clearly, the bare repetitions at best present a mode of disguise of the clothed ones that develop from sign to sign and from mask to mask and never relate to an exterior trans-iterative or non-masked reference point: there are always more masks behind every mask, with never a first.

In this context Deleuze stresses again that the two forms of repetition belong together, since the repetition only takes shape by clothing itself in disguise: 'It does not preexist its own disguises and, in forming itself, constitutes the bare repetition within which it becomes enveloped' (Deleuze 1994: 24). The differences in intensity are always enveloped by their extensive actualisations and demand to be interpreted. If above I spoke of the contemplation of virtual objects, then here the empiricist relevance of this way of speaking becomes clearer. Habits rest in passive occurrences of repetition which transpire beneath empirical reproductions related to the present and bundle together subliminal intensities. No wonder that Deleuze uses this starting point to introduce the virtual microprocesses into the transcendental structure of the (empirical) syntheses of apprehension.

> Partial objects are the elements of little perceptions [*petites perceptions*]. The unconscious is differential, involving little perceptions, and as such it is different in kind from consciousness. It concerns problems and questions which can never be reduced to the great oppositions or overall effects that are felt in consciousness. (Deleuze 1994: 108)

Consciousness results from genetic processes or is a superficial effect. It is defined in such a way that it is not coextensive with the sphere of experience in general. Consciousness is intentional (in the narrow sense), which means it actualises in or with a subject-object-structure of experience. The constitutive achievements of the passive synthesis, on the other hand, take place unconsciously, but they can be experienced as such at certain times. By means of philosophical concepts, rather than in naturalist terminology, can one relate to this experience.

It is now clear that a difference can in no way be *elicited* from repetition, since displacement and disguise are constitutive elements of repetition and thereby envelop difference. In deepened narcissistic contemplation difference is interiorised between the lines of virtual and real objects, so that the passive ego 'experiences itself as perpetually displaced in the one, perpetually disguised in the other' (Deleuze 1994: 110). Differences relating to Eros need not be opposed to the death instinct (as conceived in a material model of repetition); instead the differences are already at work in the deepest levels of repetition. With that, Deleuze properly reaches the level of the third synthesis of time. That happens because, in the transition from the second to the third synthesis, the misinterpretation of the ground of the past must be fended off, a misinterpretation that was pushed back in the concept of the disguised repetition but that can only be captured and dispensed within its full range on completion of the transition.

The ambiguity of the synthesis of memory consists in its latent determination to understand the pure past as foundational for representation. It cannot get rid of the temptation to disengage the ideal ground of time, as the ground of reason (ratio sufficiens), from fleeting and ephemeral life and pre-think the representations founded by the latter. It is precisely the specific relativity between ground and grounded that arranges the derivative appearances in a circle around a centre that is in the highest degree identical with itself. 'Always the same ambiguity on the part of the ground: to represent itself in the circle that it imposes on what it grounds, to return as an element in the circuit of representation that it determines in principle' (Deleuze 1994: 110). As Deleuze says, ideas or representations converging in the ground make up 'arcs of the circle' which participate at most in a secondary way in the quality they lay claim to. What characterises the synthesis of memory is precisely that it organises two such arcs, one is the diverging series of real and virtual objects which together relate to the synthesis of the present, and another is the passing presents which strike a cyclical arc around the past which is displaced within it. When these two arcs are superimposed, the complementarity of the series of real and virtual objects in the first arc transfers easily to the structure of the second, so, as Deleuze concludes, 'it is inevitable that the two references become confused, the pure past assuming thereby the status of a former present, albeit mythical' (Deleuze 1994: 109).

In memory the essential determinations of all the finite perspectives of representation thus seem to preserve themselves. On the other hand, the possibility opens up within memory to go beyond this ground (*fondement*) to a groundlessness (*sans fond*) in which the ground, to modify Hegel, 'grounds out' (*der Grund geht zugrunde*). Precisely the introduction of time into thought makes possible by means of the third synthesis the dissolution of the identity form of the ground and thus turns its virtual determinations toward the future.

> The ground is strangely bent: on the one hand, it leans towards what it grounds, towards the forms of representation; on the other hand, it turns and plunges into a groundlessness beyond the ground which resists all forms and cannot be represented. (Deleuze 1994: 274–5)

At this point Deleuze ties in with Heidegger, who insists on the groundlessness of representational thinking, which can ground itself only in doubtful backtracking to onto-theological premises. It is in the event (*Ereignis*) that the time structure of thinking is revealed, which cannot represent or pick up the original giving of Being in determinations relative to the being-present of beings. Where Heidegger reconciles the event of Being with the history of Being and declares it to be a mystery that should be respectfully approached, thoughtfully discussed and poetically sung, Deleuze, with Nietzsche, places it in the midst of our life. The syntheses of time culminate in the divine play – or in the purely immanent structural eventuation – of the eternal return of the same.

Blank Future

To be sure, Deleuze explains the specific transition from the second to the third synthesis through the paradox of the inner sense, set by Kant in the centre of transcendental philosophy. This paradox reflects how the inner sense 'presents even ourselves to consciousness only as we appear to ourselves, not as we are in ourselves, since we intuit ourselves only as we are internally affected [. . .]' (Kant 1999: B 152–3). The determination of undetermined existence by the 'I think' that 'expresses the act of determining my existence' (Kant 1999: B 158) must be in accordance with the form of the inner sense, that is, with time as the form of determinability. Precisely the introduction of time as the form of self-affection now implies in all consequence the just mentioned paradoxical logic that the spontaneous ego must not be identified in advance with passive existence, which alone can be determined. The one and only sensorially and phenomenally determinable existant (Dasein) thus imagines its 'own' spontaneity of thought and its 'own' intelligence solely so that it 'cannot be understood as the attribute of a substantial and spontaneous being, but rather as the affection of a passive self which experiences its own thought [. . .] being exercised in it and upon it but not by it' (Deleuze 1994: 86). The active ego and the passive self are thus fractured by the line of time, although they nevertheless necessarily relate to one another (under the conditions of a transcendental difference). For the passive existant determines itself only if it is affected by something else within time.

> It is as though the ego [*je*] were fractured from one end to the other: fractured by the pure and empty form of time. In this form it is the correlate of the passive self [*moi*] which appears in time. (Deleuze 1994: 86)

If undetermined existence can only be determined as a passive temporal self that constantly changes in the continuous variation of its degree of consciousness, then it seems more than questionable to fix its identity in such a way that in consciousness the temporal content is uniformly synthesised with the help of active functions of the understanding. Deleuze speaks of a fracture in the ego precisely because with the experience of time as form of interiority my existence is no longer to be determined as that of a spontaneous subjectivity: thanks to the time-formationally established difference, the relation between determination and undetermined Being can no longer be understood as a relation between ground and grounded, but only as affection or self-affection of the temporally determined existence, which constructs an 'infinite modulation of its degrees at each instant' (Deleuze 1997: 30). As Kant himself explains using the example of the sublime, there are givens which are too big for the productive imagination: to be sure it is persistently trying to synthesise the successive impressions (quasi-automatically), but it doesn't succeed in getting them under one concept; the apprehensions and reproductions run empty and do not find their determination in recognition.

The third synthesis of time realises itself through the dissolution of the normative (ground-validating) self-relation of human subjectivity. It nevertheless determines itself in the subjectivation form of self-affection, according to which each momentary impression is only discovered because it diverges from the previous one and on the basis of this divergence or modification becomes noticeable. When Deleuze talks about the empty formal order of pure time or about its relentlessly straight line, then he is not only alluding to the irreducible future which, from a teleological perspective, is unpredictable, but also and simultaneously to its detachment (*Ent-bindung*) from the cardinal supports of time-transcendent grounding authorities. 'Time ceases to be curved by a god who makes it depend on movement' (Deleuze 1997: 28). Deleuze makes it clear that time does not allow itself to be subordinated to extensive movement and cannot be defined as its principle of measurement. 'Time itself unfolds [. . .], instead of things unfolding within it' (Deleuze 1994: 88). Time is no longer defined in terms of events that run their course within it. As Heidegger never tired of emphasising, time is nothing chronological that transpires in time, but rather – following a formulation by Kant – the unchangeable form of becoming that lets only itself return. Ordinal time, once detached from the ground and its contents of memory, must be defined 'as this purely formal distribution of the unequal [past-future; MR] in the function of a caesura' (Deleuze 1994: 89). Consequently, Deleuze claims that the fracture in the ego comes from the caesura that conclusively sets the boundary between before and after. Deleuze uses Proust's experiences to begin to clarify how 'loss of memory' and the linearity of time fit together. For involuntary memories do not get around forgetting, they do not repeat in an actual present a present stored up in the past, but are

Subjectivity and Immanence

experienced as never having been present. Of course there are simple associations between the taste of the madeleine then and now. The decisive point is that this taste implies or encloses virtual strata of the past: Combray as it was never actually experienced, nor could have been.

> Loss or forgetting here are not determinations which must be overcome; rather, they refer to the objective nature of that which we recover, as lost, at the heart of forgetting. (Deleuze 1994: 102)

So we discover here in the involuntary memory a dimension of time that, to be sure, coexists virtually with every present, but only seldom, once upon a time, eventuates in the 'instant' (*Zeitdauer*) of a counter-effectuation. In the *Logic of Sense* Deleuze expands his ideas on the theme of 'event and time' by distinguishing between *Chronos* and the ancient Greek concept of *Aion* in its Stoic form. Chronos gathers past and future in the actual present. Aion divides past and future within a virtual instant (*Augenblick*) which designates the steadily displaced and therefore unlocalisable hiatus between what is already past and what has not yet happened.

> First, the entire line of the Aion is run through by the instant which is endlessly displaced on this line and is always missing from its own place. Plato rightly said that the instant is atopian, without place. It is the paradoxical instance or the aleatory point [. . .], whose role is, primarily, to divide and subdivide every present in both directions at once, into past-future, upon the line of the Aion. (Deleuze 1990b: 16)

Aion is the name of the pure, empty form of time, always about to happen and already passed, unhitched from present actual experiences and therefore pulled straight in its full length. The present, which controls a certain duration, divides itself to infinity into past and future and loses itself in the processes of becoming, which simultaneously flee in two directions, the 'just now' (*soeben*) and the 'right away' (*sogleich*), that never actualise as *now* (*jetzt*), but only happen in the 'feeling of absent-mindedness'. In this way not only the temporal determination of structure, but also the structural determination of time is made evident. On the one hand, the aleatory point moving ahead on the timeline always divides anew the dimensions of time, so that the past is subject to permanent structural modification. On the other hand, the temporal processes of differenciation are serially organised in the structural element of the instant and highlight singular notable points that can only be sensed. The structure, which gains its meaning from the loss of a subjective grounding authority, always encompasses at least two heterogeneous series which it determines simultaneously by determining itself. Its two-sided nature corresponds to the immanent regulation of its actualisation. That is why 'the straight line which extends simultaneously in two directions traces the frontier between bodies and language, states of affairs and propositions' (Deleuze 1990b: 167). In his book on Foucault, Deleuze will talk about the frontier between the visible and the sayable. The two series are never lines of departure, but series constituted in their relationship, which result from a process of self-differenciation and self-organisation that is immanently determined.

The three syntheses of time – present, past and future – do not construct a homogeneous whole, but constitute three different modes of repetition. Each individual mode possesses two time dimensions as integrative moment of its correspondingly determined synthesis of time. However, the transitions Deleuze describes show that one can reach a deepening of one's understanding of time by going from the first to the second and from the second to the third. 'The future, which subordinates the other two to itself and strips them of their autonomy, is the royal repetition' (Deleuze 1994: 94). In this way a singular sublimation of the 'figures (*Gestalten*) of time consciousness' takes place in the third or future synthesis. This sublimation, which in no way annuls the phenomenological significance of earlier stages that remain effective as figures of actualisation, is explicated by Deleuze within the framework of the third time synthesis. Past and present are not only conceived in a new way but as habitus and mnemosyne they must now step aside for the future (see Deleuze 1994: 94–5).

Deleuze begins his discussion of the dimensions of time within the last synthesis by determining the past *a priori* as the deficient condition of present dealings, which cannot yet be affirmed as such. In this way he expressly connects with his ideas on the sublime in Kant and on Freud's repetition compulsion, which assumes a non-representative or traumatic image that is too big for me. At any rate the past only appears overpowering from the perspective of the present because the latter supports itself on a subjective identity that has to counter and counteract the free play of differences. Thus Deleuze speaks of the necessity of a *presence of metamorphosis*: the ego is confronted with the future which possesses 'a secret coherence [...] excluding [...] the identity of the self' (Deleuze 1994: 90–1). This metamorphosis takes place in processes

Subjectivity and Immanence

of becoming-other, subjectless subjectivations that can be described as passive individuations (see Deleuze and Guattari 1987: 232f. and Deleuze 1988b: 78–110). The future brings something new into play which distinguishes it from both habit and memory. Deleuze sees its primary significance as embodying the Nietzschean idea of eternal return. 'The form of time is there only for the revelation of the formless in the eternal return, [. . .] which turns upon itself and causes only the yet-to-come [*à-venir*] to return' (Deleuze 1994: 91). In no way do identical situations, whether they be present or past events, repeat themselves on a circular formed timeline, but rather only the future repeats itself, from which a constantly new distribution of singularities result. The eternal return is the unchangeable form of change itself, which in its identity and in its Being solely expresses itself in differences and becomings. It demands a belief in the future because the Being of the past is pulled into the process of becoming and is changed with every actualisation. Only in view of the future can the differences be affirmed that in every moment have to be combined differently. The totally temporalised structure, the time that runs its course in accordance with purely immanent necessities, runs an ideal or divine lottery: a throw of the dice without set rules (every move in the game makes up its own rules or modifies given rules), without established hypotheses as to winner or loser (which numerically divide up and limit what can happen instead of fully affirming its total chanciness), without winners or losers (because the various throws are univocal, which means they are simultaneous with respect to the aleatoric point 'which always changes the rule, or coordinates and ramifies the corresponding series as it insinuates chance over the entire length of each series' (Deleuze 1990b: 59)).

Deleuze arrives at the same goal when he develops his concept of the death instinct with the help of the phenomenon of narcissism. As we have seen, the narcissistic ego, absorbed in libido-obsessed self-contemplation, interiorises the difference between the two series of virtual and actual objects. However, this phenomenon of passive selfness cannot be adequately described at the stage of the second synthesis.

> For while the passive ego becomes narcissistic, the activity must be thought. This can occur only in the form of an affection, in the form of the very modification that the narcissistic ego [*moi*] passively experiences on its own account. Thereafter, the narcissistic ego is related to the form of an I [*je*] which operates upon it as an 'Other'. (Deleuze 1994: 110)

Clearly passive (narcissistic) subjectivity covers the entire space of the time syntheses, thanks to the different forms of repetition. It undergoes the 'test of difference', a first time, a second time, a third time, so that it finally enters into an intimate relation with the death instinct. For Deleuze identifies the death instinct with the straight-running line of time insofar as it merges with the self-affection of the narcissistic ego. So Eros and Thanatos do not stand in a complimentary relationship to one another, but constitute two different syntheses. Counter to Freud, Deleuze takes the death instinct out of the material model of repetition and determines it as that 'neutral and displaceable energy' (Deleuze 1994: 113) that constructs itself out of the desexualised libido flowing back into the narcissistic ego. Deleuze cites extensively Blanchot's suggestions as developed in *L'espace littéraire*, whereby death 'refers to the state of free differences when they are no longer subject to the form imposed upon them by an I or an ego, when they assume a shape which excludes my own coherence no less than that of any identity whatsoever' (Deleuze 1994: 113). In the last text that he himself published, *Pure Immanence: A Life*, Deleuze recalls an episode in the novel *Our Mutual Friend* by Dickens, in which Riderhood, almost drowning, is for a time on the brink between life and death. In this moment the life of the individual makes room for an impersonal, singular life of immanence, 'an immanent life carrying with it the events or singularities that are merely actualised in subjects and objects. [...] This indefinite life doesn't just come about or come after but offers the immensity of an empty time where one sees the event yet to come and already happened in the absolute of an immediate consciousness' (Deleuze 2001: 29).

Intensity Differentials and the Being of the Sensible

> In the West one has always avoided thinking about intensity. [...] Deleuze has now freed it in a thought that will become the highest, the sharpest and the most intensive. (Foucault 1977a: 11)

> Est aliquid praeter extensionem imo extensione prius. (Leibniz)

Deleuze's interest in the philosophical history of the differential calculus is connected with the time-honoured question, whether infinitesimal magnitudes are responsible for the continuous variation of qualities in perceived objects. There is in the history of philosophy a wide spectrum of doctrines by naturalist philosophers, psychologists and physicalists that all take their start in one way or another from

Leibniz and his somewhat ambiguous metaphysical definitions of the differential. For our purposes we should mainly keep in mind various post-Kantian positions which precisely in light of their decidedly non-atomistic stance tie in nicely with Kant's indispensable distinction between intensive and extensive magnitudes. It is from these sources that Deleuze develops his empiricist yet radically critical approach. He applies them first to Hume and then to Nietzsche, before reverting to Leibniz himself to develop a transcendental psychology of perception comprehending both the differential and sub-representative relations of intensity and the processes of becoming which are presupposed by every objectively oriented perception.

Kant, with his doctrine of principles, certainly inspired ideas relative to the range and conditions of mathematics and nature sciences, as for example in the sections in the *Critique of Pure Reason* from the 'Axioms of Intuition' to the 'Anticipations of Perception' – ideas which Hermann Cohen later worked out in exemplary fashion. Kant also anticipated certain important questions to be raised in philosophical psychology from Herbart to Fechner and beyond, which becomes evident in the critique of psychologism later carried out by such diverse authors as Bergson and Cohen, again referring to the Kantian distinction between intensive and extensive magnitudes. These historical connections are noteworthy because when Deleuze embarks on his own fundamental criticism of Hume's classical empiricism based on Kant's theory of intensity and intensity differences, he expressly takes his cue from Cohen and, with some reservations, from Bergson.

To put it succinctly, the Humean bundles of perceptions, as extensive magnitudes (at least in the case of visual and tactile perceptions), display a degree of intensity – but it remains unclear how the two orders of magnitude are connected. Furthermore, to speak with Kant, impressions of sensation seem to be perceptions that show relatively indistinguishable characteristics of intuition and sensation. So Hume's interpretation is fraught with difficulties as long as he insists on a philosophical understanding of psychology that blocks the overcoming of its naturalistic limitations. On the other hand, however, it is precisely empiricism's obdurate and steadfast stance in wanting to base itself on experience as it presents itself that provides a starting point for its necessary phenomenological or even 'structural' radicalisation.

The central point of a post-Kantian critique maintains that no intensive magnitudes as such are ever involved in psychological facts:

they are simply not quantifiable. Now, this thesis is easily misunderstood and at first glance it is not very instructive. First it disputes quite generally the scientifically fundamental interpretation of perceptions as being intensive contents of consciousness. No doubt Bergson and Cohen choose quite different critical strategies – and Deleuze takes from both, because they each make a contribution toward a positive definition of the concept of intensity – yet they both agree that 'intensities' present measurable magnitudes only when defined extensionally as (physically-physiologically or even behaviouristically) objectifiable facts. While Bergson in the last analysis reduced all quantities to extensive quantities, Cohen not only held firm to the Kantian distinction between extensive and intensive magnitudes, but he also expanded it for epistemological reasons by construing intensities as the physical counterpart of mathematical differentials. It is just this stretching of the second Kantian principle to make it the 'principle of reality' that allows Cohen to exceed the boundaries of transcendental aesthetics and become attractive for Deleuze. Bergson, on the other hand, combines with his rejection of positivist procedures in psychology an acceptance of the distinction between actual and virtual multiplicities, whereby the latter are then also quite compatible with intensities in the Deleuzian sense.

Through Hume to Pre-Objective Intensities

Let us look again at the foundations of the empiricist theory of perception. We know that it is supposed to facilitate the realisation of a programme that founds and checks over all knowledge through reference to immediate experience. Hume introduces 'perception' as the generic term for facts of experience in general and distinguishes two types of perception according to their degree of intensity: impressions and ideas. Impressions, for their part, divide into impressions of sensation and impressions of reflection. In addition Hume emphasises that there are not only simple impressions, but also (from the simple ones) compound impressions and ideas. This addition is important because it complicates the dependency relationships of the two types of impression to one another. Hume's fundamental empiricist proposition, which is generally known as the copy-principle, frankly maintains *'that all our simple ideas in their first appearance are deriv'd from simple impressions, which are correspondent to them, and which they exactly represent'* (Hume 2001: 9, Hume's italics). The prototype-copy relation can therefore only be established on the level of simple perceptions. This is fundamentally significant because the empiricist analysis of abstract ideas depends on being able to reduce ideas to impressions and can only elicit their truth content in this way. In this context we have the principle of difference as formulated by Hume, which states that 'whatever objects are different are distinguishable, and that whatever objects are distinguishable are separable by the thought and imagination' (Hume 2001: 17). Associations of ideas cannot combine the latter in such a way that they merge or are made inseparable: precisely their 'independent separability' makes possible their empirical justification in the first place.

It has often been pointed out that for Deleuze the atomistic premises of the theory of perception and the corresponding copy theory are not feasible and force us to look back at the distinction between phenomenological and naturalistic aspects of Hume's empiricism. The atomistic premises then give way to the central thesis to which Deleuze adheres, which says that sensual intensities are genetic elements that actualise themselves in extensity as an extensive magnitude. However, they are concealed by perceived qualities that ascribe themselves to some persistent object constituting itself within the same given framework (that is, in the corresponding spatial and temporal relations). Formulated in empiricist terminology, this thesis maintains that sense impressions are first to be understood as pre-individual sense-data and only begin to stabilise themselves as associatively bundled and organised moments of perception in the order of visible objects. The postulated displacement within the empiricist field of concepts reveals itself only after a requisite appraisal using immanent criteria.

Hume himself begins rather emphatically with the phenomenological evidence of 'simple perceptions' as constituting building blocks of experience. In the much-discredited chapter 'Of the ideas of space and time' in the *Treatise*, the atomistic presuppositions of perception theory are formulated by Hume in a particularly concise way, as Anthony Flew has shown (Flew 1976: 257–69; see Hume 2001: 23–49). With the intention of rebutting the theorem on the infinite divisibility of space and time, Hume refers there to the kind of inseparable and extensionless perceptions underlying, in his opinion, all ideas of space and time.

> I first take the least idea I can form of a part of extension, and being certain that there is nothing more minute than this idea, I conclude, that

whatever I discover by its means must be a real quality of extension. Then I repeat this idea once, twice, thrice, etc. and find the compound idea of extension, arising from its repetition, always to augment, and become double, triple, quadruple, etc. till at last it swells up to a considerable bulk, greater or smaller, in proportion as I repeat more or less the same idea. (Hume 2001: 25)

In his proof, Hume combines several arguments. First he relies on the universal admission 'that the capacity of the mind is limited' (Hume 2001: 23) and can never possess an adequate image of infinity. Second, he maintains 'that whatever is capable of being divided *in infinitum*, must consist of an infinite number of parts' (Hume 2001: 23). From these two premises it follows for him that the imagination is able to comprehend minimal ideas 'which cannot be diminish'd without a total annihilation' (Hume 2001: 23). Behind this thought, which draws a conclusion from the finite limitation of the imagination to the real structures of time and space, lie further assumptions on Hume's part. Thus time and space connections of perceptions must be put together out of single, unitary and indivisible perceptions, since they otherwise couldn't exist. "Tis evident, that existence in itself belongs only to unity [. . .] 'Tis therefore utterly absurd to suppose any number to exist, and yet deny the existence of unites [sic]' (Hume 2001: 25). In addition it is assumed that ideas are especially clear and distinct if they are formed of correspondingly simple impressions and thus have at their disposal an immediately certain degree of reality. The *postulate of correspondence* between ideas and impressions asserts that that which is smaller than the smallest possible idea cannot be imagined and is therefore impossible.

Hume repeatedly says that ideas cannot be as small as you like, but reach a minimum that cannot be further subdivided. This thesis, which is here not an issue, is combined with another thesis concerned with the necessarily smallest impressions. Hume uses the ink spot experiment to illustrate what he understands to be simple impressions or *minima sensibilia*.

Put a spot of ink upon paper, fix your eye upon that spot, and retire to such a distance, that at last you lose sight of it; 'tis plain, that the moment before it vanish'd the image or impression was perfectly indivisible. (Hume 2001: 24)

From this experiment we are supposed to understand that sensible impressions have a least magnitude that cannot be further minimised and therefore are indivisible. In Hume studies one speaks of extensionless points, because each extensive size is by definition assembled out of similar simple points. We can leave aside here the problems that arise when one tries to develop a concept of extension based on these points and their addition. It suffices for the moment to interrogate the phenomenological evidence that Hume brings forth for his empiricist argument. In the last analysis the arrangement of the experiment is directed toward determining a limit to visibility, a limit that is normally invisible; this is where – more or less on the threshold of consciousness – the little, barely visible phenomena prove their irreducible atomic and discrete character. But now it seems that the intention to ground the 'logic' in an epistemological manner persistently influences Hume's descriptive analysis of the ink spot experience. The fundamental quest to uncover calculable basic units of a psychological nature compromises itself, since the description of the sense-data understood in this way is unfortunately incompatible with the phenomenological given. It isn't even necessary to harp on the multiple critiques of sense atomism from the perspective of Gestalt theory or phenomenology to argue against the assumptions Hume makes concerning the evidence of simple perceptions. In his replay of Hume's 'self-experiment', C. D. Broad summarises for the long haul the most important aspects of the way the perceptions are treated.

> At the earlier stages there certainly is a noticeable decrease in size, whilst the intensity of the blue colour and the definiteness of the outline do not alter appreciably. But, as I approach the limiting position, from which there ceases to be any appearance of the dot in my visual field, what I find most prominent is the growing *faintness* of the blue colour and the *haziness* of the outline. The appearance of the dot finally vanishes through becoming indistinguishable from that of the background immediately surrounding it. But, so long as I am sure that I am seeing the spot at all, I am fairly sure that the sense-datum which is its visual appearance is *extended*, and not literally punctiform. So I very much doubt whether there are punctiform visual sense-data. The case for punctiform tactual sense-data would seem to be still weaker. (Broad 1961: 166)

At issue here is the breaking-up of Hume's atomistic position by looking more closely at the implicit and undifferenciated reference to both extensive and intensive magnitudes. On the one hand Hume gains mathematical points of sense out of a continuous minimisation of extension, whereas on the other hand they only exist as extensionless points because they have at their disposal a gradation of intensity. Clearly the spot, when it is no longer visible, loses both its spatially extended form and its more or less intensive colour. Does that mean it is a matter of equivalent magnitudes? Broad's observations show that the minimalising of extension and the weakening of intensity are not proportional to one another. That raises certain unforeseen questions. If there are simple perceptions, don't they have to operate with an intensive magnitude that also cannot be further reduced in size? Don't elementary sense-data require elementary intensities? Can we postulate elementary values regarding intensive magnitudes? Is it at all possible to assign an intensive grade to perceptions as such? Or more generally, how should we understand the empiricist relationship between intensive and extensive magnitudes?

Hume's reliance on immediate experience and his fixation on the primordial structures of the experiential material, that is, on 'clear and precise' perceptions that have to act as the base upon which all higher-level ideas are grounded, leads him automatically to understand the individual 'sensual qualities' as indivisible homogeneous parts which allow themselves to be assembled in the sense of discrete actual magnitudes. Hume's fundamental intention of grounding a science of human nature in accordance with the Newtonian (rather than the Leibnizian) model finds direct expression in his concept of experience insofar as the perceptual process is supposed to consist in 'a mere passive admission of the impressions thro' the organs of sensation' (Hume 2001: 52), which means that it manages for the moment without any mental activity or other synthetic process. These pure, passively received and unconnected impressions are completely individualised and clearly determined, as are the ideas that result from them, and therefore 'can never, but from our fault, contain any thing so dark and intricate' (Hume 2001: 52). As a result of his scientific-mechanistic objective, Hume raises himself above the phenomenological evidence that very small perceptual givens are merely blurred or hazily perceived or even that only such things are perceived to which attention has been drawn or that somehow have awakened interest. A small ink spot is normally not noticed at all, which means of course that the smallest perceptions are not normally available and thus also fail to be represented by ideas.

The anti-atomistic implications of the phenomenological interpretation that Broad puts forward with respect to Hume's experiments in perception become better appreciated when one recalls the concept of an intensive magnitude as developed by Kant. According to Kant, intensive quantities, as distinct from extensive ones, are characterised, after all, by not being measurable precisely because they don't have at their disposal any indivisible units that can be added to one another. They designate magnitudes that are constituted not in relation to one but to zero. That is why they can be infinitely and continuously diminished: at all times they involve ever smaller genetic moments that are not synthesised successively but – as Kant says – 'in an instant' (see Kant 1999: A167/B209–11). Intensive magnitudes can therefore increase or decrease – and it is quite possible that it is exactly these self-differenciation processes that makes them perceptible – but because they do not have a common denominator, these differences cannot be located on a constant, unchanging measurement foundation. Using this concept of intensity, it is now possible to conceive of the gradation of affection (Husserl), so that inconspicuous perceptions cross the consciousness threshold at some specific point, namely at exactly the place where they (for example, the distant ink spot) become noticeable.

It follows that Hume makes his *minima sensibilia* dependent on perceptual conditions that – at least within the concrete contexts of daily life – are subject to permanent gradual modifications. Thus their unified and extensionless status no longer has any foundation. As Kant has shown, for any intensive magnitude it is a matter of a complex unit that does not consist of homogeneous parts which can be consecutively connected to one another. Even if a certain (variable) degree does define a minimum of visibility, nevertheless every quality of sensation implies an intensive and 'fluid' magnitude that 'doesn't run from the parts to the whole, that is to say, isn't an extensive magnitude', and results from the momentary synthetic apprehension of many (smaller) sensations (see Kant 1999: A167/B209). According to Kant, sensations – in contrast to intuitions – are neither extended nor divisible: they can be arranged on a vertical scale of intensities which, although it has no general standard at its disposal, yet allows one to talk about intensive degrees that fall below any particular threshold whatever. The result is that a known sensation presents a complex unit constructed out of passive syntheses of imperceptible sense-data. Not for nought does Kant call apprehension a synthesis. The givens of consciousness are in no way simple representations or bundles of simple representations, but noticeable phenomena lifted off an undifferenciated background, phenomena that result from the self-organisation of the field of experience. When these phenomena disappear, there is a continuous, not abrupt process of becoming invisible in which they become – as Broad described – indistinguishable from their background. Even though in the last analysis Kant subordinates the productive syntheses of imagination as a whole to the activity of the understanding, we nevertheless owe to his discovery of the form of the inner sense the fact that the atomistic representation of the mere reception of simple givens can be rejected in favour of a transcendental consideration of the implicit syntheses of affection.

This is a good place to clear up a fundamental problem of empiricism regarding the dispute about the Kantian objections to the premises of the Humean theory of perception. It is the problem regarding the object-relationship of simple versus complex impressions and ideas. Hume often presents simple perceptions as perceptions of objects: the empiricist sense criterion and the concept of association presume, according to Hume, already constituted objects as initial phenomena – at least in the actual practice of many of his arguments. On the other hand, he does not overlook the fact that pure incidents of experience have a 'pre-objective' nature, without however drawing from that the necessary consequences. Not without reason has one called Hume the 'spiritual precursor' of pointillism.

> The table before me is alone sufficient by its view to give me the idea of extension. This idea, then, is borrow'd from and represents some impression, which this moment appears to the senses. *But my senses convey to me only the impressions of colour'd points, dispos'd in a certain manner.* If the eye is sensible of any thing farther, I desire it may be pointed out to me. But if it be impossible to show any thing farther we may conclude with certainty, that the idea of extension is nothing but a copy of these colour'd points, and of the manner of their appearance. (Hume 2001: 27, italics MR)

Hume thus distinguishes single visual and tactile impressions from the combined total perception of an extended object. Accordingly, it seems that in the case of a perception intentionally directed at an object, we are concerned with a specifically organised association of sense-data. Yet at this point Hume fails to give a precise determination of the organisation process relating to the object, nor does he consider radically enough the quasi-objective status of the sense-data involved. Hume does not distinguish sharply enough between sense-data and objects, nor between the object-constituting syntheses of pre-individual sense-data and the resulting objects given to consciousness together with their empirical relations of association. Deleuze, in contrast, concentrates on the fact that the structure called 'consciousness – object' is predicated on genetic syntheses, so that he makes a cut between the intensive potential of virtual sense-data and the extensive qualities that can be attributed to the objects of perception. The perception of an exterior physical object implies the (habituated) unification of visual and thought processes with respect to a persistently held identity terminus. Contrary to Kant and Husserl, Hume fails to appreciate the significance of the constituting syntheses in the case of the 'identity relation'. In his opinion the identity of constant and unchanging objects is immediately perceived, that is, without the mediation of a corresponding act of thought, 'since [in the case of identity] the mind can [not] go beyond what is immediately present to the senses' (Hume 2001: 52). No doubt that Hume meticulously depicts the genesis of the belief in persistent and isolated things, yet he fails to grasp pre-objective sense-data simultaneously as preconscious moments of perception.

The whole problem of Humean scepticism can now be better judged thanks to the insights we have gained. For example, Hume treats the representation of thing-constancy or of ego-identity as natural illusions which are brought forth by the imagination thanks to many and diverse perceptions and their conventional relationships to one another. Under what conditions is this scepticism then to be considered radical or moderate, ruinous or pragmatically meaningful? In fact, the evaluation of the Humean 'doctrine of doubt' depends on the evaluation of the legitimacy of traditional epistemological validity claims. If Hume wanted to provide a foundation to the realist assumptions of *common sense*, then his philosophy falls apart thanks to its sceptical consequences. If on the other hand his critique of these assumptions is accepted and affirmed, then it is possible to develop out of it a defensible pragmatic scepticism that takes common sense to be a mutable form of opinion belonging to a historically determined imagination. When applied to the psychologism that can be found in Hume, this way of thinking means to say that the attempt to evaluate the 'laws of gravitation of the mental landscape' breaks down if no certain (causal relation depicting) recognition of facts is possible. This result is disastrous as long as one holds fast, regarding the theoretical constitution of things, to the epistemologically foundational function of consciousness. All the same, Hume points two ways out of the mess. On the one hand, his determinations of human nature and its apparent conformity to natural laws motivate one to see the continuation of the empiricist project in a physiological or naturalistic 'psychology without soul'. On the other hand, the possibility presents itself of passing beyond an empiricist philosophy of consciousness, with its descriptive analyses of experience, in the direction of a transcendental psychology that knows how to think the 'stream of consciousness' rigorously as a virtual and continuous multiplicity.

Transcendental empiricism's great strength is the way it unfolds Humean scepticism in a productive way. The subtlety of the Humean experiential method, which appears above all in critical reflections on the concept of substance and causality, is given a new 'structure' by Deleuze insofar as he undergirds transcendentally the atomistic theory of perception. It is of particular importance that little perceptions or sense-data are not given (in isolation), but are understood as virtual and intensive moments that are organised in transcendental syntheses. Only a complex unit comes to consciousness, a unit that results not from successive associations of simple sense-data but from momentary syntheses of unconscious sensibilia. These passive syntheses correspond to self-differenciation processes in the field of experience that allow something to become noticeable – and identifiable. According to Deleuze it is not a matter of indifference if the noematic phenomenon of a diffuse, not objectively localisable perception of colour is interpreted merely as the sensible quality of an identifiable object. Exclusive attention to actual and extensive givens implies disregard for precursory genetic syntheses and their specific relations of intensity. This disregard applies again to difference in itself, which can only be thought in a mediated form, starting with instances relieved of difference.

Nietzsche's Radicalism: Will to Power

In his book *Nietzsche and Philosophy* (1962), Deleuze develops a theory of active and reactive forces based on the doctrine of the will to power. In the fifth chapter of *Difference and Repetition* (1968), Deleuze again takes up what Nietzsche thought about the asymmetric relation of forces in order to give that relation an 'intensive' comprehension. The two texts are bound together thanks to Nietzsche's interest in the conception of force in thermodynamics, which shows how and why, in scientific theories of energy, intensive magnitudes appear – and are determined – only in connection with already extended physical bodies. With this in mind, Deleuze exhibits, in *Difference and Repetition*, intensity as the ontological feature of individuation processes. These processes continuously explicate the virtual structures within actual givens, but they must be defined independently from the order of explication in the sense of an order of implication peculiar to intensity.

Deleuze starts the fifth chapter of *Difference and Repetition* by interpreting difference of intensity as a constitutive factor of consciousness and its phenomenological givens. 'Intensity – difference of intensity – is the sufficient reason of all phenomena, the condition of that which appears' (Deleuze 1994: 222). From that it will be possible to derive the ontological primacy of the intensive over the extensive magnitudes founded therein. It is through the application of force or energy, the physical intensive magnitude par excellence, that extension in general can claim reality. Inspired by Nietzsche, Deleuze begins already in *Nietzsche and Philosophy* (1962) to conceptualise relations of forces or power as intensity relations. However, he doesn't succumb, any more than Nietzsche does, to the physicalist thinking that threatens to wipe out the essential difference between intensive and extensive magnitudes by way of good sense and common sense.

> This is what the will to power is: the genealogical element of force [. . .] The will to power is the element from which derive both the quantitative difference of related forces and the quality that devolves into each force in this relation. The will to power here reveals its nature as the principle of the synthesis of forces. (Deleuze 1983: 50)

With his interpretation of the will to power, Deleuze presents in 1962 the very first version of his transcendental empiricism. The crucial point is that the will to power is understood as the *genetic* and *differential* principle of force, that is, as the universal moving principle of becoming that illuminates the never-ending processes of change and the never-ending processes of interpretation of the singular constellations of force (see Deleuze 1983: 52ff.). This endogenous and dynamic principle is responsible for the fluctuating relations that constantly take place between the little energetic moments of reality, which organise themselves into variable units insofar as they affect one another, overcome one another or resist one another. The active forces that associate with one another construct physical relationships of intensity that predate consciousness and its reactive perspective. 'What makes the body superior to all reactions, particularly that reaction of the ego that is called consciousness, is the activity of necessarily unconscious forces' (Deleuze 1983: 41–2). Deleuze makes abundantly clear that Nietzsche defines quality, which corresponds to the quantity-differences in the configurations of quanta of forces, as affection. The will to power appears (*à la* Spinoza) as a capacity to affect and to be affected. 'The capacity for being affected is not necessarily a passivity [in the sense of suffering and receptivity; MR] but an affectivity, a sensibility, a sensation' (Deleuze 1983: 62). The will manifests itself as 'differential sensibility' and in this way expresses the transcendental principle of intensity that is an essential characteristic of the 'higher empiricism' (*empirisme supérieur*).

Nietzsche developed his theory of the will to power and the eternal return on contemporaneous research in physics (see Zimmerli 1999: 266ff.). However, he does not adopt established knowledge from the exact sciences. Instead he transfers certain of their theorems into his philosophical reflections. Thus although his non-mechanical concept of force is compatible with the first law of thermodynamics, it turns against the second. Nietzsche's critique of science is expressed in exemplary fashion by his rejection of the teleological notion of entropy because, at least from Deleuze's perspective, that notion concentrates on the physicalist tendency to homogenise inequalities of energy differences by attributing to them a questionable, finalistic 'plan of transcendence'. For Deleuze the becoming – without beginning and without end – of forces affecting one another, which Nietzsche conceives under the title of *eternal return of the same*, is thought in the sense of a 'utopia' of pure immanence. Thus differences of quantity – for example, chaotic differences – cannot reach equilibrium any more than they can be resolved in extension. Even though Nietzsche may want to see 'the closest possible convergence of a world of becoming to that of a world of being' in the thought of a cyclical return of identical series (see Nietzsche 1980ff., vol. 13: 375), Deleuze can certainly cite Nietzsche in order to bring difference, as the transcendental principle of becoming, into play.

To speak with Deleuze, the quanta of force, that as elements of structure stand in differential relationships and that actualise themselves in differenciated forms, remain as virtual singularities behind their actual ways of appearing. The process of becoming is never brought to rest in its effects. The micrological relations of force persist in the background of the actual phenomena that are conditioned by them. Deleuze always presents his critique of the general idea that one has concerning the erosion of differences of intensity in the field of extended bodies and their qualitative determinations with a kind of 'deep-seated' Nietzschean undertone. For if, in energy studies, force is defined as a mixture of intensive and extensive factors, then that kind of force follows the tendency to de-differenciate intensive quantities in the field of homogeneous forms of extension. Forms of energy are therefore distributed in extension, just as extensions are qualified by forms of energy, as for example, 'height and weight for gravitational energy, temperature and entropy for thermal energy' (Deleuze 1994: 223). From this, Deleuze concludes the following:

> In experience, intensio (intension) is inseparable from an extensio (extension) which relates it to the extensum (extensity). In these conditions, intensity itself is subordinated to the qualities which fill extensity. In short, we know intensity only as already developed within an extensity, and as covered over by qualities. (Deleuze 1994: 223)

This 'knowledge' leads Deleuze back to a transcendental illusion provoked by the way intensity is explicated, insofar as it tempts one to orient its description on explicit results. Thermodynamics thus empowers good sense (*bon sens*), blessed as it is with the prescience to reduce differences by forging a path from what is more differenciated to what is less differenciated. Although good sense presupposes differences, it also prescribes how they are to be distributed, unified and thus negated according to conditions reflecting ideas of physical time and space. Good sense, 'like Plato's demiurge, ceaselessly and patiently transforms the unequal into the divisible' (Deleuze 1994: 224–5). In like manner, Deleuze characterises the most general content of thermodynamic principles by asserting that 'difference is the sufficient reason of change only to the extent that the change tends to negate difference' (Deleuze 1994: 223). Of course Deleuze doesn't deny that intensity as difference tries to explicate itself. Although it is deleted within extension and its physical or sensual qualities, he certainly denies that difference is thus abolished. For difference outstrips itself or loses its very nature insofar as it is explicated, but 'as intensity, difference remains implicated in itself, even as it is cancelled by being explicated outside itself' (Deleuze 1994: 228). It is intensity's implicative mode of being that preserves it in the face of its continuous transferral into the world of already constituted individual objects and, as Nietzsche puts it, protects becoming's irrevocable inequality or disparity from 'immobilisation, mummification, or mortification in Being' (Nietzsche 1980ff., vol. 13: 375).

When Deleuze often speaks of forces and force relations, especially with respect to Nietzsche, then he is referring – in the jargon of *Anti-Oedipus* – to the 'differential coupling of streams of intensity that circulate on the body without organs'. We can avoid the jargon, which has its own problems. For Deleuze is clearly stating that the field of intensity is coextensive with the field of individuation. Connecting with concepts developed by Hume, we can say that Deleuze in no way bases the *logic of sensation* on 'impressions of sensation', but rather on 'impressions of reflection'. According to Deleuze, sensations (or forces) are affects that as such imply an individuating self-affection or folding of force on itself. The subject does not dissolve in the substanceless play of perceptions without reconstituting itself anew in what is sensible, hearable, visible or tasty. As we have seen, for Deleuze it is not a matter of the destruction, but rather of the immanent determination of subjectivation. For example, in the articles on 'literature and life' collected in *Critique and Clinique*, Deleuze makes it clear that it only makes sense to talk about 'forces' where destabilising affects are present that in their particular self-reference lead to subjectivation effects. Where Deleuze simplifies matter and talks about forces and intensities by alluding to Freud's *économie libidinale*, one could just as well substitute the phenomenological vocabulary of sensations and perceptions with respect to their individuational movements toward actualisation.

Individuation and the Intensive Origin of Time and Space

Deleuze's aspiration to radicalise Kant's critical philosophy in his book on Nietzsche turns out to be a leitmotif of his philosophical enterprise as a whole – as Daniel W. Smith convincingly shows (Smith 1997: 5f.) – and is accomplished through the genetic-structural method of an immanent determination of experience. In *Difference and Repetition* the names of Maimon and Cohen stand for the possibility of a post-Kantian transcendentalism, overhauling, thanks to Leibniz, the doctrine of time and space through a theory of differentials. In the chapter on *the asymmetric synthesis of the sensible* Deleuze makes more concrete this vanquishing of Kantian dualism and its restrictive epistemology. Transcendental conditions are not regressively exposed possibilities of presupposed experience, but genetic conditions of a developing experience that in the process of its becoming determines itself in diverse ways. Difference in intensity does not at all mark an empirical relation between various facts that in each case already have an identity. Instead this difference characterises the way the given comes about in the first place. Difference is 'that by which the given is given as diverse' (Deleuze 1994: 222). The problematical structures of ideas define themselves within experience

Subjectivity and Immanence

as differences of intensity in passive syntheses. For Deleuze the conditions of perception are thus contained within intensity as difference and cannot be established abstractly, before all experience, as pure forms of intuition.

In the last section of the chapter on ideas in *Difference and Repetition* Deleuze explains that the immanent factors in the dramatisation of the idea are space-time dynamics: they embody as actualisation times and actualisation spaces the differential relations between ceaselessly and reciprocally determined elements of structure. To be sure, the processes of differenciation differ from their results: the processes themselves (1) are simultaneously spatial and temporal, and (2) are concealed by the actual qualities and extensities that they reveal. Along with the latter two features of the (spatio-temporal) realisation of structure, there is also a third, since (3) 'every spatio-temporal dynamism is accompanied by the emergence of an elementary consciousness which [. . .] is born on the threshold of the condensed singularities of the body or object whose consciousness it is' (Deleuze 1994: 220). To clarify the third feature we will move forward to the concrete processes of actualisation in the field of individuation and the intensity relations intrinsic to it. Actual extensive and qualitative series correspond indeed to the ideal elements of quantitability and qualitability. Even so, the conditions of their actualisation are still completely undetermined. We need to find out 'what carries out [. . .] the element of potentiality in the idea' (Deleuze 1994: 221), and Deleuze quickly gives an answer. It must be a matter of spacio-temporal dramatisation, but one grounded in intensity and its relationships.

> Intensity is the determinant in the process of actualisation. It is intensity which dramatises. It is intensity which is immediately expressed in the basic spatio-temporal dynamisms and determines an 'indistinct' differential relation in the idea to incarnate itself in a distinct quality and a distinguished extensity. (Deleuze 1994: 245)

Deleuze draws a parallel between intensity's explication movement and the idea's differenciating movement. However, intensity can only then determine the structural conditions of actualisation if it can be defined independently of the differenciated or explicated results. That is possible, says Deleuze, because it has at its disposal an ontologically primary distinguished order of implication that is characterised by an idiosyncratic mode of processing. 'The essential process of intensive quantities is individuation' (Deleuze 1994:

246). Deleuze always calls the actualisation processes that can be described against the background of intensity relations individuation processes. They establish a field of communication or a system of signalising for heterogeneous series, so that the immanent structures of experience can get signs to flash and qualities to generate. In *Difference and Repetition* the reciprocal relations of the ideal synthesis of difference are treated in the domain of individuation with its fields of intensity as passive spatio-temporal syntheses. In this way the fifth chapter builds a bridge between the fourth and the second chapter: the time-syntheses of 'repetition for itself' articulate the 'asymmetric syntheses' of the individuation processes that explicate the structurally determined actualisation forms of 'ideas'. Thus it is no wonder that Deleuze in the fifth chapter focuses above all on the problem of space and places these investigations next to his analysis of time.

In connection with his reflections on the revelation-and-concealment structure (*Entbergen und Verbergen*) of intensity, Deleuze asserts 'that extensity does not account for the individuations which occur within it' (Deleuze 1994: 229). Here he follows the theoretical principle of individuation set down by Gilbert Simondon:

> Individuation does not only produce the individual. One ought not skip quickly over the step of individuation in order to arrive at that last reality that is the individual. One ought to try to know the ontogenesis in the entire development of that reality and *get to know the individual in terms of individuation rather than individuation in terms of the individual* [*connaître l'individu à travers l'individuation plutôt que l'individuation à partir de l'individu*]. (Simondon 1964: 4)

Deleuze, impressed as he seems to be by the work of Simondon, makes room for reflections on the biological genesis of the individual in the chapter on the asymmetric synthesis of the sensible. At first it is only a matter of ascertaining the origin of extensive magnitude from the intensive magnitude of original depth. 'Extensity as a whole comes from the depths' (Deleuze 1994: 229). Taking into account the paradox of symmetric objects, Deleuze makes problematic the presence of individuating factors in extensity: up and down, right and left, form and background. These factors lend depth to perception in the passively running organisation of the field of vision. In his discussions of the depth perspective that determines visibility, Deleuze has recourse, without saying so, to passages from the *Phenomenology of Perception* by Merleau-Ponty (see Merleau-Ponty 1981: 297–311).

Following Merleau-Ponty to the letter, he shows that although in perception the 'third dimension' of depth may present a possible length or breadth, for example when the observer carries out an abstract measurement, it in fact becomes in this way part of extensity and loses its heterogeneity or its genetic potential (see Deleuze 1994: 229). Deleuze agrees with Merleau-Ponty that depth arises out of a 'primordial experience' which 'clearly belongs to perspective, not to things' (Merleau-Ponty 1981: 298–9). One could say that in the (binocular) 'seeing of depth' the perceiving subjectivity is made implicit, namely in the passive syntheses of disparate monocular images. From here it is but a short step for Deleuze to associate the original relation of perception to its background, its own depth, with the coexistence of the pure past within the present. On this point as well Merleau-Ponty anticipated him:

> Perception ratifies and renews in us a 'prehistory'. And that again is of the essence of time: there would be no present, that is to say, no sensible world with its thickness and inexhaustible richness, if perception [...] did not retain a past in the depth of the present, and did not contract that past into that depth. It fails at the moment to realise the synthesis of its object [...] because the unity of the object makes its appearance through the medium of time, and because time slips away as fast as it catches up with itself. (Merleau-Ponty 1981: 240; see also Merleau-Ponty 2006: 279)

As expected, Deleuze draws parallels between the syntheses of space and of time insofar as both of them, as actualisation forms of the idea, mark out concrete individuation conditions relative to experience. The perception of extensive individual objects implies depth, which precisely in its implicative mode of Being refers to intensity. As Deleuze declares, 'It is the power of diminution of the intensity experienced that provides a perception of depth' (Deleuze 1994: 230). The power of depth is grounded in the potentiality of the idea that it is capable of actualising (see Deleuze 1994: 244). That is why the sensible or physical qualities of persistent objects presuppose fields of intensity which they explicate – and during explication cancel out. Which brings Deleuze to the question, how is it possible that intensity can be sensed independently of these constituted objects of experience? 'How could it be other than "sensed", since it is what gives to be sensed' (Deleuze 1994: 230)? With that, Deleuze arrives at the ontological aspect of the third syntheses of space and time regarding the transcendental exercise of powers or faculties (*Vermögen*): intensity, which can only be sensed – or depth, which can only be perceived. 'Depth and intensity are the same at the level of Being, but the same insofar as this is said of difference' (Deleuze 1994: 231).

Until now we have found that the structure of intensity is such that its differences cancel out or explicate themselves in a system of extension without yet sublating themselves within the framework of this system or allowing themselves to be grasped in their nature. From this derives the ambivalent or double aspect of the produced quality-as-sign within the structurally determined milieu of individuation: 'it refers to an implicated order of constitutive differences, and tends to cancel out those differences in the extended order in which they are explicated' (Deleuze 1994: 228). The problem, whose key concepts are implication and explication, is further unfolded by Deleuze through his presentation of three Nietzschean-Bergsonian features that 'deeply' characterise intensity (see Deleuze 1994: 232ff.). The first feature marks what cannot be cancelled in differences in quantity: the intensive magnitude envelops or interiorises an essential, irreducible inequality that can be homogenised but still insists within the depths of its homogenised manifestation. The second feature of intensity marks its 'profound' affirmation of difference, which only appears as negation in the domain of perfected extensities and qualities. 'Since intensity is already difference, it refers to a series of other differences that it affirms by affirming itself' (Deleuze 1994: 234). Deleuze wants to show that the negative is the inverse image of difference insofar as the negative figures of opposition and limitation are necessarily bound to differenciated forms of extension in actuality. For this purpose he examines the Platonic idea of an immanence of contrasting oppositions within a sensible quality. Large and small, thick and thin, hard and soft, etc., are for Plato challenging to reason because they each only come to mind with their opposite. Precisely the identity of oppositional characteristics, that is to say the coexistence of 'more' and 'less' as implied by sensible signs, points to the paradox of becoming, which according to Deleuze defines the constitutive character of intensity. Note the memorable passage, in the *Logic of Sense*, on growth, taken from *Alice in Wonderland*:

> When I say, 'Alice becomes larger', I mean she becomes larger than she was. By the same token, however, she becomes smaller than she is now. Certainly, she is not bigger and smaller at the same time. She is larger now; she was smaller before. But it is at the same moment that one becomes larger than one was and smaller than one becomes. This is the simultaneity of a becoming whose characteristic is to elude the present. (Deleuze 1990b: 1)

Subjectivity and Immanence

The paradox of becoming consists therefore in the simultaneity or 'identity' of two directions of sense. The present and its clear contours evaporate in the process of becoming, where past and future merge or are distributed in a new way. The intensity of becoming, that is, the implication of counter-running lines of actualisation, differenciates itself by explicating itself concurrently in two directions. When Plato makes a distinction between problematic signs and non-problematic objects of recognition and moves his exposition of the former near the asymmetric paradox of intensity, he sees, according to Deleuze, intensive quantities 'only in qualities in the course of development – and for this reason, he assigns both contrariety and the being of the sensible to qualities' (Deleuze 1994: 236). In this way, however, he misses its third feature, which has to do with implication's form of Being. For Deleuze, intensity is not only implicated in quality, but it is primarily implicit in itself, that is, implicative and implicated. This implicative self-reference of intensity is enmeshed in differential and continuous syntheses which drive forward the actualisation processes of virtual manifolds and, as processes of individuation, make them concrete. The passive syntheses are presented by Deleuze as (spatial) syntheses of implicit multiplicities (intensive magnitudes) which stand opposite explicit multiplicities (extensive magnitudes). With that, he repeats and modifies on the plane of individuation – parallel to his treatment of temporal syntheses – the distinction between virtual and actual multiplicities. This is especially apparent in the concept of distance, which is introduced by Deleuze as the implicit magnitude and partial aspect of the third feature of depth as intensive space (spatium). 'Within intensity, we call that which is really implicative and enveloping difference; and we call that which is really implicated or enveloped distance. Therefore intensity is neither divisible, like extensive quantity, nor indivisible, like quality' (Deleuze 1994: 237). The conclusive 'therefore' comes from the definition of distance, in reference to Leibniz, as a relatively indivisible and asymmetric relation that, in distinction to extensive lengths or stretches, is not put together out of discrete, homogeneous parts (ibid.).

Deleuze adopts and radicalises Kant's distinction between intensive and extensive magnitudes, exemplified by distances on the one hand and lengths on the other hand as implicit and explicit multiplicities. Extensive quantities are defined 'by the relative determination of a unit [. . .]; by the equivalence of the parts determined by the unit; by the consubstantiality of the parts with the whole which is divided' (Deleuze 1994: 237). It is a question of measurable multiplicities put together out of parts that are compatible, additive units of magnitude, all of the same order as the whole. The extensive quantities are divisible without essentially changing thereby. This is in contrast to intensive quantities, which cannot be grasped in the context of homogeneous space and time relations.

> An intensive quantity may be divided, but not without changing its nature. In a sense, it is therefore indivisible, but only because no part exists prior to the division and no part retains the same nature after division. (Deleuze 1994: 237)

The quantitative intensive unit implies only un-self-sustaining and heterogeneous partial moments that cannot be extracted as such from the whole: implied intensities as unit components would in the process change into implicit intensities as units. The Kantian determination of the intensive unit of magnitude, which 'can only be represented through approximation to negation = 0' (Kant 1999: A 168/B 210), establishes between itself and zero a gap that can be infinitely and continuously made smaller, which argues against the possibility of its being defined in terms of its parts as units of measure. Deleuze will therefore suggest that two types of multiplicities be distinguished, 'those whose metric varies by division and those which carry the invariable principle of their metric' (Deleuze 1994: 238).

In *A Thousand Plateaus* this whole problem is discussed under the rubric 'smooth' and 'striated' spaces. A smooth space is a non-metric intensive space, 'one of distances, not of measures', whereas a striated space is an extensive space, with a closed, parcelled-out or measured surface (Deleuze and Guattari 1987: 479). Deleuze and Guattari present a series of different models – technological, mathematical, aesthetic and so on – which show the existence of both spaces in their interaction and in factual interference phenomena of smooth and striated (de- and reterritorialisation). During the discussion of the mathematical model and in the context of Riemann's substantive use of the manifold, they talk about Bergson's distinction between two multiplicities. In fact Kant's reflections on the difference between intensive and extensive magnitudes are here reclaimed as well, regarding the conceptual construction of a continuous, virtual manifold that opposes any explication or striation through representational logic. However, this is not a question of an uncritical adoption of a traditional dogma. In *Difference and Repetition* Deleuze specifically refers to Cohen's 're-interpretation of Kantianism', which in his opinion 'attaches full value to the principle of intensive quantities'

Subjectivity and Immanence

(Deleuze 1994: 231). The Marburg School of epistemology is interesting for Deleuze because it connects the release from transcendental aesthetics with an orientation toward the principles of pure understanding (Kant's *Grundsätze des reinen Verstandes*). The decisive 'gap' in Kant's synthesis doctrine is for Cohen the fact that empirical intuitional material is prearranged for concepts. Kant awards a geometric extension to the pure forms of intuition 'and reserves intensive quantity for the matter which fills a given extensity to some degree or other' (Deleuze 1994: 231), whereas Deleuze, taking his cue from Cohen, attempts to derive space and time, as conditions of experience, out of the definition of the principle of intensity. For Cohen, it is a question, raised by the second Kantian principle (*Grundsatz der Antizipation der Wahrnehmung*) when understood correctly, of a constructive precept that delivers reality as infinitesimal magnitude. Deleuze, for his part, understands what is here 'delivered', that is, a spatio-temporal actualisation of ideal relations of differential moments, as it is empirically intuited, to be of extensive magnitude. The genetic syntheses of space and time present a whole made up of 'virtual parts' that are not already given as (actual) parts in advance, nor can they be so represented.

> Space and time are not presented as they are represented. [. . .] Space as pure intuition or spatium is an intensive quantity, and intensity as a transcendental principle is not merely the anticipation of perception but the source of a quadruple genesis: that of the extensio in the form of schema, that of extensity in the form of extensive magnitude, that of qualitas in the form of matter occupying extensity, and that of the quale in the form of designation of an object. (Deleuze 1994: 231)

Even though space and time cannot be reduced to concepts of the understanding, they nevertheless let themselves be integrated into the problematic field of the idea as transcendental conditions of experience – not at the outset related to extension but as 'subjacent conditions of real experience which are indistinguishable from intensity as such' (Deleuze 1994: 232).

Over against the extensive spatial relations that experience presupposes externally, there are intensive spatial relations that determine experience from within. This opposition results from the fact that for Deleuze there are also spaces in the sense of intensive magnitudes that cannot be divided up without each time changing essentially: these smooth spaces have no permanent points of reference, no constants and variables that could be assigned with respect to a stationary outside observer. On the contrary, these spaces are defined through continuous variations of their directions and points of orientation. They are not to be confused with a closed surface cut up into fixed-point intervals, but correspond to open, unbounded and multidirectional spaces on which nomads move about without sectioning them.

> Smooth space is filled by events or haecceities, far more than by formed and perceived things. It is a space of affects, more than one of properties. It is haptic rather than optical perception. Whereas in the striated space forms organise a matter, in the smooth space materials signal forces and serve as symptoms for them. [...] Perception in it is based on symptoms and evaluations rather than measures. [...] That is why smooth space is occupied by intensities. [...] Striated space, on the contrary, is canopied by the sky as measure and by the measurable visual qualities deriving from it. (Deleuze and Guattari 1987: 479)

The distribution of intensities on smooth space or on the 'plane of immanence' takes place 'nomadically' or according to the law of univocity, since it is not defined by any established transcendent reference points: smooth space cannot be defined independently of the many events that subject its surface to a steady process of mutation or metamorphosis. 'It does not have a dimension higher than that which moves through it' (Deleuze and Guattari 1987: 488) and tends to become identical with that which fills it. That is why no subjective perspectives exist *on* the space, but rather only local perspectives *within* the space, whose coordinates not only structure the particular patch, but also vary depending on the patch.

As we have seen, every relevant increase or decrease from an intensive magnitude means its qualitative change. In this sense distances were only indirectly measurable: although they can be divided if one segment is implied in another, nevertheless they cannot be assigned a common measure. Seen in this way, intensities can be compared to one another and can be given a place in non-exact and discursive relationships of order. However, a smooth space comes about primarily by means of an 'accumulation of neighbourhoods' which stand externally near one another without implying one another. In this respect he takes his cue from the model of Riemannian space as amorphous and informal juxtapositions of heterogeneous parts that 'can be effected in an infinite number of ways' (Deleuze and Guattari 1987: 485).

In spite of all that the implied multiplicities of intensity and the differential multiplicities of ideas have in common, we have held on to the fact that Deleuze wants to determine power relationships within the processes of individuation insofar as they dramatise the ideas or develop solutions for problems. In this way he sets a genetic field of passive syntheses into the middle of virtual and actual determinations of structure (differentiation–differenciation), a field that is primarily defined through the order of implication. Therefore the actualisation processes are to be described as processes of individuation, and not in terms of their outcomes as processes of explication or differenciation.

> Individuation is the act by which intensity determines differential relations to become actualised, along the lines of differenciation and within the qualities and extensities it creates. (Deleuze 1994: 246)

Structures actualise themselves when their disparate and pre-individual elements are 'tensed up' or 'coupled up' with one another or transported in a 'communicative state', which means when they express and organise themselves in a field of individuation. The virtual structures differenciate through relations of intensity that are being explicated. The latter make an effort to cancel themselves out in extension and cannot simply be separated – as *qualitas occulta* – from this movement. As we have seen, intensity does not explicate itself as such: it does not lose its differential status because it cancels itself only outside itself. It is of decisive importance for Deleuze that the intensive magnitudes cannot be derived from already constituted extensive or differenciated forms.

In this connection Deleuze falls into line with evolution-theoretical thoughts that allow individual differences to be localised in the field of individuation, that is, beneath the larger taxonomic divisions. The universality of the individual, its organic classification on the model of the family tree, must accordingly rest on previous processes of individuation: in no way do individual differences merely fill out gaps in already structured systems where points of resemblance are differenciated by genus and species. 'It is the individual which is above the species, and precedes the species in principle' (Deleuze 1994: 250). Individuation must not be understood as propagation of specification. On the contrary, specification must result from individuation. Deleuze follows von Baer's work, who situates embryonic epigenesis and the phenomena of organic de-differenciation in a constitutional milieu not defined by the criteria of representational concepts. 'The embryo is the individual as such directly caught up in the field of its individuation' (Deleuze 1994: 250). This constitutional field of individuation is generally defined in terms of sexual propagation, which expresses the 'evolutionary' principle of differenciating difference. Thus Deleuze again stresses that the differential relations only actualise themselves under the condition of individuation. 'What cannot be replaced is individuation itself' (Deleuze 1994: 258). Individuality cannot be separated from a virtual reservoir of pre-individual singularities which enable it to be drawn into unanticipated processes of becoming. The missing resemblances between ideas and their actualisation means, therefore, that only a genetic method can clear up the relations between the general and the particular, between the universal and the singular.

The field of individuation, which dramatises only (undifferenciated) differential relations – and presupposes nothing else, which is why it cannot be defined with concepts of explication or differenciation – therefore gives expression to ideas through the order of implication. The intensities imply themselves reciprocally, so that each expresses the variable totality of differential relationships. However, they express as implicational only some relations clearly, whereas they express as implied all relations confusedly. The intensive unity of the simultaneously clear-confused, which derives from the implicative nature of intensity differences, corresponds to the ideal unity of the simultaneously distinct-obscure. The clear-confused doesn't determine the idea, but rather the thinking of it, insofar as the latter expresses and works with an idea whose actualisation it determines; for indeed 'the thinker is the individual' (Deleuze 1994: 253).

Monads and Minute Perceptions – Leibniz

At this point Deleuze returns to Leibniz, who shows every sign of having succeeded, based on his theory of expression, in developing a logic that breaks with the Cartesian premise of a direct proportionality between 'clear' and 'distinct'.

> For despite the complexity and ambiguity of the texts, it does indeed seem at times that the expressed (the continuum of differential relations or the unconscious virtual idea) should be in itself distinct and obscure: for example, all the drops of water in the sea like so many genetic elements with the differential relations, the variations in these relations and the distinctive points they comprise. In addition, it seems that the expresser (the perceiving, imagining or thinking individual) should be by nature clear and confused: for example our perception of the noise of the sea, which confusedly includes the whole and clearly expresses only certain relations

or certain points by virtue of our bodies and a threshold of consciousness which they determine. (Deleuze 1994: 253)

The Idea is simultaneously distinct and obscure because it is virtually determined (differential) and actually undetermined (undifferenciated). It possesses virtual but not actual reality. The perception, on the other hand, is both clear and confused because it is actually determined (differenciated) and therefore implies virtual determinations that are not differenciated. The minute or molecular partial perceptions condense or intensify more or less in relation to our bodies and determine a threshold of differenciation across which they actualise themselves into a clearly defined perception. In this context there is also the distinction between seeing up close (*nahsichtig*) and seeing further away (*fernsichtig*) or between haptic and optic space. Whereas the smooth haptic space has no fixed points of orientation, no guidelines, at its disposal which could be unified in some kind of visual model, the optic striated space is determined by distant vision and its conditions. In close vision, and the undifferenciated perceptions belonging to it, the differential 'prototypical relations' of seeing are dramatically evident in the way they strive to make (something) visible. 'Cezanne spoke of the need to *no longer see* the wheat field, to be too close to it, to lose oneself without landmarks in smooth space' (Deleuze and Guattari 1987: 493).

In *The Fold: Leibniz and the Baroque*, Deleuze pins down the perceptual implications of his differential empiricism in connection with the problem of intensity. Particularly cogent is the chapter 'Perception in the Folds'. There Deleuze develops a transcendental psychology of perception, whereby every simple and object-directed perception contains unconscious differences that organise themselves into genetic processes. Starting from some of Leibniz's metaphysical thoughts, Deleuze remarks that every perceiving monad expresses an infinite world. Because of their finite constitution they are, however, restricted to express clearly only a small portion of that world. The world, which does not exist apart from its expressing monads, must nevertheless be implied by them in its totality. That is only possible – apart from the mentioned clear portion – as confused perceptions. Deleuze combines at this point the metaphysical thought with a psychological one, also originating with Leibniz, which Deleuze extracts – to the extent necessary – from the metaphysically burdened context of 'world syntheses' as regulated by the principle of compossibility. Accordingly, a conscious (clear) perception is assembled out of infinitely many minute (confused) perceptions that are capable of producing it in its changeable state, sort of stabilising it and then dissolving it. There are always micro-perceptions that do not integrate themselves into the present macro-perception, but prepare for the next one.

> However abruptly I may flog my dog who eats his meal, the animal will have experienced the minute perceptions of my stealthy arrival on tiptoes, my hostile odor, and my lifting of the rod that subtend the conversion of pleasure into pain. [...] Tiny perceptions are as much the passage from one perception to another as they are components of each perception. (Deleuze 1993: 87)

The relation between macro- and micro-perceptions is connected to a relation between the customary and the notable. It is thus not a question of a relation between parts and wholes, at the very least because the non-notable perceptions already have a collective character in their own right, even if they do not become conscious. A conscious perception can appear whenever at least two minute and confused perceptions determine one another or enter into a differential relationship so that they bring forth a novel singularity: thus, mixed yellow and blue colours constitute a perceptible green precisely when they alone (as two separate colours) are imperceptible. In the case of micro-perceptions, when 'differentials of consciousness' blend with one another and in this manner unfold their genetic potential in a field of individuation, they are able to call into consciousness an objective quality for the very first time.

> For example, the sound of the sea: at least two waves must be minutely perceived as nascent and heterogeneous enough to become part of a relation that can allow the perception of a third, one that 'excels' over the others and comes to consciousness (implying that we are near the shoreline). (Deleuze 1993: 88)

Consciousness in the narrow sense is therefore not impervious. Rather, it must become pervious because it itself results from passive syntheses of unconscious or inconspicuous components of perception. More exactly, consciousness is determined by structural features of bodily affectivities, as well as from the number and properties of the filters with which the continuum of singularities belonging to radical experience are 'sieved', so that the important stuff is separated from the unimportant and the expected from the unexpected. Deleuze expresses this state of affairs succinctly as follows: 'All consciousness is a matter of threshold' (Deleuze 1993: 88). Which is to

Subjectivity and Immanence

say that there are intensities below the threshold, 'smaller than the possible minimum [...] of consciousness' (Deleuze 1993: 88) that only become conscious past a certain point, that is, when they have so organised themselves that they cross the threshold or become conspicuous.

In summary, Deleuze, influenced by Kant, Maimon and Cohen's intensive understanding of the Leibnizian differential, works past Hume's classical 'pointillism', picks up Nietzsche's intensive use of force and substitutes for the Kantian 'method of conditioning' an 'internal, subjective method of genesis'. Differential relations are what filter out certain of the available hallucinatory and hazy minute perceptions and concoct out of their reciprocal syntheses a conscious perception. From that it follows that two epistemological presuppositions of Kantian transcendentalism fall by the wayside: first, space and time do not have to act as an *a priori* basis for experience in the pure form of intuition, and second, it is unnecessary to speculate about exterior objects that 'affect the mind in a certain way' (Kant 1999: A 19/B 33). The pure and empirical presuppositions of experience are instead integrated into the differential self-determination of experience: space and time can be grasped as variable actualisation forms of the differential relations among minute perceptions. The object itself is nothing that is empirically given, but rather the product of those relations in completely determined perceptions.

> Thus differential calculus is the psychic mechanism of perception, the automatism that at once and inseparably plunges into obscurity and determines clarity: a selection of minute, obscure perceptions and a perception that moves into clarity. (Deleuze1993: 90)

The transcendental field of virtual sense-data or the problematic structures of perception do not at all designate intuitively accessible ideas for some kind of infinite understanding. They just point to the dark ground (*fuscum subnigrum*) or the obscure dust of the world that is contained in each monad or in every expressive subject. Infinity means nothing more than 'the presence of an unconscious in finite understanding, [...] of a non-self in the finite self' (Deleuze 1993: 89). Tiny 'molecular' perceptions insist as 'representatives' of the world in the centre of thought – as the unthought that can only be thought. They are hallucinatory because they have no object to which they directly relate. The great 'molar' perceptions also have hallucinatory character, at least as long as they are determined in a purely immanent way (see Deleuze 1993: 93f.). Nevertheless, perceptions as conceptualised by Deleuze are radically different from those of George Berkeley and his particular phenomenal empiricism. For what is perceived is for Deleuze nothing empirically given, but rather the product of unconscious syntheses and their structurally determined implicative values (see Deleuze 1993: 94f.). Of course even Berkeley doesn't adhere to the simple thesis that external material objects are represented in perception. Rather, they are in his opinion nothing other than immaterial complexes of sensible qualities: these are immediately given to us in a certain (divinely ordained) order. Berkeley's problem – namely, the presumed identity of the perception and the perceived – consists less in the fact that he idealises the objects of perception, but rather in the fact that he idealises perception itself. In spite of Berkeley's own suggestions, it is not an innocent operation when one equates 'bundles of sense-data' with 'things'. Not so much – to make the point again – because Berkeley gets caught in the trap of an immanence devoid of intentionality. Rather, even the 'empirically-idealistically' reduced things conserve Berkeley's firmly representationalist prejudices. Things can never be given immediately because they presuppose, as always, an accustomed and unconscious act of identification: the thing that I have just seen, still see, or see again, is the *same* thing. This unifies – to speak with Kant – the faculties of apprehension, reproduction and recognition. Even if in this manner a well-determined experience can be constitutionally developed and analysed, Deleuze insists at any rate on the essential difference between non-objective perceptions and their object-related representations in the cognitive act (see Deleuze 1993: 95).

Nevertheless, the two 'floors' of body and soul remain related to a single world (or one baroque house), related to a plane of immanence that continually folds while distributing difference (on the two sections or stories). The concept of the fold (*pli*) that Deleuze deciphers in the philosophy of Leibniz connects the two sides, the interior and the exterior, in the genetic milieu of the passive syntheses of individuation and clarifies the variable relationship that exists between the thinking of the virtual on the one hand and the virtuality of experience on the other hand. The great Spinozian and Nietzschean themes – affirmation of life, becoming active and the intensification of affects – are lifelong concerns of Deleuze and find here with Leibniz their place within the self-affectational model of subjectification which is described in *Difference and Repetition* through the passive transcendental syntheses of time and intensive becoming.

Subjectivity and Immanence

But back to the psychic automism of monads! We have seen that differential relationships are responsible for the genetic syntheses of the minute, 'lilliputanical' perceptions that they cull from the teeming mass. Although the same world is perceived by all monads, yet they privilege their own particular differential relationships, each according to its nature. Therefore they have varying clear perceptions, depending on what appears noteworthy to them and thus crosses their threshold of consciousness. In this way Leibniz comes up with an evolutionary set of stages in the series of living beings that are relatively 'developed' concerning the number and depth of their differential relationships: from the naked monads to the remembering ones and finally to the reflexive monads. The reflexive monads are characterised as having the faculty of 'extending themselves and intensifying their zones' (Deleuze 1993: 92). In a moment I will have something to say about this possibility of intensifying affect, which has to do with the way affects are related to themselves. First it is necessary to touch on the constant other possibility, namely that clear perceptions are extinguished and consciousness is swamped with minute perceptions whose folds 'are endlessly unfurling on the edges [. . .] at speeds that no one of our thresholds of consciousness could sustain in a normal state' (Deleuze 1993: 93). This allows Deleuze to speak of falling asleep or passing out. In other circumstances and other books aesthetic, clinical or otherwise named phenomena are made responsible for 'deregulating the senses'. It is important to note that Deleuze, in his many and varied allusions to the event, never wastes a word on the abyss and its 'romanticised indifference'. Chaos, with its unfiltered flow of pure differences, *pli selon pli*, 'not atoms, but minuscule folds [. . .] forever agitating' (Deleuze 1993: 93), does not mark the deepest point in Deleuze's philosophy. Nor does he argue in favour of sustaining the 'normal state'. On the contrary, it is a matter of discovering ways of subjectivising on the plane of immanence, ways that interiorise difference as an ethics of intensities, deepening it and affirming even the lowest without unnecessarily explicating it (see Deleuze and Guattari 1998: 61–2, and Deleuze 1994: 244).

Reflexive monads are characterised by their ability to use the affects that they possess to expand their faculties of becoming affected. It does not suffice to say that the subject of affection, affected from without, affects itself because it is affected thanks to its ability to be affected. Of course every affection means a self-affection insofar as the minuscule perceptions in selected differential relationships must become passively connected with one another to build a noteworthy perception. Thus on this level anyway the pure passivity of receptivity is rejected in favour of immanent and not consciously strewn syntheses of sensibility. However, the monads able to influence their passive dependency on the environment possess the capability of reading the perceptible signs. As I have established, signs are something to think about because they imply virtual structures that are to be unfolded in thought. Sensory signs mark the empirical starting point of the philosophy of difference. They characterise not only the notable result of genetic processes running unnoticeably, but their notable virtual determinations can just as easily be filtered out in thought. At the same time these implicit determinations of experience are the implicit determinations of thought: problematical ideal structures (which can only be thought) that actualise themselves in intensity-determined fields of individuation (that can only be sensed). As has been demonstrated, the paradoxical structure of expression itself repeats in thought. Thinking that is compelled from the outside to think can hardly unlock the virtual structural totality of experience, but it is in position to build concepts with which, in thought, its especially important appearing aspects, that is, immanent aspects, can be helped to distinct expression. Thinking which explicates within experience the immanent determinations of the sign can discover thereby singularities that allow new facets within experiential coherence to become conspicuous. In this way thinking becomes aware of the conditions that lie at the bottom of the distinction between what is worth noticing and what is merely ordinary. Thus the interpretation of signs has perhaps as a consequence a greater sensibility for signs. The reverse is also true: that a greater capability to allow oneself to be affected – which results in more differences being integrated and sensed – will stimulate thought to pursue the various and complex virtual relations. Consequently a mutual deepening of difference will take place, so that in thought the implicit determinations of experience will be explicated, changing the genetic conditions of experience themselves. Deleuze will always say that no one knows the affects in advance to which one can be open. The 'subject', affected from without, affects itself – by feeling what it thinks and thinking what it feels – and can as a result constitute itself as the product of its affects and its thoughts.

Conclusion: Where Do We Go from Here? Lines of Flight

> A good empiricist must be a critical metaphysician. (Feyerabend 1999: 102)

Deleuze never hid the fact that *Event* plays a special role in his philosophy. Although the German concept, *Ereignis*, has been around since Heidegger's *Beiträgen* (1936–8) (see Kovacs 1992: 39ff.), Deleuze's use of *événement* is oriented more toward Nietzsche and his reflections on eternal return. One could say that Deleuze succeeds in combining two seemingly countervailing conceptions, Heidegger's event-transcendence and Nietzsche's event-immanence, into one *immanent* thought. In transcendental empiricism's concept of experience, Event links the rejection of representational thought with the affirmation of (Dionysian) becomings. Phenomenologically speaking, this has the consequence that the Event carries with it not only an abrupt forfeiture of normal customs and routines of life, but also a form of procedural continuity of a split in time or meanwhile (*entre-temps, Zwischen-Zeit*). This un-representable moment radiates through past and future, spreads itself nomadically over them and is meant to be played figurally, mimetically (see Deleuze and Guattari 1994: 158).

Many interpreters think they must choose between the idea of a nomadic allocation of Being, in tune with the third time synthesis, and the aesthetic idea of virtual counter-actualisation, in tune with the second time synthesis. Scattered intensity differences or compressed blocks of sensations? The apparent contradiction has even been explained as a change in Deleuze's thinking from a structuralist to a post-structuralist position, which overlooks the fact that *the transcendental use of the faculty of memory* is not only directed toward a memorandum that has to be remembered, yet cannot be remembered, but *belongs already to the third synthesis*. The virtual time-image of the past cannot be actualised in memory. It must be counter-actualised – in the sense of a past which was never present because it is begotten within forgetting (see Deleuze 1994: 140ff.).

Deleuze connects the transcendental exercise of all faculties with Nietzsche's carefully honed conception of immanence and becoming. This implies not only that counter-actualisation by the mime, whether as painter, dancer or whatever, relies on the nomadic production of difference among heterogeneous faculties, but also that the idea of a differential and univocal splintering of Being within becoming remains all too abstract unless we consider concurrently the concrete origin, dissolution or evolving dissemination of the actual (not to mention its relation to its virtual double). The strange 'experiential presence' of the Event always lies on the virtual level of the 'immanent presence of what isn't there' (*Anwesenheit der Abwesenheit*).

Let's take a closer look. In *Difference and Repetition* Deleuze develops his concept of the Event by describing the dissonances in the sublime or paradoxical play of those faculties which dispense with harmony and cooperation within common sense. Whereas the sensible in the empirical application of recognition is in no way restricted to being sensed only when immediately connected to an object, because that object can also be remembered, imagined or understood, the Being of the sensible as 'sign of an encounter', as Event, cannot be sensed in any other way than within transcendental sensibility. In contrast to actual representational acts, which correlate the particular operations of the faculties with an identifiable form of an object thanks to the direction of a subjective principle, the affects, percepts, phantasms and concepts communicate in sub-representational usage only because of their difference.

> The transcendent[al] exercise must not be traced from the empirical exercise precisely because it apprehends that which cannot be grasped from the point of view of common sense, that which measures the empirical operation of all the faculties according to that which pertains to each, given the form of their collaboration. That is why the transcendental is answerable to a superior empiricism which alone is capable of exploring [...] its regions. Contrary to Kant's belief, it cannot be induced from the ordinary empirical forms in the manner in which these appear under the determination of common sense. (Deleuze 1994: 143)

Deleuze's philosophical task is to show that transcendental structures of experience do not originate in the banality of object-oriented recognition, but rather out of a domain of experience that precedes the empirical givens of consciousness and is not already subject to the rules of common sense. Here we have the point of departure of

Conclusion

Deleuze's philosophy: his conviction regarding the 'derivative nature' of the model of intentionality.

> On the one hand it is apparent that acts of recognition exist and occupy a large part of our daily life: this is a table, this is an apple, this the piece of wax, 'Good morning, Theaetetus'. But who can believe that the destiny of thought is at stake in these acts, and that when we recognise, we are thinking? (Deleuze 1994: 135)

The fact of actual experience is obvious, but it is the result of finer and more difficult mechanisms. Therefore Deleuze counters it with a different image of experience, according to which each individual faculty turns in principle only toward its own incomparable and exclusive 'object', the one that is solely active for it. What we touch, see or smell is (*de jure*) not the same object, but in each case a different one. (The simple question: 'Don't you see this tree that I can also take hold of?' always comes too late and introduces a certain cognitive bias.)

Consciousness in the narrower sense, that is to say, consciousness of something actual, happens only when at least two faculties converge or concentrate upon a common noematic mediatory point (transcending as such the faculties themselves). That is why Deleuze demands a 'transcendental study' to uncover the genetic fields of intensity that are covered up by the very empirical extensions and qualities that explicate those fields (see Deleuze 1994: 236f). In this way the Event character of the implicative mode of Being, which is at first obscured, is made visible in the transcendental use of the faculties. The superficiality of what happens in immanence must not be confused with the superficiality of the world of representation. On the contrary, the flimmering perceptions and irritating sensibilia, the haunting phantasms and the cast-up concepts of virtual manifolds that do not enter experience in actuality: all these only have a chance to become events, in the temporal mode of virtual counter-actualisation, where breaks in the continuum of hardened habits open up, where transitions between clear perceptions must be produced or where unanticipated problems pose themselves.

In contrast to Heidegger, Deleuze does not find it altogether necessary to seek the Event for its own sake, although he too is fascinated by any kind of 'uplift of the soul' and occasionally gets careless. In the previous chapters I have shown in detail that Deleuze is able to determine concretely, in recourse to the empiricist interpretation of the 'pure' and passive syntheses, the dimensions of the transcendental which Heidegger freed up through his step back out of the region of representation into the field of events. Yet Heidegger's 'mysticism of Being', his low esteem of 'vulgarity' (sensuality), based on his obsession for essential truth, reflects, on his part, his ignorance of the tradition of empiricism. Deleuze, on the other hand – as did Kant and Husserl before him – profits deeply from the 'proximity to reality' of the philosophical position of empiricism. That finds direct expression in the starting point of his philosophy, for from the very beginning it is the sensual signs that can only be perceived that make thought necessary: they 'shock the soul', perplex it and force it to pose a problem. 'From the intensive to the thought – it is always thanks to an intensity that a thought strikes us' (Deleuze 1994: 144, trans. mod.).

The disturbing – or problematic – aspect of thought is the unthought, that is, that which can only be thought: for the sentiendum designates a subrepresentative area that can indeed be unfolded structurally using (virtual) concepts, but it has to be conceptualised in difference-theoretical terms in such a way that the disturbing aspect – the intensive potential of the sign – does not become sublated (*zur Aufhebung kommt*). The problem-idea, which circulates among all the faculties in transmitting its (outwardly directed) problematical power, must therefore by right be understood in such a way that it can only be sensed in sensation, can only be perceived in perception, can only be recollected in recollection. Only then, with the help of corresponding concepts, is it possible to internalise the outwardness of thought (*das Außen des Denkens*), to fold it in or to repeat it in its inwardness. In this respect, the philosophical concepts do not refer to (subjective) experience, but auto-referentially hold their own in the exposition of Events.

> The greatness of a philosophy is measured by the nature of the events [...] that it enables us to release in concepts. (Deleuze and Guattari 1994: 34)

For Deleuze this means first that the task of philosophy is to dispute the legitimacy of the moral dogmatism of representation by presenting a model of thought in which difference and repetition are situated in the transcendental service of the faculties. On this foundation of immanence the limits of experience can then be marked out in the empirical practice of the faculties and attention can be directed to their real conditions. Let me stress again, the conception of experience is carried out – in line with the ethical maxim, don't be too

Conclusion

explicit! – within the virtuality of thought. On the one hand, this makes it possible to define yet latent perspectives in the field of experience, perspectives which help heighten one's capacity to be affected while expanding and enhancing the experiential reserves one can draw upon. On the other hand, and above all, this way of thinking generates new singularities in thought, so that in their light what exists can be exposed to alienation effects, opening up new courses of action and auto-techniques for living in the world.

Yet it is not just the Event, summoned at all costs, around which the work of philosophy revolves. This is just a start in reaching for the vantage point of one's times, allowing us thereby to think over 'the advent of a new form [or new assemblages; MR] [. . .] which, it is hoped, will not be worse than the previous ones' (Deleuze 1988b: 132).

Bibliography

Adorno, Theodor W. (1981) [1966], *Negative Dialectics*, trans. E. B. Ashton (London: Bloomsbury Academic).
Adorno, Theodor W., and Max Horkheimer (2007) [1944], *Dialectic of Enlightenment*, trans. Edmund Jephcott (Stanford: Stanford University Press).
Ansell-Pearson, Keith, ed. (1997a), *Deleuze and Philosophy: The Difference Engineer* (New York: Routledge).
Ansell-Pearson, Keith (1997b): 'Viroid life: on machines, technics and evolution', in G. Genosko (ed.), *Deleuze and Guattari: Critical Assessments of Leading Philosophers*, vol. 3 (London: Routledge), pp. 1343–73.
Ansell-Pearson, Keith (2001): 'Thinking immanence: on the event of Deleuze's Bergsonism', in G. Genosko (ed.), *Deleuze and Guattari: Critical Assessments of Leading Philosophers*, vol. 1 (London: Routledge), pp. 412–41.
Aquila, Richard (1983), *Representational Mind: A Study of Kant's Theory of Knowledge* (Bloomington: Indiana University Press).
Arendt, Hannah (1981), *The Life of the Mind*, vols 1 and 2 (New York: Harvest/Harcourt).
Aubenque, Pierre (1993), 'Die Metaphysik als Übergang: Reflexionen zu einer unüberwindbaren Funktion der Metaphysik', in H. Schnädelbach and G. Keil (eds), *Philosophie der Gegenwart – Gegenwart der Philosophie* (Hamburg: Junius), pp. 161–9.
Austin, John L. (1962), *Sense and Sensibilia*, ed. G. J. Warnock (Oxford: Oxford University Press).
Ayer, Alfred J. (1936), *Language, Truth and Logic* (London: Gollancz).
Ayer, Alfred J. (1940), *The Foundations of Empirical Knowledge* (London: Macmillan).
Ayer, Alfred J. (1980), *Hume* (Oxford: Oxford University Press).
Badiou, Alain (1994), 'Zwei Briefe an Gilles Deleuze', in F. Balke and J. Vogl (eds), *Gilles Deleuze: Fluchtlinien der Philosophie* (Munich: Fink), pp. 243–51.
Badiou, Alain (2000): *Deleuze: The Clamor of Being*, trans. Louise Burchill (Minneapolis: University of Minnesota Press).
Balke, Friedrich, ed., with Joseph Vogl (1996), *Gilles Deleuze – Fluchtlinien der Philosophie* (Munich: Fink).

Balke, Friedrich (1998), *Gilles Deleuze* (Frankfurt: Campus).
Balke, Friedrich (1999), 'Den Zufall denken: Das Problem der Aleatorik in der zeitgenössischen französischen Philosophie', in Peter Gendolla and Thomas Kamphusmann (eds), *Die Künste des Zufalls* (Frankfurt: Suhrkamp), pp. 48–76.
Balke, Friedrich, ed. (2011), with Marc Rölli, *Philosophie und Nicht-Philosophie: Gilles Deleuze – Aktuelle Diskussionen* (Bielefeld: Transcript).
Baugh, Bruce (1992), 'Transcendental empiricism: Deleuze's response to Hegel', *Man and World* 25, pp. 133–48.
Baugh, Bruce (1993), 'Deleuze and empiricism', *Journal of the British Society for Phenomenology* 24, pp. 15–31.
Beddoes, Diane (1997), 'Deleuze, Kant and indifference', in K. A. Pearson (ed.), *Deleuze and Philosophy: The Difference Engineer* (London: Routledge), pp. 25–43.
Bennett, Jonathan (1966), *Kant's Analytic* (Cambridge: Cambridge University Press).
Bergson, Henri (1920), *Mind-Energy*, trans. H. Wildon Carr (London: Macmillan).
Bergson, Henri (1988) [1908], *Matter and Memory*, trans. N. M. Paul and W. S. Palmer (New York: Zone Books).
Bergson, Henri (1998) [1911], *Creative Evolution*, trans. A. Mitchell (New York: Dover).
Bergson, Henri (1999) [1922], *Duration and Simultaneity*, ed. R. Durie (Manchester: Clinamen Press).
Bergson, Henri (2001) [1910], *Time and Free Will: An Essay on the Immediate Data of Consciousness*, trans. F. L. Pogson (New York: Dover).
Bergson, Henri (2002a), *Key Writings*, ed. K. Ansell-Pearson and John Mullarkey (London: Continuum).
Bergson, Henri (2002b) [1934], *The Creative Mind*, trans. Mabelle L. Andison (New York: The Citadel Press).
Berkeley, George (1988) [1713], *Three Dialogues between Hylas and Philonous* (London: Penguin Classics).
Bogue, Ronald (1991), 'Word, image and sound: the non-representational semiotics of Gilles Deleuze', in G. Genosko (ed.), *Deleuze and Guattari: Critical Assessments of Leading Philosophers*, vol. 1 (London: Routledge), pp. 81–98.
Böhme, Gernot (1986), *Philosophieren mit Kant: Zur Rekonstruktion der Kantischen Erkenntnis- und Wissenschaftstheorie* (Frankfurt: Suhrkamp).
Borges, Jorge-Luis (1999) [1944], 'Death and the compass', in *Collected Fictions*, trans. Andrew Hurley (London: Penguin), pp. 147–56.
Boundas, Constantin, ed. (1994), with D. Olkowski, *Gilles Deleuze and the Theatre of Philosophy* (New York: Routledge).

Bibliography

Boundas, Constantin (2001), 'Foreclosure of the other: from Sartre to Deleuze', in G. Genosko (ed.), *Deleuze and Guattari: Critical Assessments of Leading Philosophers*, vol. 1 (London: Routledge), pp. 442–55.

Broad, Charlie D. (1961), 'Hume's doctrine of space: Dawes Hicks lecture on philosophy', *Proceedings of the British Academy*, vol. 47.

Chipman, Lauchlan (1972), 'Kant's categories and their schematism', *Kant-Studien* 63, pp. 36–50.

Clark, Tim (1997), 'Deleuze and structuralism: towards a geometry of sufficient reason', in K. Ansell-Pearson (ed.), *Deleuze and Philosophy: The Difference Engineer* (New York: Routledge), pp. 58–72.

Cohen, Hermann (1915) [1902], *System der Philosophie 1.Teil: Logik der reinen Erkenntnis* (Berlin: Cassirer).

Cohen, Hermann (1971), *Reason and Hope: Selections from the Jewish Writings of Hermann Cohen*, trans. Eva Jospe (New York: W. W. Norton).

Cohen, Hermann (1984) [1883], *Das Prinzip der Infinitesimal-Methode und seine Geschichte*, Werke 5.1 (Hildesheim: Olms).

Cohen, Hermann (1987) [1871], *Kants Theorie der Erfahrung*, Werke 1.1 (Hildesheim: Olms).

Cohen, Hermann (1995), *Religion of Reason: Out of the Sources of Judaism*, trans. Simon Kaplan (Atlanta: Scholars Press).

Curtius, Ernst Robert (1914), 'Das Schematismuskapitel in der Kritik der reinen Vernunft', *Kant-Studien* 19, pp. 338–66.

Davidson, Donald (2001) [1974], 'On the very idea of a conceptual scheme', in D. Davidson, *Inquiries into Truth and Interpretation* (Oxford: Clarendon), pp. 183–98.

Deleuze, Gilles (1983) [1962], *Nietzsche and Philosophy*, trans. Hugh Tomlinson (Minneapolis: University of Minnesota Press).

Deleuze, Gilles (1984) [1963], *The Critical Philosophy of Kant*, trans. Hugh Tomlinson and Barbara Habberjam (Minneapolis: University of Minnesota Press).

Deleuze, Gilles (1986) [1983], *Cinema I: The Movement-Image*, trans. Hugh Tomlinson and Barbara Habberjam (Minneapolis: University of Minnesota Press).

Deleuze, Gilles (1988a) [1966], *Bergsonism*, trans. Hugh Tomlinson and Barbara Habberjam (New York: Zone Books).

Deleuze, Gilles (1988b) [1986], *Foucault*, trans. Sean Hand (Minneapolis: University of Minnesota Press).

Deleuze, Gilles (1988c) [1981], *Spinoza: Practical Philosophy*, trans. Robert Hurley (San Francisco: City Lights Books).

Deleuze, Gilles (1989) [1985], *Cinema II: The Time-Image*, trans. Hugh Tomlinson and Barbara Habberjam (Minneapolis: University of Minnesota Press).

Deleuze, Gilles (1990a) [1968], *Expressionism in Philosophy: Spinoza*, trans. Martin Joughin (New York: Zone Books).
Deleuze, Gilles (1990b) [1969], *The Logic of Sense*, trans. Mark Lester with Charles Stivale (New York: Columbia University Press).
Deleuze, Gilles (1991) [1953], *Empiricism and Subjectivity*, trans. Constantin Boundas (New York: Columbia University Press).
Deleuze, Gilles (1993) [1988], *The Fold: Leibniz and the Baroque*, trans. Tom Conley (Minneapolis: University of Minnesota Press).
Deleuze, Gilles (1994) [1968], *Difference and Repetition*, trans. Paul Patton (New York: Columbia University Press).
Deleuze, Gilles (1995) [1990], *Negotiations*, trans. Martin Joughin (New York: Columbia University Press).
Deleuze, Gilles (1997) [1993], *Essays Critical and Clinical*, trans. Daniel Smith and Michael Greco (Minneapolis: University of Minnesota Press).
Deleuze, Gilles (2001) [1995], *Pure Immanence: Essays on a Life*, trans. Anne Boyman (New York: Zone Books).
Deleuze, Gilles (2003a) [1964, 1970], *Proust and Signs: The Complete Text*, trans. Richard Howard (Minneapolis: University of Minnesota Press).
Deleuze, Gilles (2003b) [1972], 'How do we recognize structuralism?' in G. Deleuze, *Desert Islands* (New York: Semiotexte).
Deleuze, Gilles (2004) [1981], *Francis Bacon: Logic of Sensation*, trans. Daniel W. Smith (Minneapolis: University of Minnesota Press).
Deleuze, Gilles (2006) [2003], *Two Regimes of Madness: Texts and Interviews 1975–1995* (New York: Semiotexte).
Deleuze, Gilles (2015), 'What is grounding?', from transcribed notes by Pierre Lefebvre, trans. Arjen Kleinherenbrink, ed. by Tony Yanick, Jason Adams and Mohammad Salemy (Grand Rapids, MI: &&& Publishing), available online at http://monoskop.org/images/3/3a/Deleuze_Gilles_What_Is_Grounding.pdf (last accessed 3 April 2016).
Deleuze, Gilles, and Félix Guattari (1983) [1972], *Anti-Oedipus*, trans. Robert Hurley, Mark Seem and Helen R. Lane (Minneapolis: University of Minnesota Press).
Deleuze, Gilles, and Félix Guattari (1986) [1975], *Kafka: For a Minor Literature*, trans. Dana Polan (Minneapolis: University of Minnesota Press).
Deleuze, Gilles, and Félix Guattari (1987) [1980], *A Thousand Plateaus*, trans. Brian Massumi (Minneapolis: University of Minnesota Press).
Deleuze, Gilles, and Félix Guattari (1994) [1991], *What Is Philosophy?*, trans. Hugh Tomlinson and Graham Burchell (New York: Columbia University Press).
Deleuze, Gilles, and Claire Parnet (1987) [1977], *Dialogues*, trans. Hugh Tomlinson and Barbara Habberjam (New York: Columbia University Press).

Bibliography

De Quincey, Thomas (1854) [1827], 'The Last Days of Immanuel Kant', in *De Quincey's Works*, vol. 3 (Edinburgh: A. & C. Black), pp. 99–166.
Derrida, Jacques (1988), 'Afterword: Toward an ethic of discussion', in *Limited Inc.*, trans. S. Weber (Evanston, IL: Northwestern University Press), pp. 111–60.
Derrida, Jacques (1991), 'Signature Event Context', in Peggy Kamuf (ed.), *A Derrida Reader: Between the Blinds* (New York: Columbia University Press), pp. 80–111.
Descartes, René (1998) [1637], *Discourse on Method*, trans. Donald Cress (Indianapolis: Hackett Classics).
Descombes, Vincent (1980), *Modern French Philosophy*, trans. Scott Fox and J. M. Harding (Cambridge: Cambridge University Press).
Detel, Wolfgang (1978), 'Zur Funktion des Schematismuskapitels in Kants Kritik der reinen Vernunft', *Kant-Studien* 69, pp. 17–45.
Dewey, John (1960) [1929], *The Quest for Certainty: Gifford Lectures* (New York: Capricorn).
Dickens, Charles (1997), *Our Mutual Friend* (London: Penguin Classics).
Dicker, Georges (1998), *Hume's Epistemology and Metaphysics* (London: Routledge).
Ellrich, Lutz (1996), 'Negativity and difference: on Gilles Deleuze's criticism of dialectics', *Modern Language Notes* III/3, pp. 463–87.
Fechner, Gustav Theodor (1860), *Elemente der Psychophysik*, vol. 1 (Leipzig: Breitkopf und Härtel).
Feyerabend, Paul (1963), 'Wie wird man ein braver Empirist? Ein Aufruf zur Toleranz in der Erkenntnistheorie', in L. Krüger (ed.), *Erkenntnisprobleme der Naturwissenschaften: Texte zur Einführung in die Philosophie der Wissenschaft* (Köln 1970), pp. 302–35.
Feyerabend, Paul (2010) [1975], *Against Method* (London: Verso).
Fink, Eugen (2004) [1935], 'Die Idee der Transcendentalphilosophie bei Kant und in der Phänomenologie', in *Nähe und Distanz: Phänomenologische Vorträge und Aufsätze* (Freiburg and Munich: Alber), pp. 7–44.
Flew, Anthony (1976), 'Infinite divisibility in Hume's Treatise', in D. W. Livingston and J. T. King (eds), *Hume: A Re-evaluation* (New York: Fordham University Press).
Foucault, Michel (1970) [1966], *The Order of Things: An Archaeology of Human Sciences* (New York: Vintage Books).
Foucault, Michel (1977a) [1969], 'Der Ariadnefaden ist gerissen', in M. Foucault and G. Deleuze, *Der Faden ist gerissen*, trans. W. Seitter and U. Raulff (Berlin: Merve), pp. 7–12.
Foucault, Michel (1977b) [1970], 'Theatrum philosophicum', in *Language, Counter-Memory, Practice*, trans. D. Bouchard and S. Simon, ed. D. Bouchard (Ithaca, NY: Cornell University Press).
Foucault, Michel (1977c) [1971], 'Nietzsche, Genealogy, History', in

Language, Counter-Memory, Practice, trans. D. Bouchard and S. Simon, ed. D. Bouchard (Ithaca, NY: Cornell University Press).

Foucault, Michel (1990) [1984], *The History of Sexuality, vol. 2: The Use of Pleasure*, trans. Robert Hurley (New York: Vintage Books).

Frank, Manfred (1989a), *What is Neostructuralism?*, trans. Sabine Wilke (Minneapolis: University of Minnesota Press).

Frank, Manfred (1989b), *Das Sagbare und das Unsagbare: Studien zur deutsch-französischen Hermeneutik und Texttheorie* (Frankfurt: Suhrkamp).

Frank, Manfred (1998), *The Subject and the Text: Essays on Literary Theory and Philosophy*, trans. Helen Atkins (Cambridge: Cambridge University Press).

Frege, Gottlob (1994) [1891], 'Funktion und Begriff', in *Funktion, Begriff, Bedeutung: Fünf logische Studien* (Göttingen: Vandenhoeck), pp. 18–39.

Frege, Gottlob (2007) [1884], *Foundations of Arithmetic*, trans. Dale Jacquette (New York: Pearson Longman).

Freud, Sigmund (1962), *The Ego and the Id*, trans. Joan Riviere (New York: W.W. Norton).

Freud, Sigmund (2000) [1923], *Das Ich und das Es*, in S. Freud, *Studienausgabe*, vol. 3 (Frankfurt: Fischer), pp. 273–330.

Gadamer, Hans-Georg (1987) [1971], 'Hegel und Heidegger', in *Neuere Philosophie vol. 1: Hegel – Husserl – Heidegger* (Tübingen: Mohr), pp. 87–101.

Gadamer, Hans-Georg (1994): *Heidegger's Ways*, trans. John W. Staley (Albany, NY: State University of New York Press).

Genosko, Gary, ed. (2001), *Deleuze and Guattari: Critical Assessments of Leading Philosophers*, 3 vols (London: Routledge).

George, Rolf (1981), 'Kant's Sensationism', *Synthèse* 47, pp. 229–55.

Goertzel, Ben (1994), *Chaotic Logic: Language, Thought, and Reality from the Perspective of Complex Systems Science* (New York: Plenum Press).

Goodman, Nelson (1968), *Languages of Art: An Approach to a Theory of Symbols* (Indianapolis: Bobbs-Merrill).

Habermas, Jürgen (1987) [1985], *The Philosophical Discourse of Modernity: Twelve Lectures*, trans. F. Lawrence (Cambridge, MA: MIT Press).

Hardt, Michael (1993), *Gilles Deleuze: An Apprenticeship in Philosophy* (Minneapolis: University of Minnesota Press).

Hayden, Patrick (1998), *Multiplicity and Becoming: The Pluralist Empiricism of Gilles Deleuze* (New York: Lang).

Hegel, Georg W. F. (1976) [1807], *Phenomenology of Spirit*, trans. A. V. Miller (Oxford: Oxford University Press).

Hegel, Georg W. F. (1990) [1816], *Wissenschaft der Logik*, vol. II, Werke 6 (Frankfurt: Suhrkamp).

Hegel, Georg W. F. (1991) [1830], *Enzyklopädie der philosophischen*

Bibliography

Wissenschaften im Grundrisse, eds F. Nicolin and O. Pöggeler (Hamburg: Meiner).
Hegel, Georg W. F. (1993) [1812], *Wissenschaft der Logik*, vol. I., Werke 5 (Frankfurt: Suhrkamp).
Hegel, Georg W. F. (2010) [1812, 1816], *The Science of Logic*, ed. and trans. G. di Giovanni (Cambridge: Cambridge University Press).
Heidegger, Martin (1962) [1927], *Being and Time*, trans. John Macquarrie and Edward Robinson (New York: Harper & Row).
Heidegger, Martin (1967), 'The Origin of the Work of Art', trans. Peter D. Hertz, in *Language and the Foundations of Interpretation* (Stanford: Stanford University Press).
Heidegger, Martin (1968), *What Is Called Thinking?*, trans. Fred D. Wieck and J. Glenn Gray (New York: Harper & Row).
Heidegger, Martin (1971), *On the Way to Language*, trans. Peter D. Hertz (New York: Harper & Row).
Heidegger, Martin (1975), *Gesamtausgabe* (Frankfurt a.M.: Klostermann).
Heidegger, Martin (1990) [1929], *Kant and the Problem of Metaphysics*, trans. Richard Taft (Bloomington: Indiana University Press).
Heidegger, Martin (1991), *Nietzsche*, vols 1 and 2, trans. David Farrell Krell (New York: Harper & Row).
Heidegger, Martin (1998), *Pathmarks*, ed. William McNeill (Cambridge: Cambridge University Press).
Heidegger, Martin (1999), *Contributions to Philosophy*, trans. Parvis Emad and Kenneth Maly (Bloomington: Indiana University Press).
Heidegger, Martin (2002a), *Identity and Difference*, trans. Joan Stambaugh (Chicago: University of Chicago Press).
Heidegger, Martin (2002b), *On Time and Being*, trans. Joan Stambaugh (New York: Harper & Row).
Hertz, Peter D., a.k.a. Peter Hertz-Ohmes (1967), 'Martin Heidegger's "The Origin of the Work of Art" and two chapters of "On the Way to Language"', trans. Peter D. Hertz, in *Language and the Foundations of Interpretation* (Stanford: Stanford University Press).
Hertz, Peter D., a.k.a. Peter Hertz-Ohmes (1988), 'Serres and Deleuze: Hermes and Humor' in *Canadian Review of Comparative Literature* 14:2, pp. 239–50.
Hertz, Peter D., a.k.a. Peter Hertz-Ohmes (2010), 'Sense, Being, and the Revelatory Event: Deleuze and Metamorphosis', *Deleuze Studies* 4:1, pp. 60–1, 83–91.
Hertz, Peter D., a.k.a. Peter Hertz-Ohmes (2014), 'Deleuzian Empiricism and the Potential of Chaotic Choreographies', in Arno Böhler, Krassimira Kruschkova and Susanne Valeria (eds), *Wissen wir, was ein Körper vermag?* (Bielefeld: Transcript).
Hintikka, Jaako (1972): 'Transcendental arguments: genuine and spurious', *Nous* 6, pp. 274–81.

Hintikka, Jaako (1984), 'Das Paradox transzendentaler Erkenntnis', in E. Schaper and W. Vossenkuhl (eds), *Bedingungen der Möglichkeit: 'Transcendental arguments' und transzendentales Denken* (Stuttgart: Klett Cotta), pp. 123–49.

Hirst, R. J. (1959), *The Problems of Perception* (London: Routledge).

Holenstein, Elmar (1972), *Phänomenologie der Assoziation: Zur Struktur und Funktion eines Grundprinzips der passiven Genesis bei E. Husserl* (Den Haag: Nijhoff).

Hoppe, Hansgeorg (1983), *Synthesis bei Kant: Das Problem der Verbindung von Vorstellungen und ihrer Gegenstandsbeziehung in der Kritik der reinen Vernunft* (Berlin and New York: De Gruyter).

Hume, David (2001) [1739–40], *A Treatise of Human Nature*, eds David Fate Norton and Mary J. Norton (Oxford: Oxford University Press).

Hume, David (2008) [1748], *An Enquiry Concerning Human Understanding* (Oxford: Oxford University Press).

Husserl, Edmund (1950ff.), *Husserliana, Gesammelte Werke* (The Hague: Nijhoff).

Husserl, Edmund (1956) [1923–4], *Erste Philosophie, Erster Teil: Kritische Ideengeschichte, Husserliana* vol. 7, ed. Rudolf Boehm (The Hague: Nijhoff).

Husserl, Edmund (1965) [1910], 'Philosophy as Rigorous Science', in Q. Lauer (ed.), *Phenomenology and the Crisis of Philosophy* (New York: Harper & Row), pp. 166–96.

Husserl, Edmund (1969) [1929], *Formal and Transcendental Logic*, trans. D. Cairns (The Hague: Nijhoff).

Husserl, Edmund (1970a), *The Crisis of European Sciences and Transcendental Phenomenology*, trans. D. Carr (Evanston, IL: Northwestern University Press).

Husserl, Edmund (1970b), *Logical Investigations*, 2 vols, trans. J. N. Findlay (London: Routledge & Kegan Paul).

Husserl, Edmund (1973) [1937], *Experience and Judgment: Investigations in a Genealogy of Logic*, trans. J. S. Churchill and K. Ameriks (Evanston, IL: Northwestern University Press).

Husserl, Edmund (1974), 'Kant and the idea of transcendental philosophy', trans. T. E. Klein and W. E. Pohl, *South Western Journal of Philosophy* 5, pp. 9–56.

Husserl, Edmund (1977), *Ideen zu einer reinen Phänomenologie und phänomenologischen Philosophie*, first book, first half-binding, Husserliana vol. 3/1, ed. Karl Schuhmann (The Hague: Nijhoff).

Husserl, Edmund (1982), *Ideas Pertaining to a Pure Phenomenology and to a Phenomenological Philosophy*, first book, trans. F. Kersten (Dordrecht: Kluwer).

Husserl, Edmund (1990) *On the Phenomenology of the Consciousness of Internal Time (1883–1917)*, trans. J. B. Brough (Dordrecht: Kluwer).

Bibliography

Husserl, Edmund (1999) [1931], *Cartesian Meditations*, trans. D. Cairns (Dordrecht: Kluwer).
Husserl, Edmund (2001), *Analyses Concerning Passive and Active Synthesis: Lectures on Transcendental Logic*, trans. Anthony J. Steinbock (Dordrecht: Kluwer).
Jacquette, Dale (1996), 'Hume on infinite divisibility and sensible extensionless indivisibles', *Journal of the History of Philosophy* 34, pp. 61–78.
Jacobi, Friedrich Heinrich (1993) [1799], 'Sendschreiben an Fichte', in W. Jaeschke (ed.), *Transzendentalphilosophie und Spekulation* (Hamburg: Meiner).
Jacobi, Friedrich Heinrich (1815), *Über den transzendentalen Idealismus*, Werke vol. 2 (Leipzig: Fischer).
Jacobi, Friedrich Heinrich (2009), *The Main Philosophical Writings*, trans. George di Giovanni (Montreal: McGill-Queen's University Press).
James, William (1976) [1904], 'A world of pure experience', in *The Works of William James: Essays in Radical Empiricism* (Cambridge, MA: Harvard University Press), pp. 21–44.
James, William (1987) [1909], 'A pluralistic universe', in *Writings 1902–1910* (New York: Library of America), pp. 625–819.
Kant, Immanuel (1999) [1789], 'Letter to Marcus Herz 26.05.1789', in *Immanuel Kant: Correspondence*, trans. and ed. Arnulf Zweig (Cambridge: Cambridge University Press), pp. 311–15.
Kant, Immanuel (1999) [1781, 1787], *Critique of Pure Reason*, ed. and tr. Paul Guyer and Allen W. Wood (Cambridge: Cambridge University Press).
Kant, Immanuel (2001) [1790], *Critique of the Power of Judgment*, ed. and tr. Paul Guyer and Eric Matthews (Cambridge: Cambridge University Press).
Kant, Immanuel (2002) [1772], *Prolegomena to Any Future Metaphysics*, trans. P. Carus (Indianapolis: Hackett Publishing).
Kemp Smith, Norman (1918), *A Commentary to Kant's 'Critique of Pure Reason'* (London: Macmillan).
Kemp Smith, Norman (1941), *The Philosophy of David Hume: A Critical Study of its Origins and Central Doctrines* (London: Macmillan).
Kern, Iso (1964), *Husserl und Kant. Eine Untersuchung über Husserls Verhältnis zu Kant und zum Neukantianismus* (Den Haag: Nijhoff).
Kerslake, Christian (2009), *Immanence and the Vertigo of Philosophy: From Kant to Deleuze* (Edinburgh: Edinburgh University Press).
Kitcher, Patricia (1990), *Kant's Transcendental Psychology* (New York: Oxford University Press).
Körner, Stephen (1982), *Kant* (New Haven: Yale University Press).
Kovacs, George (1992), 'The leap (der Sprung) for being in Heidegger's Beiträge zur Philosophie (Vom Ereignis)', *Man and World* 25, pp. 39–59.

Kuhn, Thomas S. (1962), *The Structure of Scientific Revolutions* (Chicago: Chicago University Press).
Lacey, A. R. (1989), *Bergson* (London and New York: Routledge).
Lange, Thomas (1989), *Die Ordnung des Begehrens: Nietzscheanische Aspekte im philosophischen Werk von Deleuze* (Bielefeld: Aisthesis).
Lawlor, Leonard (1998), 'The end of phenomenology: expressionism in Deleuze and Merleau-Ponty', *Continental Philosophy Review* 31:1, pp. 15–34.
Lawlor, Leonard (2000), 'A nearly total affinity: the Deleuzian virtual image versus the Derridean trace', *Angelaki* 5:2, pp. 59–71.
Leibniz, Gottfried Wilhelm (1966) [1702], 'Briefwechsel zwischen Leibniz und Varignon', in E. Cassirer (ed.), *Hauptschriften zur Grundlegung der Philosophie*, vol. 1 (Hamburg: Meiner), pp. 94–100.
Leibniz, Gottfried Wilhelm (1991), *Philosophical Writings*, ed. G. H. R. Parkinson, trans. Mary Morris (London: Everyman's University Paperbacks).
Leibniz, Gottfried Wilhelm (1996), *New Essays on Human Understanding*, trans. and ed. P. Remnant and J. Bennett (Cambridge: Cambridge University Press).
Locke, John (1996) [1690], *An Essay Concerning Human Understanding* (London: Hackett Publishing).
Longuenesse, Béatrice (1998), *Kant and the Capacity to Judge: Sensibility and Discursivity in the Transcendental Analytic of the Critique of Pure Reason* (Princeton: Princeton University Press).
Lyotard, Jean-François (1994) [1991], *Lessons on the Analytic of the Sublime: Kant's Critique of Judgement, §§ 23–9*, trans. Elizabeth Rottenberg (Stanford: Stanford University Press).
Maimon, Salomon (1965) [1790], *Versuch über die Transzendentalphilosophie: Gesammelte Werke*, vol. 2, ed. Valerio Verra (Hildesheim: Olms).
Maimon, Salomon (2010) [1790], *Essay on Transcendental Philosophy*, trans. A. Welchman et al. (London: Continuum).
Merleau-Ponty, Maurice (1959), 'Bergson se faisant', in *Signes* (Paris: Gallimard), pp. 229–41.
Merleau-Ponty, Maurice (1961), 'Eye and Mind', in *The Primacy of Perception*, trans. Carleton Dallery (Evanston, IL: Northwestern University Press), pp. 159–90.
Merleau-Ponty, Maurice (1963) [1942], *The Structure of Behaviour*, trans. Alden Fisher (Boston: Beacon Press).
Merleau-Ponty, Maurice (1968) [1964], *The Visible and the Invisible*, trans. Alphonso Lingis (Evanston, IL: Northwestern University Press).
Merleau-Ponty, Maurice (2006) [1945], *Phenomenology of Perception*, trans. Colin Smith (London: Routledge & Kegan Paul).
Meerbote, Ralf (1986), 'Deleuze on the systematic unity of the critical philosophy', *Kant-Studien* 77, pp. 347–54.

Bibliography

Mishara, Aaron L. (1990), 'Husserl and Freud: time, memory and the unconscious', *Husserl Studies* 7, pp. 29–58.

Murphy, Richard (1980), *Hume and Husserl: Towards Radical Subjectivism* (The Hague: Nijhoff).

Nagl, Ludwig (1992), *Charles Sanders Peirce* (Frankfurt a.M and New York: Campus).

Negri, Antonio (1995), 'On Gilles Deleuze and Félix Guattari, *A Thousand Plateaus*', in G. Genosko (ed.), *Deleuze and Guattari: Critical Assessments of Leading Philosophers*, vol. 3. (London: Routledge), pp. 1182–97.

Nietzsche, Friedrich (1966) [1886], *Beyond Good and Evil*, trans. Walter Kaufmann (New York: Random House).

Nietzsche, Friedrich (1967a) [1872], *The Birth of Tragedy*, trans. Walter Kaufmann (New York: Random House).

Nietzsche, Friedrich (1967b) [1888], *Ecce Homo: How One Becomes What One Is*, trans. Walter Kaufmann, in *On the Genealogy of Morals and Ecce Homo* (New York: Random House).

Nietzsche, Friedrich (1968a) [1888], *The Antichrist*, trans. Walter Kaufmann, in *The Portable Nietzsche*, ed. W. Kaufmann (New York: Viking Press).

Nietzsche, Friedrich (1968b) [1883–5], *Thus Spoke Zarathustra*, trans. Walter Kaufmann, in *The Portable Nietzsche* (New York: Viking Press).

Nietzsche, Friedrich (1968c) [1889], *Twilight of the Idols*, trans. Walter Kaufmann, in *The Portable Nietzsche* (New York: Viking Press).

Nietzsche, Friedrich (1974) [1882], *The Gay Science*, trans. Walter Kaufmann (New York: Random House).

Nietzsche, Friedrich (1980ff.), *Kritische Studienusgabe*, eds G. Colli and M. Montinari, 15 vols (Berlin: Walter de Gruyter).

Nietzsche, Friedrich (1982) [1881], *Daybreak: Thoughts on the Prejudices of Morality*, trans. R. J. Hollingdale (Cambridge: Cambridge University Press).

Nietzsche, Friedrich (1983) [1873–6], *Untimely Meditations I–IV*, trans. R. J. Hollingdale (Cambridge: Cambridge University Press).

Nietzsche, Friedrich (1986) [1878–80], *Human, All Too Human: A Book for Free Spirits*, trans. R. J. Hollingdale (Cambridge: Cambridge University Press).

Owen, David (1999), *Hume's Reason* (Oxford: Oxford University Press).

Paton, Herbert James (1936), *Kant's Metaphysic of Experience: A Commentary on the First Half of the Kritik der reinen Vernunft*, 2 vols (London: Macmillan).

Patton, Paul (1984), 'Conceptual politics and the war-machine in Mille Plateaux', *Substance* 44/45, pp. 61–80.

Patton, Paul (1986), 'Deleuze and Guattari: ethics and post-modernity', in G. Genosko (ed.), *Deleuze and Guattari: Critical Assessments of Leading Philosophers*, vol. 3 (London: Routledge), pp. 1150–63.

Patton, Paul (2000): *Deleuze and the Political* (London: Routledge).

Piaget, Jean (1968), *Le structuralisme* (Paris: Gallimard).

Piaget, Jean (1973) [1959], 'Genese und Struktur in der Psychologie', in H. Naumann (ed.), *Der moderne Strukturbegriff* (Darmstadt: Wissenschaftliche Buchgesellschaft), pp. 281–95.

Pippin, Robert (1982), *Kant's Theory of Form* (New Haven: Yale University Press).

Pöggeler, Otto (1987), *Martin Heidegger's Path of Thinking: Contemporary Studies in Philosophy and the Human Science*, trans. Daniel Magurshak and Sigmund Barber (Atlantic Highlands, NJ: Humanities Press).

Pöggeler, Otto (1995), 'Hegel und Heidegger über Negativität', *Hegel-Studien* 30, pp. 145–66.

Putnam, Hilary (1985), 'After Empiricism', in J. Rajchman and C. West (eds), *Post-Analytic Philosophy* (New York: Columbia University Press), pp. 20–30.

Quine, Willard Van Orman (1953), 'Two dogmas of empiricism', in *From a Logical Point of View* (New York: Harvard University Press), pp. 20–46.

Quine, Willard Van Orman (1974): *The Roots of Reference: The Paul Carus Lectures* (La Salle, IL: Open Court).

Randall, John Herman, Jr. (1965), *The Career of Philosophy*, vol. II (New York: Columbia University Press).

Reid, Thomas (1983) [1764, 1785, 1788], *Inquiry and Essays*, eds R. Beanblossom and K. Lehrer (Indianapolis: Hackett Publishing).

Reid, Thomas (1997) [1764], *An Inquiry into the Human Mind on the Principles of Common Sense*, ed. D. Brookes (State College: Pennsylvania State University Press).

Riemann, Bernhard (1882) [1868], 'On the hypotheses which lie at the foundation of geometry', trans. W. Clifford, *Nature* 8 1873; reprinted in W. K. Clifford (ed.), *Clifford's Collected Mathematical Papers* (London: Macmillan).

Rogozinski, Jacob (1996), 'Ohnmachten (zwischen Nietzsche und Kant)', in F. Balke and J. Vogl (eds), *Gilles Deleuze – Fluchtlinien der Philosophie* (Munich: Fink), pp. 80–92.

Rölli, Marc (2002a), 'Die Zweideutigkeit der Phänomenologie: Deleuze und Husserl', in D. Carr and C. Lotz (eds), *Subjektivität – Verantwortung – Wahrheit: Neue Aspekte der Phänomenologie Edmund Husserls* (Frankfurt a.M. and New York: Lang), pp. 227–42.

Rölli, Marc (2002b): 'Phänomenologie im Denken des Gilles Deleuze', *Journal Phänomenologie* 17, pp. 6–14.

Rölli, Marc (2003): *Gilles Deleuze: Philosophie des transzendentalen Empirismus* (Vienna: Turia + Kant).

Rölli, Marc (2004a), 'Begriffe für das Ereignis: Aktualität und Virtualität', in Rölli (ed.), *Ereignis auf Französisch: Von Bergson bis Deleuze* (Munich: Fink), pp. 337–61.

Bibliography

Rölli, Marc (2004b), 'Die zwei Gedächtnisse des Henri Bergson', in W. Ch. Zimmerli et al. (eds), *Erinnerung – Philosophische Perspektiven* (Munich: Fink), pp. 61–78.
Rölli, Marc (2011), *Kritik der anthropologischen Vernunft* (Berlin: Matthes & Seitz).
Rölli, Marc (2012), *Gilles Deleuze: Philosophie des transzendentalen Empirismus*, 2nd revised edition (Vienna: Turia + Kant).
Rölli, Marc, and F. Balke, eds (2011), *Philosophie und Nicht-Philosophie: Gilles Deleuze – Aktuelle Diskussionen* (Bielefeld: Transcript).
Rölli, Marc, and T. Trzaskalik, eds (2007), *Heinrich Heine und die Philosophie* (Vienna: Turia + Kant).
Rorty, Richard (1979), 'Transcendental arguments, self-reference, and pragmatism', in P. Bieri et al. (eds), *Transcendental Arguments and Science* (Dordrecht: D. Reidel), pp. 77–103.
Rorty, Richard (1990), 'Pragmatism as anti-representationalism', introduction to John P. Murphy, *Pragmatism: From Peirce to Davidson* (Boulder, CO: Westview Press), pp. 1–6.
Russell, Bertrand (1959) [1917], 'The relation of sense-data to physics', in *Mysticism and Logic* (London: George Allen & Unwin), pp. 145–79.
Russell, Bertrand (1996) [1936], 'The limits of empiricism', in *Collected Papers of Bertrand Russell, vol. 10: A Fresh Look at Empiricism, 1927–1942* (London: Routledge), pp. 313–28.
Ryle, Gilbert (2000) [1949], *The Concept of Mind* (Chicago: Chicago University Press).
Salmon, Wesley (1985), 'Empiricism: the key question', in N. Rescher (ed.), *The Heritage of Logical Positivism* (Lanham, MD: University Press of America), pp. 1–21.
Schalow, F. (1992), *The Renewal of the Heidegger–Kant dialogue: Action, Thought, and Responsibility* (Albany, NY: State University of New York Press).
Schaub, Mirjam (2001), 'Die Unerfahrbarkeit der Gegenwart: Zur Kritik am modalen Zeitbegriff bei Hegel, Heidegger und Deleuze', *Dialektik* 2001/2, pp. 151–61.
Seebohm, Thomas (1962), *Die Bedingungen der Möglichkeit der Transzendentalphilosophie* (Bonn: Bouvier).
Seebohm, Thomas (1994), 'Intentionalität und passive Synthesis: Gedanken zu einer nichttranszendentalen Konzeption von Intentionalität', in H. M. Gerlach and H. R. Sepp (eds), *Husserl in Halle* (Frankfurt a.M.: Lang), pp. 63–84.
Simondon, Gilbert (1964), *L'individu et sa genèse physico-biologique* (Paris: Presses Universitaires de France).
Smith, Daniel W. (1996), 'Deleuze's theory of sensation: Overcoming the Kantian duality', in P. Patton (ed.), *Deleuze: A Critical Reader* (Oxford: Blackwell), pp. 29–56.

Smith, Daniel W. (1997), *Gilles Deleuze and the Philosophy of Difference: Towards a Transcendental Empiricism* (Chicago).
Spinoza, Baruch (1985) [1677], *Ethics*, trans. Edwin Curley, *The Collected Writings of Spinoza*, vol. 1 (Princeton: Princeton University Press).
Spinoza, Baruch (1995), *The Letters*, trans. Samuel Shirley (Indianapolis: Hackett Publishing).
Spinoza, Baruch (2001), *Theological-Political Treatise*, trans. Samuel Shirley, 2nd edition (Indianapolis: Hackett Publishing).
Stevens, Richard (1974), *James and Husserl: The Foundations of Meaning* (The Hague: Nijhoff).
Stevenson, Leslie (1982), *The Metaphysics of Experience* (Oxford: Oxford University Press).
Strawson, Peter F. (1959), *Individuals: An Essay in Descriptive Metaphysics* (London: Routledge).
Strawson, Peter F. (1975), *The Bounds of Sense: An Essay on Kant's Critique of Pure Reason* (London: Routledge).
Strawson, Peter F. (1985), *Skepticism and Naturalism: Some Varieties* (London: Methuen).
Strawson, Peter F. (1992), *Analysis and Metaphysics: An Introduction to Philosophy* (Oxford: Oxford University Press).
Stroud, Barry (1968), 'Transcendental Arguments', *Journal of Philosophy* 65, pp. 241–56.
Theunissen, Michael (1991), *Negative Theologie der Zeit* (Frankfurt a.M.: Suhrkamp).
Tholen, Georg Ch., and Rudolf Heinz, eds (1981), *Schizo-Schleichwege: Beiträge zum Anti-Ödipus* (Bremen: Impuls).
Vuillemin, Jules (1954), *L'héritage kantien et la révolution copernicienne* (Paris: Presses Universitaires de France).
Vuillemin, Jules (1962), *La philosophie de l'algèbre*, vol. 1 (Paris: Presses Universitaires de France).
Wahl, Jean (1920), *Les philosophies d'Angleterre et d'Amérique* (Paris: Alcan).
Wahl, Jean (1925), *The Pluralist Philosophies of England and America*, trans. Fred Rothwell (London: Open Court).
Waldenfels, Bernhard (1983), *Phänomenologie in Frankreich* (Frankfurt a.M.: Suhrkamp).
Waldenfels, Bernhard (1996): *Order in the Twilight*, trans. David J. Parent (Athens: Ohio University Press).
Waldenfels, Bernhard (1999), *Sinnesschwellen: Studien zur Phänomenologie des Fremden*, vol. 3 (Frankfurt a.M.: Suhrkamp).
Waldenfels, Bernhard (2011), *Phenomenology of the Alien: Basic Concepts*, trans. Tanja Stähler, *Studies in Phenomenology and Existential Philosophy* (Evanston, IL: Northwestern University Press).
Walsh, W. H. (1957), 'Schematism', *Kant-Studien* 49, pp. 95–106.

Bibliography

Warnock, G. J. (1949), 'Concepts and Schematism', *Analysis* 9, pp. 77–82.
Waxman, Wayne (1991), *Kant's Model of the Mind: A New Interpretation of Transcendental Idealism* (Oxford: Oxford University Press).
Welchman, Alistair (1997), 'Machinic Thinking', in G. Genosko (ed.), *Deleuze and Guattari: Critical Assessments of Leading Philosophers*, vol. 3 (London: Routledge), pp. 1233–50.
Whitehead, Alfred N. (1929), *Process and Reality: An Essay in Cosmology*, Gifford Lectures (New York: Free Press).
Wiggins, David (1980), *Sameness and Substance* (Oxford: Blackwell).
Zabeeh, Farhang (1960), *Hume: Precursor of Modern Empiricism – An Analysis of His Opinions on Meaning, Metaphysics, Logic and Mathematics* (The Hague: Nijhoff).
Zimmerli, Walther Ch. (1999), 'Nietzsche's philosophy as critique of truth and science: a comprehensive approach', in B. Babich (ed.), *Nietzsche and the Sciences*, vol. 2 (Dordrecht: Kluwer), pp. 253–77.
Zschocke, Walter (1907), 'Über Kants Lehre vom Schematismus der reinen Vernunft', *Kant-Studien* 12, pp. 157–212.

Index

A-deduction, 59, 61–2, 81–8, 90–1
abstraction theory, 16, 50, 67, 71, 73–4, 112–13, 165; *see also* concepts
active synthesis, 89, 93, 99–100, 228, 230–1, 232–4; *see also* memory; recognition; reproduction; understanding
actualisation
    and immanence, 224
    and individuation, 265–6, 273–4
    and recollection, 198–200, 236–7
    and repetition, 241–2
    and structuration, 109, 203–6
    and virtuality, 17–18, 20, 178–9, 197
    see also counter-actualisation
Adorno, Theodor W., 166, 176
aesthetics, 53, 78, 107, 139, 183–4
affection
    Husserl's theory, 100, 107, 120–7
    reflexive monads, 279–80
    and sensation, 75–6, 79, 202, 257–8
    and subjectivation, 32, 264
    and will to power, 262
affects and percepts, 7, 214
affinity of appearances, 88, 114, 233
'After Empiricism' (Putnam), 8
aion, 152, 198, 247
Alice in Wonderland (Carroll), 268
analogy, 17, 169, 172, 174, 175, 182, 191
Analyses Concerning Passive and Active Synthesis (Husserl)
    affection, 122–5
    association, 111–12, 117–19
    genetic phenomenology, 100–1
    immanence, 110
    Kantian synthesis, 80, 93, 99
    recollection, 120
Anti-Oedipus (Deleuze and Guattari), 13, 24, 81, 238, 263–4

appearance
    and Being, 169, 188
    and concept, 66–7
    and perception, 82–3, 85
    and reproduction, 87–8, 91, 233
    and the 'thing-in-itself', 135–7
    transcendental, 42–3, 54, 70
    and understanding, 59–60, 62
apperception
    and association, 116, 119–20
    and intellectual synthesis, 54, 56–7
    and intentionality, 97–8
    and schematism, 139
    unity, 39, 57–8, 60–3, 72–3, 88, 90, 233–4
apprehension
    and apperception, 61–2, 88
    and association, 114, 118
    and imagination, 38
    self-affection, 46, 139
    sensation, 76, 79
    synthesis, 49, 82–6, 89, 232–3, 257–8
Aristotle, 171–5
association
    and affect, 32, 120–1
    Husserl and Hume, 99, 100–1, 110–15
    Kantian critique, 56–7, 58–60, 63, 70, 86–8, 91
    passive synthesis, 6–7, 27–9, 107
    and perception, 8, 23, 73–4, 258–9
    and reflection, 225
    and relations, 5, 29–30
    and temporality, 3, 116–20, 234–5
    transcendental, 113–14
association psychology, 213
atomism
    and affection, 124
    consciousness, 74–5, 84

Index

empiricism, 23–4, 25–7, 197
experience, 6
perception theory, 253–7, 260
time, 10
Aubenque, Pierre, 172–3
Austin, John L., 7
Ayer, Alfred J., 7, 69–70

B-deduction, 51–2, 54–5, 88
Badiou, Alain, 20
Baer, Karl Ernst von, 273
Baugh, Bruce, 190
becoming
　and Being, 176, 179–80, 182, 249, 282–3
　of concepts, 215, 222
　of forces, 261–3
　paradox, 268–9
　and time, 116, 196, 200, 202, 246–7, 281
Being
　and Cartesianism, 217
　dialectic, 189
　and difference, 16, 132, 145–8, 186–8
　equivocity, 166, 169–70, 172–5
　and event, 281–4
　Heidegger, 93, 128–9, 137–45, 244
　and intensity, 267–8
　and technology, 148–9
　and time, 115, 149–54, 184, 197, 245–6, 249
　univocity, 147, 166, 175–6, 179–83
　see also immanence; ontology
Being and Time (Heidegger), 128, 137, 141, 172
being-in-itself, 43, 134, 136, 177
belief
　and association, 28, 111, 114, 118–19
　and experience, 6, 31, 56
　and imagination, 25, 30, 71
　in truth, 158, 219–20
Bellour, Raymond, 13
Bergson, Henri
　intensity, 251–2, 268
　memory and recollection, 88, 198–9, 234–6
　metaphor of the cone, 236–7
　multiplicity, 270
　nature of concepts, 16
　temporality, 117, 197–8, 199–200, 232
　virtuality, 17–18, 131, 195–7
　see also duration
Bergsonism (Deleuze), 17, 196–7, 236
Berkeley, George, 8, 70, 278
Beyond the Pleasure Principle (Freud), 238
The Birth of Tragedy (Nietzsche), 157
Blanchot, Maurice, 194, 250
blockage of concepts, 166, 168, 171–2, 176–7, 183–6, 210, 217
Böhme, Gernot, 77, 78
bracketing (phenomenological reduction), 89, 96, 103–4, 109
Broad, Charlie D., 255–6

calculus, 11–12, 201, 250, 277
Cartesian Meditations (Husserl), 14, 101–2, 120
Cartesianism
　and common sense, 159–60
　conceptual components, 217
　and consciousness, 85
　and Husserl, 100
　and indeterminance, 191
　and Kant, 10, 19, 35, 38, 57
　and representation, 177
　and time, 46, 184, 227
categories
　Aristotelian doctrine, 172–5
　consciousness, 54–5
　objective reality, 51, 61–2, 65, 81–2, 140, 214–15
　schematism, 63–7, 79, 140
　and the transcendental argument, 56, 59–61
　see also concepts
causality, 28, 29, 30, 118–19, 181, 260
Châtelet, François, 200
Cinema I: The Movement-Image (Deleuze), 77
Cinema II: The Time-Image (Deleuze), 220
Clark, Tim, 207
Cohen, Hermann, 11, 69, 77, 251, 252, 264, 270–1

common sense
　and Being, 174, 175
　and empiricism, 8, 70, 282
　and harmony, 37–8, 39–40
　and phenomenology, 98
　and scepticism, 259
　and thought, 40–1, 43–5, 159–62
concepts
　blockage, 171–2, 176–7, 183–6
　components, 216–17, 222
　and conceptual plane, 209–10
　and consciousness, 90
　construction, 168, 215, 221–3
　Deleuze's theory, 15–16, 50, 166–8, 211–15
　and difference, 169–71, 172–5, 178, 187
　and empiricism, 45–6, 67–9, 165, 210–11, 213–14, 219–20
　as functions, 217–19
　and intuition, 11, 47, 53–4, 271
　schematism, 64–7
　as universals, 158, 160
　see also categories; pure concepts
consciousness
　and empiricism, 9–10, 258–60
　and experience, 53–8, 105–6, 108–9, 163, 243
　and intensity, 261
　and perception, 62–3, 74–5, 82–6, 96–8, 252, 276–7
　and sensation, 76, 79, 121–2, 125–6, 283
　of time, 115–17, 120, 184, 245
　unity, 90–1
　and virtuality, 17–18, 20, 196–7
　see also self-affection; thing-in-itself
counter-actualisation, 152, 198, 281–3
The Crisis of European Sciences and Transcendental Phenomenology (Husserl), 10, 102–3, 106
critical philosophy, 4, 18, 31, 34–5, 37, 135, 264; see also Kant
The Critical Philosophy of Kant (Deleuze), 19, 38, 39–40, 60
Critical Theory, 166
Critique of Judgement (Kant), 40, 78
Critique of Pure Reason (Kant)
　appearance, 136–7

consciousness, 85–7, 245
ontology, 132–3
reason, 36–7
representation, 19, 38, 183
schematism, 63–6
sensation, 76–9
three syntheses, 42, 80–3, 86–91, 129, 232–3
time, 139
transcendental deduction, 10, 49, 51, 53–7, 59–63, 101, 105–6
Critiques (Kant), 35, 37–8
Curtius, Ernst Robert, 65–6

Dasein see Being
death instinct, 241, 243, 249–50
'Deleuze and structuralism' (Clark), 207
Deleuze, Gilles
　early thinking, 2–3, 23–6, 29–30, 129–30
　work phases, 13, 155–6
　see also named works
'Deleuze's theory of sensation' (Smith), 48
Derrida, Jacques, 128, 165, 206
Descartes, René, 141, 159–60, 181; see also Cartesianism
Detel, Wolfgang, 65
dialectic, 133, 135, 149, 169–70, 186–94, 196, 208
Dialogues (Deleuze and Parnet), 5, 6, 178, 205
Dickens, Charles, 250
difference
　and concept, 209–10, 223
　empirical principle, 25–7, 178–9, 252–3, 260, 280
　and intensity, 77, 196–7, 262–6, 268, 279
　and Nietzsche, 157–8, 261–2
　ontological, 16–17, 93, 128–32, 144–8, 168–71
　and phenomenology, 95–6
　philosophical significance, 1–2
　post-Kantianism, 48–9
　and repetition, 155, 225–6, 242–3
　representation, 171–7, 183–90, 284–5
　temporality, 234–6, 249

Index

transcendental principle, 27, 45, 162–4, 190–2
univocity of Being, 166, 179–83
Difference and Repetition (Deleuze)
  anti-Hegelianism, 37, 188–9
  bare and clothed repetition, 241–2
  Being, 174–5, 179, 181–3
  Cartesianism, 159–60, 191
  consciousness, 243, 245
  difference, 17, 170, 173, 176–8, 183–4, 225
  empiricism, 1, 47–9, 156, 210–11, 282–4
  habit, 28, 226, 229–31
  Heidegger, 131–2, 155
  Idea, 190–2, 265–6, 275
  individuation, 266–8, 273–4
  intensity, 7, 27, 77–8, 260–1, 263, 268–9
  intensive and extensive quantities, 269–71
  Kant, 34, 35–6, 40–2, 56, 264
  Nietzsche, 157–8
  passive synthesis, 49–50, 80–1, 93, 185, 228, 278
  phenomenology, 95–6
  psychoanalysis, 238–41, 249–50
  representation, 14, 166–7, 171–2, 185–8, 233–4, 244
  schematism, 64–5
  structure, 193–4, 201–2, 204, 208–10, 212
  thought, 44–6, 161–2, 194–5, 214
  time, 199, 227, 231–3, 235–6, 237–8, 246–9
different/ciation, 178, 203–4, 206, 247–8, 265, 273–4, 275
differential calculus, 11–12, 201, 250, 277
Discourse on Method (Descartes), 159
distance, 269–70, 272
Duns Scotus, John, 180, 183
duration, 17, 28, 78, 196–9, 227, 236; *see also* time

Ecce Homo (Nietzsche), 158
ego, 120, 122–3, 125–6, 239, 245–6, 248–50; *see also* Being; Cartesianism

empiricism
  and concept, 165–8, 210–11, 213–14, 219
  confirmation theory, 67–9
  copy theory, 66–7, 252–3
  definition, 4–9, 29
  development of Deleuze's concept, 13–14, 155–6, 162–3
  radical, 23–4, 213, 221
  transcendental criticism, 1, 9–11, 45–6, 50–2, 70–3, 93
  see also experience; virtuality
Empiricism and Subjectivity (Deleuze)
  history of philosophy, 13
  Humean philosophy, 23–8, 31–2, 225
  Kantian philosophy, 4, 29–31
  transcendentalism, 33
empirico-transcendental doublet, 42–3, 95
Enzyklopädie der philosophischen Wissenschaften im Grundrisse (Hegel), 135, 136
epistemology
  and empiricism, 5, 9
  and Kantian thought, 34, 53, 66, 70–1, 121, 277
  Marburg School, 271
  see also scepticism
epoché see phenomenological reduction (bracketing)
Eros *see* pleasure principle
Erste Philosophie, Erster Teil (Husserl), 104–5, 109, 110–11, 112–13
Essay on Transcendental Philosophy (Maimon), 9, 11–12
Essays Critical and Clinical (Deleuze), 35, 148, 246, 264
event (Deleuzian), 15, 168, 170, 203, 237–8, 246–7, 281–5
event, enowning (Heideggerian), 129, 143–4, 146–7, 151–2, 153–4, 244
Ewald, François, 13
experience
  and concept, 66–9, 165–8
  Deleuze's concept, 6–7, 48–9, 161–4, 177–9, 282–3
  Heidegger's interpretation, 137–40
  Humean concept, 25–7, 29–31, 256
  Husserl's approach, 105–9, 110–13, 125–6

experience (*cont.*)
  Kantian concept, 53–6, 58–63, 70, 72–3, 134–5
  structure, 201, 219, 222
  and the transcendental, 10–11, 13, 14–15, 20, 284–5
  unity, 88, 102–3
  see also empiricism; sense-data
Experience and Judgement (Husserl), 111, 115
Experience and Structure (Kambartel), 75
expression, 179, 180–1, 274, 280
Expressionism in Philosophy (Deleuze), 174, 180, 181
extensive magnitude, 76–7, 78–9, 196, 251, 255–7, 261, 266, 269–73
external relations, 5, 23–4, 29–33, 112–13, 216–17, 225

faculties, 19, 38–40, 42, 161–2, 282–4
Fechner, Gustav Theodor, 126–7, 196
Feyerabend, Paul, 281
Fichte, Johann G., 129–30, 134
figural synthesis
  and intellectual synthesis, 51–2
  intentionality, 58–63
  schematism, 63–7
  transcendental deduction, 57–8, 106
finitude, 76, 129–33, 135, 137, 184
The Fold (Deleuze), 12, 48, 126, 261, 275–9
forces, 260–4
Foucault (Deleuze), 13, 95, 128, 285
Foucault, Michel
  empirico-transcendental doublet, 42–3, 95
  genealogy, 179
  intensity, 250
  representation, 14, 18
  structuralism, 193
Frank, Manfred, 158
Frankfurt School, 166
Frege, Gottlob, 217–18
Freud, Sigmund, 177, 186, 238, 240, 241, 248, 264
'Function and Concept' (Frege), 217–18

Gadamer, Hans-Georg, 133
genus, 172–5, 273

George, Rolf, 63
German idealism, 133–4, 136–7
Gestalt theory, 74, 255
Gilles Deleuze (Hardt), 2, 155–6, 181
good sense, 261, 263
grounding, 109, 129–30, 142, 145–6, 243–4
Guattari, Félix, 13, 211, 270

Habermas, Jürgen, 157–8
habit
  and activity, 229–31
  and concept, 167, 211
  and memory, 28–9, 234, 236
  and repetition, 226, 228, 238–40, 242–3
  and time, 27–8, 231–2, 248–9
  see also association
Hardt, Michael, 2, 155–6, 180–1
harmony, 37–8, 39–40, 53
Hegel, Georg W. F.
  concepts, 167–8, 214–15
  dialectic and negativity, 169–70, 187–9
  and Heidegger, 133, 140, 141–2, 144–6
  infinite representation, 48, 177, 184–8, 215
  and Kant, 37, 129–30, 132, 134
  and Nietzsche, 164
  'thing-in-itself', 135–6
'Hegel und Heidegger' (Gadamer), 133
Heidegger, Martin
  Being, 142–50, 172, 174–6
  and Deleuze, 147–8, 152, 155
  empiricism, 2–3
  enowning event, 153–4
  German idealism, 133–4, 136–7
  and Hegel, 133, 141–2, 144–6
  and Kant, 46, 80–1, 132–3, 141
  ontological difference, 16–17, 93–4, 128–32
  representative thought, 95, 154, 244
  schematism, 64, 140
  synthesis, 49–50, 88–9, 232
  thought, 44
  time, 137, 139, 149–52, 246
  transcendence, 53, 138, 281, 283–4
Herz, Markus, 59
Hintikka, Jaakko, 43, 59

Index

Histoire de la philosophie (ed. Châtelet), 200, 203, 206
Holenstein, Elmar, 100
Hoppe, Hansgeorg, 58, 63, 72, 91
human nature, 24–5, 28–33, 256, 259–60
Hume, David
 association, 56, 70, 99, 110–11, 114, 118–19
 difference, 25–7, 253
 doctrine of human nature, 24–5, 29–32
 empiricism, 2, 4–5, 23–4, 68, 71, 251
 Hume's fork, 112–13
 irrationalism, 58
 perception theory, 252, 253–9
 phenomenological reduction, 109
 scepticism, 5–6, 51–2, 72, 83–4, 229, 259–60
 subjectivity, 27–9, 225, 226, 228
'Hume's doctrine of space' (Broad), 255
Husserl and Kant (Kern), 101
Husserl, Edmund
 affection, 120–7, 257
 association, 111–14, 116–20
 Deleuze's criticism, 95–6, 98–9
 empiricism, 2, 3, 88
 genetic phenomenology, 93, 100–2, 107–8
 immanence, 109–11
 and Kant, 101, 102–7, 114
 noema, 96–8
 time, 115–20, 227
 transcendental phenomenology, 9, 10–11, 14, 52, 80, 93–4

Idea
 Being as, 141, 145
 differential, 47–9, 166, 265
 distinct and obscure, 274–5
 and impression, 252–4, 256
 problematic, 190–3, 200
 representation, 18–19, 25, 30
 structure, 206, 208
 virtual, 50, 163, 177–9
 see also association; concepts
Ideas 1 (Husserl), 96–7
identity
 and Being, 142–4
 and consciousness, 54–5, 90–1, 96, 258–9
 and difference, 144–6, 166, 169, 175
 and memory, 119–20
 and recognition, 42, 161
 and time, 115, 248–9
 see also paradox of inner sense
Identity and Difference (Heidegger), 16, 142–7
image of thought
 empiricism, 5, 13, 45–6, 155, 221
 factual and rightful, 161
 rationalist, 24, 31–2
 and recognition, 41–2, 52
 and representation, 14, 18–19
imagination
 and belief, 25, 27, 71, 111
 finitude, 253–4
 reproductive, 80–7, 90, 101
 and subjectivation, 226
 synthesis, 38–9, 49, 58, 60–3, 65, 138
 and time, 78, 93, 139–40, 227–8
 transcendental power, 9, 12, 53, 133
 and understanding, 30–1, 40, 44, 257–8
immanence
 and becoming, 262, 282–3
 and concept, 46, 209, 211–15, 221–3
 and death, 250
 definition, 19–20
 and empiricism, 27, 155, 220–1
 and experience, 15, 161–3, 224, 284–5
 grounding, 130
 Kantian, 36, 81
 and phenomenology, 98–9, 109–11
 and structure, 203, 205, 209–10
 and univocity, 180–2
 see also Being
impressions, 5, 25–8, 73, 252–6, 258, 264
individuation, 175, 181, 227–8, 260–9, 273–4, 276
inner sense
 figural synthesis, 61
 paradox, 46, 57, 234, 245–6
 schematism, 63–5, 67, 79, 140
 and time, 46–7, 52, 82, 84, 115, 139, 192
intellectual synthesis, 52–7, 59, 61

intensity
  and actualisation, 265–6
  and depth, 267–8
  differential, 77–8, 250–1, 263–5, 273
  and duration, 196
  implicative and implicated, 269, 274
  and Kantian sensation, 71, 76, 126–7
  Nietzschean-Bergsonian features, 268–9
  and perception, 11, 12, 27, 251–3, 255–7, 260–1
  quantity, 202
  space and time, 271
  and univocity, 182, 272
  and will to power, 261–2
intensive magnitude, 75–9, 126–7, 251–2, 255–7, 260–1, 269–73
intentionality
  and apperception, 56–7, 60–3
  and association, 58–9, 118
  and classical empiricism, 71–4
  derivative nature, 282–3
  and *noema*, 96–8
  passive, 100–1, 111–15
intuition
  and affection, 125
  and apprehension, 83, 84, 85–6, 139
  and categories, 59, 61, 63–5, 215
  and cognition, 62, 90, 177
  and concept, 47, 54, 271
  as continuous multiplicity, 11–12
  and reconstruction, 103–4
  and sensation, 76–9, 121, 251
  and understanding, 53, 81–2, 140, 184, 201

Jacobi, Friedrich Heinrich, 134–5, 136
James, William, 6, 7, 16, 23–4, 124, 213
Jarry, Alfred, 148

Kambartel, Friedrich, 75
Kant and the Problem of Metaphysics (Heidegger), 80, 89, 132, 133–4, 136–7, 138–9, 141, 175
Kant, Immanuel
  A-deduction, 81–3
  ambiguity, 34–5
  apprehension, 83–6, 257–8
  B-deduction, 51–2, 54–6
  empiricism, 4–5, 29, 70–3, 282
  experience, 63, 214–15, 264, 277
  harmony, 37–8, 39–40
  and Heidegger, 129–34, 136–9, 141, 154
  and Husserl, 101, 102–7, 110, 114
  Idea, 190–2
  intensive and extensive magnitudes, 251–2, 256–7, 269–71
  intentionality, 58–63
  logic, 183
  nature, 184–5
  paradox of inner sense, 46, 57, 234, 245–6
  reason, 36–7
  recognition, 41–2, 52, 160
  representation, 18–19, 38–9, 177, 233–4
  reproductive synthesis, 86–8, 232–3
  schematism, 63–9
  sensation, 75–9, 121–2, 202
  the sublime, 44, 162, 246, 248
  the thing-in-itself, 134–7
  three syntheses, 49, 80, 88–91, 232–3
  time, 46–7, 115, 139, 227
  transcendental argument, 9–11, 30–1, 42–3, 53
Kant's Inaugural Dissertation of 1770 (Kant), 85
Kant's Model of the Mind (Waxman), 83–4
Kants Theorie der Erfahrung (Cohen), 69, 77
Kemp Smith, Norman, 86
Kern, Iso, 101
Kitcher, Patricia, 53
knowledge
  and categories, 56
  and causation, 30
  and empiricism, 4, 27, 29
  ontological, 134–5, 137–8
  and representation, 18–19, 38
  see also experience

Lacan, Jacques, 235, 238, 240
Leibniz, Gottfried W., 53, 85, 187–8, 250–1, 264, 269, 274–80
Les philosophies pluralistes d'Angleterre et d'Amérique (Wahl), 23–4, 25
L'espace littéraire (Blanchot), 250

Index

Lessons on the Analytic of the Sublime (Lyotard), 34
L'individu et sa genèse physico-biologique (Simondon), 266
logic
  and aesthetics, 53, 139, 183
  of concepts, 217–19
  genealogy of, 93, 99, 107
  Hegelian, 187–8, 214–15
  and metaphysics, 144–5, 169
  representation-based, 170–1
  and structuralism, 205, 207
  and the 'thing-in-itself', 135–6
  see also external relations
The Logic of Sense (Deleuze)
  aion, 152, 198, 247
  difference, 48, 163, 178–9, 188
  Husserl, 95, 96, 97–8
  paradox of becoming, 268–9
  place in Deleuze's oeuvre, 13
  structure, 205, 248, 249
  univocity, 182
Logical Investigations (Husserl), 112
Lyotard, Jean-François, 34

magnitude *see* extensive magnitude; intensive magnitude
Maimon, Salomon, 9, 11–12, 47–8, 129–30, 192, 264
manifold
  apprehension, 82–5
  and duration, 10, 17, 28
  interiority, 48, 85
  intuition, 11, 47, 54, 60–1, 65
  representation, 38, 57, 90–1
  Riemannian, 270
Matter and Memory (Bergson), 17, 197–8, 199, 200, 232, 236, 237
mediation, 17, 49, 63–6, 79, 80–1, 187
memory
  and anamnesis, 237–8
  and association, 119–20
  and habit, 28–9, 232, 236
  and repetition, 185–6, 226, 228, 235–7
  and reproduction, 87, 88, 90, 233–4, 240
  synthesis, 243–4
  and time, 199–200, 246–7, 248–9, 281
  and virtuality, 17, 196–9

Merleau-Ponty, Maurice, 95, 128, 185, 189, 266–7
metaphysics
  Aristotelean, 171–5
  and Being, 148–50, 152
  and difference, 16, 93, 146–7, 168–71, 179–80
  and empiricism, 3, 67–8, 155, 161, 165
  of finitude, 76, 129, 131–3, 135, 137–8
  and immanence, 224
  and the logic of relations, 30
  representation, 140, 176–7, 183, 186
  see also ontology
Monadology (Leibniz), 85
monads, 275–7, 279–80
multiplicity
  actual and virtual, 196–7, 200, 252
  conceptual, 216
  and empiricism, 6
  and experience, 195–6, 201
  implicit and explicit, 269–70
  and perception, 11
  of structure, 206
  subjectivity and objectivity, 18

narcissism, 229, 238, 243, 249–50
necessity, 28, 32, 112, 215, 226
Negative Dialectics (Adorno), 166, 176
Negotiations (Deleuze), 13, 15, 155
Nietzsche and Philosophy (Deleuze), 36–7, 159, 160, 260, 261–2
Nietzsche, Friedrich
  becoming, 263, 282
  belief, 219–20
  concept construction, 165–6, 215
  empiricism, 2, 37, 156, 221
  eternal return, 249, 262, 281
  genealogy, 41
  and Hegel, 164, 188
  and Heidegger, 128–9, 131–2, 141, 244
  reason, 36–7, 157
  repetition, 130–1, 155
  and univocity, 183
  will to power, 158, 260–2
'Nietzsche, Genealogy, History' (Foucault), 179
noema, 96–8

noumena, 11, 236; *see also* thing-in-itself

objectivity
  and being, 137–9, 147–8
  categories, 140
  multiplicity, 18
  and perception, 9, 71–3, 106
  and sensation, 69
objects of recognition, 15, 18, 44–5, 234, 269
'On truth and lies in a nonmoral sense' (Nietzsche), 165
onto-theology, 93–4, 130, 131, 142–6, 149, 152–4, 182
ontology
  Aristotelian, 172–3
  intensity, 260–1, 267
  and Kant, 18–19, 132–4, 141
  ontological difference, 16–17, 93, 128–9, 131–2, 145–6
  and pure past, 197, 199, 237
  questions and problems, 193–5
  synthesis, 49–50, 105–6, 137–40
  univocity, 179–80, 182–3
  see also Being; enowning event; metaphysics
opposition, 17, 163, 169, 208–9, 268
The Order of Things (Foucault), 14, 18, 42–3, 128, 193
Our Mutual Friend (Dickens), 250

paradox
  of becoming, 268–9
  of inner sense, 46, 57, 234, 245–6
  paradoxes of pure past, 199–200, 234–5
  of repetition, 225
  sense paradoxes, 97, 205
  of transcendental cognition, 43
  of transcendental recognition, 135
  of transcendental reflection, 103
Parmenides, 142, 172–3
passive intentionality, 100–1, 111–15
passive synthesis
  and association, 3, 7, 27–9, 113–15, 117–18
  habit, 229–31, 239–40
  Heidegger and Kant, 49, 80–1, 232

Husserl, 93, 99, 101–2, 106–7, 111, 122, 126
Merleau-Ponty, 95
and repetition, 238–9, 242
sensuality, 63, 73
time, 46, 79, 227–8, 231–7, 240
see also apprehension; habit
Pathmarks (Heidegger), 141
Paton, Herbert James, 91
percept, 7, 126, 214
perception
  and consciousness, 9–10, 62–3, 74–5, 82–6, 96–8, 252
  depth, 266–7
  and empiricism, 23, 71–3, 124, 252–60, 277–8
  and experience, 6–7, 25–7, 29
  minute, 15, 18, 125–7, 274–7, 279–80
  and object, 8, 258–9
  transcendental psychology, 251, 261, 275–6
  transcendental synthesis, 11–13
  see also sense-data
phenomenological reduction (bracketing), 89, 96, 103–4, 109
phenomenology
  association, 111–15, 116–20
  in Deleuzian thought, 2, 3, 95–9, 148, 188–90, 193–4
  genetic, 93, 100–2
  and Heidegger, 128
  and Hume, 253–6, 258
  and immanence, 109–11
  and time, 115–20, 123–5
  and transcendental synthesis, 10–11, 80, 99–100, 104–9
  Urdoxa, 98
Phenomenology of Association (Holenstein), 100
Phenomenology of Perception (Merleau-Ponty), 95, 128, 266–7
The Phenomenology of the Spirit (Hegel), 133, 188
The Philosophical Discourse of Modernity (Habermas), 157–8
Piaget, Jean, 72, 207
plane of immanence, 163, 182, 209, 212–13, 214, 215, 221–3
plane of transcendence, 182, 268

Index

Plato, 141, 172, 237, 247, 268, 269
pleasure principle, 32, 238–40, 243, 249–50
'A pluralistic universe' (James), 16
pointillism, 258, 277
post-Kantianism, 9–11, 43, 47–8, 129–33, 192, 233, 251–2, 264
post-structuralism, 157, 281
potentiality, 194, 201, 203, 204–5
prephilosophical planes, 209–10, 214, 219, 220, 221–2
presuppositions
  and concepts, 212, 215, 219
  Deleuze's critique, 158–62
  and experience, 7, 15, 201, 277
  image of thought, 41
  and phenomenology, 103–4
  and the transcendental, 98
  see also association; causality
Proust, Marcel, 198, 237, 240, 246–7
psychoanalysis, 235, 238–41
psychology
  association, 114, 213
  of human nature, 24–5, 29, 31–2, 259–60
  and Kant, 42–3, 53, 102–3, 251–2
  of perception, 11, 12, 251, 261, 275
  and synthesis doctrine, 52, 80–1
  see also transcendental psychology
pure concepts, 47, 49, 53–4, 62, 63–9, 81–2, 140; *see also* categories; concepts
Pure Immanence (Deleuze), 5, 19–20, 155, 213, 250
pure past, 17, 197–200, 232, 234–7, 240, 243–4, 267
Putnam, Hilary, 8

qualitability and quantitability, 201–3, 265
Quine, Willard Van Orman, 6, 68, 74

radical empiricism, 16, 23–4, 73, 197, 213, 221
rationalism, 4, 24, 37, 53, 67, 162
reason
  Cartesianism, 159–61
  and experience, 31–2, 61–2
  and Idea, 190–3

  and Kant, 39–40, 43–4, 102, 104, 134–5
  and Nietzsche, 36–7, 157–8
  practical and theoretical, 185–6
  see also thought
reception and affection, 120–3
recognition
  and apprehension, 86
  Kantian model, 38, 41–2, 52, 54–5, 72, 160
  paradox, 134–5
  and phenomenology, 96, 98, 107–8
  presuppositions, 161–2
  and repetition, 185–6
  and representation, 19, 58, 228–9, 233–4, 282–3
  synthesis, 49–50, 61, 83, 88–91, 232–5, 239
  see also objects of recognition
Reid, Thomas, 8
repetition
  bare and clothed, 240–3
  and difference, 131, 155, 171–2, 176–7, 183, 225–6
  externality, 185
  freedom, 185–6
  and habit, 28, 111, 230–1
  and phenomenology, 107
  psychic and material, 235–6
  and psychoanalysis, 238–40
  and time, 130, 227–8, 233, 236–7, 248–50
  see also association
representation
  and common sense, 159–60, 162
  concepts, 67, 166–8, 171–2
  definition, 18–19
  and difference, 17, 25–6, 169, 282–3
  and event, 281–5
  and experience, 14–15, 52, 58–9, 61, 71–2, 228–9
  and external relations, 32–3
  and identity, 42, 54–5, 57–8
  infinite, 48, 184, 186–8, 215
  manifold, 84–5, 86
  metaphysical, 131–2, 140, 176–7, 183
  and structure, 205
  synthesis, 38–40, 59–60, 70, 87, 90, 232–4

representation (*cont.*)
   and time, 89, 235, 237–8, 243–4
   see also association; thought,
     representational
reproduction
   and reflection, 42
   self-affection, 46
   synthesis, 38, 49, 61–2, 83, 86–91,
     232–5, 240
   and temporality, 115–20
Riemann, Bernhard, 270, 272
Romanticism, 157–8, 177
The Roots of Reference (Quine), 74

Saussure, Ferdinand de, 204, 208–9
scepticism, 5–6, 51–2, 55–6, 83–4,
   112–13, 259–60; *see also* Hume;
   transcendental deduction
Schelling, Friedrich. W. J., 129–30, 177
schematism, 49–50, 63–9, 77, 79,
   139–40; *see also* categories;
   concepts
Schopenhauer, Arthur, 157, 165, 177
science and philosophy, 98–9, 109–10,
   132–3, 212–13, 251, 260–3
The Science of Logic (Hegel), 135,
   169–70
Seebohm, Thomas, 115
self-affection
   synthesis, 49, 57, 61, 63, 139
   time, 46–7, 245–6, 250
   see also consciousness
sensation
   and affection, 121–4, 264
   intensity, 76–9, 126–7, 257
   Kantian concept, 71, 75–6
   perceptions, 85, 251
   quantity, 155, 196, 202
   and temporality, 116–17
   and thought, 12–13, 45–6, 195
   see also habit
sense
   noematic, 96–8
   and structure, 205–6
   and thought, 161–2, 283–4
   and understanding, 138
   see also common sense; inner sense
Sense and Sensibilia (Austin), 7
sense-data
   and causation, 27–8

   and consciousness, 59–60, 74–5, 79
   and empiricism, 6–9, 70–1, 197, 227
   and intensity, 3, 71
   and object, 258–60, 278
   passive synthesis, 73
   singularity, 14, 69–70, 124
   see also atomism; experience;
     perception
the sensible, 45, 71, 75, 188, 282
sensualism, 60, 63, 69, 71, 75–6, 79,
   284
signs
   and memory, 199, 236
   and objects of recognition, 15, 18,
     44–5, 269
   structuralism, 204–5
   and thought, 79, 230, 280, 284
similarity, 17, 29, 118, 169, 172, 174,
   191
Simondon, Gilbert, 266
singularity
   of concepts, 212, 215, 216, 217
   and difference, 170
   of sense-data, 69–70
   and structure, 203–4, 205–6
   of substance, 179–80
   transcendental, 14, 18
Smith, Daniel W., 48, 264
space
   and hierarchy, 182
   smooth and striated, 270–2, 275
   and structure, 202–3, 206
   and time, 184–5, 253–4, 264–6, 267,
     271, 277
Spinoza, Benedict de, 168, 180–1,
   182–3
Spinoza (Deleuze), 182
Strawson, Peter F., 53
structuralism
   description, 200–1
   linguistic, 204, 208–9
   and phenomenology, 96, 193–4
   and realisation, 205, 208
   time and memory, 199, 281
structure
   actualisation, 15, 109, 265, 273
   Deleuze's concept, 199, 205–7,
     209–10, 212
   differenciation, 178, 203–4, 273
   formalisation, 207–9

Index

multiplicity, 195–7, 201
  and repetition, 242
  synthetic function, 202–3
  temporal, 232, 247–8, 249
  and thought, 195, 280
  virtuality, 17–18, 190, 193–4
subjectivation, 25, 26–7, 28–30, 154, 226–7, 264
subjectivity
  and contemplation, 226, 229–31
  continuous multiplicity, 18
  Deleuze's concept, 31
  Heidegger's critique, 93, 141–2
  in Humean philosophy, 27–8, 225, 229
  and immanence, 224
  in Kantian philosophy, 35, 141, 214–15
  and structuralism, 201
  and time, 227–8, 246, 249–50
  see also phenomenology
the sublime, 40, 44, 162, 248
succession
  and association, 111, 234
  perceptions, 25–6, 83–4
  time, 47, 78, 116, 139, 150, 227
synopsis, 83, 84, 85, 86, 139
Synthesis bei Kant (Hoppe), 72

technology, 129, 143–5, 148–9
Thanatos *see* death instinct
thermodynamics, 260, 262–3
thing-in-itself, 134–7, 138
thought
  and Being, 142–4, 147–9
  and common sense, 43–4, 159–60, 162
  conceptualisation, 13, 48–9, 79, 212, 217–18, 284
  and difference, 144–5
  and error, 44, 160–1
  and experience, 109, 230, 280, 284–5
  genealogical investigations, 36, 41
  and imagination, 139
  onto-theological, 93–4, 131
  representational, 40–1, 95, 166–8, 173, 244, 281
  and the sensible, 45–6, 194–5
  and time, 46, 132, 184, 234

  see also Cartesianism; image of thought; reason
A Thousand Plateaus (Deleuze and Guattari), 13, 126, 270, 272, 275
thresholds, 124–7, 257, 275, 276–7, 279
time
  aion, 152, 247
  and Being, 149–52, 153–4
  and event, 281
  Heidegger and Kant, 137, 139–40
  and ideas, 191–2, 196
  and inner sense, 79
  linearity, 246–8, 249–50
  and phenomenology, 115–21, 123–5
  and repetition, 130, 248
  self-affection, 46–7, 245–6
  and space, 253–4, 264–6, 267, 271, 277
  and structure, 204, 206–7
  and succession, 10, 26, 78, 82–4, 227
  synthesis, 89, 226–8, 231–8, 240, 243–5, 248–9
  and thought, 46, 132, 184
  see also duration; pure past
Time and Being (Heidegger), 128, 140–1, 147, 148–54, 176
Time and Free Will (Bergson), 17, 196, 197
transcendental
  meaning of concept, 9
  relationship with the empirical, 1, 42–6, 161–2
transcendental deduction, 10, 49, 51–61, 105–6, 133–4; *see also* A-deduction; B-deduction
transcendental psychology, 9, 12, 52, 53, 251, 261, 275–6
transcendental synthesis
  and Heidegger, 49–50, 80–1
  and Hume, 24
  and Husserl, 93, 99, 101, 104–9, 114–15
  and Kant, 10, 56, 59, 62–3, 232
  and Maimon, 11–13
A Treatise of Human Nature (Hume)
  empiricism, 24–6
  immanence, 110
  perception theory, 252–6, 258–9
  relations, 28, 30, 112

A Treatise of Human Nature (cont.)
  repetition, 226
  scepticism, 5, 52
truth
  correspondence theory, 219
  and experience, 228
  and moral belief, 158, 219–20
  pragmatic theory, 5
  and thought, 36, 44, 159–61, 221

understanding
  and association, 59–60, 88, 113
  of Being, 141, 144, 145
  doubly functioning, 106–7
  and imagination, 30–1, 38–9, 44, 140, 257–8
  and intuition, 47, 53, 137, 184
  and memory, 228, 233
  objective rules, 62
  relation to objects, 40, 72–3, 80, 81–2
  and schematism, 63–6
  and self-affection, 46–7
  and sensibility, 121–2, 138, 234
  see also categories; concepts; reason
universals, 158, 163, 188, 212
univocity, 147, 166, 173, 179–83, 223, 272
'An unrecognised precursor to Heidegger' (Deleuze), 148

virtuality
  and actuality, 20, 178–9, 194, 204–6, 282

description, 13–15, 17–18, 167
and experience, 177
and memory, 198–9, 237, 244, 247
and multiplicity, 196–7
and object relations, 239–40, 241–2, 249
reification, 208
and sense-data, 75, 258–9
see also concepts
The Visible and the Invisible (Merleau-Ponty), 189
vision, 266–7, 275

Wahl, Jean, 23–4, 25
Waldenfels, Bernhard, 109
Waxman, Wayne, 83–4
'What is grounding?' (Deleuze), 129
What Is Philosophy? (Deleuze and Guattari)
  belief, 220
  Cartesianism, 217
  classical philosophy, 13
  concepts, 167–8, 210–12, 214–15, 216, 218–19, 222–3
  contemplation, 226
  phenomenology, 95, 98
  prephilosophical planes, 221
  science and philosophy, 212–13
  thought, 43, 161, 284
  universals, 163
Whitehead, Alfred N, 229
will to power, 36–7, 131–2, 158, 260–2
withdrawal, 147, 150, 152

EU representative:
Easy Access System Europe
Mustamäe tee 50, 10621 Tallinn, Estonia
Gpsr.requests@easproject.com

www.ingramcontent.com/pod-product-compliance
Lightning Source LLC
Chambersburg PA
CBHW061706300426
44115CB00014B/2583